BACHELOR PAD E

By Aaron Clarey

Copyright © 2013 by Aaron Clarey. ALL RIGHTS RESERVED. This book contains material protected under International and Federal Copyright Laws and Treaties. Any unauthorized reprint or use of this material is prohibited. No part of this book may be reproduced or transmitted in any form or by any means, electronic or mechanical, including photocopying, recording, or by any information storage and retrieval system without express written permission from the author / publisher.

To Khanh Le

FOREWARD
By MARTY ANDRADE

Aaron Clarey saved my life.

Probably.

Maybe.

Let's just say he changed my life in a major way.

But let's not get too far ahead of ourselves. I'll have plenty of nice things to say about Aaron in a little bit. First, I want to make a difference in your life. I want to save you some time. I want to make your life better so you can enjoy whatever it is that you normally enjoy. So here it is...

Don't read Forewords.

Don't read Prefaces.

Don't read Afterwords.

And, depending on the internal structure of the book you're reading, don't read any Introductions either.

Why? These things are superfluous. They are not there to inform you, they exist to waste your time. The publishing industry treats these things as marketing tools; they're not really part of the book you're trying to read at all. They put them in there to give a book some cachet. Just ask yourself, when was the last time you were all hyper to read some great piece of marketing?

If you don't quite understand yet, let's go through it in easy-to-understand chunks.

In the Preface, the author tells the story of how and why his book came into existence. Which isn't important to us, since we're handling the book, we know it exists, and we were interested enough in the subject that we didn't need the author pushing us along trying to prove to us why it's so important to read his book. When was the last time you were reading an author's Preface and thought to yourself "holy shit, I was totally not going to read this book, but this Preface has completely changed my mind."

For whatever reason, the book you're reading was written. For whatever reason, a copy of it is now in your hands (or e-reader device, or whatever). The journey of the book from the author's brain to your hands has been accomplished. Just embrace how weird the world can be and start reading the stuff that intrigued you about the book in the first place. So, there's no reason to read the Preface.

Forewords are even worse. Firstly, if you ever see a Foreword improperly labeled "Forward" you can now laugh derisively at the person who put the book together. Hey idiot, it's called Wikipedia, it's free, and it has articles on what the parts of a book are supposed to be called. Welcome to 2003, the year after which no one ever has to remember anything anymore, thanks to Wikipedia and Google.

The Foreword is another piece of marketing. This time, it's someone other than the author trying to tell you how important the book is and why you should be reading it. The writer of the Foreword is supposed to be a respected person in the field the book is about. In effect, the Foreword is a celebrity endorsement of the book part of the book.

The problem is, if you're in the habit of reading good books, you will notice how those who write Forewords are never quite as good at writing Forewords as the author is at writing the book itself. In fact, normally the person writing the Foreword is a lesser writer than the actual author. My copy of Sun Tzu's "The Art of War" has almost 200 pages of Prefaces, Forewords, Afterwords, Introductions and Historical Notes. And it's all crap. Crap that's keeping you from the meat of the book.

Finally, it should be noted Introductions are a little tricky. Sometimes they really are necessary, and most textbooks have Introductions that aren't a total waste of time. But, once you get away from textbooks, the Introductions become another superfluous element. So, try skipping the Introduction. If you're completely lost after the first ten pages, go back read the Introduction. If not, screw it. Finish the book and get on with your life.

Depending on how many books you are going to read in your life, I just saved you a bunch of time.

Back to the primary topic of this Foreword.

Aaron Clarey and I have known each other for about a decade. We started out in radio about the same time together, and we both started blogging around the same time. We started writing books around the same time too. We both attended the University of Minnesota and live in that little slice of Soviet persistence, Minnesota. Eventually, he will convince me to learn how to ballroom dance, but that's a topic for another time.

I know Clarey, I know him well. And I can say this about him, Aaron Clarey is the one friend of mine who consistently made sense through the difficult times of my life. In fact, not only did Aaron make a lot of sense, at times his insights bordered on clairvoyance. Like many young men, I have had a difficult time making my way in America over the last ten years or so. I got one of those worthless degrees. I worked in the non-profit sector. I went to grad school and went into debt while doing it. And I ended up working a low-wage job in retail while counting pennies in order to splurge on a trip to

Subway. Things were about as bad as they could be.

And Aaron knew why. If you're a regular reader of his, you already know all the mistakes I made, but they were a mystery to me at the time.

Over the last nine years, not only has Aaron been able to explain the causes of my problems, he also offered some treatment options. His book "Enjoy the Decline" gives a framework for a personal recovery from the destruction of America. Since I read it I have found a small patch of happiness in my life; a much larger patch than I had before, and one that continues to grow.

Aaron is the only person who has consistently made sense and provided workable solutions based in reality to the problems plaguing my life. And considering the number of people I know, the number of books I've read, and the endless pile of economics and finance articles I've consumed since the Housing Crash first put me out of work in 2009, that's saying something.

This book, along with Clarey's earlier work "Enjoy the Decline," contain all the workable solutions a young bachelor is going to need. At least, all the solutions you'll need at the start of your adult life. What's nice about a little bit of guidance is it can turn into a lifetime of good judgment, requiring you to seek no more guidance. As such, this book is among those I will be gifting to young friends and acquaintances for a very long time.

Marty Andrade,
December 2013

TABLE OF CONTENTS

How to Read this Book (mandatory)	2
Chapter 1 - Leaderless, Guideless, and Adrift	4
Chapter 2 – Philosophy	12
Chapter 3 – The Basics	45
Chapter 4 – Education	96
Chapter 5 – Career	123
Chapter 6 – Entrepreneurship	168
Chapter 7 – Girls	194
Chapter 8 – Housing and Lodging	253
Chapter 9 – Cars and Transportation	290
Chapter 10 – Maintenance and Repair	305
Chapter 11 – Investing and Retirement Planning	313
Chapter 12 – Wife and Kids	365
Chapter 13 – Legal	416
Chapter 14 – Economics	437
Chapter 15 – End of Life Planning	481
Resources	500
Thanks and Sponsors	503

HOW TO READ THIS BOOK

The purpose of "Bachelor Pad Economics" is to be a reference guide for all men of all ages. Because of this it is not so much a novel that should be read from front to back, but rather topically consulted based on where you are in life. Ideally, you will have picked up this book at the age of 14 as making decisions early on have the greatest potential to improve your future. However, the book is incredibly thorough, providing guidance and wisdom for all men at all stages in life. It is chronologically organized addressing topics that affect younger men in earlier chapters (school, trades, auto-repair, girls, etc.) and topics that affect older men in later chapters (retirement planning, estate planning, divorce, etc.).

I strongly recommend all men read chapters 1-3 regardless of where you are in life. These chapters lay down the foundations to financial planning, enjoying life, the philosophy of life, and provide a "base" by which additional chapters are built upon. If you wanted to do a "quick and dirty" read of this book, those three chapters will suffice, but for practical and specific advice you will want to consult additional chapters.

Also realize many of the topics are incredibly dry and boring. Not because of poor writing, but because of the nature of the topic – taxes, 401k's, specifics of divorce law, etc. To that end I recommend using them purely as a reference for facts and data, and not so much philosophy or deep thought. Specifically, you will want to pour yourself a stiff drink before reading chapters 6 and 11. However, when it comes to chapter 11, you will definitely want to slog through the first 2/3rds of the chapter, despite it being particularly dry, so that you can get to the section "How Retirement

Works in the Real World." That is vital and mandatory reading for all men.

For those of you who have already read my book "Worthless" you can skip chapter 4 altogether as it is merely an abbreviated version of that book. Also, readers of mine will see some similar themes discussed either in my blog or "Enjoy the Decline" and repeated throughout the book. This is not to be repetitive, but because of my desire to make each chapter stand alone as people use it as a reference book and not a novel. My apologies in advance for these repetitions.

Finally, I strongly recommend reading only one chapter at a time. The sheer scope of topics this book attempts to tackle and dissect not only makes some chapters quite lengthy, but can be mentally jarring jumping from one topic to the next. One chapter you'll be reading about how to get laid, and the next you'll be reading about maximizing your tax deduction through 401k contributions. It will help your brain digest, incorporate, and retain the terabytes of information within this book.

CHAPTER 1
LEADERLESS, GUIDELESS, AND ADRIFT

As the WWII generation passes they leave behind a vacuum of wisdom, guidance, advice and leadership. Not because they didn't try to convey these things to their baby boomer children, but because their children rejected their wisdom.

Their father wasn't a *wise man who risked life and limb charging the beaches of Normandy, who had to ponder and think about the meaning of life and freedom after he killed three Germans.*

He was *"a square maaaaaan."*

Their mother wasn't *a hard-working wife who kept a clean and safe home for her children.*

She was *"an enslaved housewife, unconsciously working for the system maaaaan."*

And despite *empirically, mathematically, and factually being the most successful generation in the history of the world*, they could not be trusted because...

"don't trust anybody over 30 maaaaan."

Instead, the baby boomers replaced this established, time-tested wisdom and common sense with their own, new and modern philosophies. These new philosophies were not based in reality, but rather a self-serving idealism, and thusly corrupted nearly every aspect of American life and Western culture.

Love, romance and family, for example, have been corrupted by feminism resulting in effeminate men, masculine women, divorce, the destruction of stable families, the rise of single parents, and maladjusted children. Education has now become nothing more than a racket to extract money out of youth to enrich the education industry, while leaving the students with degrees that are useless and debts that cannot be repaid. The labor market is equally dysfunctional, with power-tripping employers requiring masters degrees for entry-level jobs that could be done by 8th graders. And the government is hopelessly corrupt, with the most vile of politicians bankrupting the nation, but not without first insisting younger generations slave away for everybody else's social security and Medicare. Nearly every aspect, facet, and corner of American civilization has declined and decayed, lessening the quality of life younger generations will enjoy.

But it gets worse.

Not only are older generations incapable of providing wisdom, leadership and guidance to the younger generations, things have gotten so bad many of them (consciously and unconsciously) actually take advantage and parasite off of the youth. Again, social security, Medicare and Obamacare are nothing more than wealth transfers from young people who have no money to old people who pissed away theirs. Education is now primarily an employment vehicle for older people with worthless degrees to extract as much as they can from younger students naïve enough to spend $75,000 on a B.A. in 16th Century French Guatemalan Lesbian Poetry. And any superficial study of the federal budget will show a mortgaging of our country's finances so people today can spend, while people of tomorrow will pay. Ergo, most elders are not only incapable of conveying wisdom, leadership or guidance, they have no incentive to even if they had any to dispense. i.e. – they need to keep you in the dark. They need to keep you ignorant. They need to prevent you from gaining wisdom. And thus, young people are left clueless about how to live their lives, how to enjoy their lives, and how to get the most out of their lives.

But there is hope and this hope has come in the form of the Internet.

Though not organized and quite unintentional, the internet has allowed for the accumulation of wisdom at a rate faster than ever in the history of human-kind. In allowing millions of similar-minded people to find each other, discuss similar topics, exchange information and compare notes, different "spheres" within the internet have formed to address the various sociological, political, economic, and romantic aspects of American and Western culture. These groups have become depositories for knowledge and wisdom that has been accruing online for the past 10 years, knowledge that has either gone to the grave with the WWII generation or was obscured (or even) purposely hidden by previous generations for political reasons. The great thing about this newly re-discovered wisdom is not only is it based in reality, and thus more effective, it explains things that have very likely been confusing you and causing you great frustration your entire life.

For example "The Manosphere."

There is not one young man alive today who has not suffered immeasurably because of the lies he was told about girls and dating. The "wisdom" his elders gave him was "to be the nice guy" or "be a caring, sensitive man." Only to find out the drug-dealing thug or the philandering athlete was getting all the girls. It wasn't until hundreds of men compiled notes and realized the advice they were being given the past 40 years was completely wrong, and set out to re-discover the truth about women. Women like tall, strong, aloof, confident assholes who ignore them and treat them like shit. You may not find that truth comfortable, but it at least alleviates the insanity millions of young men have suffered.

Another example, education.

The lies you were fed were that you could "follow your heart and the money would follow" or that "it doesn't matter what you major in, it's what you do with the degree that matters." As long as you went to college, racked up $100,000 in debt, you were doing "the right thing." Of course, working for $8/hour as a barista to pay off your student loans for your "Art History" degree has taught you otherwise. But thankfully, future generations need not suffer like you did. An educational "sphere" has formed on the internet. Countless number of websites, books, blogs, etc., are out there highlighting, if not, screaming about the risks of worthless degrees and the education bubble. All of which spare future students from the fate of crippling student loans and perpetual underemployment.

Even the media is being revolutionized.

To get into acting, theater, radio, art or writing "conventional wisdom" said you needed connections, you needed a degree, you needed to network, you needed to kiss ass. So off to theater school you went, worked for free as an intern, kissed a lot of middle-aged men's asses, only to have all the good jobs and gigs go to their children.

Now you only need skill and talent as the internet DIRECTLY connects you to your audience and prospective buyers.

Want to be a radio star?

Start a podcast.

Want to be an actor?

Start a YouTube channel.

Want to be a musician?

Sell your music on iTunes.

Want to be an author?

Self-publish on Amazon.

An entire generation has rejected the wisdom of its elders, completely sidestepping the corrupt, nepotistic, cronyistic "old" industry of entertainment and simply gone to the internet to display their talents, pursue their dreams, and make their money.

We could go on, but the larger point is these different groups or "spheres" within the internet provide the needed and necessary wisdom (and opportunity) that has been lacking. They are in a sense your "default parents" or at least "older-brother-like" sages you can seek wisdom from. However, while the internet and its sub-segmented spheres cover pretty much every aspect and corner of life, there is one area it is lacking in – personal financial advice for men.

At first, people might think, "Wait, there's a ton of financial advice on the internet," which is most certainly true. But there are some problems inherent with this particular "sphere" of the internet that prevents it from conveying its full potential of wisdom, especially to young men.

First, since financial advice has to apply to "everybody" most financial advice on the internet is too generalized and bland to be of any use. To do any good, it needs to be tailored to the individual in that each individual is different, with different goals, different finances and different circumstances. Of course no book can specifically address each of the 300 million individuals in the country, but a book focusing on a general group (say "men") is specific enough to prove very useful to those in that group.

Second, the information is too scattered. Between financial and economic enthusiasts writing blogs, to professionals trying to sell their companies' products, to financial journalists trying to be everything to everyone, there is no centralized depository or "personal financial bible for young men," that takes all the wisdom on personal financial management, organizes it, arranges it, and presents it on a logical, clear and helpful manner.

Third, most of the wisdom on the internet is "conventional."

And, therefore, most certainly flawed.

MBA-laden "Experts" consult their algorithms, look at historical economic trends, and merely regurgitate what has been regurgitated for decades past, giving no consideration to the fact that the underlying dynamics and fundamentals of financial planning is changing. For example, how many times did you hear "housing only goes up" or "any degree is a good degree?" Such advice was only conveyed because (for the most part) those rules held true in the past

...right up until the housing and education bubbles crashed, of course.

This is the major flaw in conventional financial planning. They not only fail to think outside of the box, but they have never ran or considered alternate economic scenarios, and therefore do not have any contingency plans beyond, "well contribute to your 401k some more!" leaving practically everybody exposed to a financial "black swan event."

Finally, men are the last group of people society concerns itself with in terms of economics, politics, sociology, health, romance, or any other regard. There are LIMITLESS number of articles written about women, LIMITLESS number of magazines at the checkout line for women, and LIMITLESS number of shows tailored for women. Society bends over backwards to tailor, serve, and kiss the asses of women. Very little consideration, and therefore advice, is designed, tailored, and built for men.

To this end "Bachelor Pad Economics," (though applicable to everybody) is written with the average American male in mind. Most likely single, most likely young, but every man, married or not, young or not, will benefit greatly from this book. It is the single, most comprehensive source of wisdom for young men regarding personal financial management, investing, and life from a financial perspective. It is a roadmap to financial planning that has been sorely missing the past three generations. Reading this book will surpass any number of college classes in terms of the wisdom and help it will grant you, and the younger you read it, the better off you'll be. This book, quite simply, is a must for every young man out there, so that you not only avoid the mistakes your elders made, but live better and more enjoyable lives than we did.

CHAPTER 2
PHILOSOPHY

Any financial book dispensing advice will fail in its objective if it merely tells you what to do and not why.

"Do X, but not Y."

"Invest in A, but not B."

"And heaven help you if you did Q, when you should have done Z."

The reason why is in merely barking orders you fail to explain the underlying dynamics and mechanics of a topic, therefore failing to convey the wisdom necessary for a person to make a decision on their own. Furthermore, the world of personal financial management is not universal nor identical for everyone. Every person is different, with different goals, different preferences and different abilities, rendering most generalist financial advice impractical and worthless for the individual.

Because of this it is necessary for everybody to develop their own personal financial strategy. They need a plan specific to them, that heeds their desires, will benefit them the most and one they can understand. But without any previous knowledge about economics, financial markets, financial planning, etc., how does the beginner go about designing their own optimal personal financial strategy?

The answer is found in understanding three simple philosophies or "laws" about humanity.

Finiteness
Time
Happiness (or dryly referred to as "utility" for economic purposes henceforth)

While you may not know the intricate under-workings of the stock market, or all the laws associated with 401k's, or the first thing about financing a house, in understanding these three basic philosophies about humanity you will at least have the context and perspective to construct an effective economic plan. It is akin to climbing three peaks to get the lay of a land you are unfamiliar with. By no means will you be an expert explorer or mountain climber, but viewing the land from the top of these three philosophical peaks gives you the vision and perspective to plot a general course over the financial landscape. Therefore, any time a financial challenge or question comes up, you may not have the knowledge or wisdom to immediately answer that specific question, but you will have the ability to think it through and most likely come to the answer that is going to benefit you the most.

However, beyond vision and context, these three philosophies play an even more important role – they lay the foundation for any one individual's financial strategy. They are the starting point for you, or anyone else, in developing a personal financial strategy. They are the first, necessary, and UNSKIPPABLE step you must take in going forward with planning your financial future. The reason why is that they immediately address the initial and most important part of financial planning.

You.

Understand that until you know what you want out of life, no amount of financial advice is going to help you. You can contribute the maximum to your 401k plan, buy a house with 20% down, and make "all the right moves," but it could all be for naught since you never incorporated your dreams, your desires, and what you wanted to do with your life into your financial planning. You could be wealthy, you could be rich, but you could also be miserable in that you were living your life NOT for yourself, but for what others said you should be.

Therefore, it behooves you to take as much time as possible to contemplate, think through, and ponder these philosophies. Answer the many questions these philosophies are guaranteed to raise. It could very well take years, sometimes the answers might change, and sometimes they never come. But at least in taking the time to understand these philosophies and incorporate them into your financial planning, you will be light years ahead of your modern day contemporaries and will only benefit economically in your future.

Philosophy #1 – Finiteness

If there is one primary underpinning or tenet about financial planning that should guide you in your financial endeavors, it is one simple, but very important thing – you are finite.

You are going to die.

If somebody were to ask me what the single most important bit of wisdom I ever conveyed in my entire life was, I would say, without a doubt it was getting people to realize...

"You are going to die."

And the reason is simple.

You *ARE* going to die.

You are finite. You will end. You will be here one nanosecond, and gone the next.

All this life and waking up every day, trying to figure out what to do with yourself, and how to maximize your pleasure out of it, will come to an end very soon, at a date way too early. Your consciousness that you take for granted – the ability to think, the ability to observe, the ability to pontificate – will just "poof!" be gone and your entirety will cease as the rest of the universe continues on without you. You will return to blackness and non-sentience just like it was before you were born as the world quickly forgets who you were, why you were here, and what you did.

Unfortunately most people fail to incorporate this very important fact into their financial planning, let alone life. And so off they go, lackadaisically living life, making grand and horrible mistakes, squandering their one and only short experience on this planet. But while the concept of finiteness and death makes for some very interesting (and serious) philosophical contemplation, it also puts things in the ultimate context because it conveys the single most important thing in planning your financial life – urgency.

I often say near-death experiences are good things because they light a fire under people's asses. They remind people they could be snuffed out at any second and the life they have lived up to that point is (usually) a sad and pitiful one. They make people take inventory of how they've led their life in the past and whether they wish to continue to do so into the future. Do they want to continue leading their craptastically boring lives, watching Jerry Springer, getting drunk at the bar, listening to lousy rap, being overweight, and watching sports on TV? Or do they want to achieve something unique, interesting, and different? Do they want a life of happiness, joy and accomplishment, or one of misery, boredom, and commonness? Fitness and health, or obesity and bad sex?

In short, realizing you're finite will trigger the sense of urgency you need to not only start making plans, but translate those plans into reality. But we're not talking about grandiose things like climbing Mt. Everest or racing in the Tour de France (though, those certainly would apply). We're talking about everyday things that affect every aspect of your life. Your career, your physical life, your social life, your education, your family, your intellect. Realizing you are finite will force you to put every aspect of your life under a microscope and ask "How can I achieve what I want in this particular aspect of my life?"

As to what those specific achievements are, it is ultimately up to you and what you want to do with your life. But whatever it is you choose, realize as long as it is what you want to do, then it doesn't matter. It is only what will make you happy.

Do you want to be a family man instead of a corporate man?

All the more power to you.

Would you rather be a high powered career man, instead of an international playboy?

By all means.

Does being a computer geek, playing Dungeons and Dragons with your nerdy friends sound better than jet-setting around the world picking up chicks?

Who is anybody to judge?

But none of that will matter until you put forth the effort to actually realize these dreams.

It is here mortality and its consequential urgency become your best friends because they fight the number one obstruction people face in achieving their dreams – procrastination. Mortality and urgency prompt you to get off your lazy ass and do what needs to be done to realize your dreams. *Precisely* what specific actions need to be taken? Well, there are no universal rules, but in general there are three actions you must take to reach your goals:

1. Set goals
2. Develop a plan
3. Establish a regimen to reach those goals

Set Goals

This may sound stupid, but it only sounds stupid because so few people do this. But have you ever taken the time to think about and plot out your life? Have you ever sat down with a large sheet of paper and took inventory of your life and what you'd like to achieve with it? Have you spent even an hour in the past year contemplating this very important question? Could you even name one person who has done this and, thusly, who knows what they want out of life?

The reason most people are so miserable is because they never take the time to ask these questions of themselves. They rush into life, inefficiently slaving away for reasons they're not entirely too sure of. They go to college for a worthless degree because "their parents told them to." They work for abusive bosses because "good employees tough it out." They buy sports cars and McMansions they can't afford because the marketing industry told them "it was cool." And they have kids because "that's what you're supposed to do." And soon, be it the "career woman" who realizes at 42 she really just wanted to be a mother, or the CEO who suffers a stroke at 57 who just wanted to fish, it's too late as life has passed them by and will never give them another shot. Don't become these people. Find out what you want in life and establish your goals *first* before putting effort into it.

Develop a Plan

The second thing you need to do is develop a plan to achieve those goals. The details and answers may not all be there, but in at least knowing what your goals are, you'll be set on a path or trajectory to reach them (and, as it just so happens, you'll tweak and adjust your plan as you go along as more and more information comes your way indicating what is feasible and what is not). Of course, there is no guarantee your plans will work or your dreams will be realized, but, again, compare yourself to your "plan-less peers." How many people do you know who are drifting aimlessly through life, waiting for some external force to "change everything for the better?" Waiting to "win the lottery" or "marry rich" or "get that big promotion?" Whatever it is they're waiting for, it won't happen because they're waiting for something *outside of their control* to happen. In having a plan of your own you put your fate *in your hands*. You take concrete steps to bring yourself closer to achieving your goals and increase your chances of success. And though there is no guarantee you will be successful, you definitely stand a better shot than your plan-less peers, wasting their lives adrift, hoping "good things will just happen to them."

Regimen

Finally, you need to follow through. You need to constantly, regularly, and religiously carry out and execute your plan. You need to get up, you need to work extra hours (outside your day time job), and you need to sacrifice. You need to dedicate yourself to achieving those goals. But it's not enough to merely develop a plan and pursue it at your leisure. You need a *regimen*, something that forces a definitive, daily schedule on you. Perhaps nothing as detailed and drastic as, say, basic training in the Army (where every waking minute of your life is scheduled), but you need to have a schedule of sorts that you religiously adhere to, forcing you to relentlessly advance and close in on your goals.

None of this will be easy and it will take a superior amount of self-discipline and control, but in doing so you will enjoy a superior life and become a superior person. You will not be talking about the latest Kim Kardashian episode around the water cooler with people you hate at a job you loathe. You will not be working as a barista for $7 per hour, constantly self-rationalizing your stupid decision to blow $125,000 on a Masters in Creative Writing degree with all the other emo kids. You won't be living check to check as you make payments on a house you don't need, a wife you don't like, and children you can't afford. You will be living your dream, whatever it is, enjoying your one, finite, and precious life on this planet. And if at anytime you feel tired or lazy and just want to procrastinate a little bit, just remember…

…that out-of-control truck is just about to jump the corner,

…that stray bullet is just 200 yards away,

…and that vicious, aggressive, and untreatable cancer cell is just 10 seconds from metastasizing in your blood stream.

Philosophy #2 – Time Theory

In the movie "The Matrix," Neo (played by Keanu Reeves) finds out that the world he lives in is not real. It is just a computer program running in his mind. The real world is a dark and scary place run by artificial intelligence machines, and humans are nothing more than satiated thermal batteries to power these machines. In the final scene Neo has an epiphany that allows him to see the Matrix for what it truly is. So instead of seeing walls, a room, floors, and people, etc., he sees nothing but the code – the 1's and 0's, the bits and bytes that make up the entirety of the Matrix world. Because he can see the basic unit, the individual building block of the Matrix, he becomes invincible as he can fully understand and manipulate the Matrix at its most fundamental level.

However, "The Matrix" analogy above is not too unlike our own real world. Matter of fact, it is eerily similar to our real world in that everything around you is actually not as it seems. This book in front of you, the computer on your table, the chair you're sitting in, the room around you, even the clothes you are wearing right now are indeed NOT

a book,
a computer,
a table,
a chair,
a room,
or your clothes.

They are nothing more than human time.

If you think about it, the cotton that composes your clothing would never be cultivated, let alone sewn or transported without the human time necessary to plant it, grow it, reap it, sew it and deliver it in its current form. The materials used in the sheet rock, the framing, the flooring and everything else used to construct the building you're currently in would still be in the ground or stored in trees. The cell phone you have would still be rare earth metals, silver, sand and carbon strewn across the planet. And the video game you intend on playing later tonight would never even exist without human time let alone the console you intend to play it on. Practically EVERYTHING you see in your environment only exists in its current form because human time has been expended on it turning it from raw materials to its current-day incarnation. In other words, everything around you are not "things." They are human time.

And so, just as Neo realized the Matrix was nothing but 1's and 0's, you now also realize your entire environment, your entire world is composed of nothing but human time.

Of course, having this epiphany yourself will not grant you "economic invincibility," answering every question you'll ever have about economics, finance, and your future life. However, in understanding on the cellular level how an economy and society works you are infinitely ahead of your peers (and most economists) in being able to intuitively understand what economics and life is all about. This perspective (like realizing you are finite) provides you with additional context, perspective, and understanding that will enable you to think things through and further bolster your fundamentals in planning your financial future. However, while pondering the ramifications of human time theory may seem fanciful right now, there are already practical applications you can make to your life because you understand the concept of human time.

First, the most obvious benefit is that you now know what economics is all about. It is not "big businesses," "governments," and "people" just all mushing around in some kind of economic primordial goo. It is merely an exchange of human time.

You really didn't buy my book. You bought MY TIME to put it together. And with the money you gave me I am going to purchase some other individual's time to do something for me (say, make some gasoline or make me a sandwich or repair my car). In short, an economy is nothing large, complex, mystical or magical. It's nothing more than you, me, and the remaining 6 billion people on the planet exchanging time via the products and services we make, and in doing so helping each other out.

Second, you can now fully and completely understand what money is. It is merely a tool by which people convert and exchange their time with other people. The reason for money is because the goods and services we offer each other are not divisible nor does everybody want them. For example, say I need a new motorcycle. I face two problems. One, what if the motorcycle builder doesn't want a copy of "Bachelor Pad Economics?" And, two, it is unlikely I can get ONE motorcycle in exchange for ONE copy of "Bachelor Pad Economics." I need to sell MANY copies of my book in order to purchase a motorcycle. Money solves this problem by allowing me and everybody else to convert our labor into a divisible currency that everybody wants. So whereas the motorcycle builder would not accept a single book for a single motorcycle, he WOULD accept $10,000. Money is the tool that allows this exchange to happen.

Third, you truly understand the value of your time, specifically the concept of wages. Since we all can't build motorcycles, grow our own food, write books, do our own dental work, etc., that means we must specialize in one particular skill or trade. But what that skill or trade is ultimately determines the value of our time, i.e. our wage. If you want to become an English teacher in a *country that already speaks English*, you are offering nothing of value to other people. They in turn are unlikely to sacrifice any portion of their time laboring away to buy your services, thereby explaining why English teachers make so little money. But if you are willing to become a heart surgeon or an electrical engineer or a computer programmer the value of your time increases multifold because you offer a rare and highly demanded service. This not only explains why surgeons and computer networkers have such high wages, but also explains why you should go to school FOR THE RIGHT DEGREE (for more information about choosing the right degree see the book "Worthless").

Fourth, in having a higher wage you can command other people's time and thus enrich yourself. Understand that while the money you receive from somebody is in exchange for your labor, it is *also a claim or right to other people's labor*. If I have $10,000 I can "command" a group of people to give their time to me via making me a car. Once again, I am exchanging $10,000 of my time for $10,000 worth of theirs. In a very basic theory the number of hours I sacrificed earning up that $10,000 should be the same number of hours everybody spent building the car, but what if my wage was $500/hour while the average auto-manufacturer was only paid $50/hour? My ONE hour will buy TEN of theirs. I only sacrificed 20 hours of my life to buy 200 hours of theirs, netting me 180 hours of additional time.

This once again emphasizes the value of having a skill or a trade, but also shows you how to become "wealthy." It is in making that same hour of your time much more valuable than other people's time. It is in doing so you can sacrifice a small fraction of your time, for multifold amounts of other people's time. This surplus time, of course, does not manifest itself in the form of an extended life-expectancy, but rather riches in the form of money or material goods.

Closely related is, fifth, investing. Money is not only a claim on other people's time, it is also a way to STORE the purchasing power of your time if you don't need to buy anything right at that moment. You may also want to store your time away in the form of money for large purchases you plan on making in the future. A down payment for a house. Your kids' college fund. And most likely and commonly, your retirement.

Money, for the most part, stores your time well. If in a year from now you wished to pull some money from your savings account to buy a car, you could. The purchasing power of your money will not erode significantly in that year. However, over time, or during bouts of high inflation, your money, or "stored time" WILL lose its purchasing power, prompting you to *invest* it.

In investing your money, your past labor will not sit idle in some savings account as inflation eats away at it. Your labor, via money, can be lent out or invested to other people. These people can take your time (in the form of money) and invest in factories, plants, new technologies, that will produce goods and services other people want. Hopefully, these ventures will be successful, and not only return your original investment of time, but other people's time in the form of *profit*. In other words, forget "401k's" and "IRA's" and everything else you've heard about investing. All it is, is lending your time to somebody else with the expectation you will get more time in return.

Sixth, how much money or other people's time do you need? Do you want to slave away for all 79 years of your life expectancy? Work up millions of dollars-worth in time and then die, never getting to spend it or enjoy it? Or do you want to have a little fun in life? Go travelling, eating good food, driving fast cars, and imbibing in quality booze? Life is not about slaving away and working all the time. It is about enjoying life and living it. But you cannot just have fun all the time, just as you cannot work all the time. There has to be a balance. This is what economists call the "leisure-labor trade off."

Every hour you work is one less hour you can spend on leisure or enjoying yourself. And every hour you spend on leisure is one less hour you can spend on labor. There is no right or wrong balance as it is up to the individual tastes and desires of each person, but if there is an observation I have had in my two decades of economic experience it's that humans tend to OVERVALUE labor and UNDERVALUE leisure.

The reason is simple – unless you were born in a third world shithole your life expectancy is the same as the richest of people. In other words, Bill Gates, despite his billions, is likely to have the same life expectancy as you, me, or any other regular schmoe making $40,000 a year. Ergo, as long as you are not desperately poor, to the point it adversely affects your health, you and Bill Gates can expect to have the exact same amount of the only resource that matters – human time.

It is here you have to ask yourself a question (which will have important consequences for your financial plans) – *"Is it worth slaving away to make all of that extra money?"*

For some people this answer is "yes." They like working, they thrive on producing, and they just excel in a corporate environment. They want big, expensive toys, insist on high quality food, expensive travel, and luxury clothes. But for most people the answer is "no." Having fun, relaxing, and enjoying life is more important than life in the office. Of course, I do not want to tell you what is the correct course of action as that will ultimately depend on your personal preferences. However, I do want to prevent you from the fate of Steve Jobs – an entire life working up billions of dollars, only to (tragically) have no time to enjoy it.

The final immediate benefit of having the "human time epiphany" is one of morality. Specifically, removing morality when making economic and financial decisions and replacing it with logic, math, economics, and reality.

As you will find out in later chapters in this book, the economic and political environment in the US (and most of western society) is one trending towards "forced sharing" or "socialism." Also, since the US and most of western society are democracies, this means society has voted *upon itself* these rules, laws, and, specifically, taxes that you must also obey and pay. Because of this you can expect to pay roughly a 40% tax over the course of your life. 40% OF YOUR WORKING LIFE will be spent working up the money to pay taxes. Normally you would expect that 40% to go to government programs that benefit you (defense, roads, police, etc.), however, in reality 70% of that money goes to other people (in the form of welfare, food stamps, WIC, health care, etc.). Mathematically translated this means out of a 50 year career, 14 of those years are literally you being a slave to other people.

This has serious ramifications for your "labor leisure" decision, not just because it provides a great deterrence to work, but it also raises the question as to whether or not you should be on the receiving end of government welfare. It is here you need to remember that morality has little to no place in affecting your economic decisions. Understand that in a *DEMOCRATIC* society voting in and forcing these rules on you any morality in economic decision making has been removed from you and abdicated to them. And whereas you may have some moral issues about being a veritable economic parasite, understand that it would be akin to being a professional football player who refuses to take steroids when the NFL makes all steroids legal – you are only hurting yourself. You have this one shot at life. You should take as much legal advantage as you possibly can.

Philosophy #3 – Happiness (aka "Utility")

The third and final philosophy you must understand is happiness. Because if you're not happy, then what's the point? There's just no purpose in living. You are merely wasting your one and only life on this planet being *miserable*. So before you even start thinking about making economics and financial decisions you need to figure out what is going to make you happy in life.

The problem is that the concept of happiness is an intangible one. What is happiness? What triggers happiness? How do you measure it and how do you attain it? According to economists it is dryly considered the "utility" you derive from the "consumption" of material items. So when you eat ice cream you are happier than you were before. When you drive a sports car you are happier than when you were driving a Kia. And when you have $500 you are happier than when you only had $200. Unfortunately, while the above may be true, it is also misleading as it equates being wealthy with happiness. In reality happiness transcends material wealth as it includes many other psychological, emotional, and physical components. A person who is clinically depressed because he lost his wife to cancer can have all the money in the world, but he won't be happy. A person with Bill Gate's wealth, but no friends, will not be happy. And somebody who bought his first cigarette speed boat who is in constant physical pain due to an illness will not be happy. There are many non-monetary or non-material things that influence one's happiness, making happiness much more complicated than "having a lot of money."

Because of this complexity happiness eludes most people. Most people believe what the media, government, schools, and marketers tell them, flinging themselves into the rat race in the vain hopes of making it rich…only to be in debt, living paycheck to paycheck, suffering the same miserable and ordinary existence as everyone else. But the real reason why most people fail to achieve happiness is because they never put the time into understanding the concept of happiness. Happiness is not a certain amount of money you can save up or a position you get promoted to or a fancy sports car you buy. It is merely a state of mind. A state of mind that, when you're in it, nothing else matters because…

you're happy.

Are you dirt poor, barely getting by, living in a squalid studio apartment, but still happy? Then what does it matter? *You're happy.*

Are you making a billion dollars per year, drinking the finest scotches, driving fast boats and fast cars, and somehow "still" manage to be happy? Then what does it matter? *You're happy.*

It is in sitting down and taking the time to think things through (much like we did with the previous two philosophies) to answer important questions about yourself and what you want out of life that will make you happy. And though the answers will vary for each individual, there are some universal "components" or "requirements" to happiness that apply to us all and are key to achieving and maintaining happiness.

Health – The first requirement to being happy is to have your health. Most people do not appreciate their health because, for the most part, they have it. It is only when it's gone do you really appreciate it and desperately wish to have it back.

Have you ever met somebody on kidney dialysis? You ever meet a diabetic who had their feet amputated? Ever meet somebody with triple-bypass surgery? Not a lot of happy people in those groups as they constantly suffer physical pain, have to worry about premature death, and are physically impaired to the point they cannot fully enjoy life. This isn't to say that if you have health problems you can't be happy, but it certainly makes it difficult.

Therefore it is MANDATORY you do what you can to maintain your health. Of course this is not completely within your control as you may have a genetic predisposition to cancer or a meteorite could clonk you in the head at any time, but common sense things like diet, exercise, avoiding smoking, etc., allow you to do what is within your power to maximize the length and quality of your health.

The primary challenge you will find, however, is not so much knowing you need to stay in shape as much as it will be staying in shape as you age. During your youth you can allow yourself some vices and ignore your health for a while. But inevitably *you will get old* and *still have half your life to live*. Ergo, maintaining your health is not so much for when you are young, as much as it is when you are old. At the age of 50 will you be able to run 4 miles, hike in the Grand Canyon, and touch your toes?

Or...

will you constantly need an oxygen tank, one of those motorized wheel-chairs at Wal-Mart, and your daughter to wipe your ass because you stroked out at 52?

The lesson is simple – stay in shape.

Security – Economists are not entirely off focusing their attention on material wealth. The reason why is, until very recently in human history, there was not much wealth to go around. Most humans lived in a subsistence economy, barely producing enough food, clothing, and shelter to merely exist. Until the industrial revolution poverty was the norm and nearly 100% of a human's miserable life was spent just staying alive (imagine Scrat from "Ice Age" constantly and frantically trying to secure his beloved acorn). This behavior or psychology has been engrained and reinforced in human DNA for the past 200,000 years (and millions of years before that if you consider the previous creatures we evolved from). Consequently, this instinct is **incredibly strong** and attaining happiness will prove difficult until you actually achieve security.

However, today "security" has a different meaning than it did in 10,000 B.C. when cavemen were staving off saber-toothed tiger attacks. Security today, more often than not, means you don't have to worry about feeding, clothing or sheltering yourself into the foreseeable future. Your basics are covered and you can relax, perhaps even consider some luxurious pursuits. This translates into you having an adequate source of income, and not just a source of income, but a reliable and long-term source of income. In reality, however, this is rare. Recessions can cause you to lose a job. Divorce can cause you to lose your assets. And health problems can immediately impair your finances. Unless you are independently wealthy, securing enough income to feel "secure" will be a recurring, though hopefully, rare event in your life.

Still, like your health, there are things you can do to mitigate your risk and increase your security, notably, your wage. For example, a surgeon friend of mine has suffered a mere fraction of the strife, worry and fretting I have since he took the time and effort to develop a highly-compensated skill – heart surgery. When men were committing suicide during the 2008 financial crisis, the "Great Recession" was nothing but a mere annoyance to him. Also, avoiding financial liabilities or mistakes in your life can do a lot to achieve security. Imagine how little you need living as a bachelor in a studio apartment driving a cheap car as opposed to the father of six in a McMansion with three car payments and a spend-happy wife. You may not have a Lexus or a house in the burbs, but at least you have financial serenity. In short, a combination of wise, frugal decisions when it comes to income and spending will go a long way in helping you attain security in your life.

<u>Freedom</u> – Man is happiest when he is free. The reason is simple – in being free you get to spend your time on what you want. You get to benefit from the majority of your labor. You get to live life how

you want. Because if you aren't spending your time on what you want, then you are by default spending your time on somebody else. At best this is called "work," at worst it's called "slavery." Nobody can be truly happy with either.

However, while it is obvious you aren't a free man in countries like Iran, North Korea, or Burma, it isn't just governments or countries that can prevent you from being free. There are other entities and individuals, even in a free country, that can limit your freedom. Namely, any kind of authority figure or liability.

Parents, for example, are an authority figure of which you are not "free" from until you move out of their house and *no longer accept any form of financial subsidy from them*. This isn't necessarily a bad thing as they are your parents and in exchange for their authority you get free lodging, wisdom, guidance and love as a child. But inevitably you do need to move out from underneath their yoke to live your own life. Otherwise, you can expect your mom to lecture you at the age of 32 about curfew, who to date, and going to church as you live in her basement. And that is definitely not a life of the free.

Employers are another example. Again, they aren't necessarily a bad thing as they do provide you with a job and compensation in exchange for your labor, but how many jobs have you had where you're truly doing what you want? Are you really free? When there's that first beautiful 80 degree day in spring, can you just up and leave or do you have to sit in some god-awful meeting as your idiot boss blathers on incompetently? Even though you are compensated, you are still a kept man. Your goal should be to become independently wealthy as quick as possible never needing an employer again. Until that time you're just another unhappy corporate cog.

Infinitely worse than an employer, however, is a nagging wife or controlling spouse. You want to make your life miserable? Then marry the wrong woman. I've seen more men VOLUNTARILY sell themselves into matrimonial slavery than there were actual slaves in the Roman Empire. But that is what makes it so much worse. It was VOLUNTARY. One day they were 29 years old, employed, having a good time, drinking beer, and truly happy; the next day they were married, with kids they couldn't afford, a wife who gained 40 pounds, and a purse they needed permission to get their balls out of. A starving bachelor in North Korea is infinitely freer and happier than his married-to-a-bitch American counterpart because at least he isn't controlled 24/7.

And finally, liabilities. You can be the freest man in the world. You can be self-employed. You can have all the friends and fun in the world. You can be living the dream. But you buy a house or car you can't afford, take on credit card debt, or (worse) bring a kid into this world, kiss all that freedom good-bye because now you have a liability. Understand living with your parents and at least some up-front employment early on in life are necessities to get yourself established. But going into debt or bringing children into this world are SELF-IMPOSED liabilities. You needn't take them on. But if you do realize until you pay them off or get them out of your house, you are no longer working for you, you are working for them. You have an obligation to them and owe them a part of your finite life. You are not free.

We could go on as there are certainly other entities, organizations, and people in life that will either impede or prohibit your freedom. In general, though, you simply want to avoid these people or entities, or use them only to advance yourself towards total freedom. This doesn't mean you shouldn't get married or have kids or have a job, but it does mean you should marry the right girl, only have kids you can afford, and only work for an employer as long as it pays off. Your overarching goal, however, should be to attain total freedom where all of your life is spent doing what you want. In short you want to be like Steve McQueen where he said:

"I live for myself and answer to nobody."

<u>Purpose and "Agency"</u> – In the WWII mini-series "Band of Brothers" there was an episode where Major Winters (one of the main characters) was told to take some time off as he had been on the frontlines too long. His commanding officer gave him leave and sent him to Paris where he could enjoy some good food, drink some good wine, relax and recoup. However, when Major Winters got to Paris, he didn't know anybody and was, thusly, bored. Through the cinematography you see many shots of Major Winters sitting by himself at a café, taking a bath in absolute silence, or not saying a word to anyone. In the documentary you find out later he actually didn't like the vacation as he missed his men and felt useless just sitting in Paris. It wasn't until he got back to his battalion and returned to war did he feel "functional" or "normal" again.

While I cannot attest to the value women place on having a purpose in life, I can attest, without a doubt, the value of having a purpose in life is to men. It is not "valuable." It is not "highly valuable." It is "an absolute necessity."

Without purpose or "agency" a man will become depressed, lethargic, even angry. A common problem among recently retired men is that they no longer have a place to go work every day and often fall into a depression, sometimes committing suicide. This isn't to say at the age of 27 you are going to commit suicide if you don't have a job or get laid off, but it is to say happiness, especially for men, is heavily contingent on having a purpose in life. What that purpose is depends on the individual. Some men want to be fathers, some want to be soldiers, others want to be businessmen, but whatever it is, you have to have something to do in life.

The problem young men face today, however, is one of a changing economy and their role in society. In 1950's America the man's role was very clear – he was the father, bread winner, head of the household, and protector of the nation. Also the economy was booming, providing jobs for any man who wanted one, as well as careers for any man willing to work for it. Today the economy and society are different. The economy is growing at only half the rate it used to, offering fewer employment prospects and making the "life-long career" a myth. Women are also entering the work force divvying up what jobs there are (and often times causing unnecessary workplace drama and problems). Government is also replacing men in the roles of father and head of the household. In providing women and children with daycare, food, health care, shelter, and many other services, the government has rendered many men unneeded and obsolete. In short, the focus of society and the economy has shifted from one of men and the household to that of the government and the commune, leaving men with no clear point or purpose in life.

With a diminished role in society men will have to come up with their own replacement roles. This will shift the focus of purpose and agency from the traditional "career, father, provider, protector" type roles to roles that are more hobby-like in nature. The reasons are multifold. One, a hobby is not dependent on the health of the economy. An accountant who aspires to be an author can work on writing regardless of whether he's employed or not, and thus still have purpose in life. But a man whose purpose or agency is in being an "accountant" is at the mercy of a worsening and more hostile economy. Two, the primary reason in becoming an "accountant" or an "engineer" was to be the provider for your theoretical family. But with the government progressively supplanting men in that role all men manage to achieve in having a "real job" is

working more

to pay more taxes

to pay the government

to do the job they used to.

If a man is going to be forced to pay for a family that either isn't his or he cannot command, then why work so hard, let alone define yourself as an engineer? Become a "home-brewer" or "gear head" instead.

Finally, as society places less value on a man's career, his profession and his ability to support a family, it will be his leisurely pursuits that define him. Women are infinitely more impressed with a man's ability to be a salsa dancer or a motorcyclist than his ability to do "discounted cash flow analysis" (and trust me, I know, I can do all three). Society won't care that you can program a Cisco router or firewall, but they'll be mighty impressed if you can bench press twice your weight. And your date isn't going to care that you are making a new alloy in your lab, but she will be impressed you travel a lot. Since society increasingly values men less in terms of "provider, protector, bread winner, father" you might as well become a "cook, marksman, weight-lifter, motorcyclist."

The larger point is that as society and the economy go through this shift there will not only be less economic opportunity to fulfill your role as "father, protector, provider, and bread winner," there will be less appreciation for such roles. Therefore, to make sure you have purpose and agency in life, you need to find hobbies and interests that are not dependent on economic circumstances and cannot be supplanted by government intervention.

Fun – Because of the Darwinistic programming you have, many men will approach life from the angle of attaining financial security first, and THEN relaxing and enjoying life. You will get everything in order, get your degree, get your career, pay off your debts, pay off your house, and then, once financially stable, finally permit yourself to enjoy life. There is just one minor problem with that approach:

Life doesn't work that way.

Not only is it very unlikely you will attain financial security in your 20's (because society just plain doesn't give younger people the opportunity), but because of the chaotic nature of the economy you cannot plan that far or that reliably in advance. It will take at least a decade of incredible fiscal discipline and self-control to achieve such financial stability and in that decade the economy or your life is bound to have some bad luck that will derail your plans. This doesn't mean you shouldn't try or work hard to achieve your financial goals, but that you do occasionally permit yourself to have fun along the way.

Buy yourself some ice cream. Take that trip to Europe. Buy the convertible. Take your date to that fancy dinner. Splurge on that video game. Get hammered on high end scotch. Go on that road trip to Vegas. Whether it is a large ticket item or small, in order to be happy you need to do the occasional fun thing, because otherwise what is the point of living? You weren't put on this planet to work all the time, you were put here to have fun. And if you play more than work chances are you will have a happier life.

<u>Other Humans</u> – If *"You are going to die"* is the best economic advice I've ever given, then the second best economic advice I've ever given is:

"The only thing that matters in life is other humans."

The reason why is two-fold.

1. It makes financial planning incredibly simple and
2. It makes people have the happiest life possible.

At first glance it may not be obvious how my second-most important bit of advice can simplify your financial planning and give you eternal happiness, but the trick is to understand why other humans are the only thing that matters in life.

Consider two items.

The most advanced Xbox entertainment system

and

a human.

No matter how advanced Microsoft makes its latest Xbox console, in the end that device is finite. It is limited. It can only interact with humans in a way OTHER HUMANS have programmed it. It is incapable of thought, having an opinion, or making independent decisions. It is also incapable of humor, wit, charm, love, irony and adoration. In the end, the most you can do is play it as far as its human programming has allowed it to be played. Beyond that, there is nothing else it offers to you.

The human on the other hand is mentally infinite, it is dynamic, it is capable of independent and sentient thought and is unlimited in the way it can interact with you. Humans are also able to cut a joke, make you crack a smile, make you fall in love, make you adore somebody and reciprocate feelings. Because of this humans are by far the most interesting, engaging, and valuable thing on the planet. And no matter how far science advances, no material item will ever be able to replace the interactivity, complexity, and limitlessness of a human. However, there is a key additional advantage humans have over material items that has huge ramifications for financial planning:

They're free.

This is the greatest news possible for anybody interested in financial planning because it tells you the most important thing in life is FREE.

The Xbox one? $500.

The F-22 Raptor plane? $150 million.

The Ferrari F430? $125,000.

A human being capable of infinite thought, engagement, challenge, emotion and humor? Free.

Because of this, financial planning is infinitely simplified because if you look at what the majority of humans spend the majority of their money on it is unnecessary and unneeded ~~crap~~ material items that come nowhere near to rivaling the value, engagement and happiness humans can deliver.

That BMW with the leather seats will never replace the value and entertainment you derive from playing poker with your buddies, but it will set you back three years' worth of your salary.

That McMansion in the suburbs will never replace the value and entertainment you'll derive from watching your children play soccer, but it will enslave you for the 30 year duration of the mortgage.

That $5,000 diamond necklace will never replace the value and entertainment you'll derive when your husband farted in church causing everybody to laugh including the pastor (true story), but it will prevent you from enjoying a family vacation together.

In short, if you can realize that it is humans that are the most important thing in life and not material items, you will spend (at least) 60% less money on said material items, meaning you need to work 60% less in life. With your life expenditures lowered by 60%, financial planning becomes a breeze as you need nowhere near the amount of money previously thought. However, the true benefit in reducing your work load by 60% is that you get to spend all that additional time on the only thing that can make you truly happy – other humans.

The trick of course is getting people to realize that humans ARE indeed more important and valuable than material items. This is difficult, especially for younger people who have been bombarded and brainwashed by advertising, marketing, and media telling them they need that fancy sports car, they need those expensive clothes, they need that advanced degree, and they need that McMansion in the suburbs. However, to prove it to you consider a phenomenon you can see now almost on a daily basis – texting. And not just texting, but texting in social or beautiful surroundings.

For example I recently did a motorcycle ride from Minneapolis to Hyder, Alaska. Enroute I spent some time in Banff and Jasper National Parks. Below is a picture testifying as to just how beautiful the entire area is:

What do you suppose nearly every kid (and dare I say) nearly every woman under 30 was doing while surrounded by such beauty?

Texting.

The planet's most beautiful scenery with glaciers and mountains and lakes and these people couldn't pull their eyes away from their smart phones.

However, the reason is simple. Unconsciously, and on a primal level, they valued the attention they were getting from other humans far away more than the spectacular vista Lake Louise provided. The witticism, the flirty e-mail, or the lewd sext meant more to the recipient than the breath-taking view Athabasca Glacier was offering. Of course we can criticize people for doing so, but it doesn't change the fact humans value human interaction and attention above all else. Realizing this, accepting this, and combining this important philosophy with the previous two will ensure your financial planning is infinitely more effective and your life a very happy one.

CHAPTER 3
THE BASICS

With a strong philosophical foundation about financial planning, economics, and the purpose of life, you at least have the wisdom and insight to make well-thought out financial decisions. You can also start taking the initial steps in establishing some lifetime goals, build a tentative game plan on how to achieve them, and make some changes in your life to ensure you do. But the scope of financial planning and managing your economic life is wide and nearly limitless. Over the course of your 79 years of life expectancy you can expect to make hundreds of decisions regarding your 401k's, life insurance, car insurance, health, what kind of degree do you get, should you take the promotion, should you live in the US, how about precious metals, and the list goes on. Instead of tackling these in a random and chaotic manner, it is best to approach personal financial management in a logical and structured way. The first and best step of which is to go over the basics.

While the basics won't cover everything, if you follow the advice in this chapter, you will at minimum "not fuck up your life." Matter of fact in reading these first three chapters you will be ahead of most other people when it comes to personal financial management. You could, in theory, set this book down, never to revisit it again and do "just fine" in your financial and economic life. But beyond a "quick and dirty" solution to your life's financial plans, it pays to have a thorough understanding of the basics in that it lays the foundation for you to understand more advanced financial and economic topics later. Topics that may prove in the future to be the difference between a happy man with a life, and a rich, happy man with a life and no financial worries.

Budgeting

The most basic, simple, elementary, financial lesson everybody needs to learn is to spend within their means.

All

not "some"
not "most"
not "the vast majority"

ALL FINANCIAL PROBLEMS come from people, companies and governments spending more than they make.

If people, companies, and governments spent less than they made there would be no need for this book, let alone the entire financial advising industry. If people, companies, and governments spent less than they made, we wouldn't have recessions, depressions or economic crises. If people, companies, and governments spent less than they made, most wars would not occur.

It is the most basic and simple of financial lessons – *spend less than what you make.*

If you can learn this very basic mathematical lesson, you will never have any self-inflicted financial problems in your life.

Of course, the issue really isn't one of mathematics. It's psychological. The human brain can understand mathematically "don't spend more than you make." It's a very simple and logical concept. But that very same brain will execute the most insane mental acrobatics to excuse and rationalize spending money it doesn't have. The reason is simple — people wish to maximize their happiness or "utility" by consuming as many material things as possible whether they can afford it or not.

The ice cream
The sushi
The sports car

You name it, your brain is biologically predisposed to consume and enjoy the MAXIMUM amount of stuff the world has to offer. So much so, it will ignore that very important and mathematically undeniable law (that you can't spend more than you make) and tell itself the MOST FANTASTIC OF LIES to excuse you for violating that law.

This, unfortunately, is the instance where all financial problems begin. And so if we address this problem at the psychological level and not the logical or mathematical level, you can be "vaccinated" against the "disease" that causes nearly all financial problems.

The solution is very simple — a budget.

I personally can't force you to have the psychological epiphany to realize and incorporate into your brain that you CANNOT spend more than you make. That is up to your own mental temerity, fortitude, and honesty. I can, however, provide you a tool that will help you adhere to the unviolatable law of "don't spend more than you make." And that tool is the "budget."

Naturally, everybody knows what a budget is. You list your income, you list your expenses, and hopefully you have something left over in the end. It is an issue of having the self-control and discipline to adhere to the budget that is the problem. Because of this there are many ways or "tricks" financial advisors recommend to help you stick to your budget. Some of them recommend a "cash only" budget where you do not have any credit cards, pull out a certain amount of cash each paycheck, and FORCE yourself to live on that cash alone. Once the money runs out, too bad, you're out of money and have to deal with it. Others recommend an "envelope" budget where cash is put in envelopes dedicated towards paying certain expenses. Again, once the cash runs out, too bad, you can't spend any more money until the next paycheck. Even I have a purposely-set low credit limit on my credit card to ensure I minimize my spending.

We can go on as there are as many variants of personal budgets as there are financial advisors, but in general there are two types of budgets that will help you depending on your personality and financial situation - the "Detailed Budget" and the "Lazy Bachelor's Budget."

The "Detailed Budget" is precisely that – it's detailed. It is one where you list your income and then list every imaginable expense you'll ever have. There are already templates out there on the internet, not to mention personal budgeting software like "Microsoft Money," but below is an example budget from a free template offered by Microsoft:

INCOME
Wages
Interest/dividends
Miscellaneous

Income totals

EXPENSES

<u>Home</u>
Mortgage/rent
Utilities
Home telephone
Cellular telephone
Home repairs
Home improvement
Home security
Garden supplies
Home totals

<u>Daily living</u>
Groceries
Child care
Dry cleaning
Dining out
Housecleaning service
Dog walker
Daily living totals

<u>Transportation</u>
Gas/fuel
Insurance
Repairs
Car wash/detailing services
Parking
Public transportation
Transportation totals

Entertainment
Cable TV
Video/DVD rentals
Movies/plays
Concerts/clubs
Entertainment totals

Health
Health club dues
Insurance
Prescriptions
Over-the-counter drugs
Co-payments/out-of-pocket
Veterinarians/pet medicines
Life insurance
Health totals

Vacations
Plane fare
Accommodations
Food
Souvenirs
Pet boarding
Rental car
Vacations totals

Recreation
Gym fees
Sports equipment
Team dues
Toys/child gear
Recreation totals

Dues/subscriptions
Magazines
Newspapers
Internet connection
Public radio
Public television
Religious organizations
Charity
Dues/subscription totals

Personal
Clothing
Gifts
Salon/barber
Books
Music (CDs, etc.)
Personal totals

Financial obligations
Long-term savings
Retirement (401k, Roth IRA)
Credit card payments
Income tax (additional)
Other obligations
Financial obligation totals

Misc. payments
Misc #1
Misc #2
Misc #3

The first thing you'll notice is just how long and detailed this budget is. It includes scores of different expenses, some of which you most likely never thought of. It also has a "miscellaneous" section where you can enter in your own expenses should they not be found in the long list above. Each day or week you spend hours pulling out your receipts or printing off your credit card statement and enter into each category the amount you spent. You then compare the amount you actually spent versus what you budgeted for and hopefully you spent less than what was allocated.

The major drawback of the "detailed budget" should be plainly obvious— it's prohibitively cumbersome.

In this template alone you have around 70 individual items on your budget, most of which wouldn't occur to you to list, some of which you've never heard of or seen before. The time it would take the average person to document and record each of his or her expenses for just a DAY would at least be an hour of that person's time. Furthermore, no matter how detailed, no budget can fully account for all the different expenses and expenditures for all people. I guarantee you that in just 3 days of using the above budget you would be adding accounts because your personal spending is unique to you and not accounted for in the above template.

Because of this there are only two instances or reasons you would want to use this traditional type of budget. One, you have that kind of personality and REALLY like to know in extreme detail how and where you spend your money. There's nothing wrong with this as some people have that psychology (and they make great accountants). But most people do not have the patience, personality, or time for such detailed work. Two, you are on an incredibly tight budget and have to make sure every penny counts. This may be the case when you are in college or if you are facing severe financial problems (the two most likely times you'll be your "poorest" in life). But beyond those two instances the time it takes to adhere to this budget is not worth your time.

The "Lazy Bachelor Budget" on the other hand is not so much a budget as it is a philosophy or a way of life. Instead of wasting your time tracking every nickel and dime, comparing whether you overspent or came under budget, you follow one simple rule – spend as little as you can. In following that one simple rule you dispense with the chore of tracking and categorizing each individual expense, and instead replace it with a simple, default spending policy – spend as little as you can. You may not know where all of your money is going, but it doesn't matter, because in following that policy you will likely never spend more than you make.

There are many benefits to this approach over more traditional and detailed budgets. The time savings alone make the Lazy Bachelor Budget worth it. You'll never have to balance your checkbook because you will always ensure you spend less than you make, and you'll never have to save receipts because you don't care how the money was spent. There is also a lot less stress as you don't fret over whether you can afford something or not, because otherwise you wouldn't have bought it. And because it is easier to follow the Lazy Bachelor Budget, chances are *you'll actually follow it.* Rarely does anybody stick with a detailed budget for long, let alone replace it with a simplified version (like the Lazy Bachelor Budget). Sure enough they simply revert back to their old spending-spree ways, never solving their original financial problems in the first place.

All of these benefits combined, however, are dwarfed by the single largest benefit of the Lazy Bachelor Budget, a benefit that ensures you'll never have any financial problems in your life – you develop the habit and preference for cheap living. At first this may not seem like such an advantage. Who wants to live cheaply, let alone have a preference for it? But permit me a story to explain.

A couple I knew made a cumulative income of $350,000 a year. They were very well to do, with both the husband and wife having high-paying, successful careers. So I was confused when the husband approached me one day and asked me to consult them about their personal finances. I couldn't figure out what possible problems a family could have where the cumulative income was $350,000 per year.

But I soon found out.

- They both had luxury cars to maintain appearances at their respective offices and social gatherings.
- They had an additional SUV so they could tow their kids around to the various sports and activities they had.
- Their children were spared nothing. Nothing but the best. The best clothes, the best sports gear, the most expensive trips and brand new cars.
- The house was also so huge, they had an entire floor dedicated to storing all the toys and gadgets their kids no longer played with.

When all was said and done, yes, they made $350,000 a year, but spent more around $400,000.

While you might think this is rare, the truth is it's actually the norm. The majority of people tend to spend as much as they make, regardless of how much they make (and then probably a little more). It's why you can have a family making $350,000 and *still* have financial problems. But once again, this testifies to how the biggest hurdle to budgeting is not mathematical, but psychological, and shows you the value of following the Lazy Bachelor Budget. If you can get yourself psychologically accustomed to cheap living you directly address and negate the single largest threat to your personal finances – the psychological predisposition to maximize your spending.

A successful (though extreme) example of this is another friend of mine. He drives a cheap Asian import car and nothing else. It doesn't have air conditioning, power steering, automatic locks, or powered windows. He has a humble house in an uncoveted suburb. He fixes his own car, does his own home repairs, gets his clothes from the Salvation Army, and when he goes out, rarely spends more than $12 on a dinner at Perkins.

He is a multi-millionaire.

He bills out at $300 an hour to do high-level computer networking and security work. He easily made over $200,000 for each of the past 20 years, only to reinvest the proceeds in rental property and stocks. He has no debts, owning a small real estate empire outright, and works, at most, 20 hours a week. But in spite of spending a mere fraction of what the $350,000 per year couple does, he is infinitely happier. He has no stress. He has no worries. The man is truly free, capable of doing whatever he wants, whenever he wants, however he wants. And what he "wants" to do only reiterates that very important philosophical lesson from chapter 2 – the only thing that matters is other humans. He spends the majority of his free time conversing with friends over coffee and spending time with his dad as they work on various housing projects. The man leads a "rich" life and it isn't because of his money.

Of course, not everybody is going to become a $300/hr computer networking guru who shops at Goodwill for clothes, but the story of my friend reiterates some key and important points about budgeting and personal finances. If you replace a detailed budget with a simple policy or philosophy of minimal spending instead, not only is it easier to follow, but you will likely never have any financial problems. In forcing yourself to develop a taste for cheap living you not only eliminate the desire to purchase material items, but never suffer the financial stress that comes from purchasing things you can't or "can barely" afford. And finally, you'll realize happiness is not contingent on how much money you make or how many toys you buy, but how much free time you get to spend with family and friends. All of this can be achieved by adhering to the "Lazy Bachelor Budget."

***

Accounting

Over the course of your life it is guaranteed you will run into many instances where it will prove valuable to have some basic accounting skills. Nothing as detailed as "double entry bookkeeping," but specifically the ability to read the two most common financial statements:

The Income Statement

and

The Balance Sheet

The reason these two statements are key is because they are the two primary tools by which financial information is conveyed about a company, a person, even a government. And if you can read and interpret these two financial statements you will be able to make much more sound judgments in many areas of your financial life. Specifically;

Stocks, Bonds, Mutual Funds and Other Investments – You will be able to analyze and assess the profitability and financial health of a company (or mutual fund) and therefore determine whether you'd like to invest in it. This will play a vital role in your retirement planning as stocks, bonds and mutual funds are the investments that will account for the majority of your retirement funds.

Employers – You will be able to assess the financial stability of a company and whether or not you would like to work for them. This is important because it could mean the difference between a life-long career at a stable company or a short 4 month stint where you and everybody else gets laid off as the company files for bankruptcy.

Government Finances – As you live in a democracy you have a responsibility to your state, county, city, nation and fellow citizens to be informed about the finances of the various levels of government. You want to be able to know how much you're paying in taxes, where that money is going, and how that money is being spent. A responsible citizen informs himself about such matters to ensure he makes a wise choice when voting.

Taxes – In being able to read financial statements you'll also be able to do your taxes. Of course, sometimes tax law is so complicated it requires you pay an accountant to do them for you, but at least you will have the ability to understand them...sort of.

Applying for Loans – It is a near guarantee at some point in your life you will apply for a loan. Be it student loans, a car loan, or a mortgage, you will have to compile both a personal income statement and balance sheet every time you apply for a loan. It will also help you understand how banking and lending works, as well as how to keep your credit score in good standing.

Starting and Running a Business – Many of you will invariably become entrepreneurs, running your own business. Not only will this likely require you apply for a loan, but in order to determine whether you're profitable or not you will need to learn how to compile and read financial statements.

There are other instances where being versed in financial statements will prove useful, but nearly every major aspect of your economic and financial life will require some literacy in the income statement and balance sheet. There is, however, some good news.

You are already conceptually familiar with these financial statements.

Understand there is NO difference between your personal finances and that of a government, an employer, or a corporation. The only major difference is that a corporate financial statement might have an extra 6 zeroes tacked onto it. But beyond that, there is no functional or fundamental difference between the two. It is merely a matter of semantics. Therefore, in order to read them it is merely a matter of familiarizing yourself with the terms a company or a government might use in their financial statements as opposed to what you might use in yours.

The Income Statement

Whether it's your "income taxes," your "personal budget," a corporation's "profit and loss statement" or the "US Federal Budget" all of them are merely variations of the same thing – an income statement.

An income statement in its simplest form lists the sources of revenue for an entity and then subtracts out the expenses leaving a "profit" or "loss" at the bottom. In a very general sense every budget, tax form, profit and loss, and income statement follows this simple structure:

Revenues
-Expenses
=Profit

There are of course more details, but no matter how complex, even the US federal government's $4 trillion budget follows this basic layout.

The Personal Budget – While we have addressed personal budgets previously, keep in mind there is no "universal" or "standard" template for them. They can be as simple as the chart above or as detailed and complex as the Microsoft template we used before. Regardless, using a truncated version of the earlier template you see the general layout of a personal budget:

Income	
Salary	$20,000
Other Income	$2,000
Total Income	$22,000
Expenses	
-Rent	$7,000
-Insurance	$1,200
-Food	$3,000
-Phone	$1,200
-Clothing	$2,000
-Booze/Games/Beer	$4,500
-Tuition	$6,000
Total Expenses	$24,900
Profit/Loss	-$2,900

The key items to point out in a personal budget are that as you age you will likely have multiple sources of income. It isn't just your job that generates income, but you might have some interest on bonds, dividends from stocks or some other source of income. You should also note that your income is always AFTER-TAX as you do not get to keep all of your income. Roughly, anywhere from 10% to 60% will be taken out to pay for taxes depending on how much money you make and what state you live in. You may also have noticed in the example above the individual has a "net loss," spending $2,900 more than he took in. This is a likely scenario for many young people as they attend college and therefore have to borrow money to make up that short fall.

<u>Personal Tax Return</u> – Akin to your personal budget is your personal

tax return. While a budget is used primarily as a tool to track and limit expenses, your tax return is used to estimate your overall tax bill and whether you need to pay into the system at the end of the tax year or whether you get a tax refund. Everybody has to file a federal tax return, but not everybody has to file a state tax return because some states do not have an income tax. Regardless, the most common tax return you will see is the IRS form "1040" which is the standard tax form most people fill out when filing their federal taxes.

Page 1: (next page)

Form 1040 — Department of the Treasury—Internal Revenue Service (99)
U.S. Individual Income Tax Return — 2012

OMB No. 1545-0074 | IRS Use Only—Do not write or staple in this space.

For the year Jan. 1–Dec. 31, 2012, or other tax year beginning , 2012, ending , 20 | See separate instructions.

Your first name and initial | Last name | Your social security number

If a joint return, spouse's first name and initial | Last name | Spouse's social security number

Home address (number and street). If you have a P.O. box, see instructions. | Apt. no. | ▲ Make sure the SSN(s) above and on line 6c are correct.

City, town or post office, state, and ZIP code. If you have a foreign address, also complete spaces below (see instructions).

Foreign country name | Foreign province/state/county | Foreign postal code

Presidential Election Campaign
Check here if you, or your spouse if filing jointly, want $3 to go to this fund. Checking a box below will not change your tax or refund. ☐ You ☐ Spouse

Filing Status
Check only one box.
1. ☐ Single
2. ☐ Married filing jointly (even if only one had income)
3. ☐ Married filing separately. Enter spouse's SSN above and full name here. ▶
4. ☐ Head of household (with qualifying person). (See instructions.) If the qualifying person is a child but not your dependent, enter this child's name here. ▶
5. ☐ Qualifying widow(er) with dependent child

Exemptions
6a ☐ Yourself. If someone can claim you as a dependent, do not check box 6a . . . . .
b ☐ Spouse . . . .
c Dependents:
(1) First name Last name | (2) Dependent's social security number | (3) Dependent's relationship to you | (4) ✓ if child under age 17 qualifying for child tax credit (see instructions)

If more than four dependents, see instructions and check here ▶ ☐

Boxes checked on 6a and 6b
No. of children on 6c who:
• lived with you
• did not live with you due to divorce or separation (see instructions)
Dependents on 6c not entered above
Add numbers on lines above ▶

d Total number of exemptions claimed . . . .

Income

Attach Form(s) W-2 here. Also attach Forms W-2G and 1099-R if tax was withheld.

If you did not get a W-2, see instructions.

Enclose, but do not attach, any payment. Also, please use Form 1040-V.

7 Wages, salaries, tips, etc. Attach Form(s) W-2 . . . . | 7
8a Taxable interest. Attach Schedule B if required . . . . | 8a
b Tax-exempt interest. Do not include on line 8a . . . | 8b |
9a Ordinary dividends. Attach Schedule B if required . . . . | 9a
b Qualified dividends . . . . | 9b |
10 Taxable refunds, credits, or offsets of state and local income taxes . . . . | 10
11 Alimony received . . . . | 11
12 Business income or (loss). Attach Schedule C or C-EZ . . . . | 12
13 Capital gain or (loss). Attach Schedule D if required. If not required, check here ▶ ☐ | 13
14 Other gains or (losses). Attach Form 4797 . . . . | 14
15a IRA distributions . | 15a | b Taxable amount . . . | 15b
16a Pensions and annuities | 16a | b Taxable amount . . . | 16b
17 Rental real estate, royalties, partnerships, S corporations, trusts, etc. Attach Schedule E | 17
18 Farm income or (loss). Attach Schedule F . . . . | 18
19 Unemployment compensation . . . . | 19
20a Social security benefits | 20a | b Taxable amount . . . | 20b
21 Other income. List type and amount | 21
22 Combine the amounts in the far right column for lines 7 through 21. This is your total income ▶ | 22

Adjusted Gross Income

23 Educator expenses . . . . | 23
24 Certain business expenses of reservists, performing artists, and fee-basis government officials. Attach Form 2106 or 2106-EZ | 24
25 Health savings account deduction. Attach Form 8889 . | 25
26 Moving expenses. Attach Form 3903 . . . . | 26
27 Deductible part of self-employment tax. Attach Schedule SE . | 27
28 Self-employed SEP, SIMPLE, and qualified plans . . | 28
29 Self-employed health insurance deduction . . . . . | 29
30 Penalty on early withdrawal of savings . . . . . . | 30
31a Alimony paid b Recipient's SSN ▶ | 31a
32 IRA deduction . . . . | 32
33 Student loan interest deduction . . . . | 33
34 Tuition and fees. Attach Form 8917 . . . . | 34
35 Domestic production activities deduction. Attach Form 8903 | 35
36 Add lines 23 through 35 . . . . | 36
37 Subtract line 36 from line 22. This is your adjusted gross income . . . . ▶ | 37

For Disclosure, Privacy Act, and Paperwork Reduction Act Notice, see separate instructions. Cat. No. 11320B Form **1040** (2012)

Page 2:

[Form 1040 (2012), Page 2 — tax form image]

(for a more legible sample visit the following site: http://www.irs.gov/pub/irs-pdf/f1040.pdf).

Although very complex, tax returns do follow the general format of an income statement, listing your income first, and then subtracting various expenses. The goal however is not to find out "how much money you have left in the end" but rather to calculate your "taxable income" which is in turn used to calculate your total tax bill. This number is then compared to what you already paid in over the year to see whether you owe or are owed money.

Because of its complexity (and the fact people are afraid of getting in trouble with the IRS) most people pay an accountant to do their taxes. However, I would strongly recommend doing your own taxes at least once just to get a feel for how taxes are calculated and so you can better understand your tax return should you pay an accountant to compile them for you.

<u>Corporate Income Statement</u> – Just like people, corporations have to pay income taxes as well. However, in addition to the government, corporations must answer to another group of people – the shareholders. As it is the shareholders who own the company, they want to know how much profit the company is making and whether or not the company will pay out any of that profit in the form of "dividends." To show this companies issue an "income statement" sometimes also called a "profit and loss statement" or just "P&L" for short. Like any other budget or tax return it lists how much in sales the company has and then subtracts out its expenses (below is Target Corporation's 2012 income statement, note the official title of "Consolidated Statement of Operations").

	2012	2011	2010
Sales	$ 71,960	$ 68,466	$ 65,786
Credit Card Revenues	$ 1,341	$ 1,399	$ 1,604
Total Revenues	$ 73,301	$ 69,865	$ 67,390
Cost of sales	$ 50,568	$ 47,860	$ 45,725
Selling, General and Administrative	$ 14,914	$ 14,106	$ 13,469
Credit Card Expenses	$ 467	$ 446	$ 860
Depreciation and Amortization	$ 2,142	$ 2,131	$ 2,084
Gains on Receivables held for sale	$ (161)		
Earnings before interest expense and income taxes	$ 5,371	$ 5,322	$ 5,252
Net Interest Expense	$ 762	$ 866	$ 757
Earnings before income taxes	$ 4,609	$ 4,456	$ 4,495
Provisions for income taxes	$ 1,610	$ 1,527	$ 1,575
Net earnings	$ 2,999	$ 2,929	$ 2,920

However, companies have different expenses than humans and so some general and standardized expense terms are used.

COGS stands for "cost of goods sold" and is what the company paid for in terms of raw materials or goods it purchased for resale. So for example when Target buys all of its products that it is going to resell on its shelves that expense is considered "COGS." SGA stands for "selling, general, and administrative" expenses and is sometimes used as a catch-all phrase that includes all the operating expenses of a firm that are NOT COGS. So for example utilities, salaries, interest expense, and insurance are usually all lumped into SGA and not listed individually. There are also "other income" and "other expense" accounts that account for miscellaneous sources of income or expenses that otherwise don't fit into any of the above accounts. And at the very bottom, after we have accounted for all sources of income and expenses, you have "net income" or "net earnings" or "net loss" or "net profit" aka "the bottom line." This is the amount of money left over that can be paid to the shareholders or be reinvested back into the company.

The problem with corporate income statements (and corporate

accounting in general) is that there are as many types of expense accounts as there are companies as each company and industry has its own unique set of expenses. For example if you decide to start a law firm your income statement will not show COGS because you are selling a service, not a physical product. Oil drilling companies have an expense called "depletion" which you will not find anywhere else. Airlines have a whole slew of maintenance and operational expenses that can only be found in the airline industry. And making matters worse, sometimes accountants use multiple terms to describe the same account (sales is also called revenue, net earnings is the same as net income, etc.). In short, to be able to become literate in reading income statements you really do need to take a course in accounting or spend a lot of time pouring over income statements, familiarizing yourself with them. This is beyond the scope of this book, but if you are really interested I teach an online class titled "The Analysis and Valuation of Stocks" which does an exemplary job. You can find it by searching the following site:

www.ed2go.com

Government Budgets – Once again, as this is a democracy, you have an obligation to society to become an informed voter. Part of that is familiarizing yourself with the finances of the country as well as your state. So you have a choice:

Be the typical, ignorant, moronic 20 something that likes to spew BS about how we don't spend enough money on the children, the poor, health care, education, puppies, flowers, and unicorns, and if we just did that then the world would have no problems and we could sing Kumbaya around a camp fire, or

be an adult and spend the whopping 20 seconds it would take to look up the federal and state budgets online.

The federal budget can be found here: www.budget.gov, though the level of detail may be a bit overkill. For a simplified version Wikipedia does a decent job of breaking it down.

Regardless, the federal budget, just like all other forms of income statements, follows the same general flow and layout, but it is actually better viewed in pie chart form. This gives the viewer a quick synopsis of where the majority of our taxes go and in what proportions.

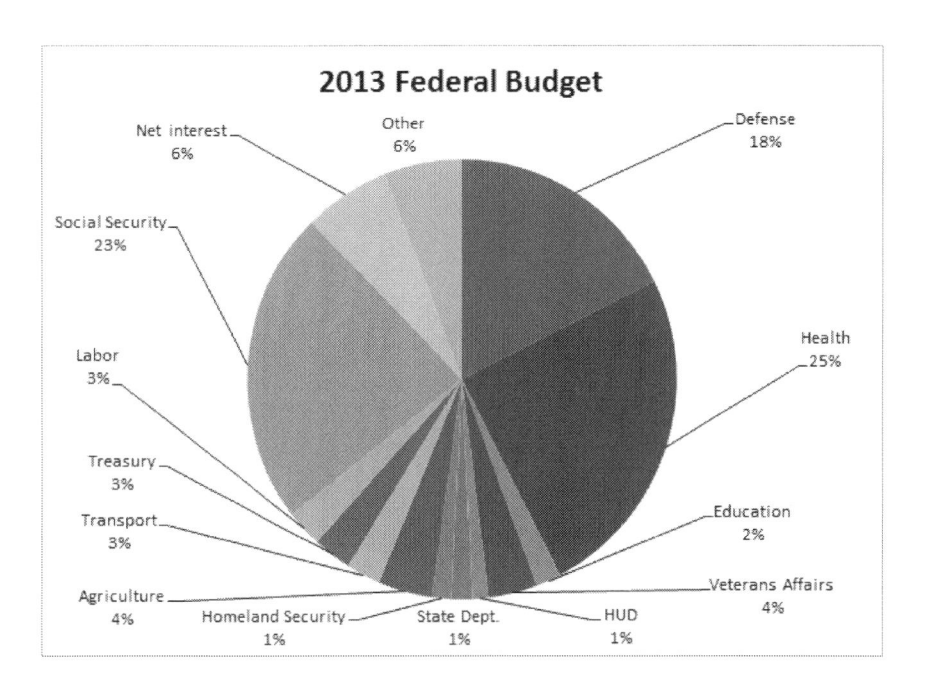

2013 Federal Budget

- Net interest 6%
- Other 6%
- Defense 18%
- Social Security 23%
- Health 25%
- Labor 3%
- Treasury 3%
- Transport 3%
- Education 2%
- Agriculture 4%
- Veterans Affairs 4%
- Homeland Security 1%
- State Dept. 1%
- HUD 1%

Again, like a corporate income statement the government has expenses that are unique to governmental finances (social security,

Medicare, defense, transportation, etc.) and it will take some time for you to familiarize yourself with those accounts. However, there is one thing missing from the pie chart and that is how much money the government took in.

For the above budget (2013) the government spent $3.8 trillion, but only took in $2.9 trillion. This was a shortfall or "deficit" of $900 billion. Since taxes were not adequate enough to cover all of the government's spending, the government had to borrow that money adding $900 billion to the "national debt."

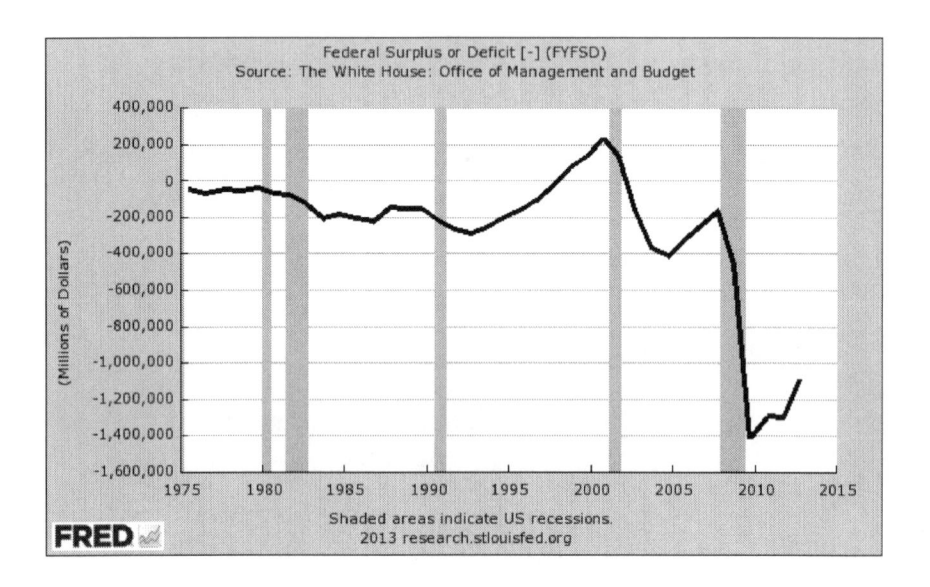

This issue (the deficit and the debt) is the single largest economic problem facing the country and will have ramifications and consequences to your financial future. Because of this the topic will be addressed in more detail in a later chapter.

The Balance Sheet

While the income statement shows you how much money a person or entity is making, the balance sheet shows how much that person or entity **owns** versus how much it **owes.** In short, it shows an entity's "net worth" or "how rich it is."

For example, it is a common mistake to assume that middle aged man driving that $70,000 luxury car living in that $3 million McMansion is "rich." The truth is most people who drive $70,000 luxury cars and live in $3 million McMansions are poor. Yes, they own a $70,000 car and a $3 million house, but they have a $70,000 car loan and a $3.5 million mortgage. In other words, they owe more than they own resulting in a NEGATIVE "net worth" of -$500,000. Contrast that with your average waitress with a $4,000 used car, $7,000 in her checking account and a small $100,000 condo, who owes nothing on the car and has a $50,000 mortgage. She is infinitely richer as her net worth is a positive $61,000. But if all you looked at was what people "owned" and not "owed" you would never know the young waitress is a more stable and fiscally responsible person.

This is the primary benefit of being able to read a balance sheet because not only is it important you can assess your own personal finances, but chances are you will at some point lend an individual or a company money. A family member or a friend will be in a rough spot and will need to borrow some cash. Or you will be interested in investing in "bonds" (which is nothing more than lending money to large organizations like governments or businesses). In both instances the way you can tell if they are capable of paying you back is by looking at their balance sheet to see if they have enough assets to cover their debts.

The balance sheet is really, very simple.

- On one side you list everything you own, aka, your "assets."
- On the other side you list everything you owe, aka, your "liabilities" (or sometimes "debt").
- The difference is "how rich you are" or your "net worth."

And just like an income statement, the balance sheet follows a general outline or structure regardless of whether you're a person, a company, or a government:

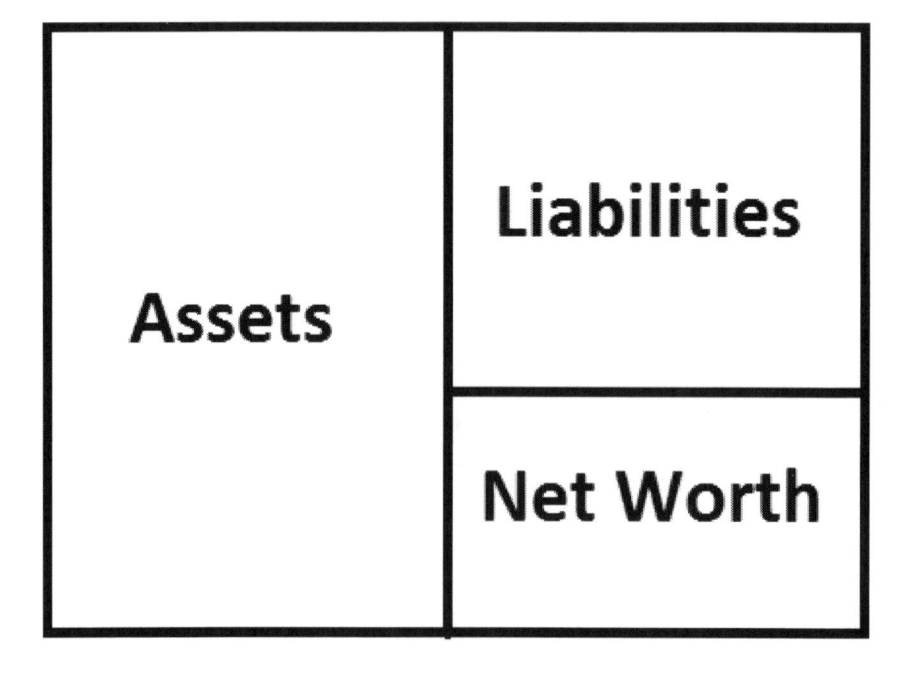

Assets	**Liabilities**
	Net Worth

However, the two most likely instances you're going to need to be able to read a balance sheet is when you are assessing your own personal finances and when you are looking to lend money out as an investment. Because of this we will focus only on personal balance sheets and corporate balance sheets.

Personal Balance Sheets – Like the income statement there will be some semantical differences between a personal balance sheet and a corporate balance sheet, but the layout and structure is still the same:

List everything you **own** on one side
List everything you **owe** on the other side
And the difference between the two is your "net worth" (which hopefully is not negative).

The problem people have when compiling their personal balance sheet, however, is the same one when compiling their budget – they forget a lot of details.

If I were to ask you to list ALL of your assets, chances are you would include large items like your X-Box, your flat panel TV, your computer, your smart phone, your car, and your furniture.

However, what about your clothes?

The beer in the fridge?

The pens and paper in your desk?

Understand you don't just list the large or "expensive" assets when compiling your balance sheet, you list EVERYTHING because everything you own is an asset.

The same thing applies with what you owe or your "liabilities." Most people will list their car loan, their student loans, and their mortgage. But what about the credit card? The $5,000 loan your father gave you? Or all those utilities you will have to pay at the end of the month? No matter how small you need to consider EVERY liability or debt you have. When it's all said and done a personal balance sheet should look something like this:

Personal Balance Sheet

Cash	$ 428,168	Short Term Notes Due to Financial Inst.		
Securities	$ 19,600	Short Term Notes Due to Others		
Cash Value of Life Insurance		Insurance Loans		
Homestead	$ 400,000	Installment Loans/Contracts		
Other Real Estate	$ 525,000	Mortgage on Homestead	$	99,933
Profit Share/Pensions		Mortgages on Other Real Estate	$	75,498
Retirement Accounts	$ 241,238	Taxes		
Automobiles		Credit Cards	$	6,500
Personal Property	$ 85,000	Other Liabilities	$	23,328
Due from Others				
Value of Business	$ 2,970,591	**Total Liabilities**	**$**	**205,259**
Other Intangibles				
Total Assets	**$ 4,669,597**	**Net Worth**	**$ 4,464,338**	

While the above example is one of a rich person and we could point out several things, the most important thing to note is the issue of "liquidity." If you look at the details, the majority of this person's wealth comes from his business. Nearly $3 million of his $4.5 million in wealth is in the form of a company. But let's say his son is struck with a medical emergency and needs an immediate $3 million procedure.

Could the father just sell his $3 million business in a matter of minutes? Probably not.

This is the concept of "liquidity" and is just as important as "net worth."

Understand a person may list the value of an asset at $3 million, but if that asset needs to be sold in a rush, its price would have to be reduced significantly because there aren't a lot of immediate buyers with $3 million cash in hand. Contrast that with, say, silver or stock in IBM. Both are considered "highly liquid" because they can be converted into cash quite easily. Ergo, a balance sheet doesn't just tell us the net worth of a person or how rich they are, but also how "liquid" they are.

This is an important concept as many people can be considered "rich," but not liquid, meaning they are still a high risk when it comes to lending. During the housing bubble there was no limit to the number of middle-aged, desperate real estate developers who listed the value of their real estate empires in the multiple of millions of dollars. But if they ever had to actually sell those properties in a pinch, they would only receive a fraction of that value. Unfortunately the "pinch" came in the form of the housing crash and most of these former "real estate moguls" ended up filing for bankruptcy because of *liquidity, not net worth*. Therefore, while there are certainly other things to analyze when looking at the balance sheet, the two most important ones every novice needs to learn first is net worth and liquidity.

Corporate Balance Sheets – People for the most part intuitively understand their own personal balance sheet and, like the income statement, it is just a matter of learning some new accounting terms to understand a corporate balance sheet. You won't recognize all the accounting terms in Target's balance sheet below, but you should be able to visually identify the assets, liabilities and net worth sections (also note in this case it is not a side by side balance sheet, but just one long list of account items). An excellent exercise, however, would be to look up each of the account items listed on the balance sheet below (I recommend using www.investopedia.com). Not only will you familiarize yourself with some standard accounting items in a balance sheet, you'll also have the lesson of liquidity reiterated as companies list their assets and liabilities in order of liquidity (example on next page)

Assets	
Cash and Cash Equivalents	784
Credit Card Receiveable for sale	5841
Credit Card Receiveables, net of allowance	0
Inventory	7903
Other Current Assets	1860
Total Current Assets	16388
Property and Equipment	
Land	6206
Buildings and improvements	28653
Fixtures and equipments	5362
Computer hardware and software	2567
Construction in Progress	1176
Accumulated Depreciation	-13311
Property and equipment net	30653
Other non current assets	1122
Total Assets	**48163**
Liabilities and Owners Equity	
Accounts Payable	7056
Accrued and other currently liabilities	3981
Unsecured debt and other borrowings	1494
Nonrecourse debt collateralized by credit card rec's	1500
Total current liabilities	14031
Unsecured debt and other borrowings	14654
Nonrecourse debt collateralized by credit card rec's	0
Deferred income taxes	1311
Other noncurrent liabilities	1609
Total noncurrent liabilities	17574
Shareholder's investment	
Common stock	54
APIC	3925
Retained earnings	13155
Pension and other benefits liabilities	-532
Currency translation	-44
Total shareholders investment	16558
Total liabilities and owner's equity	**48163**

***

Minimalism

"Minimalism" is like "The Bachelor Budget," but instead of following the simple policy of "spend as little as you can," it takes this policy and turns it into a full-blown way of life. It isn't just about spending the least amount of money possible to stay within a budget, but applying a minimalistic philosophy to all aspects of your life in order to get the most out of that life. The benefits of such an approach are numerous. You minimize the amount of financial risk in your life. You minimize the amount of work you must do in your life. You minimize the amount of wealth that can be stolen from you. And consequently you maximize the total amount of freedom and happiness you have. But in order to understand and apply the philosophy of minimalism to your own life, you must understand the one underlying principle it hinges on:

Stuff is evil.

At the core of minimalism is the fact that assets are not assets at all, but rather liabilities. At first this may not make sense. You may be asking the question,

"Well, if I own this electronic entertainment system and I paid cash for it, is it NOT an asset? Does it NOT have value?"

which of course is true. That IS an entertainment system. It DOES have value. And if you don't owe anything on it, you have an asset with a positive value. But what you are not accounting for are three "indirect" or less-obvious costs:

1. The lifetime ancillary, supporting, and maintenance costs of owning that asset.
2. The "opportunity costs" or "what could you have done with the money, had you not purchased that asset."
3. The stress the comes from owning it.

First, to purchase that entertainment system you had to forfeit 50 hours of your life at a job you hate, answering to a boss you loathe. Second, is the entertainment system worth the stress at work and the 75% increase in the chance of a stroke? Third, you now have to have an apartment large enough to house it. Fourth, especially if you're younger, you get to spend more time, energy and sweat lugging that thing around every time you move. There are others, but when all of these ancillary costs are considered in their entirety, more often than not the ownership of the asset is just plain not worth it.

Now take that concept and multiply it by

every asset you own,
every asset *you think you need to own*, and
every asset *you are going to own in the future*.

Every vehicle, every computer, every piece of furniture, every video game, and every little POS trinket the ladies in your life will insist on cluttering your house with. When you consider the enormity and totality of stuff a normal person acquires in his life you can see just what a large unforeseen lifetime price you are paying for all this "stuff." In the end you don't end up owning the stuff as much as the stuff ends up owning you.

However, a mere paragraph or two getting your brain to view stuff as "evil" cannot undo the trillions of dollars companies, media and governments have spent over the decades brainwashing you to buy as much stuff as possible. Citing stress at work is probably not enough to get you to seriously reconsider Microsoft's latest Xbox console, and citing moving costs is probably not enough to get wifey to reconsider the new furniture set. You and everybody else have been conditioned to like stuff since the day you could watch television. Ergo, a more detailed and literal review of the benefits of minimalism will not only convince you of its merits, but show you exactly how it works and why you might want to incorporate it, at least partially, into your life.

Lodging and Storage – Arguably the single most important benefit of minimalism is when you apply it to housing. If you think about it, the single largest expense in most people's budget is what they pay for housing. Be it rent or a mortgage, every month hundreds of millions of Americans spend trillions of dollars on housing. But what precisely are they housing?

If all they were housing was themselves, then technically all a human needs is a tent. But if you look into any home or any apartment you will soon realize that the vast majority of those trillions of dollars are not, in fact, spent on housing people as much as it is storing stuff. This is a very important distinction to make because, for the most part, you pay for housing based on the amount of square footage, not the number of heads in the household. Therefore, if you can eliminate the amount of stuff you own you can eliminate the amount of square footage you need for housing, and therefore drastically reduce the single largest expense in your entire life.

To what extreme you want to go is up to you. I personally was able to minimize my personal possessions down to a futon, a coffee table, an LCD projector, a laptop and some weights. All of my worldly possessions could fit conveniently in one room, and when moving, the back of a pickup truck. A friend of mine suggested a hammock or blow up mattress for even more minimal living. And there are communities of people who live in their cars (some out of necessity, others out of a curiosity as to whether they could do it or not). Of course, that is perhaps too bare-bones for most people, but if you were to be honest with yourself you could get rid of at least 50% of your stuff, thereby cutting your lifetime housing expenses in half.

Time Savings of Cleaning and Maintenance – It's very simple – the less stuff you own, the less maintenance and repair it needs. A 10,000 square foot McMansion will require at least a day of human labor each week to clean, while a small studio apartment can go months without cleaning (trust me, I know). A small Kia with no frills has infinitely fewer things that can break than a luxury BMW with all the bells and whistles. And a boat you rent twice a year only needs gas, while the person who owns it gets to clean it, maintain it and store it. Therefore, in addition to paying increased rent to store your stuff you get to have the honor and privilege to repair and maintain your stuff as well. That is time that could be spent fishing or playing video games if you just got rid of all that stuff.

Mobility – Arguably the most underrated benefit of a minimalist lifestyle is mobility. Because if you can get rid of your stuff, your ability to travel, move, and take advantage of opportunities increases exponentially.

For example, take the IT guy I worked with back in my banking days. All he wanted to do was sell his house, get rid of all of his stuff, grab his backpack and laptop, and go backpacking in Mexico until he died. It is possible for every person to do that, but the reason it is so rare is because nearly 99.9% of people have stuff that needs storing. This means they have to essentially pay for two residences – one to house them while travelling and another to house all their stuff while they're gone. This doubling of lodging expenses prohibits nearly everybody from travelling around the world as it financially anchors them to their stuff back home.

Also, one may consider minimizing their stuff because of the nature of today's job market. Gone are the days of finding that one reliable employer in town where you work 35 years, get your gold watch and retire in the same community. The economy today is fluid, dynamic, and constantly changing meaning the best job opportunities may be 2,000 miles away, not to mention they may require you to travel a lot. Additionally, there is no loyalty between employers and employees anymore. Employers have absolutely NO problem laying off thousands just to make an extra 40 cents. The consequences are that the average time a person stays on a job is only 4.4 years and only 2 years for younger generations. Therefore, since loyalty is not rewarded and most economic opportunities will require mobility, then why buy a house, let alone a lot of stuff? This leads to the largest benefit of "packing light" and being mobile:

Moving fucking sucks.

It doesn't "just suck".

It *"FUCKING* sucks."

Chances are you are going to move at least 12 times in your life and probably more if you're younger. Why make such a horrible and repetitive experience more painful than it has to be? Get rid of your stuff and moving goes from the most painful thing in the world to just a mere annoyance.

Less Theft/Less Legal Risk – When you don't own a lot of stuff then that just means less stuff for other people to steal or take. This will happen in two forms in your life. The first being theft. While living in Minneapolis some of the local scum stole my 1985 Cutlass Supreme. When it was recovered it was so damaged there was no point trying to salvage it. The good news, however, was that I only paid $500 for it. I spent more insuring it than I did the car itself. So when it got stolen (or dinged, or scratched) I didn't care. If you don't have a lot of stuff (or at least a lot of nice stuff) when somebody damages it or steals it, you won't care. The second way is law suits. As America becomes a more litigious society chances are increasing you will be sued for frivolous reasons. The good news though is that people only tend to sue people or companies with deep pockets. If you don't have a lot of assets, then there's nothing for them to sue. And even if they do, and they win, you simply declare bankruptcy, forfeit what meager assets you own, and move on with your life.

Lower Taxes/Government Benefits – Somewhat related to theft is taxation. The government likes to get paid and if it doesn't it has this nasty habit of charging you fees and throwing you in jail. However, the federal government (and most states) have a "progressive tax system" where the more you make the higher the percentage of your income you pay in taxes. As a minimalist, however, you benefit the most from this system as you make the least amount of money possible and are therefore taxed at the lowest rate (below are the federal income tax rates for 2013).

Rate	Single Filers	Married Joint Filers	Head of Household Filers
10%	$0 to $8,925	$0 to $17,850	$0 to $12,750
15%	$8,925 to $36,250	$17,850 to $72,500	$12,750 to $48,600
25%	$36,250 to $87,850	$72,500 to $146,400	$48,600 to $125,450
28%	$87,850 to $183,250	$146,400 to $223,050	$125,450 to $203,150
33%	$183,250 to $398,350	$223,050 to $398,350	$203,150 to $398,350
35%	$398,350 to $400,000	$398,350 to $450,000	$398,350 to $425,000
39.6%	$400,000 and up	$450,000 and up	$425,000 and up

However, the tax benefits to minimalism do not stop there because the less you make the more government benefits you qualify for. These can range from anything from "tax credits" to qualifying for food stamps to getting free housing (all of which will be addressed in more detail in a later chapter). Of course there is a moral aspect to taking a government handout at the expense of the taxpayer, but morality aside, understand these are the rules and laws society, via democracy, voted in. To be purely economic and literal about it, you might as well take as much advantage as you can.

Less Spending/Less Work/Less Stress – Finally, the most direct and obvious benefit of practicing minimalism is the direct cost savings. Since you are pursuing the "Lazy Bachelor Budget" your demands for money are drastically lowered and therefore your demand for work is drastically lowered as well. You needn't work as much, you needn't answer to an abusive employer, and the stress that normally comes with three credit cards, a car payment, a student loan, and a mortgage payment simply doesn't exist in your life. Of course you aren't going out for sushi every night, but you are immune to recessions, you can afford all you need, and you live a much simpler and happier life.

***

Debt

As mentioned before all financial problems in the world are caused by people, governments and companies spending more than they make. And if they simply spend less than they make then all the world's financial problems would go away. But most people don't do this and so the cumulative sins of spending more than you earn manifest themselves in the form of debt. It's not like "oops" you spent $25,000 and you only made $20,000, well, be more careful next time. By the fact you spent $5,000 more than you had means somebody had to lend you that $5,000 and they will very much expect you to pay it back. And if you don't they will hunt you and haunt you for the rest of your life. But most people's financial problems are not on the order of a mere $5,000. They are usually on the order of $250,000 and in many instances the debt is so great there is no way people can actually work up enough money to pay off those debts.

The solution is simple – don't go into debt.

Of course on the outset such a solution seems obvious and insultingly-simplistic.

"Really, don't go into debt and I won't have any financial problems? No kidding? Just like that? Really?"

But the benefit of such a simple solution is hidden by its naïve, child-like simplicity – what if people just didn't go into debt? What if people didn't have credit cards, car loans, and so forth? What if we could change people's psychologies and behaviors so that they wouldn't ever take on debt? What you would soon realize is that we have nothing short of the silver bullet to *all of the world's financial problems*. Since it is only debt that can cause financial problems, if people simply refuse to go into debt there will be no financial problems. And that isn't "simplistic" or "naïve." It's logical and binary. Without debt you are immune to financial problems. Without debt it is *impossible* to have any financial problems.

The real issue is can a person really avoid debt 100% in their lives? There are things in life that cost a lot of money, practically forcing you to borrow to pay for them. How are you supposed to afford a house? Aren't you wasting rent all those years? Would it not be worth taking on debt in the form of the mortgage so you build up equity in 30 years? What about college? How are you supposed to pay for that? At 18 you don't just have $50,000 laying around. Would it not be worth taking on some debt to get an education so you can get a higher paying job? And cars? How are you supposed to afford a good, quality car for reliable transportation so you can get to work every day and make money? Are these things not worth going into debt for?

The answer is, sadly, becoming, "No, not really."

Take the four primary things you will borrow money for:

Cars
Consumer spending (credit cards)
A house
College/Education

Cars and consumer spending should be obvious. Those are merely material items that will wear out and need replacing. They are not investments where you expect them to pay off, but rather clothes, food, booze, video games, etc. that will have a zero dollar value when you're done consuming them. All you manage to do in signing up for that $700/month lease (loan) of a sports car you can't afford is impoverish every other aspect of your life, force yourself to suffer a job you hate, and cause you unneeded and unnecessary stress during the life of the loan.

Housing (which we shall delve into later) ironically you can never own. Even if you buy a house, pay it off, and have a zero balance on your mortgage, you still have to rent it from the county by paying property taxes. You also get to pay insurance and pay for any maintenance which every house has. You really don't own that house, you own a liability that you have to pay for anyway. Additionally, like the $700 sport car lease, your $3,000/month mortgage payment only forces you to be a slave to your boss for the next 30 years.

And finally, education. It should be very apparent now with the bursting of the education bubble and the high under-and-unemployment rates of young college graduates just what a waste and scam most colleges and universities are. Kids are graduating with masters degrees only to work in coffee shops and grocery stores. Yes, of course there are good programs and good degrees that still may be worth the investment, but the majority of students do not study those topics. All they've managed to do is destroy their financial futures by taking on $70,000 in student loans to study tripe and party for 4 years as they make $8/hour mopping floors.

But there is a very positive other side to this coin. If it's a better deal NOT to borrow to pay for these things, then you're actually quite free. If you take those four major purchases out of your life, the amount of money you need to make and the number of hours you need to work drops dramatically. For example I've always found it odd kids actually want to go to college. What, you want another 4-8 years of high school v. 2.0? Paying bloated tuition as you sit in some beige classroom listening to some hack professor blather on like Ben Stein in "Ferris Bueller's Day Off?" Staying up till 3AM to study for finals eating ramen noodles? What if you just learned a trade, worked in construction, made some decent money, rented a cheap place, got drunk every night, chased girls and travelled around the world? Would that not be preferable to going into massive amounts of debt to go to college?

The thing to understand is that society has programmed people into thinking they HAVE TO go to college and they HAVE TO get a house and they HAVE TO have kids and they HAVE TO have fancy cars. But in reality, you don't. And when you take away these falsely-premised demands you eliminate nearly all the reasons you'd need to go into debt and consequently eliminate the vast majority of any would-be financial problems.

***

Don't Do Stupid Shit

Chances are you are a young dumbass.

I say this not out of condescension, but the expectation you are a young male, and thus inexperienced and thus clueless about most things in life. Of course, I mean this in a loving-older brother sort of way, but you're still a young dumbass none the less. And truth be told, the majority of life-crippling mistakes men make are when they are young dumbasses.

The primary way people screw up their financial lives is not through bad luck or having something random happen to them. It is through their own idiocy and stupidity that they torpedo their finances and thus ruin their lives forever. In 99.9% of cases where people have financial problems it is self-inflicted. The trailer trash, single mom of 6 in Wyoming did not innocently contract the "Trailer Trash, Single Mom of 6" disease, where one day she was on her way to become an engineer, got bit by a mosquito and then – **POOF!** – got infected with the "Trailer Trash, Single Mom of 6" disease. She made stupid decisions over the course of her life that got her there. The crack head was not on his way to a great investment banking career when, out of nowhere, a snake bit him infecting him with the "Crack Head Sitting on the Corner Begging for Money" disease. He made stupid decisions that led to his miserable life.

However, a lot of times the line between a good decision and a bad one is not always so clear. Not to mention, that line can be blurred with alcohol or emotion, two items that many young men are susceptible to.   These "less obvious" bad decisions are particularly dangerous as they can wreak just as much damage on a young man's life as a patently stupid one. Thus, a review of the most common mistakes young men make to screw up their lives (both obvious and less so) is called for.

<u>Bad Friends</u> – Say you are the most honest, nice, reputable, ethical person out there. You are not a criminal, but some of your friends

have had run-ins with the law, do/deal drugs, get in bar fights, etc. You have the fullest of intentions of becoming a surgeon and will start school in the fall. Thankfully, you can afford college because you worked hard, had a 3.9 GPA and got a full scholarship. One day, on the way back from dropping your friend off at his house you get pulled over for a taillight being out. The cop is a K-9 unit and as the dog comes near your car it starts barking furiously. The cop searches your car and finds some crack-cocaine in a plastic wrapper that is obviously your-less-than-trustful friend's. Even though it isn't yours, you can now you kiss college in the fall goodbye, you can kiss your scholarship good-bye, you can kiss your career as a surgeon goodbye, and now you get to face possible prison time.

If I were to estimate it, I would say about 70% of the people in prison right now are not criminals, but rather victims of having bad friends and being at the wrong place at the wrong time. One "friend' of mine would drink booze while I was driving. My pothead brother has left more than one "gift" in my car. And there's been more than one instance at a bar where fights instigated by my "friends" were breaking out and the cops would have been well within their rights to arrest us. Of course, as you age you eliminate this element from your group of friends, but especially when you are younger, testosterone, booze, and drugs are ample, all of which is a bad mix for getting a criminal record and thus a severely impaired professional life.

<u>Bad Girlfriend</u> – If having bad friends is bad, having a bad girlfriend is a nightmare. The reasons are many. You will tend to love (or at least have feelings for) your girlfriend. This impairs your ability to think logically and only acts as an enhancer to your testosterone. If things go wrong with your girlfriend you typically react not with

calm thought and logic, but uncontrolled emotions – rage, anger, and hatred. Also, there ARE women out there who sadistically get off on playing mind games and creating drama with men. It has happened TWICE that I've had a psychotic bitch screaming at the top of her lungs in my car while I was driving on a busy interstate. Both drove me to the brink of nearly hitting them, which would have guaranteed me jail time. Third, they are female. ANY, and I mean ANY domestic violence charges, whether real or fake, will result in you going to jail and an up-hill battle in court. Finally, one bad girlfriend probably has three or four other guys she's stringing along. Guys who, because of their emotion, will view you as a threat and come out swinging or worse, carrying a shotgun.

You put all this together and you got a volatile mix that results in fights, jail time, false domestic violence charges, sometimes false rape charges, jealous husbands, violent ex-boyfriends, headaches and mental abuse, all of which will impair, if not at least scar your life. No girl is worth that.

Fights – Being a man you have a biological, darwinistic desire to stand up for yourself and fight. To maintain some level of justice. To ensure you are treated properly. This is so thoroughly engrained in your brain that it is a visceral and incredibly strong reaction. And so when you are assaulted or challenged by men (and sometimes women) to fight you have this desire to get in there and start throwing punches.

Don't.

No matter how right you are, no matter how much they deserve it, do not get into a fight with another person. It just isn't worth the risk of jail time or a criminal record. However, while that logically explains why you should avoid fighting, it does nothing to assuage your anger and genetic desire to just open up and start wailing on the guy. But perhaps this will.

Understand who has what at risk when fighting.

Most people who start fights do not have lives or futures. They're losers. They probably have some minor criminal record and their best hope for a career is to be a shoddy roofer as they try to work off their hangover. In other words, they have nothing to lose.

You, however, probably have a lot more going on. You might be an officer in the military. You might be in grad school on your way to become a surgeon. You might have a great political career ahead of you. Heck, you just plain have a family. All of that is at risk when you get into a fight. This isn't to say you don't defend yourself if your life is threatened, but it is to say don't get into a bout of road rage because somebody cut you off.

Drugs and Alcohol – As for drugs, just don't do them. Wait till you're rich and don't need a job. Until that time, just don't do them. As for alcohol, remember it has a tendency to land you in jail either through DUI's, domestic violence, or fights.

Cars (and Other Expensive Shit You Can't Afford) – Especially when you are young, you will want to have a nice car so you can drive fast and impress the ladies. The problem is since you are young you have no money and earn a low wage. So when you buy a brand new sports car at 19 you are making arguably the worst financial mistake of your life as it can impair your finances well into your

30's. The same thing with clothes, fancy dinners, or any other luxury items you can't afford, but think are going to impress the ladies.

The truth is, it won't impress them because there will always be a tell in some other aspect of your life that will let them know you really don't have the money. You live with your mom. The past-due notices in your mail. The fact you work at Wal-Mart or are going to college. You just plain cannot compete against the 30 and 40 something men who DO have the money. Besides, your time will come, but not if you bankrupt yourself at 23.

Health and Car Insurance - Especially when you are younger, you may think you can get by without having health or car insurance. Don't get by without it. Get it. Though there is no guarantee you will get into an accident or you will get sick, when you do you will be begging and pleading for a time machine to send you back in time so you can purchase it. It may be unlikely you'll even need it, but all it takes is one accident or one appendicitis and you once again have impaired your finances well into your 30's.

Stupid Degrees – Though there is an entire chapter dedicated to this, in short, do not spend $120,000 on stupid degrees. When you are being asked to spend that amount of money you better damn well make sure you get your money's worth. And the most effective way of doing that is choosing a major that has a high employment rate and a high starting salary. You can search starting salaries by major to see which ones are in demand today, but it doesn't take a genius to know a "Masters in French Poetry" isn't as employable as a 2 year tech degree in welding.

Stupid Career Choices – Chances are society, your teachers, your parents, and the government have told you that you can become anything you want.

No, you can't.

We all can't become astronauts. We all can't become musicians. And we all can't become president. And if you spend time pursuing a career you just don't have the aptitude or ability for, you will not only fail but waste a significant percentage of your youth. A perfect example is one that simply devastates the black community – rappers and professional athletes. Nearly every young black male dreams of becoming an athlete or rapper. However, only 1 in 19,000 people actually become a professional athlete and there's 1,000 times more "aspiring rap artists" than real ones. For the remaining 18,999 failed athletes and 999 failed rap artists they merely wasted their youth chasing a dream that was never going to be caught. However, had they taken serious inventory of their skills or merely had a "Plan B" you would have many black men becoming high-paid engineers, doctors, mechanics, etc.

Be smart and be realistic. Choose a career you can do.

Pay Your Fucking Taxes – Life will prove difficult enough. Finding a job, making ends meet, paying for college, finding the right girl, avoiding trouble, saving for retirement, and everything else you have to do in life just to survive. There is no need to make it doubly stressful by running into trouble with the IRS or your state revenue collection agency. Paying taxes may suck, especially if you are younger and need every penny to survive. However, skimping on your taxes is a quick way to simply end up having to pay *more* in taxes (via fees and penalties) or get a criminal record if you are particularly blatant and egregious in your tax evasion. But the primary reason to avoid trouble with the IRS is that it just takes too much time to resolve. You are going to spend many more hours in wasted labor just trying to make things right with the IRS than anything you could possibly save with just "a little bit of cheating."

<u>Never Have an Illegitimate Child</u> – Without question the single most damaging decision you can make in your life is having an illegitimate kid. Take all of the above mistakes, combine them, multiply them by 1,000 and you still don't come anywhere near to the life-destroying mistake of having an illegitimate kid. The reason why is that kids are the number one cause of poverty. This is not debatable. This is not up for discussion. This is not a matter of opinion (and if there is any doubt, please look up the poorest countries in the world and see what their birth rates are). It is simply a matter of math.

Poverty is measured in terms of income per capita. That "capita" means person, which includes any children you may just happen to bring into this world. The problem with children, however, is they don't work for at least the first 12 years of their lives and are by default (and in a non-pejorative sense) parasitical. This means YOU get to work up the extra money to pay for them.

However, there are other major reasons illegitimate children are the death knell to any young man's (or woman's) life. First, there are the financial costs. These can vary but the average kid today costs over $250,000 to raise until the age of 18. This not only makes college tuition look like a joke, but pretty much makes attending college an impossibility. Second, it isn't just the financial costs, but also the labor costs. Even with all the government help in the world the child cannot be left alone for any significant amount of time until they are at least 12. That is 12 years of CONSTANT supervision which prohibits you from pursuing any other pursuits in life. In having a child your life is over as it is immediately superseded by the child's. Finally, it takes two to tango, which means there is invariably another parent involved and more often than not that person will not see eye to eye with you. This can make having an illegitimate child a nightmare as you are constantly pulled into court for more child support, accusations of abuse, and a never ending litany of minor and petty fights. No illegitimate child is worth the 10 second orgasm.

There is, however, an added insidious twist every man must know about when it comes to illegitimate children:

Many women have no problem in tricking you into getting them pregnant.

As disgusting as that might sound, its disgust is only outdone by the shame this problem even exists and the severity of its consequences. This **IS** a real phenomenon and there **ARE** women out there like that. All one has to do is search on Google "how do I trick my boyfriend to get me pregnant" and you will come up with

not hundreds,
not thousands,

but

millions of hits.

This means men must take precautions when sleeping with various women. Even if they say they're on birth-control you must assume they are not. You must make it a policy to always use condoms, take a male contraceptive pill (when they become available), or have a vasectomy the second you determine you do not want children. Otherwise you run the risk of being in the uncomfortable and compromising position of having to negotiate for an abortion (which you may be religiously against) or aiming for Tom Leykis's patented "Hail Mary."

CHAPTER 4
EDUCATION

With the basics and underlying philosophy about financial management addressed, we can move on to more specific topics, specifically the most logical next step in a young man's life – education. Education will play a vital role in your life in that it will inevitably give you the skill or trade you need to command a higher wage for your time. However, there are several economic and political factors affecting the current education industry, making your education a minefield capable of helping you achieve your dreams or destroying you, impoverishing you, and ruining your life.

The Education Minefield

Ideally, the education industry would be first and foremost for the students. From kindergarten to college the entire focus, purpose, and concentration should be to educate, train and prepare students for the real world so that they may do their best, achieve their most and, hopefully, live better lives than their predecessors.

Ideally.

For while we view the education industry as a group of caring teachers, principals, administrators and counselors, selflessly dedicating their lives towards the noble goal of educating our children and the future, all while working for subpar wages, the reality is anything but. The truth is the vast majority of people in the education industry are there first and foremost for themselves. The children are a mere after-thought, and sometimes worse, a political pawn to advance a political agenda and secure more funding.

The problem is that most people cannot fathom this as they cannot separate the education industry from the children they portend to be educating, giving the industry a child-like innocence and unassailable reputation. Therefore, if you ever dare to suggest that we might hold teachers up to performance standards, or that spending per pupil has increased five-fold while performance has remained flat...

Why if you're not for education, then you must be against the children! Why do you hate the children? Don't you know they're our future?

This not only has put the education industry beyond critique and beyond reproach, but also makes it susceptible to corruption, allowing it to be infiltrated by arguably the most hypocritical, despicable group of charlatans and scammers on the planet. For instead of truly being selfless and dedicating their careers towards educating and helping out children, most teachers, principals, professors and administrators use students as hostages, demanding more money for their industry while letting educational standards suffer, all so they can have an easy job that more closely resembles baby-sitting than educating.

Of course, this is quite a damning claim to make and because of the education industry's impeccable and unassailable reputation, many people are shocked I would dare criticize something as noble, sweet, kind and charitable as teachers. But are teachers and professors really that holy and sacred? Is the education industry really that pure and noble?

Well, consider your own educational experience.

Last I recall there were only five teachers and professors in my 17 years of education that were good, let alone taught me anything. All the others were mean, boring, didn't like children, and were so dispassionate about their jobs it really felt like they were reluctantly baby-sitting. Chances are if you were to take inventory of your teachers as well and be intellectually honest about it, a very small minority of them would qualify as genuine "teachers" and most as disinterested "baby-sitters."

Second, did you enjoy school or was it more like a prison? This isn't a testament to how boring school is, or what a "bad student" you were, but rather just how poor most teachers are. Any subject, no matter what, can be made to be interesting to a student if the teacher is passionate about it. But the vast majority of children are not engaged, not intrigued and not intellectually stimulated because, once again, most teachers are not there to educate, share a passion, or inspire students as much as they are to collect a check. This is why kids spend 13 years of K-12 education tortuously fighting to stay awake, wanting nothing more than the bell to ring so they can go home.

Third, let's not kid ourselves. If you can remember back to high school (or college), who were the types and caliber of people declaring education majors? Was it the IT geek valedictorian? Was it the accountant who wanted to become a CPA, work in the industry and then retire as a teacher to share his world experiences and wisdom? Was it the med student who would teach part time at the local university after establishing his medical practice? Or was it the lazy student who didn't want to try hard, didn't like math, wanted three months a year off, but covered it all up by saying, "I want to change lives" or "I like working with children?" The reality is that deep down inside they didn't give a damn about the children as much as they cared about choosing an easy major with an easy job at the end. And if you don't believe that, ask anybody why they're majoring in education. It's almost a near guarantee they'll list "3 months a year off" as one of their top reasons. It's not only why the majority of teachers today are horrible at their job, but why education majors have the lowest average IQ of all majors.

Bad as all this is, however, it gets a lot worse in college. For while you don't have to pay for K-12 education, you do have to pay around $200 per credit for college. And not only $200 per credit, but fees, pre-reqs, books, parking, etc. Nearly half of the classes you take have nothing to do with your major, and if you thought your teachers didn't care about you, just wait till you get a professor with 700 students in his lecture hall and 20 supporting "teacher assistants."

Ultimately, you have to step back and honestly ask yourself if education is so important then why do we make it so difficult and expensive to attain? If the children and students are our future why do we send in the least qualified and most boring people to teach them? And if the entire future economic productivity of the United States (and the world) relies on people getting a degree and learning a trade why do we throw up hurdles like unnecessary pre-requisite classes, insanely-high tuition costs, and charge thousands of dollars per semester for books?

The answer is because the education industry is not a charitable, non-profit entity there to help educate the precious little children, but rather a for-profit industry intent on milking every penny of profit it can, indifferent about whether they actually educate the children or not. Again, if you don't believe it, all you have to do is look at the sheer size of the education industry. Every year in the United States we spend $1 trillion on education which is more than we spend on our domestic "big oil" industry. And given how "evil and corrupt" we all assume the oil industry to be, an even larger industry, 75% of which is government spending, is guaranteed to be infinitely more corrupt.

The larger point of this long screed against the education industry is not to villainize it, but to warn you what you're dealing with when it comes to seeking an education – a $1 trillion industry, heavily financed and politicized by the government, that has been intent on taking advantage of you since the age of 5. Yes, there are legitimate fields of study. And yes, you can get an education that will prove immeasurably beneficial to your life. But the industry as a whole is a minefield, fraught with risk, designed to extract as much money from you as possible. From K-12 there is a cacophony of teachers, counselors, professors and administrators spewing propaganda and bold faced lies to get you to blow $100,000 on their industry:

"You NEED to go to college."
"Follow your heart and the money will follow."
"You should get a masters or doctorate. That will help you get a job."
"You need to be a well-rounded person."

"Employers look for critical thinking skills."
"It isn't all about the money."
"It doesn't matter what you major in, it's what you do with it."

And if you believe these lies, failing to identify the education industry for the monster it truly is, you run the risk of ruining your life as you graduate from college with a worthless degree, $100,000 in debt, working as a stockboy for $8 per hour. To prevent this from happening, you need to understand the real reason you should pursue an education.

The REAL Purpose of an Education

Let us be very clear what purpose an education serves and why you should get one:

It is an investment you make to increase the value of your time so you can charge more for it and thereby increase your income and wealth.

That's it. That's the entire purpose of an education.

It is not to have "the college experience."
It is not to "meet and bang hot chicks."
It is not to "get hammered and party."
And it sure as hell isn't to "become a well-rounded individual."

It is to increase the wage you can command for one hour of your labor.

Period.

Of course teachers, guidance counselors, society, media and your parents might tell you otherwise. They want college to be a romanticized experience, a fun time you'll remember fondly. A time where you can grow as a person and get "an education in life." The problem with that is they are treating college like it is a consumer good and not an investment. That college has merit unto itself and (as you will commonly hear) "it isn't all about the money."

The problem is it HAS TO BE ABOUT THE MONEY because of the price you are being asked to pay for it. If education was free, then sure, knock yourself out. Get a triple doctorate in Art History, Puppetry, and Lesbian Transgender Renaissance Festival Unicorn Studies. But since you are being asked to drop (at least) $50,000 of your money and 4 years of your youth earning that education, you simply cannot afford it NOT to pay off. You have to get a positive rate of return on your investment because if there isn't then you will absolutely cripple your finances for decades. Anybody who contends otherwise is either spectacularly ignorant of math or purposely trying to scam you.

While this may not be what you wanted to hear, it does simplify the problem of choosing a major or discipline. It makes it one of simple mathematics – which degrees or majors pay the most? And the answer is simple – STEM.

"STEM" stands for "Science, Technology, Engineering and Math" and includes degrees like engineering, chemistry, computer science, medicine, etc. They are no doubt the most difficult degrees (some of which take 5 years to earn instead of 4), but they are the ones that are going to increase your wage and command a higher salary.

The reason they command a higher salary is simple – STEM graduates create the stuff people want in society.

Compare two degrees.

English and electrical engineering.

What precisely does the English major provide that the rest of society wants?

We already speak, read, and write English in this country, most people being fluent and literate by age 5. We don't read books by English majors (because, ironically, most English majors never get published, let alone write anything good). And no kid in the history of kids ever listed "English lessons" on their Christmas wish-list.

But compare that to the electrical engineer.

Society is helplessly dependent on the constant and reliable generation and transmission of electricity, so much so, without it society would collapse in about 3 days. We all want more fuel efficient cars, solar power, wind power, batteries, etc. And there isn't one kid (let alone adult) who doesn't have some kind of electrical doodadery on their Christmas wish-list.

In short, it boils down to the basic economic laws of supply and demand.

Everybody demands the services of electrical engineers.
Nobody demands the services of English majors.

There is a short supply of electrical engineers because of the difficulty and rigor of their discipline.
There is a glut of English majors because it's easy and anybody can major in it.

This difference between the relative supply and demand for different majors manifests itself in the form of "starting salaries." Starting salaries are nothing more than the numerical economic reality of the labor market. And if you look at the starting salaries between electrical engineering majors and English majors, you see electrical engineering majors are more valuable.

2009 Starting Salaries (Source: NACE)

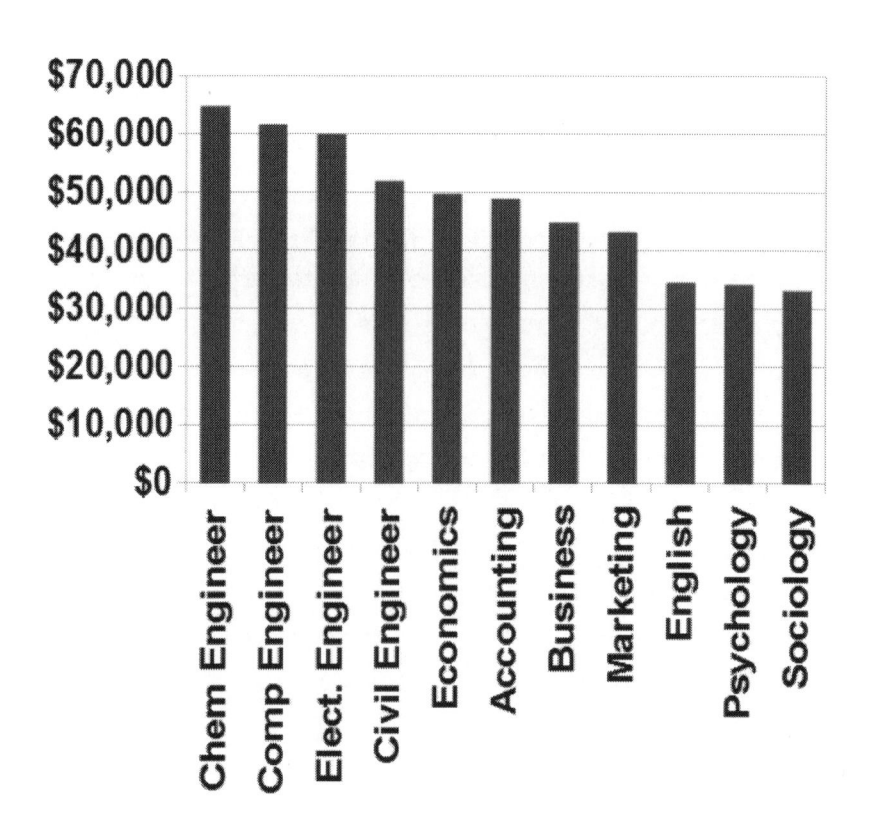

Of course, most English majors will take umbrage and insist they are just as important as electrical engineering majors. And, yes, poetry majors will take offense and insist they are just as valuable as chemistry majors.

The problem is they're not.

They *factually and numerically* are not because society, through the labor market, mathematically tells us so by placing a higher value in the form of higher starting salaries. People willingly forfeit over $500 for Apple's latest electrical gadgetry. People willingly pay anything for the latest touch-screen device. But few, if any people, pay for English lessons in an English-speaking country. This doesn't mean English majors are evil or that poetry majors are dumb. It just means nobody wants to hire them. And that is something neither you nor they can afford after dropping $70,000 on an education.

Naturally, not everybody can become an electrical engineer or a computer scientist. People just don't have the aptitude or interest. The trick is to find something you like, have an aptitude for and pays well. This requires a fair amount of soul-searching, trial and error, researching the labor market, and sample-studying different fields. And truth be told, it takes most people years to find out what they're good at and what their true calling is. The key thing, however, is not so much choosing the right major as much as it is avoiding the wrong one that can financially cripple you. To this end I recommend the following bits of advice in addition to merely looking at starting salaries:

Avoid the Liberal Arts and Humanities in General – Though many people will disagree, the humanities "aka" "the liberal arts" are largely worthless degrees. They do not teach you any skills society wants or the economy demands. Worse still most liberal arts departments have become corrupted by politics and no longer serve as genuine institutions of learning as much as they are tools of indoctrination and the Democratic party.

Can It Be Replaced By the Library? – That being said, the liberal arts are very interesting. Just because a degree in the humanities doesn't pay doesn't mean you shouldn't read up on philosophy or history. But, since it doesn't pay, why pay $3,000 per class to some washed-up professor to teach you about Plato when you can go to the local library or the internet and read Plato for free? You get the exact same education (probably better) with the exact same employment prospects, sans the student loans.

Is the Primary Source of Employment Merely Re-teaching? – Speaking of washed up professors, what do people in those fields do for employment when they reach the masters or PhD level? Are they hired by NASA? Do they go and work at the R&D labs of Merck? Are they developing new surgical techniques at the Mayo Clinic?

Or...

do they just go back to the same classroom and re-teach the stuff they were taught 3 years previous to new students?

The tell-tale sign of a worthless degree is when the only or primary application of the study is to merely re-teach the same stuff to new and future students. This tells you the "study" has no practical application outside academia and therefore technically has no value.

Does It End in "Studies?" – Most, but not all worthless majors end in "studies." "Engineering" implies its purpose and value. "Metallurgy" does the same. But if you asked me what I was majoring in and I just said, "African American" or "Transgender" you would be confused. If I added "Studies" to each then it might make a little more sense. The truth is if it ends in "Studies" or has a hyphen in it, you are not studying anything that will teach you a skill or an employable trade. You are merely paying $250 per credit to study the traits of a group of people. It might be interesting, but will do nothing to increase your wage.

Repeat Classes – Understand because worthless degrees offer nothing of value it is hard to extrapolate a full 4, 6, or 8 year degree out of those majors, let alone multiple classes. For example, everything about education could be summarized in a 50 page booklet. But to get a doctorate in education you have to read thousands of pages which merely regurgitate the same thing a hundred different ways. Because of this classes and their material tend to repeat themselves offering you nothing new to learn and making it nearly impossible to read their textbooks.

Made Up Language/Pablum – From the University of California's Women's Studies Department's web page:

"The Department of Gender & Women's Studies offers interdisciplinary perspectives on the formation of gender and its intersections with other relations of power, such as sexuality, race,

class, nationality, religion, and age. Questions are addressed within the context of a transnational world and from perspectives as diverse as history, sociology, literary and cultural studies, postcolonial theory, science, new technology, and art."

Did you understand any of that? Neither did I. What do you suppose the chances are it's a worthwhile degree?

"Worthless" – Finally, I STRONGLY recommend EVERY high school and college student read my book "Worthless." Not because it is going to enrich me, but the book fleshes out in more detail the key topics we are covering here and serves as a great guide towards choosing the right major. Besides, it's $12 on paperback and $5 on Kindle, both of which are significantly less than the $75,000 you'll be asked to spend on a degree.

Choosing a College

If you were to listen to your teachers and parents you would think you only have two options after graduating from high school – either go to college or don't. The truth is you have many more options which is a good thing because not every young person fits into this "black and white" "college or not" dichotomy. However, where your parents are right is you can't just graduate from high school and hope to make a decent living. You do need to develop some kind of employable skill otherwise you will forever be that stock boy. And choosing the right type of college is the first step in developing that skill.

Public University – Public university, or what I like to refer to as "regular ole college." These are state universities, subsidized by your state government so they are made affordable to the majority of people. Every state in the country has at least one campus, the vast majority of them having multiple campuses for your convenience (ergo why you have University of California – Davis and the University of California – Los Angeles, etc.). As long as you are a resident of the state you qualify for "in state tuition" which is cheaper than what they charge out of state residents.

For the most part these colleges are merely average in the quality of education they provide. Some unique campuses have better reputations for specific fields (for example the University of Illinois – Urbana Champaign is a highly ranked tech school, while the University of Michigan – Ann Arbor is one of the top tier law schools in the country), but by and large companies and employers don't come banging down the doors to hire graduates from these schools. That being said what you major in will be the primary determinant of whether you find a job after graduating from one of these schools.

Private University – Private colleges are precisely that – private schools that are not part of the state system. In being so, tuition is much higher since they do not have the state subsidizing their tuition. In theory because they are private and because you are paying more they are presumably better schools than the public ones. However, the truth is their quality and caliber varies greatly. There is no limit to the small, tucked away private liberal arts college, nestled within the hills of the east coast that charge an arm and a leg for tuition, only to dump their graduates into the unemployment line. If you are going to attend a private university, then you want one that is either highly ranked or considered part of the "Ivy League."

<u>The Ivy League</u> – Schools in the "Ivy League" are considered the country's top schools. Your Harvard's, your Yale's, your Princeton's. Students who get into these schools are practically guaranteed to be financially successful. Because of this they are incredibly hard to get into, requiring you to have a near perfect GPA, top notch ACT and SAT test scores, an exemplary student resume, tons of extra-curricular activities, and so forth. But while acceptance into these schools will likely result in a six figure salary, there are just two major drawbacks to attending these schools.

One, you pretty much have to give up your childhood to get into them. Kids that get into these schools are the ones whose parents force them to take violin lessons at three and never have any free time to do their own thing. If you haven't been pulling a 4.0, performing a piano concerto at the age of 12, and have a marginal SAT score, then you're unlikely to be accepted, but thankfully you at least had your childhood. Two, these schools are considered "the best" not because they're actually the best, but because they provide students with the best connections, nepotism, and networking. In reality, a Harvard graduate is no better or smarter than a University of Ohio graduate, it's just that he "went to Harvard" while the other guy went to Ohio. This means your success will not rely on studying and excelling in your passion, as much as it will your ability to schmooze, kiss ass, and brown nose.

<u>Tech School/Community College</u> – Despite the focus and emphasis on attending a four-year school, not everybody is cut out for college. This doesn't mean you're less intelligent, it just means you don't have the personality for it. There are many people who don't have the patience to sit in a classroom, listening to some boring

professor blather on about the Battle of Waterloo. They are more hands on. They are more practical. They want to get to work.

For these types of people tech school or "community college" or "votech" may be their best bet. Unlike four year colleges, tech schools teach a specific skill or a trade such as welding, plumbing, computer networking, etc. Thankfully, most of these programs only take two years to complete and graduates have better employment prospects than most people graduating from a "real college" today. Sadly, however, in the past and even today, tech school was advised against, even ridiculed by most teachers and counselors. Students were pushed into attending four year colleges while dismayed from specializing in "the trades." However, the labor market has proven them wrong. Plumbers make a commendable wage of $20/hr while your average "Masters in Women's Studies" graduate makes $7/hr pouring coffee.

The other benefit to attending a community college or tech school is that you can get your "pre-requisite" classes in before transferring to a traditional four year college. The primary benefit of this is that tuition is often much cheaper, parking most likely free, and the professors more down to Earth.

Military – While many people are familiar with the military in terms of the GI bill, most people do not know that the military has a ton of training programs, schools and classes you can take within itself, most of which will either transfer to an actual degree or some kind of certification. Of course, you wouldn't join the military solely for its educational benefits, but if you were considering joining the military it is helpful to know that there are educational opportunities within.

Self-Study and Certification – There are several industries that are receptive to hiring somebody, not on the basis of whether you sat in classrooms for four years, but whether you can prove you are capable of a certain skill or trade. A perfect example is the computer industry. Millions of people are employed as computer networkers, computer technicians, repairmen, etc., not because they went to college, but because they passed their "Cisco Certification," their "A+ Certification," or their "Microsoft Certification." There are other industries that do this, but the point is why go to school when all you need is to pass a test and get certified? Of course, this requires the discipline to force yourself to self-study, but the time and cost savings alone makes such a non-traditional education a viable option.

Additionally, there is an added benefit to the "self-study/certification" education model – it is likely to gain popularity in the future. With the internet more and more classes are being offered online for free. MOOC's (Massive Open Online Courses), Khan's Academy, Ed X are all examples of an increasing number of classes that allow people to teach themselves the skills necessary to land a job, get a certification, or start a whole new career. Of course, such classes may not be viewed as "legitimate" by most employers today, but in the future, as it becomes apparent the internet can educate just as effectively as colleges can and at a fraction of the cost, more and more employers are likely to consider people who are self-taught and self-certified.

"Degree Mills" – Previously I indicated just merely graduating from high school was not enough. That you had to do something, anything beyond high school in order to be successful. The truth is I was wrong. There is something much worse than just graduating from high school.

You could attend a degree mill.

Degree mills are a derogatory (but well-deserved term) for "unaccredited schools." Understand every real college, university, trade school, or community college needs to be certified by one of six "regional accreditation boards" in the United States. If they aren't then they are considered an "unaccredited school" and their credits cannot be transferred to other schools.

You have likely seen advertisements for these schools during daytime TV. They usually offer degrees that *"in 16 short months can lead to an exciting career in"* you name it;

Law enforcement
Medical transcriptioning
Travel and hospitality
Veterinary science
Etc.

But the two dead give-aways they are scams is if they offer a culinary program or their classrooms are in a strip mall versus a genuine college campus.

These schools are scams. They are bottom-feeder schools that prey off of the worst students who performed so poorly in high school, they could not get accepted anywhere else. With nowhere else to go, these students gladly pay an exorbitant price for tuition only to be given a "degree" that is invalid and not recognized by other colleges, let alone most employers.

Ensure you NEVER attend one of these schools:

http://en.wikipedia.org/wiki/List_of_unaccredited_institutions_of_higher_learning

Financing an Education

The only thing more difficult than passing your classes in college is how you're going to pay for them. Tuition is climbing at three times the rate of inflation. Between classes and studying you already effectively have a 50-60 hour per week job, prohibiting you from working. And given the economy, it is unlikely you'll be starting off making $60,000 with benies and plenty of excess cash to pay down those student loans. However, while you may not be able to pay cash for your education, you can do some basic things that will at least keep your student loans manageable upon graduation.

<u>Work</u> – Though it may suck, I strongly recommend working while in college. I don't want to hear any complaints. I worked an average of 42 hours per week and attended school full time. Of course, I dropped 30 pounds, was sleep deprived, and would get sick for months at a time because of malnutrition, but it "technically" was possible to pay for college. That being said, I would never recommend working fulltime while attending college, but at least aim to work 10, preferably 20 hours per week. This will go a long way in at least paying for your living expenses while in college, perhaps even making a little dent in your tuition bill as well.

Work **Smart** – If I told you I also graduated six months early and with a 3.96 GPA while working 42 hours per week, would you still believe me?

Well, it is true. I graduated 5th in my class, in 3.5 years, all while working full time.

However, there was a trick. I worked as a "campus cop."

While a lot of my shifts involved patrolling campus or walking girls to class at night, if you gained enough seniority you were promoted to building shifts. These shifts were highly coveted because you would make one or two patrols an hour, but for the remaining 90% of the shift you would sit at a desk and…

study.

This was ideal because I could now kill three birds with one stone. I was able to earn some money, I was able to study, and because I was alone and uninterrupted for so long I was FORCED to study thereby boosting my GPA. Contrast that with working as a waiter or a janitor, you don't have the benefit of studying while you work. To this end, I strongly recommend finding a job where you can study on the job. Matter of fact, unless you're particularly desperate for money, I suggest refusing a college job unless you can study. It just isn't worth it otherwise.

Scholarships – The irony of scholarships is that they are primarily for high school students with high GPA's, because once you enter college you probably won't have the time to apply for them. Between classes, studying, and work you won't have the time to…

"Write an essay of 500 words or less on why you think work ethic is important to society!"

especially when there are 127 other applicants doing the same. It's almost a guarantee you'll make more money working the hours you would have spent applying for said scholarships. So if you're in high school and have a decent GPA, by all means go for it, but if not, your time is better spent working.

Live With Your Parents – Tuition has become so expensive and the job market for young people so bad, there is no longer any shame in living with your parents. Yes, it may suck. And yes, you may lose a little bit of freedom, but if you can attend college near your parents and cut rent from your budget, that alone will go a long way in reducing your total student debt come graduation.

"A Room" – Some people will live in the dorms. Some people will live in a studio. Some will go so far as to split a one bedroom. I recommend finding just "a room." While the majority of housing on campus will be dorms and apartments, you should be able to find a house where the landlord rents out by the room. You then share the kitchen, the bathroom, etc., with 3-6 other guys paying around $200 a month. Quarters are cramped and rarely do things get clean, but you're not going to college to have fancy living quarters. You just need a place to sleep.

The Military – Unless you are dead set against it, joining the military has a lot of benefits, namely, they pay for *everything*. Food, clothing, shelter, health care and education. Admittedly, there are risks to joining the military and it isn't for everyone, but there are a lot worse ways to pay for your education.

Take Your Time – The truth is there aren't any jobs out there for young people today. This could of course change, but the current unemployment rate for young people (20-24) is 13% and the underemployment rate is closer to 50% (depending on which measure you use). i.e.- there won't be a high-paying, challenging job for you upon graduation. Therefore, there's no rush. You can enjoy college. Leisurely take a class here or there, play hacky sack with some peers outside, work during the day time as a bartender, play some video games at night. Not only is this more enjoyable, the costs of college are spread out to the point you could very likely pay cash for them, never having to take on student loans.

It is OK to Take on Some Debt – The problem a lot of people have is they worry or fret about borrowing money regardless of what it's used for. This makes sense if you borrowed $250,000 to buy a Ferrari but only make $40,000 a year. But as a college student making a paltry $10,000 a year it can be quite intimidating borrowing $20,000, even for something as legitimate as college. The key is to know the difference between an investment and a hobby. A degree in computer science is an investment. A degree in "communications" is a hobby. One is going to pay off. The other isn't. As long as you are applying the funds towards a wise degree it's perfectly alright to borrow some money.

Find a Sugar Mama – By all means, if you possibly can, find yourself a sugar mama. While divorce has wreaked havoc on the country, the silver lining is that it has made available millions of 30 and 40 something women who are desperate to be convinced they are still young, still beautiful, and still capable of attracting a young man. Again, like applying for scholarships, I would not dedicate too much time towards it, but it might be worth poking your head into the local cougar bar to see if you can't get an older woman to finance a couple months' rent and groceries.

A Miscellany of Advice

Grad School – After graduating with a bachelor's or "undergrad" you will of course have the option to continue on and get your masters or doctorate. Bar becoming a doctor, it usually isn't worth it. Most advanced degrees in the liberal arts only serve to get you a low-paying teaching position that does not warrant the $150,000 in tuition and eight years of college. Most advanced degrees in STEM are unnecessary as you are immediately employable with just a bachelor's. And nearly all advanced degrees in business or law are worthless as there is a flood of MBA's and lawyers. This isn't to say grad school isn't worth it, but whether you should pursue an advanced degree will become more apparent once you graduate and spend some time in your field.

Internships – When you go to college, time will be scarce. You'll have to attend class, you'll have to study, and you'll probably have to work. What little time you have left will be incredibly valuable. Do not waste it interning.

While the idea of internships may seem appealing the truth is the vast majority of them are nothing more than a scam companies use to get cheap, or outright free labor. Worse, the work is never challenging. It is usually mundane clerical work like filing, faxing and other simple tasks that you could literally have done in the 4th grade. In short, they're nothing more than abuse and you should avoid them.

There are, however, incredibly rare instances of internships that are legitimate. You get paid, you get to do real work related to your degree, and they increase your chances of employment. Unfortunately, you'll spend more time finding that magical internship than what it may be worth. Therefore, if you insist on interning, be incredibly picky and quick to judge. If you show up for work and they have you file, you walk out. No excuse, no reason. You walk. If you show up for work and they say, "Sorry, we don't have the budget to pay you, but it is worth the experience," you walk out. No excuse, no reason. You walk. Hopefully, you find that "one" internship, but your time is more often than not better spent drinking and chasing girls.

School Location – Unless you are a particularly independent minded individual, where you go to college will likely determine where you end up living during your 20's and 30's. And unless you really have your heart set on a particular program at a particular school, I suggest looking at other ancillary traits to determine where you would like to go to college as location will have a huge effect on your happiness.

For example, climate. There is no godly reason to go to school in the upper Midwest. Winters are harsh, you get to deal with snow emergencies, and just see how much fun it is driving on "black ice." Instead, I would strongly recommend relegating your search for schools in Texas, Florida, Arizona, California, Georgia, etc.

Another example, landscape. Were I to do it again I would have attended Black Hills State University in Spearfish, South Dakota. The reason why? Because I love mountain climbing, hiking and fossil hunting. Whatever your hobbies and passions are, why not attend a college where those passions and hobbies are in your backyard and not 2,000 miles away?

Finally, welfare. You are likely to be your poorest during college. Why not avail yourself of the generosity of the country's most liberal and leftist states? California, Oregon, New York, etc. Even if you're paying out of state tuition, the bevy of government handouts may more than offset those costs. Of course, once you graduate and start making money you would look to leave the state immediately, but at least while you're poor let them pay for you.

The Difference Between a University and a College – I mention this only because nobody told me, but universities are different than colleges and this can cause confusion for college-bound men in high school. A college is a school that offers degrees in a certain field. For example, the Columbia School of Journalism or the Carlson School of Management are individual colleges, they are not universities. A university on the other hand is nothing more than a campus full of different colleges. When you apply to school you apply to the individual college you wish to attend. This will depend on which major you wish to declare, but if you ever decide to change your major and that major is in a different college, you will likely have to re-apply.

The reason this is important is because different colleges have different application standards. The "College of Liberal Arts" at the

University of Minnesota, for example, has the following requirements of their applicants.

1. Must have a pulse
2. Must be human
3. Must have a positive high school GPA
4. Must be stupid enough to apply here

The "Institute of Technology" at the University of Minnesota requires you:

1. Have a 3.0+ GPA
2. Have decent ACT and SAT scores
3. And demonstrate some kind of aptitude for STEM

Ergo, if you want to major in a certain field, understand the college that offers that degree may have higher application standards than the rest of the university. This means you have to either work hard in high school or (if already graduated from high school) apply to a lesser college at the university (usually their liberal arts college), boost your GPA there and then re-apply to the original college of your choice.

Underemployment – Even if you major in a legitimate field, graduate with honors, and do everything right, do not get too excited about your employment prospects. The reason is that you can have the greatest resume in the world, but without jobs at the other end all that education and training is moot. Sadly, this is the current state of the US economy today. Economic growth is half of what it used to be which means demand for jobs has also been halved. Taxes and regulation have also grown considerably resulting in companies and employers going overseas instead. And generations before you have failed to save up enough money for retirement, forcing them to work longer, leaving less room for promotion and opportunity for younger generations.

***

In the end you must approach your education as what it was always intended to be – an investment. But you must also be keenly aware that with a trillion dollars a year being spent on the industry it attracts some of the most manipulative, charlatan scum. This results in a world that "isn't what it seems" as teachers, professors, principals, counselors and deans all claim they're there to help you, but in reality are there to take your money. Navigate this world carefully ensuring you get an education that is going to pay off. You simply cannot afford otherwise.

CHAPTER 5
CAREER

Upon graduating you will have invested a significant amount of time into your education and training. On the low end, if you just went to trade school you will have been going to school for 15 years. On the high end, if you decided to pursue a doctorate you will have spent a total of 21 years in school. These will respectively represent 75% and 81% of your total life on this planet upon graduation. You would think with such an enormous amount of education and training a human would be nearly capable of anything. You can learn to brew beer in a couple of hours. It only takes a couple weeks to learn to weld. And it only took 140 hours to train WWII fighter pilots.

So what does the real world of work have in store for you?

Nothing that will ever come close to your total potential.

The sad truth about the labor market is that the opportunities come nowhere near to what you are capable of or what you trained for. Unless you are in a highly specialized skill (say, brain surgery) you can expect, at most, to be used at about 20% your total capacity. Additionally, since you are younger, you will not be taken seriously nor given the opportunities to prove yourself. Worse still, while you languish in this environment your skills and what you learned during college will start to atrophy, as will your creativity and innovation. In the end, most of the jobs you will have before you're 30 could be done by a competent 5th grader and will rarely be rewarding, challenging, or well-paid.

The reason for such a difference between your capabilities and what is out there for jobs is multi-fold. First, there just isn't the economic growth to warrant as many and as highly trained/skilled people that we are graduating from our schools today. If the economy was booming like it was during the 40's and 50's, then there might be enough demand, but the economy today is only growing at half that rate. Second, an army can't have all generals and no privates. In other words, employers need to make a profit, they need to produce things. If all they have is a bunch of college-educated managers and nobody working on the front lines, then that company won't be in existence for much longer. Third, you were lied to by the education industry and (even) your parents about the importance of an education. Truth be told, you really could be released from school in the 5th grade, and if mature and responsible enough to show up on time, you could do most jobs people under 30 are doing today. Jobs today just do not require all the schooling and training "Big Education" forces you to take.

The result of such a disparity between what you are capable of and what the real world has to offer is a working environment that not only will spectacularly fail to meet your lofty expectations of challenge and reward, but crush your hopes and dreams of the future. After nearly two decades of schooling it will take you months just to land an interview, sometimes years to find a job. After flirting with the likelihood you'll have to go on welfare, you will have a bit of "luck" and maybe land a job. You will desperately take it just so you can make ends meet, but you will soon find out it is tedious, mundane, and nothing like what your employer said it would be. You will think you're just "unlucky," that not all employers are like that, and it's just a matter of finding another employer. But you will soon find out, job after job, that all employers are indeed "like that."

The reason why is employers now have millions of the most educated, trained, and indebted job applicants in the history of the country desperately throwing themselves at them. Because of this employers can afford to be increasingly arrogant and petty in what they demand to see in an employee. Never mind you're more than qualified for the job. Did you:

Wear the right tie to the interview?
Answer the HR (human resources) lady's questions about "dogs and cats" the way she wanted you to?
Commit to getting your masters without the company paying for it?
Give the HR lady your Facebook password so she can spy on you?
Agree to spend hours outside the office participating in corporate social responsibility events?
Spell out "don't" as "do not" in your reports because your boss doesn't like contractions? (true story)

Sadly, none of this is made up. That's how bad the current working environment really is in America. Your success is not contingent on capabilities or skill, but rather your ability to be political, jump through hoops, walk on eggshells, and have near-mystical powers to interpret the constantly changing desires of HR and management. And barring some miraculous economic growth it is the labor market you will get to face when you enter it.

The question is how can you make the best of this bad situation? Realize you will be spending the plurality of your waking hours at work and not with the children or the wife. So yes, money is a factor, but so is your mental health. And no matter how hard you try to fight it, men have a genetically engrained desire to live up to their full potential – an impossibility in this current environment. Thankfully, dire as modern day corporate America may be, you are not relegated to be employed there. You have several options when it comes to choosing a "career path," all having their pro's and con's, suiting different people with different personalities. But whichever route you take (or combinations thereof) the key is to remember that it is a two-way street. It is not just you selflessly throwing yourself at the mercy of a charitable employer, kind enough to grace you with employment, but rather you using them to help advance and achieve your aims and goals. Any other approach will result in a miserable working life.

The Corporate Man

Though the introduction excoriated the idea of becoming a traditional, reliable, company man, many people will actually thrive and succeed in this environment. Additionally, as it just so happens, most people will have to work in corporate America at least once in their lives either to make ends meets, build up capital and money to start a business, return to school, etc. So whether you want to make corporate America your permanent home or are using it as a temporary stop-gap measure, a more thorough review of the "corporate career" and how to navigate it is warranted.

Understand when you enter a corporate or "traditional" working environment you are sacrificing individuality, freedom, happiness, excellence, and capacity for security and stability. As mentioned before you will never reach your full potential, but you will have that steady reliable paycheck. You will never be challenged, but the job will likely be there tomorrow. You may not be able to spend time with your family, but the health benefits are killer. The reason this system works (and accounts for the majority of employment in the country) is because it is efficient on the company level. Everybody working together at the direction and desires of the corporation can, as a group, achieve greater things than the individual. In short, it is like working for the "Borg" where the collective is more important than the individual.

Because of this the most valuable trait an employee can have is CONFORMITY, nothing else. It doesn't matter if you know of a better way to do things. It doesn't matter if you know the current way of doing things is wrong. It doesn't matter if you've identified a spectacular opportunity that would make the company billions or a horrific threat that is sure to bankrupt the company. Unless you are the CEO, the single largest contribution you can make to the collective is obedience.

Once you understand this you can at minimum survive in a corporate environment and (if you choose to) excel. You shed whatever individuality you have and obey. You shed whatever opinions you might have and conform. You shed whatever morality you might have and comply. You be a good little boy, do what you're told, don't ask any questions and in two or three decades time you might get promoted.

However, there are HUGE and multiple drawbacks to this kind of corporate culture and mass-compliant psychology. Drawbacks that will test your sanity, ruin your family and social life, risk turning you into a sociopath, and sometimes result in you losing your job. And even though you may be able to psychologically separate yourself from your job, over the course of decades it will still affect you.

The most obvious drawback is the consequences of a "hyper-compliant" work force. Namely, obedient behavior replaces profitable behavior. Normally this isn't an issue as (hopefully) the leaders and executives of the company make wise decisions that will lead to profit. And given the collective and efficient structure of the corporation, as long as people obey, the company will make money. But what if the leaders of the company are wrong? What if they start making bad decisions? In a hyper-compliant environment nobody is there to stop them because nobody dares risk the punishment. They simply comply, accelerating the collapse. The housing crash, the Dotcom bubble, the accounting scandal, Operation Market Garden were all doomed to fail because nobody in the compliant, obedient employee ranks dared challenge or question the top-down, dictatorial leadership.

This is the single largest risk of working in a traditional corporate environment – massive layoffs. One day everything is going great, you did what you were told, the paychecks aren't bouncing, and you're getting your 401k match. But because management has the horse blinders on and nobody dares to toll the bells or sound the alarms, they miss a major threat to the company that ends up torpedoing the entire firm. The next day you're laid off and you find out your 401k was never funded.

Another drawback is the toxic psychological environment that results from a hyper-compliant work force. Because compliance supersedes profit, the focus is no longer on performance, but obedience. Therefore, if you want to get ahead you need to "obey more" than the other guy. It soon becomes a race to the bottom where your performance is not based on how much ass you kick, but how much ass you kiss. Making matters worse is where does it end? At least with profit and production certain tangible measures could be used to assess your performance, but with brown nosing and ass kissing, the sky is the limit.

This problem manifests itself in several ways. As mentioned before, with a surplus of applicants HR directors and hiring managers become progressively petty and demanding on what they expect from applicants and employees. So much so they request Facebook passwords, demand "masters degrees" for jobs that are entry level in nature, and on multiple occasions have been caught demanding "five years experience" in software that has only been around three. You are required to attend "diversity training," "sensitivity training," are forced to sit in meetings that have nothing to do with your job, and "kindly" requested to donate time outside of work for the company's various "CSR" or "corporate social responsibility" projects.

There is also the problem of "progressive credentialism." Again, with so many applicants employers can demand irrational levels of education and training as merely a means to filter applicants. This forces students to spend another 2-4 years in college getting an advanced degree, another $75,000 in tuition, not to mention hundreds of hours studying for certifications beyond their advanced degree. Not that they're ever going to use this education and training on the job, it is merely to be "slightly" more qualified than the next applicant. Just a big, completely unnecessary $75,000 hoop to jump through.

And then there is just plain sadism and abuse.

With so many people tripping over themselves to obey and comply managers and bosses cannot help but get an ego and go power tripping. This is displayed no clearer than when bosses refuse to spend the time actually leading and training, and instead say things like "must hit the ground running," or "steep learning curve." So arrogant and lazy are they, they refuse to do the most basic of duties like *train in their staff*, preferring instead to force their staff to spend $75,000 of their own money on advanced degrees and certifications. But worse is the guilt tripping. Instead of giving direct and clear orders, as well as the tools to complete the job, most modern day bosses show you around your first day of work, recluse to their offices, and then it's up to you to walk around the office and pull people's teeth just so you can just merely do your job. If your performance suffers or you dare need some kind of guidance, leadership, or just plain extra work, your boss attempts to shame you for requesting his time by saying, "*Look, you have to figure it out yourself. I'm too busy with my own work,*" when indeed, his "own work" is to lead you.

You add all this up and corporate America is no longer a meritocracy where hard work is rewarded, but it is an inhumane, toxic psych-ward sure to cause mental damage to anybody unfortunate enough to stay there over the long run. Therefore, you need to take serious inventory of your own self and your life goals to see if this is really the path for you.

Are you the type of person who doesn't care about promotion, just wants a paycheck and can tune out the psychological drama?

Then a corporate career might work for you.

Are you the type of person who NEEDS to be a CEO or an executive, has no problem putting on a fake smile, and are sociopathic in nature?

Then a corporate career is *definitely* for you.

But if you are a person who needs to have some kind of challenge, some kind of progress, and insists on a basic level of self-respect and mental stimulation, then a corporate career is antithetical to you. The best you can hope for is a temporary stint in corporate America, merely to bolster your finances or raise some capital so you can move on to bigger and better things.

The Entrepreneur

Be it the highly skilled surgeon or the lowly roofer, the two have something in common – they are both self-employed. They are entrepreneurs. Though one may seem more glamorous than the other, aside from their skills they are nearly identical. Neither of them have a boss, they have "clients." At any time they can refuse service to somebody. And instead of being relegated to the work an employer gives them, they can work as much or as little as they want as it is they who find and determine their own work.

Self-employment may not be for everyone. It is unreliable at times, you have to drum up your own business, not to mention, manage all aspects of the business. But as traditional employment becomes more hostile and psychotic, the freedom and simplicity of self-employment makes it an increasingly attractive alternative (and sometimes your only option).

Though nothing official, there are very roughly four general categories of self-employment.

The "independent contractor" is typically a tradesman with a special skill needed by most people. Plumbers, truckers, welders, roofers, carpenters, painters, chimney cleaners, even realtors, and consultants. They are usually small one person operations, peddling their trade as people need it. Commonly, they start out working for another company or "apprenticing," but once they hone their skill they usually set off on their own, starting their own small business.

The "specialist" is just like an independent contractor, but has a highly specialized skill. Surgeons, dentists, computer networkers, accountants, lawyers, etc. Again, a bit more glorified and certainly requiring more schooling, but functionally the same business model – sole-proprietor offering their skill, working out of their office.

There is the "artist," people who don't necessarily offer a skill, but create something of value hoping to sell it for a profit. Writers, musicians, fashion designers, etc., but it isn't necessarily relegated to what can be considered "traditional art." Computer programmers who create "apps" for smart phones or custom builders like "Count's Kustoms" where they rebuild custom-made cars and motorcycles are also artists in their own regard. These people usually value their passion more than profit and are consequently happier, even though they may not be making a lot of money.

Finally, there is the "business owner." A true entrepreneur, this man is not just a one-man operation a la the independent contractor, but rather a genuine "capitalist." He has employees, he has staff, he runs a factory, and he manages all aspects of the company. The business can be something as small as a restaurant or something as large as Mark Zuckerberg's Facebook. Though not as simple as being a welder, he leverages the assets and size of his company to make himself infinitely richer either through large profits or, perhaps, selling his company to a larger firm for millions.

There are certainly more "categories" of entrepreneurs and some of these fields certainly overlap, but in every case the man is his own man. He answers to no one. He sets his own work schedule, determines the path of his company, and, consequently gets to enjoy all the benefits (and costs) that comes with self-employment. But self-employment is not for everyone. It takes a certain psychology and tenacity to do it. Not to mention, determination and an adamancy to be free. It also attracts idealists who love the idea of being their own man, more than their ability to make it a successful reality. To that end a serious consideration of the pros and cons is necessary before committing yourself to the path of self-employment.

Pros:

<u>Your Own Boss</u> – The single largest benefit of being self-employed is you are your own boss. You get to select your clients and ultimately you have the freedom to fire your clients. This is a huge advantage, not because of the power you have, but because bad clients are the single largest threat to the success of a firm. Clients who don't pay.

Clients who consume an inordinate amount of your time. Clients who are just plain difficult. They not only cause financial difficulties, but mental strife as well. Problems you normally would have had to tolerate back when you were "working for the man," but not anymore because you are the man now. Less mental, political, and psychological problems are one of the key benefits of self-employment.

Rapid Decision Making – Rapid decision making also ranks highly as a benefit to self-employment. Anybody who has sat in a meeting knows just how pointless and inefficient they are. There needs to be consensus, there needs to be commune, you need input from everybody, when nobody wants to be there and couldn't care less about the meeting. While "meetings" grind companies to a halt, the self-employed man simply "decides" that is going to happen.

"We are doing X"
"We are doing Y"

This results in a more nimble and responsive company. A company that can move faster, poach larger company's business, resulting in larger market share and higher profits.

Implementation of Ideas – Related to decision making, self-employment also allows for the rapid implementation of good ideas. For example, I worked at a bank that was the 2ND WORST BANK IN THE STATE by all measures and accounts. They wanted improved efficiency, improved profitability, streamlined processes, blah, blah, blah. So when I presented them a comprehensive marketing plan, identifying and outlining specific actions that could be taken to achieve those goals, the

CEO
Senior VP
Regional Presidents
And every other executive

never looked at it.

Matter of fact, I guarantee it is sitting in their files or buried in their e-mail servers right now. To this day they still haven't turned a profit and I'm sure they're holding hours-long meetings where they talk how to improve profitability.

In being self-employed when there are problems or opportunities and you come up with an idea to solve them or capitalize on them, there is no debate about it, there are no meetings held about it. You simply implement those ideas and do it. This again gives you an advantage over your competitors as well as leads to increased profits.

Mobility – Unless your business is anchored to a building like a restaurant or factory, you have the ability to move and capitalize on any economic opportunities, regardless of location. For example, there is no limit to the number of welders and machinists who are bringing down six figures in North Dakota's Bakken Oil field. Had they been traditionally employed, however, their economic success would be tied to their employer and the local economy. Being self-employed and having a universally pliable trade makes the world your oyster.

<u>You Never Have to Deal with Human Resources Ever Again</u> – That 25 year old ditz who does the "screening interview," asking you questions like

"What's your favorite color and why?"
"Dogs or cats?"
"Where do you see yourself in 5 years?"

for a chemical engineer position of all things?

The one who then hires her BFF or a guy she'd like to fuck and not the most qualified candidate?

Yeah, you NEVER have to deal with her ever again.

<u>You Can Kick Ass Instead of Kiss Ass</u> – Since you are the boss there is no boss' ass to kiss. Additionally, since you are no longer working for a company or a corporation, performance is no longer based on compliance and obedience, but rather performance and profit. Ergo, no more office politics, no more work place drama, no back-stabbing, no pointless meetings, and no more ladies gossiping over the water cooler. You are free to spend every waking second making sound, logical decisions that maximize profit and performance. The ensuing psychological serenity alone makes self-employment worth it.

<u>Tax Write Offs</u> – In order to understand how "tax write offs" work you need to understand the concept of "taxable income." The government does not tax companies on the total amount of money they take in, they tax them on the amount of money remaining

after companies subtract out all of their expenses, aka "taxable income."

So for example, say you have a painting company and you brought in $100,000 for the year. The income tax rate is 40%, so if the government were to tax you on TOTAL INCOME, you would have to pay $40,000 in. But you would say,

"Whoa, whoa, whoa! Wait a minute! I got all of these expenses! I have to pay $30,000 for paint, $10,000 for labor, and $10,000 for insurance. If I gotta pay for all those AND $40,000 in taxes, then there won't be anything left!"

And you would be right.

But this is why you are taxed on TAXABLE income, not TOTAL income. You are allowed to "deduct" or *"write off"* all legitimate expenses related to the firm.

Thus, your income statement would look something more like this:

Revenue (Total Income)	$100,000
-Paint	-$30,000
-Labor	-$10,000
-Insurance	-$10,000
Taxable Income	$50,000
-Tax (40%)	-$20,000
Profit to You	$30,000

In the above example your "write offs" saved you $20,000 in taxes. Without them your tax bill would have been $40,000, but in "writing off" all your expenses, you only paid $20,000 in taxes. So you can see the value in having as many write offs as possible.

Now consider a person who has a two hour, 100 mile round-trip commute. Every day he wakes up, spending $12 a day in gas, $5 a day in parking, and $500 a year in maintenance. That adds up to roughly $4,600 a year in transport costs.

Does he get to write those off from his taxes?

No, because he's a corporate man. He gets to eat those costs in full.

But if you're self-employed you DO get to write those expenses off from your taxes because they are a necessary and legitimate expense in order for you to conduct business.

This is one of the best benefits of being self-employed – you get to write off expenses you would normally incur anyway as a regular person, but because you're now self-employed, those expenses can be deducted. Take your computer for example. Nearly everybody, self-employed or not, has to buy a computer. But only the self-employed people can write it off as a viable business expense. Your commute, same thing. Nearly everybody has to drive somewhere to work. But only self-employed people can write it off from their taxes. Cell phone, insurance, rent, there are many expenses you would have to pay anyway that you now get to write off against your taxes.

Of course, you don't want to abuse "write offs." This is where the infamous, *"I'll just write this dinner off, we talked about business right?"* write-off comes from and is also the type of illegitimate deductions that will land you in jail with the IRS. But there are at least thousands of dollars in tax deductions you can write off being self-employed that regular ~~working stiffs~~ "corporate men" cannot.

Cons:

Who Needs Who More – Key to your success as an entrepreneur is who needs who more. Not just for financial reasons, but mental health reasons as well. A brain surgeon not only commands a high wage, but because he is in such high demand he does not have to tolerate one single micro-gram of crap from anybody. He gets to operate on his terms, his rules, and if anybody gives him the slightest bit of guff he can find another gig in a matter of minutes. Not only is he guaranteed income, he also has a stress-free career. Contrast that with a relatively unskilled trade like snow plowing. You likely aren't the only snow plowing service in town. You can't charge exorbitant prices. And if you get a lippy client you may just have to suffer it. This doesn't mean we all have to become brain surgeons, but you should definitely consider becoming a "specialist" as opposed to a mere "independent contractor."

Bankruptcy – The quickest way to bankruptcy is by starting a business. Specifically, a stupid business. I've seen all manner of stupid businesses and business ideas. Horse farms, bobble shops, sports bars, you name it. But the stupidity of such ideas belies the biggest threat self-employment poses to people – that they fall in love with their ideas and dreams…ideas and dreams that just aren't profitable.

Because of this people are not only wedded to a failing business idea, but blinded to the fact they're losing money. They're "doing what they love and that's all that matters," when in reality all that matters is whether you're making money or not. Soon, not only does the company go under, but the business owner exhausted all of his or her personal financial resources, borrowed money from friends and family, drained their retirement account, all for an expensive and, ultimately, destructive hobby.

Ensure your business idea is not a stupid one.

Seasonality – Not a huge drawback as much as it is an annoyance, a lot of businesses are seasonal or cyclical. This doesn't pose a huge problem, but can result in irregular cash flows and income. This necessitates you budget for a "slow season" or at least learn how to diversify your business to take advantage of down time (for example bike shops also selling skiing or snowboard gear).

Accounting and Management – In being the boss you are ultimately responsible for everything. You may be a great plumber or a great computer security consultant, but you are likely a lousy accountant or employment law expert. But just because you don't "like" accounting or employment law doesn't mean it goes away. It still has to get done. Most people are smart and outsource this to a CPA or a lawyer. Others aren't so smart and either try to do it themselves or just never do it at all. The latter always ends up in bankruptcy.

Banks Hate Self-Employed People – A huge drawback in being self-employed is that you will be considered a higher lending risk by most banks and financial institutions. You could be making $1 million a year, sitting on $5 million in cash, but in the end you will pay a higher interest rate for a car loan or mortgage. The reason is that as a whole self-employed people are not your surgeons or Bill Gates of the world, but rather your failing horse farm hobbyist, drunk trucker with child support payments, and generalist "business consultant" who lives in a trailer. Therefore, most banks' lending policies discriminate against the self-employed.

Constant Recertification – A lot of industries (notably, accounting, law, medicine, etc.) will require constant certification and recertification. In many (and an increasing number of) industries you have to not only prove you can do the job, but get "continuing professional education" or "CPE" credits to further prove you are presumably staying abreast of the most recent developments in your field. This "progressive credentialism," though called for in some instances, is becoming nothing more than a money-making scam for a lot of industries (the CFA, CPA, human resources, education, etc.) and is becoming so bad it renders several previously lucrative professions unviable.

The Government Worker

If all of the above sounds like a lot of work, you're right. It is. Whether you're employed by a company or self-employed they're both going to require a lot of work, toil, sweat, education and abuse. But what if you wanted to find a job that was easier. And not only easier, but higher paying and more secure? Well, the answer is government work.

The blunt, cold, honest truth is that government work is easier than private sector work. That may be insulting. That may ruffle the feathers of government workers. But that doesn't change the fact it's true. Because government workers are not constantly pushed for profit or efficiency, government work is easier and more lackadaisical than private sector work. Also, because there is no incentive for cost control, government workers are paid (depending on which statistics you want to use) anywhere between 10-50% more than their for-profit counterparts for equivalent work. The benefits of government work don't stop there because of...well...the benefits. Unlike the private sector you get a pension (something practically unheard of nowadays) and if you log enough hours you can retire at 55. Tuition reimbursement not only for yourself, but likely your spouse and kids. You can "double dip" on your pensions if you have multiple jobs within government, and your health care premiums are just a fraction of what people in the real world pay. With effectively twice the pay for half the work it leads any logical person to conclude "If you can't beat 'em, join 'em!"

But just like any other line of work, there are drawbacks. If you think you weren't going to be challenged in the corporate world, then just wait till you get into government work. A parking lot attendant buddy of mine parks cars for the State of Minnesota, the employees of which never stop complaining about how they do nothing at work. Notice they're not bragging. They're *complaining*. The human mind is not meant to sit and stagnate for eight hours a day, it's meant to be engaged. While on average you can expect to spend 80% of your time "looking busy" in the corporate world, you can expect 90-95% of your time to be spent "looking busy" in the public sector. Some particularly lazy and union-esque people can do this. Most intelligent people can't.

Another thing is the people you get to work with. Again, blunt and truthful, they are on the average, inferior. They have no drive, they have no incentive, and they tend to be lazier than their private sector counterparts. But what makes things worse is because of their environment they are spoiled, leading them to believe they are more intelligent than they really are and their jobs more important than they really are. All one needs to do is hang out with elementary school teachers (which I have) and listen to them not just complain about how hard their jobs are, but how important it is to educate the children, when in reality their job is nothing but glorified baby-sitting. Social workers are another example. A colleague of mine has a girlfriend whose job (as a social worker) is to visit injured children in the hospital, assess whether they were wearing the right safety equipment, and then hand out safety literature if they weren't. The anecdotes are endless, and certainly not all government employees are like this, but most government jobs are nothing but welfare with a make-work job attached to it to bolster the ego of the employee. Ergo don't expect to be sitting next to Steve Jobs discussing how to cure cancer while working at the Department of Motor Vehicles.

Finally, it is unlikely you will become an "executive." The public sector requires doctorates for nearly every executive position in nearly every field, no matter how unnecessary it is. If you want to become a "superintendent" you need your doctorate. You want to become the head of the social work department, you need your doctorate. Want to rise through the ranks at the library you need a masters in "library science." This not only forces you to torture your brain for 2-4 years, studying a subject that only has a weekend-long seminar's worth of material, but you now get to play politics. As you get higher up in government positions you will spend more and more of your time lobbying for taxpayer money. Regardless of your political beliefs you will have to become a democrat, or at least fake like you are one. And if you think "looking busy" is draining, just try living the lie you're a socialist for 20 years. In the end, unless you can suffer a pointless graduate degree, lying through your teeth, and being somebody you're not, it is best to be a lowly ranked government employee, taking advantage of its overly generous benefits, having the taxpayers pay for your easy life. In the wise words of my 47 year old realtor:

"If I had just become a teacher, instead of working 80 hours a week in the real world, I would have been retired by now, and that's only working nine months a year."

The Military

Lucrative as government work may seem, if I were to do it all over again, I would have joined the military. The reasons are compelling as they are endless.

First, especially when you are younger, you can't just go and find a decent paying job. You need to go through *at least* a three year phase of "entry level positions." Positions that barely pay a living wage and will ensure you flirt with true poverty for those years. If you haven't experienced poverty, you don't want to. You will experience true hunger, you will lose weight, you'll get sick, you will constantly fret and worry about money, and you will rarely get to enjoy any luxuries in life. But if you join the military you can avoid this hellish existence.

The reason why is while most people focus on the risk of death when pondering the military, they completely ignore the simple fact that as long as you are in the military they will pay for your

food,
clothing,
shelter,
and
health care.

This is an often overlooked benefit to joining the military, especially if you are younger and come from a poor family. Yes, basic training is hard. Yes, there is always that risk of getting killed. And yes, you may get stationed in "Bumfuckegyptstan." But you don't have to worry about where your next meal is coming from, you don't have to worry about whether you can afford rent, and you don't have to worry about whether you can afford your medical bills, because the military is taking care of you. This is a huge advantage over your starving 18 year old, college-attending counterpart as they go to school full time, study part time, work some $8 per hour job, all while still accumulating $80,000 in student loans.

Second, speaking of student loans, you're not going to have any. The reason why is because the military will pay for it. Whether it is the GI Bill or the educational opportunities offered while you're in the military, your education is bought and paid for by the military. However, the **NUMBER ONE COMPLAINT OF ALL MY 30-40 SOMETHING FRIENDS WHO WERE IN THE MILITARY WAS THAT THEY DID NOT FULLY AVAIL THEMSELVES OF THE EDUCATIONAL OPPORTUNITIES OFFERED TO THEM**. This indicates the problem isn't that these opportunities aren't being offered, but rather young men are too busy scoring passes off base, goofing off, and being a bunch of dumbasses instead of appreciating the once-in-a-lifetime opportunities presented to them by our generous military. The problem is most young men think the military "sucks" and can't wait to get out when in reality, the real world is a lot worse, especially for uneducated, untrained young men. Trust your elders and men who rue not taking full advantage of their military careers when they had the chance. The grass is not greener on the other side, stick with the military until you have all the education and training you need.

Third, along the same lines, there is no better place to get real world experience for young people than the military. Understand nobody in the real world is going to take you seriously until you are at least 35. This is largely in part due to your peers ruining the reputation of "young people." Yes, *you* may show up on time. Yes, *you* may not do pot or show up for a shift drunk. But enough of American 20 somethings have to the point you will never be given the opportunity to prove yourself until you start growing gray hair.

The military, on the other hand, cannot afford to have you lollygagging about, driftlessly roaming around base, doing nothing. They will put you to work immediately, and not just work, but train you in skills that will help get you employed once you leave the military. Mechanics, logistics, computer networking, electronics, accounting, you name it. Also, you don't have to wait until you get out of the military to pursue your college degree. There are a plethora of programs that allow you to get college credit while in the military ranging from online classes to college classes offered on or near base. All free and all to your advantage.

Fourth, since nobody is going to take you seriously until you reach the age of 35, you might as well stay in until you're 38. The reason "38" is the magical number is because if you entered when you were 18, and stuck around for 20 years in the military, you would qualify for a pension. And not just any ole pension. A lifetime pension. A paycheck, every month, for the rest of your life. Of course, to the young 18 year old committing 20 years to anything, let alone the military, seems like an eternity, not to mention 38 seems "old." But understand those 20 years will fly by faster than you think, and 38 really isn't that old. But more importantly, bar some incredible luck or connections, you really aren't going to miss out on any career or economic opportunities during those 20 years because of the bigotry against younger people. If you joined the military, stayed for 20 years, had them pay for everything, got your degree in a legitimate field as well as some training, and then retired, not only would you be in the top 5% of 38 year olds financially, but you would have better employment prospects than most. And if you don't believe that, just look at most non-military 38 year olds today and see if they have it any better.

Admittedly, the military is not going to be for everyone. Some of you may have some moral objections, others may know in their heart of hearts it isn't for them, and some of you have medical conditions that would preclude you from military service. But out of everything society offers to its youth, the military is hands down one of the best deals you can avail yourself of, even considering the risk of death.

The Minimalist aka "Going Galt"

The minimalist or "Galtist" does not hate work as much as he hates authority. So much so he or she is willing to minimize their lives, thereby lessening their need for employment and, consequently, minimizing the time they need to "suffer" working under an authority. They value their time and freedom above all else and couldn't care less about a mortgage, a car, or other standard staples in life. Long as they're not answering to some boss or clocking in at the factory they are happy.

Because of this their "job" isn't to make money, but rather to minimize their spending. However, to what extent they pursue this depends on the individual. At some basic level, everybody is a minimalist. Nobody likes work and we'd prefer to never work again if given the choice. Therefore, we may downsize our house or cut out the cable to make ends meet and avoid taking another job. However, true "minimalists" go to the extreme, living in trailers, generating their own electricity, and getting by on less than $5,000 a year. What extremity of minimalism you might wish to achieve depends on your own personality. But somewhere between "cutting back on sushi" and "living in a trailer using car batteries for electricity" is a happy medium that may suit a lot of people.

For example, there are a lot of "minimalist" jobs out there where you have to answer to an "authority," but you rarely see their face. Being a security guard is a perfect example of this. You rarely see your boss. You rarely tolerate office politics. As long as you show up on time and are sober you are allowed to be left alone for eight hours a night, permitted to work on your hobbies or just goof around on the internet. A truck driver is another example. Bar some minor office work up front, you can just drive around the country, looking at its beautiful landscape, listening to the radio or your thoughts. There are other jobs that minimize your face-time with authority, but the larger point is that you *can* find jobs conducive to a minimalist mindset. That added income can be the difference between a life of living in a cheap studio apartment or out of a van down by the river.

Another approach is to "suffer" working a real job for a certain amount of time, only until you save up enough money or have a side-business going that allows you to never work again. If your expenses are minimal, say, $7,000 a year, and over the course of a decade you manage to save $140,000, you have 20 years' worth of savings. This, of course, requires you spend some time in the real world, but if you can tough it out and adhere to tough fiscal discipline, you could retire well before most of your debt-laden peers.

However, a cynical, though poignant question to ask is why have a job at all? Setting morality aside, with such minimal spending it is possible just to get by on the government dole. Matter of fact, it's almost *impossible* not to. In having such minimal spending, you need an equally little amount of income. So little income, it almost guarantees you will receive more in tax benefits, refunds, tax credits, and general government services than what you paid in. Matter of fact, half of all Americans do not pay federal income taxes, as they are heavily subsidized by the rich, mathematically making most of us default economic parasites. Therefore, the issue of whether you should be "moral" and work hard is moot and academic, especially if you're deciding to "go Galt." You already are living off the system. It is merely up to your own personal moral code as to whether you'd want to engage in work to make yourself feel better about it.

Moral debates aside, though, there is one final huge and often unforeseen benefit to minimalist living:

You stand a much higher chance of becoming rich, even more so than the most obedient and ass-kissing of MBA's.

Understand what makes people rich is not being the good little corporate man or being the good little obedient wage slave. It's ideas and innovation that makes people rich. Ideas and innovation most normal corporate cogs have not the time nor energy to dream up of, let alone pursue as they finally pull into their driveway after a ten hour work day and two hour commute, creative and conscious as zombies. However, the exact opposite can be said of minimalists or Galtists. If anything these people have plenty of time on their hands to dream. And not just dream, but think through. And not just think through, but actually pursue.

Take Douglas Adams for instance, author of "The Hitchhikers Guide to the Galaxy." He came up with the idea while working as a security guard.

Have you heard of "Harry Potter?" The boy would never have existed had its author, J.K. Rowling, not benefited from the British taxpayers' generosity financing her bills and writing career as she collected welfare.

And your fancy little Apple doo-dad wouldn't exist if Steve Jobs and Steve Wozniak were working on TPS reports at Initech instead of tinkering in their garage.

Authors and anecdotes aside, the truth is if you're constantly occupied with a 9-5, mind-numbing job, you won't have the time, energy, or desire to pursue any dreams you might have. But if you are a minimalist, working barely 10 hours per week, the human mind will find something else to do with the remaining 30. And usually what it picks isn't mind-numbing or boring, but your hobby, your interest, and your passion. And in being your passion it will inspire you to dedicate even more time to it than you would a normal job, thereby ensuring it is uniqueness and quality. And it is high-quality, unique things that act as a lightning rod to riches.

There is no guarantee of course you will make it rich, sitting inside your studio apartment, drinking Weasel whiskey, smoking cigarettes, contemplating the next great work of fiction or "Angry Birds" app for smart phones. But it is a guarantee you stand better chances of becoming a millionaire than the mass-produced MBA slaving away 80 hours a week, hoping for that promotion, as his employer secretly files for bankruptcy.

A Miscellany of Advice

Regardless of which route you choose or whichever career path you take, there are some universal bits of advice that will come in handy. However, the following advice is unconventional as most "conventional" advice is outdated, obsolete, and will usually only serve to harm your career instead of advance it. No "career planning experts" would ever make the following recommendations, but therein lays the benefit of the following advice. Since everybody is doing what the "experts" say, none of them are doing anything special, and therefore will achieve nothing special either. It is in standing back, opening your mind, and assessing the real world labor market for what it truly is that is going to allow you to make wise decisions, based in the real world, that will deliver superior results.

Experiment While You're Younger – Much shame and beratement is laid on the younger generations for being "unprofessional" or "immature." And while this criticism may apply to the majority of your peers, but unjustifiably to you, you might as well take advantage of it and experiment a little bit. Since (once again) nobody is going to take you seriously until you are older you have carte blanche to test, agitate, experiment and risk everything.

For example, three years after I left banking, I was solely making a living on dance classes and books sales. It was 1PM in the afternoon, I was drunk and playing video games, when I received a call from a bank that was wondering if I'd come in and consult them. Infuriated with the whole industry from before (and perhaps a bit too inebriated) I just cursed and yelled at the guy over the phone.

"What the fuck? Another shitty community bank? Wait wait wait. Lemme guess, you still have a bunch of old farts sitting there wondering why their real estate portfolio has gone down the toilet? And now you want somebody to come in and clean up your fucking mess for you? Am I right? Oh, and, wait, lemme guess. Nobody's had the balls to fire those guys so you never clean up your bad loan portfolio and now I would get to deal with these morons and their

moron clients who constantly need more money and never have a hope in paying it back. Am I right?"

The guy asked what I charged per hour. Indifferent, I said,

"$75 per hour and no bullshit."

I started the next week at $65.

The point is most employers are so sterile, so politically correct, anybody who stands out, for better or worse gains notoriety. And while notoriety can both be good or bad, in the corporate world it tends to take on its absolute value. Think about the HR rep who has to sift through hundreds of resumes that do not significantly deviate or vary from one another…until she gets to yours which is made of blue construction paper. While logic would say she would toss it in the garbage, ironically it would at minimum pique her interest and result in a much higher chance that you'd be called for an interview. Another example, say your immediate supervisor refuses to listen to a great idea you had. Go over his head. That guy not listening to you? Go over *his head*. You keep on going until you get all the way to the CEO if you have to. Because what's the consequence? You lose your lousy, low-paying job that wasn't going anywhere anyway?

The larger point is not that you should be sending out resumes on blue construction paper or harassing CEO's, but one of experimenting and taking risks in your younger days. Since employers will discriminate against you because of your youth, you have nothing to lose testing the limits of their idiocy and bigotry. And consequently, testing this idiocy will send up enough flags (both good and bad) that important people with decision making power will notice.

Confidence – Realize the labor market is a two way street. Not only do you need an employer, but your employer needs you. Because of the high unemployment rate, however, employers have developed a bit of an attitude, offering low pay and lording jobs over applicants. Therefore, when you are inevitably offered a job it is likely going to be a low-ball figure. Always negotiate for more.

Yes, you may be desperate.
Yes, you may really need that money.

But there's always welfare and sleeping on a couch instead.

While there is a chance they may rescind the offer if you ask for too much, it is much more likely they will counter with a significantly higher amount than their original offer. This is good for two reasons. One, it tells the employer you are not going to be taken advantage of and, two, it lays the foundation or "base" for all your future starting salaries and raises. This is important in that raises and starting salaries tend to be somewhat "exponential" or "compounding." Ergo, if you start at $50,000 not only will your next job have a higher starting salary, but a 7% raise on $50,000 is much higher than a 7% raise on $30,000.

Job Hop – "Job hopper" is a derogatory term used to explain somebody who isn't loyal and has a tendency to jump from job to job. While this term may have carried some shame 50 years ago, today a job hopper is just somebody smart enough to know when a job was sold as something it wasn't and has enough self-respect to quit it and find another one.

The truth is the vast majority of your jobs are not going to be a good fit and it's going to take some time to find that "right one." However, this only reinforces the value of job hopping in that it is very analogous to trying to find a spouse. You don't find the love of your life by "toughing it out" and sticking with the first girl you date for years. You dump her ass and find a new girl. And if that girl starts giving you guff about being a Republican or how you like to own guns, you dump her ass and find another one. You keep doing this, girl after girl after girl until you find "the one." The same thing applies to the job hunt. You don't stay with an abusive boss, doing a job you hate. You get rid of that job ASAP and find another one. And if that next one doesn't prove to be a fit, you quit that job ASAP and keep going. You keep job hopping until you find "the one" because suffering 20 bad jobs to discover the 21st one is the job of your dreams is infinitely better than loyally working a job you hate for 50 years.

Try Jobs You Think You'd Hate/Be Bad At – If you had asked me when I was younger if I would ever become a ballroom dance instructor, a radio show host, or an author, I would have laughed in your face. Never in a million years would I have ever thought I would become any of those things. But I did. And the reason was shocking to me.

I was really good at them.

Understand just because you don't *think* you'd be good at something or you don't *think* you'd like something, doesn't mean you won't. Matter of fact, most people have no clue what hidden talents and abilities they have, and when accidentally discovered are surprised they have a new-found passion.

This is great news because most people relegate themselves to fields they *think* they like and jobs they've trained for. But there are nearly a limitless number of careers, jobs, and fields you likely have a hidden and surprising aptitude for. Ergo, if your chosen career path in life is proving more difficult than you previously thought, why not just try a completely different industry or field you thought you'd never go into? Military, used car salesman, medic, dog walker, yoga instructor, jazz musician, stripper, you name it, you might as well at least try it. The worst you'll do is simply go from one job you don't like to another, but at best you might just find your passion, a passion you never knew you had.

Networking – "Networking" is nothing more than a euphemism for "kissing ass." It takes form in all shapes and sizes, but in general it is where you go and "network" to meet people in the vain hopes they might land you a job, get you a contract, or generate some business. So you attend seminars, join professional associations, join the chamber of commerce, sit in lectures, go to company sponsored-happy hours, attend job fairs, etc., all while wearing the fakest of smiles, feigning the fakest of interest.

Networking, by all means, should be abolished for the detestable waste of time it is, but sadly it is a necessary evil you and anybody else who wants a "successful career" must suffer. The reason why is that networking has reached such a critical mass and has become so engrained in corporate culture it is now standard and required. Therefore, if you take a job and wish to excel at it, you must engage in this hypocritical hoop jumping as this is how "most business gets done."

Thankfully, however, younger generations may get a reprieve from this despicable business practice as social media sites (like Facebook or LinkedIn) have supplanted the jobless "job fair" and pointless "professional association." Instead of wasting your precious free time driving to, flying to, and attending networking events, you can be much more directly connected to relevant people via these web sites who have a genuine business interest in you. Until this time comes, however, you can expect to waste at least 20% of your career networking.

<u>"You Don't Need the Money" Position</u> – Either through minimizing your expenses or avoiding debt, arguably the single best position to be in your career is where you simply "don't need the money." What this position allows you to do is negotiate for the absolute maximum amount of pay because if they refuse to pay it, what do you care?

You don't need the money.

This results in an ironic, but very beneficial spiral where you make...well...even more money. Since you can afford to bid out at the highest rate or wage, you will inevitably only take the highest paying jobs. This not only results in you having to work less to make the same amount of money, but requires any future jobs you take thereafter to be even higher paying than that. Thus, when another opportunity comes along you can demand even MORE money, because...well, again, you don't need the money.

One would think you would have to be a surgeon or a highly skilled individual who is in such demand they can name their price, but the truth is you just need to be a minimalist. In being a minimalist you achieve a position of *truly* "not needing the money." This in turn grants you the position to bluff for more pay...while, ironically, not needing it.

Have a Part Time Job/Always Be Looking for a Job – Especially if you've just graduated from college and have student loans to pay, it's going to prove difficult to get into the position of "not needing the money." However, you can still achieve the same effect and superior bargaining position if you have a part-time job or are constantly looking for a job. In having a part-time job you at least have some secondary income to fall back on in case things sour at your job. And in constantly looking for a job, you are likely to have multiple-job offers which will give you considerable leverage against your current employer. It may take a bite out of your free-time, but running a strategy like this, especially in the early years of your career, can prove to be very beneficial in accelerating your salary.

Refuse Their Health Insurance If Too Expensive – Employers will offer health insurance as if it were a benefit, but then charge you $350 a month in premiums for it. If you are old and already have a condition, this is great. But if you are young you are simply getting screwed over.

Understand why employers offer health insurance to young people. It isn't because they care about you or want you to be healthy. They need you to pay exaggerated premiums to subsidize the health insurance of older employees. A catastrophic insurance policy for a young, in shape man only costs $125 a month. Demand employers pay you cash instead and that you will get your own insurance.

Older is Not Smarter or Better – When I was 22 I thought people who were 30 had their act together, and if they were 40, then they were light years ahead of me in terms of knowledge, experience and wisdom. The reality was they were just older.

I came to this epiphany during the housing bubble when, time and time again, my boss would criticize my reports which were indicating there was a surplus of housing and that there was a strong chance the housing market would crash. It was particularly frustrating when he'd ask me to rewrite my reports, recalculate my figures, and in general lecture me about the quality of my work as it led me to believe I was doing a bad job. I never questioned him because I thought since he was older, he **must** be right. My work was inferior, I was doing a bad job, and I was a bad employee. However, the reality was my boss was compensated based on sales, not profits, and wanted as many loans to come through regardless of their quality. Ergo, I wasn't a bad employee, I was just in his way.

It wasn't until my boss got a cease and desist order by the FDIC at his new job and the housing market collapsed did I realize he wasn't "more experienced" or "wiser" than me, but was a scheming, greedy, scumbucket who is the reason bankers have the reputation they do. But what was particularly enraging was the years I spent under him and other bosses thinking somehow my work was inferior and there was something wrong with me, when in fact, there wasn't.

This is the true risk of assuming older people are smarter or wiser than you – it will drive you insane simply because it's not true. Remember, to get ahead in today's employment world it is not intelligence, smarts, or innovation you need, but compliance and obedience. Therefore, if you have a senior-level manager or a 50 something boss, it is a guarantee they got there by being a good little corporate cog, not being a ponderous innovator or genuine leader. Worse, as the corporate world deteriorates, people can get ahead faster by kissing ass and mastering office politics. This means the higher up you go, the more amoral and corrupt these people likely are. In the end you do not have brilliant, intelligent, and honest leaders in management, but conformists, politicians, Machiavellians, and sociopaths.

But they face a problem.

In order to maintain their positions of power they cannot let younger employees find out just what frauds and incompetents they really are. They need to protect their "reputation," maintain their authority, and hide the fact that nearly 90% of managers and bosses in America could be replaced by well-trained, under-30 somethings. Thus, to protect their white collar, middle-management fiefdoms they construct a massive and elaborate façade to keep younger workers in the dark. Younger employees are berated, lied to about their performance, given little to no training, given little to no opportunities, and are forced to walk on eggshells and jump through hoops, all to have them so thoroughly confused they are fooled into thinking they really are inferior to the 52 year old thug running the company into the ground.

Thus, the lesson is simple – don't assume somebody who is older than you is somehow wiser, more experienced or better than you. If you do, you not only let these people take advantage of and abuse you, but you will have to suffer the maddening experience of trying to reconcile what you know is right with what an incompetent manager is telling you is wrong. Additionally, you will never let yourself advance in your career as you constantly underestimate your abilities and skills, abilities and skills that likely surpass your superiors. While this borders on arrogance, an intellectually honest assessment of yourself and your abilities, without the constant subterfuge on the part of inept bosses, is necessary for you to achieve your best.

Lie on Your Resume – Companies and employers lie every time they put out a want ad. They make the job sound better than it actually is and always put the "ad hoc work as needed" as a catch-all to ensure that they can make you do whatever they want. They also lie about their pay being "competitive," they lie about promotion and advancement potential, and they lie about what kind of education is truly needed to do the job.

The solution is simple – you lie right back.

While you can't lie about things that can be confirmed (school attendance, GPA, etc.) you can lie if you ever got fired or not (you never did), lie about previous job duties (you weren't filing or faxing, but "streamlining office logistics"), lie during the interview (HR can't confirm anecdotes), and if you can, get a friend to lie for you (I had one friend claim I was his employee to fill a two year gap in my resume, gave me a great reference!)

While none of this is right or moral, in today's modern labor market it's called for. If companies are going to

- force you to unnecessarily spend two more years and $50,000 in grad school,
- only to get a job that is truly entry level,
- where 70% of the duties listed were bogus anyway,
- and not even bother to train you in

then the least you can do is return the favor and be as deceitful and dishonest as they are.

Feminized Workplace – The introduction of women into the work force has been both a blessing and a curse for society. While their additional labor results in increased economic productivity, their innate differences have caused consequential sociological, psychological, managerial, and sexual problems in the work place – sexual harassment suits, sexual discrimination, affirmative action, sensitivity training, etc. But while most of these problems have been minor and never presented a real threat to the functionality of the labor force, current and future generations of women not only present new and very real threats to male employees, but may very well undermine the entire labor market today.

Most obvious is the "feminist NARC." As more and more young girls are indoctrinated with socialist, feminist thought, they pompously believe they have a "higher" or "secondary" calling beyond merely doing their job. Namely, one of fighting against sexism, "patriarchy," bigotry, etc., wherever they find it. This takes form in anything ranging from women filing faux sexual harassment suits (because they simply didn't agree with what a man was saying in a personal conversation that didn't involve them) to a Nazi-eqsue level of tyranny where women will search for and forward personal Facebook posts or "tweets" of male employees to their bosses that they found disagreeable in an attempt to get them fired.

This may seem outlandish, idiotic, and childish but the outlandishness of it all is only outdone by the fact that not only are more and more young women doing this, but employers are actually acting upon it, firing men for having political opinions or making off-color comments on social media sites that have nothing to do with their jobs. Adria Richard's narcing out two otherwise sophomoric computer programmers at a convention for cutting sexual jokes is shocking, not because 20 something men were cutting sexual jokes, but because their employer actually fired them based on her childish whining. Quin Pu's forwarding of sexts to her ex's boss in an effort to avenge his dumping her is only further proof to the childish mentality young women have been brought up with. And the firing of a man named "Pax Dickinson" for having a personal twitter account that was certainly not feminist-friendly, is merely another example. Anecdote after anecdote can be provided, but what you must realize is that modern day employers have become so sensitive to the slightest of complaints, they deem it their right to intrude and eavesdrop on your own personal conversations over the internet. And the fact alone they will bend to the wishes of tattle tales, narcs, and narcissists renders an ever-increasing percentage of employers inhospitable to normal male behavior.

You are therefore faced with a choice. Stick with an environment that will become progressively more and more Orwellian in nature (and thereby be forced to watch every word you speak and every comment you post on Facebook), or strike out on your own allowing yourself the sanity and freedom most real men need.

Another genuine risk to male employment in today's labor market is the gatekeepers of employment – HR.

Let us be clear what "Human Resources" (HR) really is. It is nothing more than an affirmative action program designed to get more women employed in the corporate world without putting them in genuine positions of power. They can't do accounting. They can't do math. They can't do computer programming, but they can ask you some mean questions about where you see yourself in three years or whether you've ever had a disagreement with your boss and "how did you solve it and why?"

The real threat, however, of HR is not that they are idiots put in charge of vetting labor, but they are now the primary vehicle by which the government is infecting socialism and leftism in the corporate sector. "Diversity," "affirmative action," "going green." None of these things have anything to do with the sole purpose of a corporation – profit. They are merely psychological viruses designed to co-opt and corrupt the private sector into becoming another arm to advance the aims of politicians and socialists, not to mention provide talentless women with a "job" or "career."

All of this, on the basic, genetic level, is antithetical to men. Men are generally for progress, production, profit, excellence, advancement, and achievement. Things normally the private sector and competitive corporations would advocate and epitomize. But as the corporate sector is co-opted more and more with egalitarian idealism of "going green," "carbon footprints," "diversity," "feminism," etc., your performance is no longer going to be rated on effort, hard work, intelligence, discipline, rigor and effort, but (once again) commune, negotiation, ass-kissing, brown-nosing, lying, politicking and things as bigoted as the color of your skin, sex, and sexual preference.

Finally, as more and more (feminist) women enter the workforce, the corporate culture will change from one solely focused on profit for the shareholders to one that focuses on using the corporation as a tool for parasites to advance their own personal, financial, and political aims. More emphasis will be put on "Corporate Social Responsibility" than "net profit" because a score of leftist women (and men) can be employed by such a bogus department. The United Way will make its extortionist rounds in your office and if you don't donate you will be scarlet-lettered for the rest of your career. You may have genuine and real work to do, but you need to attend diversity training, sensitivity training, and sexual harassment training, all so that consultant who's doing the training can bill out at $200 an hour. And finally, you will be degraded to wearing pink for an entire month, because if you don't, then you hate women and you want them all to get breast cancer.

In short, as more and more young girls, infected with socialist, leftist brainwashing populate the workforce and as more and more non-profit ogranizations infiltrate their way into corporate America, you can expect a forever increasing percentage of your time to be donated towards completely leftist, idiotic, political bullshit at the cost of genuine work, production and excellence.

It is an environment that is simply intolerable and unacceptable to most self-respecting men. But one that is becoming more common and one you must prepare yourself for.

Go on Welfare if Necessary – Until you work in the real world, it is hard to convey just what a hostile environment it can be. Petty co-workers, vindictive HR reps, sociopathic bosses. There's a reason Dilbert is so popular and that reason is because this stuff is true. But while no job is perfect, a lot of them are unacceptably hostile to the point they're mentally abusive and damaging. If it gets that bad, then there is no shame collecting a government check. Again, taking morality out of it, just because unemployment is above 7%, doesn't give employers the right to be abusive, petty, psychotic, and test your sanity on a daily basis. If they do, at least have the self-respect to walk off the job, collect a check, and enjoy the fact that those people now have to work that much harder to support you. This doesn't mean you should abuse the system, but that you shouldn't let any system abuse you.

However, this doesn't mean you can just "walk" and start collecting an unemployment check. There are different rules and laws governing whether you qualify for unemployment and welfare in each state. THOROUGHLY consult these laws before telling your boss to take his job and shove it.

Sue If You Have the Chance – There have been two instances where I could have sued an employer or potential employer and won. One was when I was told if I were black they could hire me. The other was when a student of mine showed up drunk for class and punched me. I didn't sue in either case because (in the case of not being black) I was a young 21 year old and didn't know any better and (in the case of getting punched) I liked my employer…until they let the kid back in after expelling him because they needed his tuition money.

Understand companies and corporations are soulless, mindless entities, indifferent about you and your future. They couldn't care less if you lost your job or were out on the street starving because their job isn't to ensure your livelihood, but to make money. If they can make an extra $100 by laying off 4,000 people, they will. Because of this employers do not deserve any loyalty, and like they use you, you should also use them. Therefore, if the opportunity ever presents itself to legitimately sue a company, do it. There is no guarantee a company will commit some egregious transgression against you, but it certainly is a possibility over the course of a 50 year career. The issue is whether you can realize there is no morality or benefit in "taking the high road," in that most employers and corporations would turn around and do the exact same thing to you.

Of course, conventional wisdom will advise against suing employers, saying it renders you unemployable for life. But this is operating from the obsolete premise that there's a viable career out there for you to ruin in the first place. Unless you stand a really good shot at a great career or have a job and an employer you really like, the only thing you do in not suing a company or employer is let an injustice against you go unpunished and pass up on the money you could have won in a law suit.

CHAPTER 6
ENTREPRENEURSHIP

Though addressed in the previous chapter, entrepreneurship deserves a chapter unto itself as it is not only a much larger topic, but is in every man's psychology to be free. Free from tyranny, free from oppression, free from authority. Because of this most men will be happiest working for themselves. But being an entrepreneur is not for everyone, nor is it possible for everyone. It requires hard work, innovation, foresight, creativity, and tenacity. But whether it is in your blood or not, entrepreneurship in some capacity or another, even if you have a regular job, is a great skill to have because it provides the following benefits beyond generating your own income.

- It will provide you a valuable "Plan B" in case of being laid off
- It gives you an excellent negotiating position with employers in that you technically "don't need the money"
- It grants you the luxury of being able to walk out on abusive bosses, narcing coworkers, Nazi HR departments, and inhospitable working environments
- It is the only way your passion will ever be your job
- It is likely the only way you will ever excel and achieve your best

But attractive as entrepreneurship and "being your own boss" is, it is incredibly risky. Most people do it wrong, make mistakes, and end up going bankrupt. Worse, they ruin their personal financial lives, impair their retirements, and even impair the lives of family, friends and loved ones who sympathetically lent them money.

Therefore, if you are going to become an entrepreneur you need to do it right.

The Entrepreneurial Mind Set

The first thing you need to have in order to succeed is the entrepreneurial mindset or psychology. This is a rare thing to have since the day you were five you were programmed to be an employee, not an entrepreneur. Starting in kindergarten you have been conditioned to "go someplace everyday" in the morning and not return until the night. You have been conditioned to endure a commute either on a school bus or in rush hour. And you've been forced to take at least 13 years (more, if you went to college) of boring, mind-numbing classes in school, which is nothing more than preparing you for the boring, mind-numbing jobs you will have in the real world. To buck this brainwashing you either had to drop out, endure it, never swallowing it whole, or have somebody explain to you there was an alternative.

But merely "not liking school" or "not liking work" isn't enough to become an entrepreneur. You also need to take action. This is the largest psychological hurdle most people face in that you can't just have a great idea and then "someday the time will be right." That is merely procrastination. You need to have a carpe diem attitude and commit yourself to doing it as soon as possible. Nearly every person I know has a business idea or dream they'd like to pursue. The only thing stopping them is their procrastination.

Fearlessness is another trait you need to have. Many people are intimidated by the prospects of leaving the "safe world" of traditional employment and regular paychecks, but more daunting than that is the fear of failure. This is why most people will delay filing for an LLC or business bank account. Not because the paperwork is intimidating, but that it makes it official and commits you to follow through. The trick is to understand nothing is guaranteed in life and that an even bigger risk than failure is regret. Regret you'll have, wondering if you should have started that pizza company as you lie there in the stroke unit because the strife from your corporate job sent you there.

In addition to beating back fear and procrastination you will also need an inordinate amount of discipline. Most people take years to write a book. I wrote one in three weeks and another in just under 60 days (real ones, not 20 page pamphlets or essays). The way I achieved this is I forced myself to do it. Didn't matter how I felt. Didn't matter if I was tired. Didn't matter if there was something I preferred to do. I committed myself to doing it and expended the effort and time to see it through. You must also do the same with your business. You need to set a goal, you need to set an objective and then you need to work tirelessly until it is complete. Approaching a business lackadaisically is just another form of procrastination, but with even more time wasted.

Finally, you need independent thought. Successful entrepreneurs are not conformists who somehow accidentally find themselves starting businesses or unintentionally discovering great opportunities. They are men and women who have different perspectives, think differently, observe things others don't, and constantly question if there isn't a better way to do things. It is because of this independent mindedness they are able to identify opportunities to profit that most others just plain don't see. This isn't to say being a good, reliable employee is a bad thing, or that there's something wrong with you if you aren't constantly rethinking and questioning everything. But if your brain isn't constantly racing to find a better way to do things or you've never rammed heads with authority, chances are you lack the independent thought necessary to become an entrepreneur.

A Viable Business Idea

One of my sadistic pleasures is watching "Restaurant Impossible" where the host, Robert Irvine, goes into financially troubled restaurants, assesses what's going on, and then makes harsh and blunt recommendations to the owners as to how to turn the restaurant around. The reason it's a sadistic pleasure is because always, without fail, the owners of the restaurant are galactically stupid and naïve about the basics of running a restaurant. Invariably, though, the reasons the restaurants fail are the precise exact same reasons most businesses fail.

The Owners "Thought It'd Be Fun" – Let us be clear about something. Running a business (unless you are incredibly lucky) isn't "fun." It's "less annoying and agitating than working a real job." People who go into business to start a "horse hobby farm" or start a "sports bar" aren't serious entrepreneurs who stand a shot at becoming successful. They are lazy people who naively believe starting a business is an easy out and doesn't take a lot of effort.

It's Been Their Dream – Dreams are things people typically enjoy doing. But that's the problem with dreams – people typically enjoy doing them, which means they'll willingly do them for free, which means you can't charge them. In short, the profit isn't there to start a "doll making shop," becoming a "food critic," or some other such childish idea because who would pay for it?

A Complete Lack of Leadership – Part of running a business is actually...running the business. A lot of fake entrepreneurs, however, only like one fun aspect of their business and focus solely on that aspect. This leaves the remaining 95% of running a business unattended. Management, hiring, firing, decision making, strategic planning, legal, accounting, taxes, licensing, inventory, etc., any one of which, if left unattended, will sink a company.

There are other individual reasons, but in the end they all boil down to people's desire to run a business outstripping their ability to, or falling in love with a business idea that just isn't viable. The absolute best outcome of this is that you run an unprofitable business which just ends up becoming an "expensive hobby." But the worst outcome is you ruin your financial life, cause undue stress on your family, get divorced, deplete your retirement savings, and declare bankruptcy. All the more reason to ensure your business idea is viable.

What constitutes a "viable business idea," however, depends on you, your abilities, your insight, the economy, and a limitless number of other variables. But as long as it's profitable, then it is viable. The real problem will be whether or not you are intellectually honest with yourself. Do you want to be like everybody else and run a night club? Do you think "it'd be really cool" to breed dachshunds? Then prepare to fail miserably unless you are exceptionally talented. But if you can program a new logistical management software or develop a new alloy stronger than titanium, then you may have a good business idea on your hands. This isn't to say things that aren't science or technology-based can't be profitable, but to emphasize the importance of not letting your emotions or what you'd "like" to do blind you to the fact whether a business is profitable or not.

(For a more detailed breakdown of what industries and businesses have higher failure rates than others, as well as reasons for those failures, consult the following site:

http://statisticbrain.com/startup-failure-by-industry/.

You may also be interested in which industries are more profitable than others. "Risk Management Associates" measures the profitability of many industries and by company size as well. The reports do cost money, but you may be able to find them for free at your local library
http://www.rmahq.org/)

A Business Plan

Once you know what kind of business you want to run, the next step is to develop a business plan. Not just for financing should you require a loan, but for your benefit as well so you know what the hell you're doing. Just because you have a viable business idea doesn't mean you can't screw up in the execution. Developing a detailed business plan helps carry you through each step necessary to achieve success in establishing and running your business. It may even point out major flaws you hadn't seen before, saving you from making a horrible and life-crippling mistake. Thus, it is vital you develop a thorough and detailed business plan.

There are thousands of "business plan templates" on the internet available for free and they vary in detail as well structure (depending on the industry you're in), but all follow a general outline:

I – Summary/"Executive Summary"
II – Company Description/Mission Statement
III – Product or Services
IV – Market Analysis
V – Strategic Plan
VI – Management Structure and Team
VII – Financial Plan

Again, there are many resources on how to write a business plan, but the SBA's tutorial and outline is a very good starting point:

http://www.sba.gov/category/navigation-structure/starting-managing-business/starting-business/writing-business-plan

The final stage in developing a business plan is, ironically, the one thing most commonly missing from business plan templates – an exit strategy.

Most business plans assume you are going to run the business forever, but this is simply not the case in the majority of instances. You might sell your company once it becomes profitable. You might hand off the management of a company to a full time manager, taking a silent partner position. You may run it into the ground and need to sell it. Nothing lasts forever. However, it is usually when you sell a business that you make the most money on it, not the annual profits from year to year operation. Because of this, the exit strategy is arguably the most important part of the business plan. The key is to know what your exit strategy is so when the optimal time to sell presents itself you can capitalize on it.

Ideally, you would never sell your business because you love it so much. You love being a plumber and will be a plumber until you're dead. This case is one of the rare instances you have no exit strategy. Your exit strategy is "death" and your only concern is who to leave your business to. You may not get a big "payoff" in the end, but you enjoy your work so much you would never sell your business in the first place.

Another exit strategy is where you purposely build up a company with the sole intent of selling it. A lot of software companies do this, fully intending on larger companies like Microsoft of Electronic Arts to buy them out, or smaller biotech firms who develop some kind of patented drug, dreaming of the day Merck or Pfizer buys them out. This requires an intricate knowledge of the industry to ensure you develop a product somebody wants, otherwise you are left with a company you don't want to run and a product nobody wants.

A third exit strategy is to simply pay somebody to manage your firm. In this sense you "exit" the business work wise, but still retain ownership and are entitled to its profits. The trick is to find a reliable and trustworthy manager who will manage the firm in your interests and maintain its profitability. It technically isn't a full exit strategy as you still own the firm, but you can at any time sell your interest in the company.

Finally, morality set aside, you can pull a "Solyndra." This is where instead of building up a company to make a profit, you merely get financing to start a business you "claim" is aiming to make a profit. In reality, you are using the company as a shell to pay yourself a large executive salary. This happens more than you think as charlatans, con artists, and politicians get financing to start businesses that never had any hope of making any money whatsoever. They then pay themselves $500,000 a year each and after three years the company files for bankruptcy, but not without each executive making $1.5 million. It isn't a moral business plan, but it is a legal and profitable one.

Choosing a Business Type, Location and Registration

Once you have a thorough business plan drafted, you can now start implementing it and turning your business dream into reality. The first step is to determine where you want to register your business and what kind of legal business entity you would like it to be.

It is here we run into a significant amount of complications and technicalities because there are 50 different states, resulting in 50 different tax codes, not to mention a whole host of intra-state tax laws regarding residency, repatriation of income, and things like "tax nexus." This is all beyond the scope of this book; therefore, it is strongly recommended you spend a couple hundred dollars with a tax accountant or lawyer who can recommend something more specific to your situation. Regardless, in general you want to register your company in a state that does not have an income tax.

This confuses people at first in that they just assume they need to register their company in the state they live. However, understand what a company is – it is a separate legal entity from yourself. You are merely the owner of that company. Just as you can own property in a different state, you can own a company in a different state. Therefore, it is in your best interests to register your company in a no income tax state. As of 2013 there were only five states with no *corporate* income tax.

Washington
Wyoming
Nevada
Texas
Ohio (though it is strongly recommended you do not invest in Ohio for other reasons)

Not to make matters more complicated, but depending on the business type you choose you may only pay *personal* income taxes. There are nine states with no *personal* income tax.

Washington
Nevada
Wyoming
South Dakota
New Hampshire
Alaska
Texas
Tennessee
Florida

Naturally, for legal and tax reasons, not everybody will be able to register their business in one of the above states. But if you can help it certainly avoid states that are high tax and anti-business.

California
Minnesota
New York
Illinois
New Jersey
Wisconsin
Rhode Island
Ohio

(You may also wish to consult the Tax Foundation's "State Business Tax Climate Index" which is published on an annual basis:

http://taxfoundation.org/article/2013-state-business-tax-climate-index)

Upon selecting a state to register your business in, you now need to determine which type of legal "business entity" you want your business to be. This is where terms and acronyms like LLC, S-corp, C-corp, etc. come in. These are merely different legal entities you can form a business under, each with the pros and cons.

Sole Proprietor – This is the easiest business to form in that you're not even forming a business. You are merely declaring you are starting one. You don't have to fill out any forms, you don't have to pay any registration fees, you just start your business and come tax time fill out a "Schedule C" on your tax returns, and boom! You're done.

This is OK for beginners or people with small businesses that verge on becoming hobbies, but it leaves the owner susceptible to law suits and creditors. Since you have not registered your business as a separate legal entity and are operating under your own personal name, you are now personally responsible for anything that goes wrong with your company. Therefore, it is strongly advised to form some kind of company, completely owned by you, but legally separated from you.

"Single Member" LLC – The most likely legal entity entrepreneurs will use is the "single member LLC." LLC stands for "Limited Liability Company" and "single member" merely implies there is only one owner. Because it is a "limited liability" entity, it means only the entity or company can be sued or go bankrupt and not the individual who owns it. This allows the entrepreneur to carry out his business, pay himself money out of the LLC, and leave the LLC as merely a separate legal entity to conduct business with (or take the brunt of legal and financial problems, thereby protecting his personal assets). Also, in this LLC being a single member LLC, the owner only needs to fill out a "Schedule C" on his taxes. It is generally wise counsel to form a single member LLC instead of just operating as a sole proprietor.

LLC – An LLC is just like a single member LLC, but has multiple owners. All the same legal and financial protections apply, but since there is more than one owner you have to file a partnership tax return. This takes a little more time and cost when preparing your state and federal tax returns.

The reason you might register a multi-member LLC is because you do not have enough money to start the business on your own and must go into some form of partnership with other people. But beyond these few items, there are no major differences between single and multi-member LLC's.

S-Corp – An S Corp can be considered a slightly larger LLC. It can have multiple owners (100 max), and unlike a C-Corp (a "normal" corporation) you do not have to pay corporate income taxes. This prevents "double taxation" where a C-Corp is taxed on its corporate income and that income taxed once again when paid out to shareholders. Additionally with S-Corp's, you are not considered an employee unless you are paid a salary by that company. If you instead receive your share of profits (aka "distributions") those payments are not subject to the 15.3% tax for Social Security and Medicare.

C-Corp – A C-Corp is what most people think of when you hear the word "corporation." This is typically a larger company, can have a limitless number of shareholders, and often goes "public" becoming a publicly traded company, selling shares of stock that you can buy on the stock market. However, unless you need a large amount of capital to start your business, it is unlikely you will start off as a C-Corp.

There are many other types of legal entities you can form, but the above are the most common and beneficial to entrepreneurs. For more details consult the IRS' web page about the tax treatment and benefits of different business entities:

http://www.irs.gov/Businesses/Small-Businesses-&-Self-Employed/Business-Structures

Upon settling on a business type, you need to go to the state's "Secretary of State" department and register your business. This requires a nominal fee around $100 and some paperwork. After a few days to a week your application will be approved and you will officially own a company. This allows you to set up bank accounts, obtain credit cards, and other necessary business items for your company. You will also have to apply for a federal Employment Identification Number which will allow you to employ people and assign your business its own "social security number." The rest of it is completely up to you and your entrepreneurial acumen to make it a success.

Applying for a Loan

Depending on the financial needs of your company, you may have to apply for a loan. If this is the case then your entire business is dependent upon obtaining that financing. This means you not only need to convince the bank to lend you the money, but that the bank is now a business partner of yours. This banking relation is arguably the most important relationship you are going to have in your business and you can save an inordinate amount of time and money if you strictly adhere to some good financial habits. This will help you not only obtain a loan, but any future financing needs your company might have, as well as lower your interest rate.

First, thoroughly contemplate and think through your entire financing needs both present and future. **NOTHING** pisses off bankers more than a person who comes in for a loan and then constantly changes the amount they need, requests changes to the terms of the loan, or requests completely new loans a week after closing on the first one. It not only shows you have not given adequate thought to the financial management of your company, but lowers your chances of getting approved.

Second, if it is a new company you need to have a good business plan. By "good" I mean "clear and succinct." It doesn't need to be 400 pages because if it is you will likely harm your chances of getting a loan. Just a good, solid, comprehensive business plan that is digestible in one sitting. Once you develop this business plan you should approach several banks to play them against each other and see if you can get a better rate. You will likely have to make a presentation in person to a banker or (if a large enough loan) a committee of bankers. Ensure you are rehearsed, well-spoken, and able to predict and answer any questions they might have. If they are interested they will have you fill out a loan application.

Third, you need to provide ALL of your financial statements. These include:
- Three years of your personal tax returns
- Three years (if available) of your company's tax returns
- If a new company, three years' worth of projected income statements
- Year to date income statement of your company (as tax returns only show your profit up to the previous year's end and banks like to know how you've done in the interim)
- An updated balance sheet of your company
- An updated personal balance sheet

Banks do not just lend money to people based on trust. You need to prove to them you have the ability to pay them back and if you don't, you have enough in personal assets to pledge as collateral.

Fourth, your financial statements ***need to be current.*** If you are one of those people who cannot get your taxes in on time, constantly file extensions, and claim you're too busy to file on time, then don't bother applying for a loan. The reason is if you can't even pay the IRS on time, then you're certainly not going to pay the bank on time either. Also, as it just so happens, federal regulations practically prohibit banks from making loans until they have current financial statements. So just make it a good habit to keep your financial statements up to date.

Accounting

Once in operation you need to start accounting for your expenses and sales. This is often a purposely overlooked chore as people just don't like accounting. Unfortunately, "not liking accounting" is like "not liking gravity" or "not liking that water is wet." It is a mandatory fact of running a business and failing to do proper accounting will destroy your business.

However, unless you are running a huge company, you needn't install a horrendously complex accounting system. You don't even need to install Quickbooks (which is what I recommend). You just need a simplified accounting system that you understand and captures all your expenses and income.

For example, "Shoe Box Accounting."

In "shoe box accounting," you get a shoe box and throw in all your receipts over the course of the year. At the end of the year you simply categorize and tally up those expenses in MS Excel. You then present this spreadsheet to your accountant and have him fill out your Schedule C in your tax return.

This is of course very simplistic and won't work if you're running a larger company (in which case you would presumably outsource this to an accountant), but it does highlight the two key traits of a good accounting system – simplicity and thoroughness. In being simple it makes sense, is logical and is organized. It is also something you can do. It isn't that hard to save your receipts and fill out a spreadsheet, so you are likely to do it instead of sweep it under the rug. The shoe box method is also thorough. ALL of your relevant expenses are filed in one location and at the end accounted for when you tally them up. However, being thorough is more a function of good accounting habits than a simplistic accounting system. These are some accounting habits every entrepreneur should have:

#1 Keep personal accounts separate from company accounts. In having a separate checking account and credit card for your business, you needn't worry about whether one expense is personal or another is business. This makes tallying up your expenses at the end of the year infinitely easier.

#2 Use your company credit card as much as possible. Credit cards usually have some kind of "budgeting" function that tally up your expenses. If the majority of your business purchases are done through the card (as opposed to cash or check) then the majority of accounting work can be done by this tallying function.

#3 Save your receipts. For non-credit card purchases get into the good habit of always asking for a receipt. There will be times you pay by cash or check and those expenses add up. You want to get every penny of legitimate tax deductions possible.

#4 Account for your mileage. There are two methods you can account for mileage. Either by saving all your receipts, insurance payments, gas receipts, oil changes, and all the other expenses that go into maintaining a car, and then pro-rate that by the percentage of miles that was used for business versus personal

or,

write off 58 cents a mile.

The mileage rate (currently 58 cents a mile) is established every year by the IRS and is the amount you can write off per mile. I personally prefer this method because it's easier, you only need to account for your mileage. However, there is an added benefit to this method – you can actually make money.

In Wyoming my car broke down in late October, leaving me only with my motorcycle. Desperate to have some kind of heated transportation for the ensuing winter I bought a beat up, run down Pontiac Grand Am for $1,500. The oil leaked. The coolant leaked. One door was smashed in. And there were cigarette burns all over the upholstery. But when I was sent on business I could write off 58 cents a mile. The fortunate thing was each of the branches at the bank I was working for were at least 100 miles apart from each other. Additionally, we couldn't e-mail attachments because our e-mail system only supported attachments of 50MB or less, which meant I would have to drive files to different branches. Over the course of the winter I put over 3,000 business miles on that car which netted me a total reimbursement of $1,740. This not only paid for my car, but also the gas I used for transport.

In short, the 58 cents per mile rate includes some kind of consideration for depreciation. But if you have a cheap used car, it's already depreciated to the point your write off ends up actually paying you. So if you are a poor fellow or just don't care what kind of car you have, save yourself some time, not to mention, make some money and use the 58 cents per mile deduction.

#5 Get into the "write off psychology." As previously addressed in chapter five, remember to ensure you maximize your tax deductions. Did you write off your cell phone bill? How about that trip you had to go to Target to get some office paper? And the time you had to pay somebody to fix your computer? Ensure you get every legitimate deduction. Consequently, do not abuse your write offs or tax deductions. That dinner you had where your best friend asked you how the company was coming along does NOT qualify as a tax deduction. The time you flew to Vegas to gamble but happened to buy some office paper at Target does not permit you to write off your flight, hotel and gambling losses.

#7 Don't forget quarterly taxes. Since nobody is taking money out of your paycheck for taxes, now you have to. And if you don't, Uncle Sam will get very upset. Every quarter you need to make an estimated guess at what you owe, fill out a "1040 ES" tax form, and send that with your estimated tax payment into the US Treasury. The IRS has a horrendously complex worksheet that helps you calculate your tax bill, but the truth is it's unusable. I instead prefer to ballpark it, intentionally overpaying it so I don't have to worry about any shortfalls or fees.

There are certainly more techniques and habits you can use, but the key thing is to ensure you do have an accurate and thorough accounting system. This can be something as simple as the "shoe box method" or "envelope method" or complex as hiring it out to an accountancy or CPA. But whatever you decide upon, you MUST have an accounting system in place. Because if you don't have an accounting system, then you don't have a company.

A Miscellany of Advice

Start a Business on the Side – Very few entrepreneurs are working a regular full time job one day and then BLAMO! The next day they're running a profitable corporation. Businesses just don't form that way. They usually start out as an idea or even a hobby, and from there slowly grow into full time occupations for their founders. This means if you have a good business idea you should pursue it ASAP. Because even if you have a day time job, the sooner you start the sooner it will grow into a full time occupation.

But whereas most people think of starting a business when they're 30 or 40, the ideal time would be to start when you're 18. Again, nobody is going to take you seriously until you're 35. And most of the jobs you're going to have in your 20's are not going to be challenging anyway. You may as well be pursuing your dream or your passion on the side in the meantime. And if you're lucky, by the time you're 30 your business, however small it may be, will have grown to the point you don't ever need to work a real job again.

Start Working on Your Company at Work – One of the great things about most jobs in America and Western Civilization is that about 80% of your time is wasted at the office looking busy. Managers are incredibly inefficient and more often than not underestimate your capacity for work. Take advantage of this and instead of "acting busy," *actually be busy* developing your own business.

This isn't to say you use company computers or resources to run your own personal office supply store out of the basement, hocking your employer's supplies. But it is to say if you have any down time to start, at minimum, drafting ideas, outlining thoughts, thinking things through, and researching stuff on the internet. Nearly half the effort you're going to burn through starting a business is work that does not require a computer or a spreadsheet. It's going to be thoughtful work, strategic planning and brain storming. Naturally, you won't be able to fully plan and launch your company from your cubicle, but you can knock out at least 60% of the work...all while getting paid for it too!

Align Your Business With Your Interests – While I've mocked and ridiculed people for being naïve for starting businesses like horse farms, doll shops and sports bars, this doesn't mean you force yourself to start a business in a field you hate. If you don't like metallurgy, then you're not going to be happy making alloys even if it makes you a billionaire. You need to pursue something you enjoy. Thankfully, humans have a wide variety of interests, most of which they're unaware of. The trick is to find one you enjoy and is also profitable. But the primary reason for founding a business in something you enjoy is that the primary driver or engine of your success will be your passion. Passion is what causes a person to work 80 hours instead of 30. Passion is what keeps you up late at night working on your latest project. Passion is what is going to carry your company through. If you do not have passion, then you do not have a business, so ensure you start a business you're going to enjoy.

The Fewest Moving Parts – My girlfriend at one time owned a BMW. This evil machine, made in the deepest, darkest depths of hell by people who would give the devil a good name, had so many bells and whistles on it that at least once a month something would break. But that was the primary problem – it had a ton of bells and whistles. It just had more shit that could (and did) break.

A company is the same way.

You want your company to be as simple as possible. You don't want it complicated. You want a bare-bones, stripped down, but well-oiled machine. The reason is because you want to focus on making money, not repairing things or putting out fires. And the fewer moving parts you have in your company, the less time you're going to spend fixing them. This means as few employees as possible, as few suppliers or vendors as possible, as few vehicles, computers and other physical assets as possible. Ideally, it would just be you and a laptop that would comprise the entirety of your company.

Naturally, not all businesses or business models are conducive to this. If you are manufacturing you need a factory and employees. If you are a restaurant you need suppliers and vendors. But unless you absolutely need to make billions of dollars or insist on going into manufacturing, one of the biggest benefits of self-employment is less headaches and simplicity. So when choosing a business to start as well as how to structure your business make every effort to get by with as little people and components as possible. It only means less headaches in the future.

Avoid Business Partners – In all my years in banking every "partnership" I saw consisted of a business partner who did all the work and provided all the money, while the other business partner merely loafed around and parasited off of the other. DO NOT TAKE ON BUSINESS PARTNERS. They are the single largest risk to your business.

Other Business Opportunities Will Arise – There is no other way to describe it, but as you go about managing your business, more and more opportunities to profit will arise. For example, when I taught dance classes it became very apparent I had a captive audience. It also became very apparent none of my students would become the next Fred Astaire in my short hour-long dance classes. So I decided to film instructional dance videos and charge $15 a pop. In one night alone (though sadly not the norm) I sold over $300 in DVD's. However, when I first started teaching dance classes I never foresaw this particular opportunity for profit. The same thing will happen to you.

Like climbing mountains, you will see your business as this sole, single mountain in front of you to scale. But as you climb it and get to the top, you have additional vision and vantage points you previously didn't have, and because of this you will be able to spot additional mountains and opportunities for profit. A buddy of mine aligns tires, but also found it a profitable side business to sell them as well. Another buddy is in lumber, but also founded a "used pallet" company. And of course there's me with my instructional dance videos. Whatever it is, your business is practically guaranteed to have more than one potential source of income. So keep a keen eye out and always be thinking of a way to leverage your current position into making more money.

Location Independence – One of the biggest mistakes beginning entrepreneurs make is one of pride and ego – they get an office they don't need. They do this because they want to "feel" like they're an entrepreneur and want to show off to other people. The irony, of course, is that if you're just starting out you can't afford to lease an office you don't need, and you're likely hurting yourself and your chances of making your business successful in the long run. Instead, what you should be aiming for is "location independence."

Below is a picture of one of my offices.

Here's another.

And here's a third.

With the advent of the internet and with most work being able to be done from a laptop why would you anchor yourself to an office, let alone pay for one when your office views can look like this and change any day you want?

CHAPTER 7
GIRLS

The single largest plurality of a man's life will be spent in the pursuit of girls. You will go to clubs to meet girls. You will go to parties to meet girls. You will spend hours on the internet flirting with girls. You will spend years in college and decades at work to attract girls. If you think about it, nearly all of your conscious time on this planet is either directly or indirectly spent on getting girls.

While at first this may seem a bit pathetic, understand there is nothing wrong or pathetic about it as you are psychologically hard-wired and genetically programmed to want, desire and pursue women. It's very natural and, truthfully, there's something wrong with you if you don't have this biological imperative (the exception of gay men duly noted). But because of this women present an incredible risk. They are likely to be your greatest single source of happiness, just as they are the greatest single source of pain and misery. They will consume the greatest amount of your time and resources, an investment of which may never pay off. You see this risk play out in everyday life:

The sad, cowardly nerd who never gets the courage to approach women, and consequently lets their absence ruin his life.

The reliable, stable family man. Father of three, happy as can be, until she delivers the divorce papers.

The high school football captain/player who has a full scholarship and a bright future...until he knocks up the wrong girl.

Or the desperate middle-aged man who orders a mail order bride until she leaves him once she gets her green card.

The examples are endless, but you get the point. Women can be the single greatest blessing or curse in your life.

Because of this the topic of women, how to pursue them, how to be successful with them, and (above all else) how to do it effectively and economically is arguably the most important part of this book. The problem is the sheer scope and breadth required to thoroughly address the topic of women. For millions of years men have opined, theorized and speculated about the nature of women and have still come up with nothing. And one lowly chapter, let alone a thousand books on the topic, will fail in the same regard. However, instead of approaching the topic of women by attempting to address each and every one of their eccentricities with the corresponding "advice" or "wisdom" (which has never worked anyway) it is best to take a top-down approach about women, operating from a model or "general theory" and from there fill in the specific details and advice.

The Economic Model

Religious leaders will contest.
Psychologists will argue.
Feminists will scream.
And your mother will disapprove.

But the cold hard truth is that the relationship between men and women is not explained through religion, psychology, politics, feminist theory, or your mother's time-tested wisdom, but rather...

Economics.

Specifically, supply and demand.

Supply and demand for what?

Supply and demand for sex.

If you harken back to your high school economics class you will remember that economics is all about people who supply a good and people who demand it. These "suppliers" and "demanders" meet in a market, negotiate and haggle, finally settling on an "equilibrium price" for said good, and then you draw some funky charts. And in this particular market it is women who are the suppliers of sex and men who are the demanders of sex.

The question is how do men pay for sex and the answer is key, as well as a vital insight into the psychology of women:

With attention.

Attention is the currency all women crave. Women crave attention so much one could argue it is actually the men who are the suppliers (of attention) and sex is the currency that women pay for it with. But neither here nor there, it is generally assumed in "psycho-sexual-economic" circles that women supply sex and men pay for it.

However, it isn't simply just a matter of lavishing a woman with attention and she starts disrobing. If that were the case any nerd could flood the captain of the cheerleading team with texts and notes, and end up nailing her in the locker room during lunch hour. There is something else going on.

Enter "Sexual Market Value."

"Sexual Market Value" or "SMV" is the concept that one person is sexually more desirable than another. So if you have a handsome man who works as an investment banker his sexual market value is higher than say a fat, single mom on her third divorce. Keeping consistent with the economic model, your SMV is very much like your currency or cachet. If you are trading in US Dollars it is unlikely you would be trading with people in Venezuelan Pesos. Conversely, people trading in gold, are unlikely to trade with you. This puts the entirety of your romantic and sexual success with women in your ability to increase your sexual currency or SMV. How this is done is very simple – figure out what the opposite sex wants and deliver.

It is here our forefathers haven't completely wasted their time. For the most part everybody knows what men want in women and what women want in men.

Men want a woman who has:
- Big tits
- A tight ass
- Long legs
- Long hair
- Youth
- Nobody else's children
- Isn't a financial or legal risk
- And isn't batshit insane

Women want a man who has:
- Money
- Brute strength
- Security
- Charm
- Leadership
- Confidence
- Intelligence
- Who is a bit dangerous
- And is a badass

The real issue is whether people are actually willing to invest the time and resources to achieve these qualities and traits and therefore attract a mate. And if you look at the general population, most people aren't. The majority of Americans, both men and women, are fat, obese, lazy, unattractive, uninteresting, boring, mundane wastes of human protoplasm that inspire neither attraction nor desire from the opposite sex. They'd rather watch TV, stuff their faces, watch internet porn, read Harlequin romance novels, and come up with any excuse to avoid improving themselves. The result is a slothful population that lives their sexual and romantic lives vicariously through celebrities, the movies and the internet.

However, this is actually an opportunity for you. With such low and decreasing standards, you have very little competition. Matter of fact, if you can run just three miles without dying by the age of 35 you are already physically in the top 20% of men that age. The issue is whether you are willing to commit the effort and discipline to achieving the above traits.

Some of these traits are actually easy to obtain over time. Others just plain suck and are going to be a chore for the rest of your life. And some just plain don't make any sense (especially to a younger man). But a review of the importance of each of them, as well as an explanation of why women view them as attractive, will hopefully not only explain why you should attain such traits, but provide the necessary incentive to achieve them.

Money – Women do not so much like money as much as the financial and material security it can buy. Remember, in the olden days humans lived miserable existences where food and clothing were hard to come by and secure. And just like it is hard-wired into a man's brain to work hard to secure his future, so too have millions of years of evolution hard-wired this into women's brains. This does NOT mean they are somehow "cheap" or "shallow," but rather is merely how they biologically and darwinistically are. Of course, many women will abuse a man for his money, but it is up to your guile and cleverness to determine this for yourself.

Regardless, you need to at least be able to demonstrate you earn a good living and are a "good provider" in order to attract a woman. So prepare to hit the books or get a trade or start a business, because nothing repulses a woman more than an unemployed nerd living in his mother's basement.

Brute Strength – Revisiting their darwinistic, biological brain, women desire physically strong men. Not because there is anything inherently attractive about muscles, but because those muscles in eons past have protected women and their children from other men, hungry animals, and a whole horde of other threats. Once again, it is hard-wired into their brains to find stronger, taller men attractive than skinny, shorter men. While you can't do anything about your height, you can do something about your arms and that is hit the gym.

Unfortunately, lifting weights is by far the most mind-numbing, boring, painful chore you will ever have to endure in your life. However, you will be much more successful with women spending time at the gym than you will at the bar or nightclub. It is arguably the single best thing you can do to attract women. Just suck it up and accept that over the course of your life you will have to spend thousands of hours on your new part-time job – lifting weights.

Security – Akin to brute strength you need to be able to demonstrate you can provide security for a woman. However, not just by being physically stronger than other men or making more money than other men, but by being willing to fight. This is why practicing martial arts or even owning a gun goes a long way in increasing female attraction in you. It shows you will go to the mat for her (and your would-be children) to protect them.

Dangerous/Badass – Having a dangerous streak and being a bit of a badass *proves* you have gone to the mat in the past and have followed through on providing security. You occasionally get into a fight. You have a small, inconsequential criminal record. You display rage at times. Whatever it is, there is a "bad, dark, sinister" aspect of your past that shows you have thrown down and thrown a couple punches. The paradox, however, is that being a badass can land you in jail and seriously impair your financial future.

Thankfully, *just merely being dangerous* does not.

Ergo, hobbies like riding motorcycles, sky-diving, hunting, martial arts, etc., are all legal, but still convince her little hindbrain that you do not fear danger and threats do not deter you. Also, though it does not mean you did anything dangerous, getting a tattoo for some reason convinces women you did. However you pull it off, being the "bad boy" or "badass" is somewhat of a balancing act. You want to display danger and criminality, without actually putting yourself in danger or a jail cell.

Confidence/Leadership – Women love a leader not only for the security and financial reasons, but leaders are also usually the center of attention.

And, remember,

women

love

attention.

Therefore, if you are a leader in some capacity or another (a teacher, an entrepreneur, a rockstar, a senator, etc.) women will throw themselves at you so they too may bask in that glorious attention (just look up Sen. Dennis Kucinich and his girlfriend). But the single largest determining factor in whether or not you become a leader is whether you have confidence, and women seek out confident men like a junkie does heroin.

Sadly confidence cannot be faked. It needs to be genuine. You need to have confidence in yourself and conviction in everything you do. There can be no hesitation on your part or fear of failure. You need to approach a girl at a bar who is nestled within a herd of her female friends. You need to ask the girl out without a care or concern she might say no. And (my personal favorite technique) you don't ask the women for permission to take her on a date like some simpering wimp, but tell her, "I'm taking you out on Friday." The key is to realize that failure is the necessary first step to success. You will fail. There is no avoiding it. Matter of fact, you should embrace it. Once you get over that and accept it, you will have confidence.

Charm/Intelligence – It is very simple – women love to laugh. You need to be able to tickle their fancy, flirt with them, keep them smiling, and keep them on a dopamine high, all of which requires intelligence, wit, charm, and charisma. However, when you demonstrate intelligence, wit, charm, and charisma understand you are not only entertaining them, endearing them to you more, but demonstrating you can think quickly on your feet and observe things others can't. All of which merely parlays into more security, more safety, and more wealth for them. It's why "The World's Most Interesting Man" has more women surrounding him than the big, dumb jock who can throw a ball "real good."

Just like confidence, however, you cannot simply "flip a switch" and start being witty and charming. It will take time and maturity. But you can accelerate the process by reading philosophy, watching brilliant comedians like Victor Borge and Eddie Izzard, and studying the likes of Sean Connery, Cary Grant, and Walter Matthau. This isn't to say you will become James Bond by the age of 25, but you will certainly be more charming than your 20 something peers who fashioned themselves after Will Ferrell and Seth Rogen.

There are certainly more "traits" or "characteristics" one can aim for, but if you achieve all of the above you will dramatically increase your SMV and therefore increase the quality of women you can attract. Of course, none of these traits are achieved without work and effort, for if they were, then nobody would stand out, be special, or even be considered "hot." But understand that is the key to sexual and romantic success with women – it is because the aforementioned traits are so difficult to attain and require so much effort that very few men do these things and therefore enjoy success. It is up to your mental temerity, rigor, and constitution to suffer what others won't, stand out from the rest, and ensure you are more attractive than most other men.

There is, however, one last final and VITAL economic lesson. And that is one of desperation.

Understand the "Law of Supply." If you flood the market with something, it becomes worthless. This is why diamonds are valuable and dirt is not. There is nothing inherently valuable about diamonds just as there is nothing inherently invaluable about dirt. It is merely an issue of the supply of both. There are very few diamonds, but there is literally tons of dirt.

Your attention is the same thing.

If you flood women with attention, even if you have a high SMV, you will drive the value of your sexual currency and cachet down.

Therefore **DESPERATION IS THE SINGLE MOST DAMAGING THING** to your SMV.

At first glance this doesn't make sense. Logic would say that if you like a girl you should approach her, and lavish her with your "high SMV" attention, and win her over. But understand women do not operate by psychology or logic, but rather economics. If you "lavish" her with your attention, no matter how high your SMV, you are simply flooding the market, undermining the value of your SMV, and will consequently scare her away.

It is here you must learn "The Tao of Steve."

Based on a 2000 movie by the same name, "The Tao of Steve" is basically a "What would Steve McQueen do?" philosophy. It is broken down into three steps or parts and helps explain precisely how you mete out attention and expend your SMV currency:

1. Absolve all interest – You cannot have an interest in a girl because if you do, she will be able to sense it and think she already has you in the bag. This will result in her trying to extract even more attention from you, which only puts you in a catch 22. If you absolve any interest in her, however, and merely "hang out" you plant doubt in her mind. Doubt that will grow into fear that you may not find her attractive, making her more likely to go out with you. This doesn't mean you treat her poorly, but with indifference and aloofness.

2. Excel in her presence – Every man, no matter how nerdy or sad, has something they excel in. It could be chess, it could

be auto-mechanics, it could be being good with dogs. Whatever it is, you do that in front of her so she sees you have a skill and thus a higher SMV.

3. Retreat – After demonstrating your value, you simply retreat. Again, following the Law of Supply, to make your time and attention more valuable you mete out very little. You keep it scarce. This doesn't mean you never contact the girl again, but when you do (say a week after meeting her) that attention is so rare she will be much more likely to go on a date with you, as opposed to the guy texting her four times a day, sending her flowers.

In the end, you should have an idealistic scenario. You have worked out, kept yourself in shape, developed a devastatingly charming personality, some skills on the side, a good career, and the confidence to strategically deploy these assets at will to seduce the ladies. You are also following The Tao of Steve, limiting the amount of attention you dish out. In theory, it should all work out. Soon you'll have a portfolio of women to date at your beckon call, and perhaps one or two might make great candidates for marriage. But as you'll quickly find out, no matter how good your game is, no matter how ripped your muscles are, and no matter what your take-home pay is, it's precisely that.

"Theory."

Complications

Understand there is another side of the equation.

Women.

You can control yourself all you want. It is within your power to improve yourself, perfect yourself, lift weights and do everything within your power to become a real-world incarnation of "The World's Most Interesting Man." But what you do not control is the other half of the formula – women. And it is here where the majority of your problems will lie.

Understand there have been some major changes in the past 50 years as it pertains to the relationship between men and women in the United States as well as western civilization. And whereas the previous economic model has held up to time-well-tested for the previous million years, sociological and political changes have occurred that now challenge this economic model.

Specifically, the three major changes that have come about are:
- Feminism
- The government replacing men
- The destruction of the division of labor between men and women

All three changes go against millions of years of genetic, biological programming, but worse, have corrupted modern day western women to the point most of them are damaged goods.

Naturally, such a damning accusation will receive criticism and critique. However, this accusation is not made lightly as its ramifications and consequences overshadow the harshness of its condemnation. One must understand that the most important thing in life is the opposite sex. Not only is it what you are genetically programmed to enjoy, but they (women for men, and men for women) are likely to be the primary source of happiness in your life. Feminism, the government, and the consequential destruction of the division of labor have destroyed both men for women, and women for men, thereby denying the greatest gift life has to offer for both sexes.

This will likely be the single largest source of grief in your life as modern day political fancies and fads will corrupt, brainwash and ruin several generations of women. Making matters worse, any criticism, pointing-out-of, and mere observations of this will result in a scathing accusation of sexism, bigotry, misogyny and hatred, preventing a solution to this problem.

Have you ever been called "shallow" for expressing your preference for skinny women?
Have you ever been lectured for not liking "her fat friend?"
Has any woman ever set you up with an actual "hot friend" and not another affirmative action case?

Sadly, it gets even worse than that, as being called "shallow" for not liking fat girls is the least of your concerns. Now false rape charges, frivolous divorce, career-destruction, and tricking men into getting women pregnant are the new landmines the modern day man gets to negotiate on this increasingly hostile battlefield. Therefore, it is very important to know how these three major factors have changed men and women and the dynamics between them, thereby allowing you to develop more effective strategies, have more success with women, not to mention...

cover your ass.

Feminism

While much can be written about feminism, in a very general sense it has gone from a political movement for the equal treatment of women to a radical movement hijacked by Marxists to transfer wealth to women. To this end feminism and feminists have used whatever tactics and strategies, moral or not, they can to achieve this aim. Affirmative action, victimization, sexism, misogyny, redefining rape, redefining domestic violence, diversity, "male privilege," "fat acceptance," shaming language, etc. A nearly endless list of political phrases, terms, and propaganda has been concocted from whole cloth for the sole purpose of creating the reason and rationale to simply steal other people's money. However, such a dishonest movement requires a huge amount of disinformation, propaganda, and just outright lies to keep such a legal extortion racket going. Disinformation, propaganda, and lies that ruins the lives of both men and women.

Lie #1 – "She Can Have It All"

The first and arguably most destructive lie (especially for young women) is the canard that "she can have it all." "Have it all" meaning a career, an education, children, and a husband. While for a lucky few this can be a possibility, the sad truth is there just isn't enough time in a woman's life expectancy to get a master's degree, have a successful career, have a husband and effectively raise a family. She may be able to do all four, but she will do all four poorly. Ergo, a woman may have a great career as a "highly successful lawyer," but pays a nanny to raise her children and gets divorced by the age of 42. Or the PhD candidate who finally graduates from college, is forced to work until she's 40 to capitalize on her education, by which time she is too old to attract a husband, and too old to bear children safely.

The problem is that this lie is told to women at a very early age starting in elementary school and reinforced throughout college. One could even claim with shows like "Sex and the City" this façade is kept up well into their 40's. It isn't until it's too late do they realize "no, you can't have it all," as their world never turns out to be what was promised to them by feminism.
Naturally, this does nothing short of completely destroy the lives of millions of women, but from a male perspective it essentially puts you dead last on their "to do list." Yes, they might date you. Yes, they might have sex with you. But you will always play third fiddle to their education and career, perhaps even fourth if they already have children. In the end they'll be ready to consider you when, ironically, you no longer have an interest in them as their 20's, and thus their best opportunity to find a spouse, are long gone (for a hilarious parody of this phenomenon look up the YouTube video "29 31" by Garfunkel and Oates).

Lie # 2 – "She Doesn't Need a Man"

Similar to the above, some feminists will contend women don't even need men in the first place. All they need is a career, some friends, a successful social life, and boom! "Fish bicycle!" Even if they want children, just get in-vitro-fertilization!

While it is technically true a woman can physiologically live on just bread and water, this does nothing to address the millions of years of genetic and biological engineering that is screaming at them to find a man and have children. It also does nothing to address the fact humans are the most important thing in life, let alone humans of the opposite sex can provide different and necessary forms of attention the same sex cannot. This is why you will have the most glitzed up of party-going girls, pushing every man away at a night club, only to go home and cry because there's no man in her life. Regardless, the lie of "She Doesn't Need a Man" has the same effect as the lie of "You Can Have It All" – men are put at the bottom of the priority list and a girl is likely more interested in her career than forming a quality relationship with you.

Lie # 3 – "You're an Independent Woman"

One of the biggest lies of feminism is not a lie at all, but rather how feminists have been successful in redefining the meaning of the word "independent." Independent means you do not need anybody else to survive. You are self-supporting. You are not parasitical. Sadly it has been co-opted to mean *independent-minded* which has nothing to do with whether or not you are actually independent.

Hypocritically, though, if you look at where the vast majority of feminists are employed you will realize as a group they are actually quite dependent and parasitical. Nearly every women's studies department at every university relies heavily on state and federal money. Outside academia nearly all of feminist work is "non-profit," charitably relying on the donation of others. Feminism's entire political platform calls for the constant and continual transfer of wealth from others through government programs, and they beg for legislation that gives preferential treatment to women. In the end you'll find the most "independent" feminists are actually some of the most parasitic people on the planet. But while blatant examples like this are easy to point out, the sad truth is the majority of female employment (feminist or not) is actually quite dependent and non-self-supporting as well.

If you look at where the majority of women are employed, they are not employed as engineers making Apple products or surgeons patching up people's hearts, but are rather concentrated in industries that really produce nothing of economic value for the rest of society – government, non-profit, and education. These industries are not only easier, but are in all honesty and reality affirmative action programs built to provide make-work jobs for people who want to avoid difficult disciplines and industries.

The elementary education industry is NOT about educating the children as much as it is an over-glorified (and incredibly expensive) baby-sitting operation for people who can't do math.

Social work is a joke of an industry that has failed miserably at solving society's sociological problems despite the trillions that have been spent on it.

And HR is merely the single largest private sector affirmative action program to employ women.

All of these "professions" are cake, taking absolutely no academia rigor to major in, and in the end produce nothing of economic value people want. Consequently, the rest of society has to pick up the extra slack, producing the food, electronics, cars, and other goods that actually have value, while these people get to delude themselves into thinking they're a "self-supporting adult."

But what makes it worse (and doubly rich) is these industries are not freeing women from "oppressive womanly duties" that kept them in the kitchen during the 50's, but merely outsourcing those same "oppressive duties" to other women. Daycare providers, school teachers, cafeteria workers, social workers, guidance counselors, non-profit directors, you name it, the entire panoply of non-profit, public sector, and education type employees are merely doing the jobs stay-at-home mothers used to do half a century ago. All women have achieved in dominating these fields is outsource the care of their own children to other women, while they raise and rear the children of complete strangers. To add insult to injury, they now get to pay taxes as they are now compensated for work that in the past was tax free.

The problem for men, however, is the attitude these "faux careers" and this "faux independence" imbue in women – intolerable arrogance. They actually think they're real professionals, supporting themselves, earning their keep in society as if they were chemists or accountants. They think working nine months a year with six year olds is "tough" and on par with "designing electric engines for hybrid cars." Matter of fact, some even get a superiority complex as they think there is no nobler calling than working for the precious little children or the poor. But worst of all, they are so ignorant about government finances, they don't realize it is you (and millions of women with real jobs) who have to pay extra taxes to create these make-work industries, to keep up the façade, and to shelter their egos.

In the end, you can fully expect to be a petroleum engineer, sitting there on a date with a young woman who won't shut up about her "Masters in English." She'll unconsciously tell you how people (i.e.

"you") don't pay enough in taxes to provide the funding she needs to get her "Doctorate in English." She will actually view you as inferior in terms of education because you only have a "bachelor's" degree in chemistry, and she'll manage to fit into the conversation just what an "independent woman" she is at least four times. Of course, her independence still won't prevent her from expecting you to pick up the check...

and then you'll yearn to date an accountant.

Lie #4 – "Big is Beautiful" aka The Destruction of Physical Beauty

If you read enough feminist doctrine or websites you will see a persistent and relentless campaign against what has traditionally been considered "beautiful" in women. A shapely figure, long legs, long hair, big boobs, beautiful eyes and a comely face are all bad, all evil, and all shallow. And not only are men shallow for liking these physical traits in women, women who have these physical traits are traitors.

This may not make sense to a normal, rational individual. Why would feminists care what men find attractive in women, let alone be upset if a woman had natural beauty?

To answer that you need to ask what does the average feminist look like?

The truth is most feminists are ugly. Not because they don't have the capacity to be beautiful, but because *they choose not to.* They choose not to be beautiful because being beautiful requires effort.

And this is the key to understanding why feminism yearns to destroy beauty.

Consider all the effort you have to spend on making yourself attractive to women. Lifting weights, majoring in a tough subject, working hard, etc. Women must also expend that same amount of effort in order to be attractive to men. However, most feminists plain don't have the work ethic or temerity to put forth the effort. They simply aren't willing to commit to the effort required over a lifetime to attain and maintain their beauty.

This would be fine if that's all there was to it. Feminists would not work out, not eat right, not do up their hair, be ugly and leave well enough alone. The problem, however, is they don't. Beautiful women remind them of their ugliness and laziness. And men who pine for pretty girls simply reinforce this fact. They cannot brook the fact there are prettier girls in the world and men apply higher value to said girls. Therefore feminists need to eliminate female beauty and aim to do so by mocking it, ridiculing it, shaming any man who wants it, and villainizing any girl who has it. Anything to rationalize and excuse away their sloth and laziness.

This is, of course, nothing short of psychotic. It's delusional. Not only do feminists think by mere shaming they can undo millions of years of evolution and biological programming in men, but think they have the moral right to tell others what they should and should not find attractive. They have gotten so insane one of the larger initiatives in feminism today is the "Fat Acceptance Movement" (look it up). Naturally, because of its outlandishness, one would think feminism's aim to eliminate female beauty would fail miserably. However, they have been successful on three fronts to varying degrees.

One, they have been able to convince a significant percent of young, impressionable women to simply disfigure themselves. From the grunge movement of the 90's to today's tatted-up, tramp-stamped, lip-pierced, staph-infected trollop, feminists have convinced a significant percentage of younger women to make themselves as unattractive as possible. Gone are the days where women wore cute dresses and skirts, accentuating the beauty of the campus, and in are the days where you can't tell if it's Marilyn Manson or not. Sadly, young men today pay the price as they are deprived the benefit of looking at physically attractive women.

Two, while they have not convinced every woman to disregard their physical beauty, they have convinced nearly every woman that their looks are a non-vital part of attraction and that men are shallow for not liking them solely for their personality. This is not only misleading, but damaging as the REALITY is a woman's physical beauty is the most important of several vital requirements for a man's long term attraction and commitment. No matter what propaganda is disseminated, no matter how shallow women may think men are, the truth is the number one thing men value in women is physical beauty. Operating on any other premise will result in failure.

Third, they've even convinced many young men there actually is something wrong with them for not finding somebody attractive solely on personality. This doesn't override their genetic hard-wiring, and never will. But it does cause a great amount of confusion and guilt in young men for simply being...well...normal young men.

In the end, this assault against beauty causes confusion for both young men and women as it goes against their biology. But worse, any belief or adherence to it lowers the quality of women men have available to them, and lowers the quality of men a woman can attract. All so feminists can fool themselves into thinking they too are beautiful.

Lie #5 – "Victimization"

As per typical leftist political strategy, feminists will always play the victim card so as to beget additional government funding and preferential treatment. They will claim women are oppressed, women are beaten, women are kicked in the shins, etc., and the solution is *always* more government money.

In the end, there is nothing complex or particularly clever about this strategy as every ethnic and racial group has been using it since the late 80's. However, in the case of feminism three key bogus statistics will constantly be touted as proof to their oppression, rationalizing a further confiscation of your money...and sometimes worse.

One, the wage gap. The wage gap, which claims women only make 75% of what men do, is actually true. Women on average earn only 75% of what men do. Feminists will use this as proof positive that they are oppressed and men are discriminating against them. They then go on to demand preferential hiring treatment in the labor market. The reality, however, is that women major in easier subjects, have easier jobs, work a fraction of the time that men do and, consequently, produce only 75% of what men do. It is a statistic that has been debunked time and time again, but is still resurrected from the dead in the vain hopes it fools some of the more ignorant people.

Two, the "1 in N" women are raped on campus statistic. I say, "N" because it always changes depending on which campus and which feminist you consult. Regardless of what it is (1 in 3, 1 in 4, 1 in 2) this is nothing more than a ruse to create the illusion there is a "rape epidemic" on campus and the women's shelter (once again, staffed by unemployable women's studies majors) needs more taxpayer money to fight this plague.

Sadly, more government money is the most noble of their motives, because for whatever sick, sadistic reason, some feminists are so filled with hate for men they've gone to the extent to redefine rape, rendering sex a very risky proposition for most men.

If a girl was drunk and couldn't remember, it's rape.
If a girl was peer pressured and really didn't want to, it's rape.
If a girl just didn't like you afterwards, it's rape.
Some feminists claim all sex is rape.

What feminists consider rape, however, is not the real threat. It's the risk of a false accusation of rape. And with such diluted definitions of rape, more girls are incented to make false rape accusations, especially with the encouragement of feminists. Incredulous and disgusting as this might sound, it is a risk you cannot afford to ignore as a false rape accusation will wreak an incalculable amount of damage upon you. Besides, if you still don't believe this happens all one has to do is look up Antioch College's infamous "sex policy" or look at the sheer number of young men being falsely accused of rape to see this is a very real and very serious threat.

Three, "women earn the majority of college degrees." This is not in the genre of "victimization," but is thrown out there in conjunction with the wage gap statistic to show just how oppressed they really are. *"Why, if women are earning the majority of degrees, then it's even more insulting they only make 75% of what men do!"* It is also thrown out there to make men feel ashamed they are getting beat by women in academic performance. The reality is that yes, women earn the majority of college degrees, because the majority of degrees being awarded to women are in worthless humanities and liberal arts fields. Nearly two-thirds of worthless degrees are awarded to women, while 80% of engineering degrees go to men. In short, it doesn't take anything to get a degree in "15th Century French Lesbian Poetry Studies" while it does take infinitely more rigor to get a degree in "Computer Engineering."

The intended goal of these three bits of disinformation is not only to attain "victim status," but also to get women to distrust men and view them as the enemy. They are the oppressors. They are all potential rapists. They are abusers. You combine that with idiotic concepts like "male privilege" or "rape culture" and impressionable young women can be led to believe men are actively, consciously, and purposely oppressing women. At best such propaganda makes dating much more difficult than it already is. At worst it can ruin a young man's future with a bogus rape claim.

***

There are certainly more lies and bits of deceit on the part of feminism, but understand what feminism is and the consequences it has for your interaction with women. It is a political movement that aims to use women as a means to absolve themselves from as much work and responsibility as possible. It paints women as victims, oppressed by men, who need more and more government money and intervention to "make things right."

Ironically, however, it causes just as much damage to women as it does men because it lies to both about the realities of each other. Women are led to overvalue and overestimate themselves, as well as ignore the desires and realities of male sexuality, thereby severely impairing their chances of ever finding true love and having a successful family life. Also, feminism wreaks havoc on men as their propaganda not only lowers the overall quality of women for men, but increases men's taxes, increases their chances of divorce, ruins dating, makes sex a legal risk, and lowers their chances of having a stable, sane, enjoyable family life. While such an evil and vile political movement should fool no one, sadly it has made significant inroads by playing off of the naivety and ignorance of young women. Therefore, it is important, not just for your success, but your safety and sanity to be able to identify feminist thought in women, avoid it, and if necessary, disarm it.

Government Replacing Men

The second major change having a profound and detrimental effect on women is the government replacing men. In the olden days, it was usually the man who made the money, protected the home, and served as the head of the household. Matter of fact, it was the man who was the nucleus of society and the government was a subservient entity there to help assist the man in leading his life and maintaining his family. However, especially since the advent of women's suffrage, men's roles in society have been increasingly taken over by the government.

There have been several factors leading to this change. First, with women winning the right to vote, voting patterns changed favoring democrat/labor/leftist/socialist parties and causes. This was nothing malicious or evil as much as it was the natural consequence of women's more caring and compassionate nature. Women tended to vote for the children, the poor, the elderly and the destitute. And whereas previously such charity cases were handled via the church or charities, women viewed the government as the ideal mechanism to address these social ills.

Second, the Great Society merely took what was a voting trend and made it official. The government would now be an official provider for children and families, guaranteeing them a basic level of income and assistance. But while noble and well-intended, the Great Society started to encroach upon what was traditionally the territory of men – providing for their families.

Third, the social acceptance of divorce. Once "no-fault divorce" became law and the social stigma of divorce was removed, a boom in the divorce rate occurred which broke apart the traditional nuclear family. But without the physical presence of a father two interesting things happened. The first one was that a man was no longer in charge of how the family's budget was spent. By merely being commanded to make child support and alimony payments to the mother, he could no longer insist on standards being met before releasing those funds to family members. Now his ex-wife (and kids) could spend it however they pleased as there was nobody to attach conditions or strings. The second thing was if the father was a deadbeat then the mother and kids needed some form of income. Welcome in EBT and WIC, financially supplanting the man's role as provider with the government and with equally no strings attached. In short no-fault divorce physically and financially removed fathers from their families.

Finally, the social acceptance of illegitimate births. By removing the requirement a mother and father be married, society gave its blessing to not having a father around at all. A man could simply inseminate the woman and instead of having a "shotgun wedding" leave, while the woman would just replace him with a government check. This removal of man's last role in family participation completed the full transformation of man from the head of household and nucleus of society to that of a....

sperm donor.

With such a dramatic decline in status, the question is precisely what value does a man bring to society today? What can he offer a woman that already isn't being offered by the government? And the answer is...

nothing.

Bar donating genetic material, men today simply cannot compete against the government as a potential suitor. And to see the devastating effects of this, all one has to do is look at the black community.

How exactly does a black man compete against Barack Obama for the affection of a black woman? Not President Obama as a person, but the trillions of dollars in government spending he directs every year? Simple, he can't. The average black man, let alone any man cannot offer a woman:

Unlimited spending money
Unlimited food
Free housing
Free transportation
Free education
Free internet
Free telephones
For the rest of her life

He just plain doesn't have the money, let alone the job stability to make such an offer, let alone the ability to deliver on it. But the federal government with trillions of taxpayers' money can.

But making matters worse for any man unfortunate enough to try to compete against the government for the affection of a woman is that the government won't hold her to any standards. The federal government doesn't care if she sleeps with another man. The federal government doesn't care if she's looking for a job or not. The federal government doesn't care if she does drugs or treats her kids right. The federal government is an emotionless, insentient, non-judgmental entity. It is incapable of opinion, let alone holding people to standards. But if a man parts with a percent of his finite life to work up the money and then gives it to a woman, he is going to insist on attaching some strings and hold the woman to some standards. And that, sadly, is a deal breaker for many young women today.

While this cannot be said for every woman, it is a factor that must be considered in that your cachet with women is being marginalized by the benefits and riches the government offers them. Not all women are going to be so shallow, opting to take a cold government paycheck over a warm, loving human being. But with enough indoctrination, enough government benefits to sweeten the pot, and enough male roles supplanted, many women can be convinced to dump you and hook up with Sugar Daddy Government. And if you don't believe that just look up Peggy Joseph, Sandra Fluke, or "The Life of Julia."

Destruction of the Division of Labor and the Family

All of economics, and consequently, the standards of living of everybody in every economy, relies on a very simple economic principle – the division of labor.

The division of labor is the logical reality that letting people specialize in individual skills is better than requiring everyone to be poor masters at everything. In other words, it's best to have one individual be a chef, another individual be a mechanic, a third individual be a surgeon, and a fourth individual be a farmer rather than require everybody to be all four (could you imagine the quality of your food if your chef had to be a surgeon, mechanic and farmer all at the same time?).

However, the division of labor also applies to families and family management. This is why, over millions of years, men have generally been the bread winners, going out to work every day, while women typically stayed at home and raised the children. This isn't to say that women couldn't work or that men couldn't stay at home and rear the children, but that it was a more effective system to divide the labor, allowing for one person to specialize in home maintenance and child rearing and another to specialize in earning a salary to pay for said home and children.

Historically this system has proven to be the optimal family structure. No more than 50 years ago when the nuclear family was the norm, a family could get by on one income, have a parent at home to raise more stable and productive children, and still have all their financial needs met. During this time the economy was growing at roughly twice the rate it is now, unemployment was half of what it is today, and crime was not the issue it is today. The reason was simple – this model of family produced superior, more-productive, more-honorable people resulting in the pinnacle of human achievement in all of history.

However, with the advances of feminism, socialism, and the state, demands have been made to destroy this traditional system. As discussed before the government has replaced men in the role of father, husband, and provider, and women have now outsourced their traditional roles of child rearing to the state. This not only increases taxes to the point you now need two incomes to support the same family, but results in a whole host of other societal ills. Children are brought up poorly, not to mention by complete strangers, resulting in maladjusted adults, incapable of supporting themselves, who are more prone to crime, drugs, disease and poverty. Economic growth has collapsed not only because the state consumes a larger share of the economy and crowds out the private sector, but because people today have nowhere near the work ethic of previous generations. Divorce continues to be high, destroying the lives of millions of young husbands and wives. And don't forget about the children destroyed in the process, who will go on to populate future dysfunctional generations.

In short (and history will prove this true), feminism's and the state's intrusion into family life has resulted in the decay and inevitable destruction of society. But the largest cost to men, however, is not so much the general destruction of society, but that the only thing that gives a man point or purpose in life has either been taken away from him or destroyed – his family.

Revisiting Chapter 2, one must remember that it is other people who are the most important things in life. And the most important people in life will be your wife and your children. Your family is the single most important thing in your life. But with political forces pushing the destruction of the division of labor in the family and the tearing up of traditional roles between men and women, it is infinitely more difficult for men today to find a quality wife and raise a successful family than it was 50 years ago.

For example, the most necessary and required step to start a successful family is to get a wife. Sadly the quality and caliber of young women have been decimated by feminist thought, indoctrinating educations, bad parenting, and Miley Ray Cyrus. Most modern day women are arrogant, entitled, and completely delusional about what it takes to be a wife, let alone a successful mother. Worse still, divorce is now a completely acceptable option, so much so women have "starter marriages." This not only makes marriage a risky proposition, but should make you think twice about who will be the mother of your children.

Another example is leadership. All organizations, families included, need one clear leader in order to succeed. Anytime you have two or more leaders the organization will fail as it cannot be directed by two opposing leaders. Historically, though not always, it has been the man who has been the leader in the family. But today with media, education, and other forms of soft brainwashing women have been told they *need* be the leader, just as much as men. However, this presents a paradox for women as they ideologically want to be a leader, but biologically are not attracted to men who aren't. Thus, if a husband abdicates his leadership to the wife, more often than not she loses respect for him, or worse, leaves him for a man who will lead. This then results in a forced "co-leading" or "co-parenting" situation that is impossible. Arguments arise, disagreements turn into points of contention, and more time is spent on how to solve problems rather than solving the problems themselves. Ultimately the integrity of the family is undermined which more often than not results in the dissolution of the marriage.

Another thing men must consider is the economy no longer offers the average man the employment opportunities necessary to solely support a wife and children. By default both the husband and wife need to work so they have enough money to support themselves and pay taxes, which makes the government an unwanted family member. Therefore, time cannot be spent raising your own children as you and your wife must both work to pay the taxes to raise other people's children via the state. This behooves the question, if you or your wife aren't around to raise or spend time with your own children, then what was the point of having a family? The reality is government teachers will spend more time with your kids than you will.

And finally, what kind of world would you be bringing your children into? The current national debt, combined with "unfunded liabilities," means any child being born today is immediately saddled with around $300,000 in debt. Unemployment for younger people is roughly twice that of the national average. And this says nothing about the deteriorating quality and caliber of other people's children, the kids of which your children will have to grow up with and endure.

The question these issues pose to every young man considering or desiring a family is, "is it worth it?" Though you are genetically and biologically programmed to desire a wife and kids, understand society has fundamentally changed the rules as to what it means to be a father and a husband. It has forced the state into your family as an unwelcomed third party, it has ruined women's ability to be a loving wife and effective mother, it has ruined the economy to the point a family needs two incomes, and it has seriously impaired the future to the point your children will be born with a horrendous economic handicap. Never has it been so risky and difficult to be a father and husband than it is today. One must seriously weigh the costs and benefits before committing to having a family.

Deprogramming

Just as women have been brainwashed and indoctrinated, so too have you. For it isn't just women who have been led to believe outright lies and propaganda, but men as well. It's just our lies are different.

Whereas girls were told,

"Be obnoxious, arrogant, and have a lot of moxie."
"Men should like you for you."
"You can have it all."

Boys are told,

"Be kind, sensitive, caring, and nice."
"Women are shallow for wanting your money."
"You are privileged and have all these advantages being male."

Much of this brainwashing has already been debunked in this and previous chapters. However, there are still some major brainwashing, lies, and falsehoods you must be made aware of in order to clearly see what is going on around you, and so you can make more effective decisions in life.

<u>"It's Not You, It's Society"</u>

After roughly 13 pubescent years of tortuous experiences with girls, I was at my wit's end. I was by no means a failure with women, but for all the success I had with them, it was not worth the price in terms of the pain, agony, drama and general bullshit I had to endure. Girls standing me up. Girls screaming on the interstate because I didn't buy them a soda. Girls being an hour late. Girls buck naked in my bed, but then refusing to sleep with me. Nearly every unimaginable thing that could happen with girls happened to me, and I could not for the life of me explain it.

Was it bad luck?
Was it I was "looking in the wrong places?"
Or perhaps my mother was right. I "just attracted the wrong type of girl."

But then something happened. My brain started to permit itself to ask a question I had been wanting to ask, but it was so outlandish and statistically impossible I refused to.

"What if the problem wasn't me, but the rest of society?"

Understand why this is an incredibly arrogant question to ask. You are essentially saying there's nothing wrong with you, the ONE individual, but rather the remaining 150 MILLION women in the country. Naturally, you can see why such thinking would be debunked. Statistically speaking it **HAS TO BE YOU**. You **HAVE TO BE** the one with the problem, because what are the chances everybody else is wrong? On top of it, it's incredibly arrogant. What kind of individual has the hubris to blame his individual problems on the rest of society?

But as mentioned before, I was at my wit's end. I did everything right, did what everybody told me to do. And not just that, but tweaked and tried every possible permutation and variation in my tactics. Every variable of every one of my strategies was deployed, only to come back with either miserable failure or yet another floozy that had daddy issues. I had so thoroughly exhausted every option and strategy the only explanation left was that there was something wrong with society. And so for just this once I would permit myself to think there was something wrong with society and not me.

I have never gone back.

Upon having the bravado to ask the forbidden question of "Is it society that has the problem and not me," the reality of the world became very apparent. There was *indeed* something wrong with society and not the individual. Girls and boys had become political pawns of politicians, professors, teachers, media moguls, fashionistas and others, thus ruining both for each other. Girls didn't like "sensitive, caring 90's men," they liked strong, brutish men as they always had. And boys didn't like nose-pierced "independent women" on the cutting edge of grunge fashion, with advanced liberal arts degrees, but girls with big boobs, nice legs and an agreeable demeanor as they always had. It wouldn't matter how many stupid poems I'd write for that cute girl working at the coffee store, I was flooding her with too much attention and thus driving the market value of my attention down. It wouldn't matter how many times I'd ask her out in a witty manner (Power Point presentation, it WAS clever), I already asked her out too many times and it was never going to happen. I should become aloof, hit the gym, follow "The Tao of Steve" and if that didn't get a girl, to hell with her, there are others.

The results were a rough "tripling" of my success. I scored more numbers, scored more dates, got laid more, and never tolerated a temper tantrum on the interstate ever again. But arguably an even greater benefit was the clairvoyance that came with this epiphany. It was like going from a trench in WWI, getting the absolute shit shelled out of you, having no clue what was going on around you, to a satellite command center with a detailed and precise bird's eye view of exactly what was going on in that battlefield. There was also the elation that "no, I wasn't insane" and that I would never be confused like I was in my teens and twenties ever again. I had finally figured it out.

What many male internet philosophers call this experience is "taking The Red Pill." It is a reference to the movie "The Matrix" where Neo chooses to take the red pill which shows him what the real world truly is. And it is an experience every young man needs to go through if he is to be successful with women.

The reason is very simple – basing decisions in reality will prove more successful than basing them in lies, falsehoods and propaganda. The problem is society has lied to men and women about reality. They've convinced men that women like "sensitive men who write poems" just as much as "football players with their dad's BMW." And they've convinced women that "big is beautiful" and "men value educated women." But making matters worse, society shames you and punishes you dare you think outside the box or adhere to reality. A woman who admits her biological desire to "just be a stay at home mom" is EVISCERATED by feminists and liberals. And a man who dares to date multiple women and avoid marriage is considered an enemy of the state. Thus, it does take a significant amount of courage, independent thinking, even risk to "swallow The Red Pill," but once you do you will have more success in life.

There is, however, a problem.

The Red Pill can be abused by men who are intellectually dishonest and just wish to find an excuse for their poor performance with the ladies. If you're a fat ass living in your mom's basement at 32, playing World of Warcraft, and offer absolutely nothing of value to the ladies, then the temptation to just say,

"All women are fucked up. Screw them! They don't deserve a guy like me!"

is just too great. You are no different than the deluded feminists pushing for "fat acceptance."

But, if you are in shape, decent looking, have your act together, and still don't understand why she stormed out of the restaurant after you ordered the veal, then an intellectually honest consumption of The Red Pill is needed.

Ultimately, what The Red Pill is, is nothing more than allowing yourself to have self-respect and sanity. If you did everything right, are physically attractive to women, and improved yourself to the point there is no real reason or excuse for a girl to turn a guy like you down, then you have eliminated yourself as a potential reason for your failure. The Red Pill then allows you to forgive yourself and focus your efforts and strategies on where the real problems lie – society.

You Are Not the Enemy

One of the most despicable and childish political movements is the "privilege" fad. The reason it is so detestable is it presupposes those with "privilege" are unaware they have it and therefore unaware they are "oppressing" other groups. If you are white you have "white privilege," but don't know it. If you are male you have "male privilege," but don't know it. But what is truly sinister and cowardly of this faux "privilege" movement is that it makes the accusers the sole judge and jury over whether or not you are indeed oppressing somebody.

Leftist – "Oh, you're male? You have male privilege! Pay more in taxes."

You – "But I don't oppress anyone."

*Leftist – "That's because you're **unaware** you are oppressing people, because you are blinded by your privilege. Sexist!"*

Inanity aside, all the "privilege movement" is, is nothing more than the latest leftist political strategy being used in a never ending political war between them and the right. This war has been going on since the dawn of time and it will continue forever into the future. But just like real wars there is collateral damage. And just like real wars, there are innocent victims. And whether you're aware of it or not you are likely a victim of this political war.

When I was in school, it was just the blanket assumption sexism existed and there were *some* evil, ignorant men who oppressed women. 30 years since, the volume on sexism has been turned way up with the introduction of sexual harassment, male privilege, affirmative action, and more into the political arena. All of these on the face seemed to be well-intentioned, honorable, and noble ways to achieve equality between the sexes, but sadly they have been co-opted by feminists for political aims. So whereas in 1981 I was merely told,

"Don't discriminate against girls. It's not right,"

today, I can only imagine what a six year old boy must endure in school:
- 24 year old female teachers,
- who really don't care about the children and only wanted an easy job,
- fully steeped in feminist indoctrination fresh from college,
- cheer on girls for the most mundane of achievements,
- while pumping boys full of Ritalin for acting...like...well...um...boys,
- who then try to jam political propaganda down the throats of boys who don't know any better and just want to play in the sandbox,
- and are so deluded they actually think 6 year old boys are capable of having "male privilege."

The result is nothing more than a war on boys.

This is not a statement of whining or complaining. Nor is it a statement of "woeismeism" to beget undue pity for boys. But it is intellectually honest assessment of how the war being waged on our country's political stage, specifically the tactic of "victimization," ensnares boys as innocent victims. With victimization politics, you need a victim and a villain. And the narrative has been "males" are oppressors and "females" are oppressed. But this is not reality. It isn't true. It is just propaganda. However, this doesn't stop politicians from unforgivably forcing it down the throats of children, using said children as political pawns. And so from the age of six, all the way until he's 22, a confused young boy is constantly accused of

"male privilege," and
"sexism," and
"misogyny" and
"discrimination," and
"domestic violence,"

when all he wanted to do was play in the sandbox at 6 and play with a girl's boobs at 16.

In the end, it is a very "South Parkian" reality where the adults are all insane and the young boys aren't. The boys are caught up in the political battles of their parents, but have the honesty and purity to make the right choice. The adults attempt to convince the boys to engage in whatever political tomfoolery, but the boys merely point out the emperor has no clothes and refuse.

It is the same thing today.

Men of all ages need to realize that they are not the enemy. You are not oppressors, you are not misogynists, you do not hate women. Understand there is a huge political movement to paint all men as "the bad guys." This movement is so evil, so disgusting, and so desperate they now employ a tactic like "male privilege" which claims you are "oppressive, *you just don't know it."* Worse, they are so vile **they have no qualms against using it on children**. But deep down inside you know for a fact whether or not you "discriminated" against a girl. You know for a fact or not whether you "hate women." And no matter what feminists say, no matter what the news anchors say, no matter what teachers say, and no what matter politicians say, you know whether you are a good person or not.

There is Nothing Wrong in Desiring Physical Beauty

You are genetically programmed to like girls with:

Big boobs
Long legs
Long hair
A pretty face
A tight ass
Who has a kind and sweet demeanor.

That is reality. It cannot be changed. It is not optional.

Therefore, if women complain about this, they are the ones with the problem. Not you. Have no shame in finding what you do attractive.

Never Listen to What Women Say

Many of you will logically seek the advice and counsel of women as to how to be successful with women. You figure they are women, so they would know what women want.

It is the single worst thing you can do.

Understand that though they are indeed women, they have absolutely zero experience in dating and having sex with women. So when you ask them for advice about all matters female they will give you the worst advice you could possibly imagine:

"Be yourself."
"Buy her flowers."
"Compliment her on her shoes."

And other such nonsensical garbage.

If you want advice on dating women ask people who have experience in dating women – other men. They will not only give you advice that will work, but won't lie to you to spare your feelings (which many women do).

Also, ignoring the advice of women has practical applications beyond dating. In a world of single mothers, absentee fathers, female school teachers, and an effeminate media, most men today have likely been brought up under a heavily female-skewed environment. This doesn't mean your single mother didn't love you, or that your teachers weren't trying to educate you, but it does mean that your upbringing has been incredibly biased. You need to listen to men and have male role models in your life to balance out this deficit. Therefore, if something isn't working right in life (career, education, girls, etc.) it is wise to seek the wisdom of your male elders who have been down this path before.

Yes, The Quality of Women is That Low

It is a near-guarantee that if you follow the advice in this chapter and you dedicate the time and effort to improve yourself and increase your SMV, you will have success with women. However, understand this success will largely be **quantity, not quality**.

Bragging set aside, of the now-over 300 girls I've dated in my life, I've dealt with:

- Drama queens who would scream while I was driving on a busy interstate
- Three suicide threats
- One assault (after I told her I would never sleep with her again)
- A girl who screamed at me for looking at her phone
- A girl who kept me from her parents because I wasn't Asian
- Two girls who were buck naked in my bed, but wouldn't have sex
- Scores that were saving themselves for Jesus
- Three that went back to abusive boyfriends
- Three girls whose ex-boyfriends stalked me and hunted me down
- Three who would dry hump my leg, but not have sex
- One who said "if you're having sex and the girl says 'stop,' one more thrust is rape"
- One who was married, but failed to mention that during the three months we were dating

and this doesn't include the scores of girls who would be late, stand me up, cheat on me, fail to mention she had a kid, or any other behavior that passes as "acceptable" nowadays. In all honesty, only three girls, less than 1%, were anything that would approach marriage material.

Naturally, because of all these problems and drama I thought I was just having horrendous luck. Girls not calling me back. Girls throwing temper tantrums. Girls on drugs. It "must have been me." I must be "going to the wrong places." I must "just attract the wrong girl." But as I got older and older, and dated more and more girls, I came to a horrifying realization – **This was NORMAL! This is what the average American girl is like!**

I cannot emphasize enough the damage 20 years of K-college brainwashing will cause in the average American girl. You have the education industry kissing her ass telling her she can become anything she wants. You have the media kissing her ass convincing her she is a beautiful princess deserving of all the attention in the world. You have her parents kissing her ass merely reinforcing this. And you have the government kissing her ass providing her financing for college, preferential treatment in the job market, and a backup-provider if needed. From the age of five to 25 young women are celebrated, pampered, and exalted in society, so when they're finally dumped out into the dating market you are dealing with the most narcissistic, spoiled, batshit insane people in the history of the world (and if any woman wants to contest this, then by all means I will listen to her when she dates 300+ American women).

What this means for you, be you a young man about to enter the dating field, or an older man looking to revisit, is that:

"No, you're not insane. It is really that bad."

You will at first think you are just having bad luck. Then you will try to hit different bars or clubs, change your tactics, etc. But like me, you need to take a bit of The Red Pill and realize it doesn't matter where you go, or what you do, it is a society-wide phenomenon. Get used to the idea that you are going to have to kiss 100 frogs before finding yourself a quality princess.

Reality Will Always Win in the End

Ultimately, no matter what political or social forces try to do to ruin women and brainwash men, in the end it will never overcome the much more powerful forces of reality and evolutionary biology. The trick is to not listen to the propagandists, feminists, politicians, media, academians and other "thought-leaders" in our society, but instead trust your own eyes and the behavior of women. This won't be easy as reality requires you to expend a significant amount of effort improving yourself and all the aforementioned thought leaders will ridicule you, mock you, and accuse you of being a whole host of "ists" and "isms" (sexist, misogynist, bigot, etc.) But if you swallow The Red Pill and base your strategies and actions in reality you will have much more success with women than the effeminate 54 year old Peace Corp veteran trying to make rent for the month who did everything the thought leaders told him to.

A Miscellany of Tactics, Strategies, Advice and Wisdom

While the task of "summarizing women" is an impossible one, hopefully the above at least provides a working model as well as some much-needed vision, clarity, and guidance. But while the above will certainly help, it does not address every potential situation you will run into with women, let alone provide the specific action you need to take. In other words you have a great overall strategy, but very little in the way of specific, executable plan or policy. Sadly, there aren't enough trees in the world to provide the paper necessary to document and addresses every potential scenario you might run into with women. But after consulting with various colleagues, philosophers, "pick up artists," and authors, we have settled on what we believe to be some of the key bits of advice that will serve you best in the field. They won't address everything, but they will hopefully address the majority of issues you will face when courting women.

Failure is the Key to Success

Ask any man who is deemed successful with women and he will tell you his secret is "failure." While I may have dated 300+ women, I have EASILY asked out 10 times as many.

That's **2,700 rejections.**

But people don't see that. They only see the success.

Ironically, the "success" people do see can't even be considered "success" as it is usually the most psychotic bitch ever. The third hottest girl I ever dated was a bi-polar, bulimic, drama-queen and if I could do it again, I would trade her in for a fat chick with an illegitimate child. Regardless, you must learn to embrace failure as there is no other path to success. Sadly, you must also remove a bit of your humanity and not take a woman who rejects you personally, but view her as just another emotionless hurdle to jump before crossing the inevitable finish line. Ergo, failure is not a measure of you failing, but your effort and inevitable success.

The 505025 Rule

The rule states:

"50% No x's 50% Show = 25% Go"

This means there is a 50/50 chance a girl says yes or no to a date. However, just because she says yes, doesn't mean she'll actually show up for the date, thus the 50% "show." Therefore, you only stand a 25% chance of actually going out on a date at any given time (empirically, however, it is more like 30% No x's 30% show, resulting in a real world "show rate" of about 21%). Regardless, the moral of this lesson is with a 70% flake rate NEVER expect a girl to follow through on her word. You will waste valuable buddy time, drinking time, and video game time, setting aside a Friday night for a date only to have 70% of them bail out at the last minute. Matter of fact, you should bank on the fact girls will flake, relegating dates to a "Plan B."

The 20/80 Rule aka "The Alpha Male"

OK Cupid (a dating site) posted a study that showed women found 80% of men's profiles to be "unattractive." This lends credence to a theory going around intellectual circles that 20% of the men (called "Alpha Males") end up attracting and sleeping with 80% of the women. This "monopolization" however, leaves the remaining 20% of women to be impossibly chased after by 80% of the men.

This is why you need to increase your SMV. You need to be in the top 20%. Because as charming and intelligent and nice and kind as you may be, nothing replaces big muscles, some sharp clothes, and a bit of badass aloofness. If you want to be successful with women, you need to be in that top 20%.

"I Have a Boyfriend"

If a girl tells you she has a boyfriend, that's like saying she breathes air or has boobs. You should not let it faze you or stop you, because in two short weeks she'll be single or out with a new guy. Additionally, if she's going to cheat on her boyfriend, it might as well be with you and not some other guy. Only unless a woman says she's *married* should you let it deter you.

The "Shit Test"

Women will both consciously and unconsciously test men to see if they have the spine to stand up to them. Because if a man can't stand up to a woman, then he certainly cannot be a good defender and protector. At first you will be confused, asking

"Why is she complaining about me getting her the wrong cough syrup?"

Then you'll get angry,

"What!!! That was just a test!!! She was just trying to test me!!! What kind of a woman does that!!!????"

Then you'll understand,

"Wait, they don't even know they're doing it. And if I can identify and pass these stupid tests, then I'll just wrap them around my finger all that much more!"

The key to passing the shit test is to either ignore it, dismiss her, or put your foot down. The correct response depends on the context and type of test, but whatever you do, do not fall for it. More can be learned about "passing shit tests" by researching the internet.

The Backhanded Compliment

Like being able to identify shit tests, you must also become a master at backhanded compliments.

You NEVER compliment a girl directly or honestly. You will simply inflate her ego, make her think you like her, and give her the upper hand. You need to make her feel insecure and that you really couldn't care less about her. This is where backhanded compliments come in.

Specifically, backhanded compliments are compliments hidden within an *unintentional* insult. Women's insecure nature will naturally default to the insult instead of focusing on the compliment, seeding doubt and insecurity in their minds. There is no way to become "good" at backhanded compliments other than to practice. But some good ones are to relate an aspect of the girl to your grandmother.

"Say, nice perfume. It reminds me of my grandmother."
"Those are some very mature slacks you have on."

"Did you pick that up at a vintage store? I love the 40's look. Reminds me of my Gram-Gram."

It may sound childish and sophomoric, and it is, but it does work.

The Fat Girl vs. the Hot Girl

"It's easier to make a fat girl thin, than a hot girl nice."

Dinner for Schmucks

You never take a girl to dinner. You meet her for drinks. Dinner is frequently becoming a means by which women score free food out of tools they have no interest in. Drinks are how women relax/excuse themselves for sleeping with a man they do have an interest in.

You want to be the guy getting them drinks. Not the guy paying for dinners.

Booze, Booze, Booze

Booze is your greatest friend in getting laid. Again, this is why you pay for drinks, not dinners. However, it is always wise to have an ample supply of it at home, even a spare bottle of it in your car. An old school silver flask is also a classy way to get a woman to imbibe outside of drinking establishments.

"We're Not Having Sex"

There will be many times where you'll be out with a girl and she'll invite you into her house. She will then give you the obligatory *"Just so you know, we're not having sex."*

This means two things.
1. She's thought about it
2. You're likely to get it.

Maybe not that night, but it is definitely a good sign. Pour her another drink.

The "After Sex Happy Text"

Though unlikely, you cannot afford the risk of having a false accusation of rape. Sadly, the chances of being falsely accused are increasing as the definition of rape becomes more liberal and modern women become more narcissistic. All it takes is a failure on your part to return her call, and soon your night of consensual passion turns into a night of rape. Soon the cops are at your door and you are in a world of trouble.

To avoid this horrible fate all you have to get is the "After Sex Happy Text."

To do this you just have to text the girl the next day with the goal of getting her to send you a friendly reply proving the sex was consensual. Anything polite and kind will do.

"Hey, had a great time last night."

"Hey, thanks for last night."
"Last night was a blast!"

Typically, you will get an equally agreeable reply indicating she also enjoyed herself, putting you in the clear. Ensure the text and number are saved with a screen shot and back up all those life-saving texts on a thumb-drive. Again, it is unlikely and a very off-color topic to discuss, but this is unfortunately the world we live in.

Motorcycles

You need to get a motorcycle. Do not ask questions. Your first step after finishing this book will be to go and purchase one.

Takes Time to Ferment Interest

A major mistake young men make is they assume it is just a simple matter of asking a girl out and she says yes. This becomes a problem if you have tickets to a concert or some kind of event you would like to take a date on. Unfortunately, getting a date is not like picking up a pair of boxer shorts at Wal-Mart. It is more like cooking something in a crock-pot – it takes time to brew and stew. Therefore, you need to slowly "grow" girls into cultivatable fruit before you can date them. Flirting at school, talking to them at work, running into them at regular hangouts, etc., is just the natural course of building up a rapport with them so you can date them later. Some "pick up artists" would contend you should just go for numbers and try to close on a date within a week, but that takes time and effort. Your background "game," something you're constantly, but effortlessly doing, should consist of slowly teasing and flirting with girls that already exist in your life, slowly morphing them into dating material.

Never Date Born Again or Super Religious Girls

Unless you are a Christian or a particularly religious fellow, you want to avoid super religious girls or "born again Christians." Not that there is anything wrong with Christianity (or any religion for that matter), but most of these girls do not adhere to the religion for anything as noble as "God" or "Jesus." Instead they abuse the religion as a tool to lord power and superiority over others.

This not only means no sex for you, but you will constantly be compared to Jesus, lectured about how you aren't as "good a person" as she is, and a whole host of other headaches and hypocrisies your life is just too damn short for. The second you hear she is "born again" or "doesn't believe in pre-marital sex" you bid her farewell and adieu.

Ranking

Ideally, if you find the right girl and fall in love she will be #1 in your life and you will be #1 in hers.

Ideally.

For while that would be nice, there have been some sociological trends in society that put men further and further down a woman's ranking system.

If she is incapable of selflessness, love, and altruism, you are default ranked #2
If she already has a kid, you are default ranked #3.
If she "has Jesus in her life," you are defaulted ranked #4.
If she has a "super important career," you are default ranked #5
And if she has an overbearing mother she's incapable of telling off, you're default ranked #6.

In theory you can be ranked #100 if the woman has enough false gods before you, but the general rule is that you insist on being #1 otherwise you walk.

Lie About being a Criminal

Women lie all the time.

Push up bras, make-up, extensions, heels, you name it. Women lie.

So there's nothing wrong with telling an innocent little white lie about your non-existent criminal record.

You don't want something that will scare them away like "murder" or "manslaughter," but something sexy like a jewel thief, bank robber, or assault while nobly protecting your younger sister. Of course "this was all in the past when you were foolish and young," but having a little bit of a sordid past (true or not) doesn't hurt.

Single Moms

As you age it is an inevitability you will run into the prospect of dating single moms. Conventional wisdom says, "date them, have sex with them, never marry them." However, this may not be an option if you're 55 and all the women in your dating age range have children.

Try anyway.

First, you will always be ranked second in their lives. Second, being a single mom is an indicator of poor decision making ability, both in life choices, and mate selection. Third, you WILL be paying for a child that isn't yours either through time or money or both. Fourth, men can always date younger where you'll hopefully be able to find some childless women.

Does this mean all single moms don't make great candidates for marriage? Of course not. But with limited time and resources, not to mention this is your one and only life, ideally you'd have the self-respect to demand a woman who is your one and only wife, not a time share between you, her previous husband, and their children.

The Manosphere

A final resource you may want to consult as it comes to the pursuit of women is a sphere within the internet called "The Manosphere." As alluded to in Chapter 1, wisdom from our elders has been lost over the generations, but different groups over the internet are reconstituting this wisdom. The Manosphere is reconstituting the wisdom of men. This means if you have a question or are looking for some kind of guidance, you may not find it in this (or any other) book, but you are practically guaranteed to find something written about it in The Manosphere.

There are scores of blogs, podcasts and vlogs that constitute The Manosphere, and any general search on Google will pull them up, but some of the flagship blogs you may want to consider are:

Tom Leykis
Roosh
Chateau Heartiste
Vivalamanosphere
Delusion Damage
Captain Capitalism
A Voice for Men
The Spearhead
Dalrock
The Rational Male
The Art of Manliness
Judgy Bitch
Sunshine Mary
Dr. Helen
Grerp

There are also some key articles you may wish to read that go beyond and into much more detail than what was capable here:

"How to End Cockblocking as We Know It" – Roosh V
"Final Exam – Navigating the SMP" – Rational Male
"Women in Love" – Rational Male
"War Brides" – Rational Male
"Just Get It" – Rational Male
"Plate Theory" – Rational Male
"The Catalogue of Anti-Male Shaming Tactics" – Exposing Feminism
"Good Examples of Readers Passing Shit Tests" – Chateau Heartiste

"The Misandry Bubble" – Singularity 2050/The Futurist
"The Hail Mary" – Tom Leykis
"7 Ways Feminism is Destroying American Women" – Roosh V
"The True Nature of Women" – Roosh V
"3 Principle Types of Game" – Roosh V
"Deondra" – Captain Capitalism
"Chicks Dig Guns" – Captain Capitalism
"The Death of the Night Club" – Captain Capitalism
"Milk, Cow, Dancing" – Captain Capitalism
"Fractional Reserve Speed Dating" – Captain Capitalism

In general, however, you can view The Manosphere as the hundreds of older brothers you never had, the fathers you never knew, and your uncles your mom did not approve of. They are there for you and more than willing to help.

CHAPTER 8
HOUSING AND LODGING

Conventional Wisdom

Rent is the single largest expense you are likely to have in your life. Depending on where you live and how expensive your tastes are, you can roughly expect to drop around $1,000 a month on rent. Assuming you move out at the age of 18 and live the standard 78 years of male life expectancy, that would add up to a lifetime total rent expense of $720,000, and certainly over $1 million when accounting for inflation.

But what do you get in exchange for rent? What do you get for $1 million in a life-time inflation adjusted rent expense?

Nothing.

Absolutely nothing.

When you rent, realize you are spending money on a service, not a product or a physical asset. You are paying somebody to allow you to sleep under their roof, bathe in their shower, and use their toilet. You do not get the rights to that property. So when you end your lease you leave with absolutely nothing to show for the thousands of dollars you spent on that service.

Because of this it is considered "conventional wisdom" to get out from underneath renting and into a house as soon as possible. And though you will have to pay a monthly mortgage, you will no longer be "wasting money on rent" as instead you are slowing building up equity in your home. But there are more benefits to homeownership than just "not wasting rent anymore." Over the course of the mortgage you will inevitably pay off your entire house leaving with you a sizeable asset that will help during your retirement years. And upon paying off your mortgage your monthly budget will improve dramatically as you've eliminated the single largest expense in your life (be it rent or a mortgage).

Because of these benefits, people largely consider homeownership a good thing and inevitably make it one of their lifetime financial goals. But homeownership is also fraught with risks. Since your house is likely to be the most expensive asset you'll ever buy, housing can easily wreck your personal finances despite its clear financial advantages. Additionally, homeownership in America isn't what it used to be. With taxes, a slowing economy, and other political trends your biggest asset may just be your biggest liability. So before you become George Bailey and commit yourself to spending $500,000 of your time on your piece of the American Dream you need to know all the risks and ensure homeownership is for you.

The New Strategy

Traditionally, homeownership has been the goal or centerpiece of the American Dream. The truth is, however, that homeownership no longer makes sense for the majority of people in the majority of instances. The primary reason is that the economy and labor market are no longer conducive to homeownership. Long gone are the days of dependent employers and stable jobs, where you could reliably work for 30 years at the same place. And even if you are fortunate enough to have the same employer for 30 years today, chances are they will require you to move. In short, today's economy and labor market demands mobility more than anything else. And to anchor yourself to one physical location for 30 years, especially during your younger years, will impair your life as well as your career.

The arguments against homeownership, unfortunately, do not stop there. There is also a huge and unspoken political risk in being a homeowner today in America. Realize nobody in the United States really owns their own home. If that were the case, upon paying off your mortgage, the only expenses you would have would be insurance and maintenance. But there is one other contemptible expense:

Property taxes.

Every house in every county in every state in the US has a property tax levied against it. What this means, from a fundamental and literal economic perspective, is that you don't truly own your own house. You can never own your own house. You are merely renting that house from the state.

Normally, property taxes have been low enough that this has not become an issue. Additionally, property taxes usually go to finance the local school district as well as pay for various infrastructure projects that support the house (roads, sewer, etc.). However, as local governments and the public schools have become increasingly corrupted and politicized, property taxes, especially in large, liberal metropolitan areas, have skyrocketed. So much so people may be able to afford the mortgage, but not the property taxes (this is typically the case where you hear about an old couple getting kicked out of their home. The mortgage is paid off, but they cannot afford the ever-increasing property taxes).

The ultimate problem property taxes pose to homeownership is it takes something that was traditionally an asset and turns it into a liability. Previously, you were buying a home where you could reliably assume property taxes would be kept to a minimum. But now, with property taxes in some cities increasing 400% every 10 years (*cough-cough wheeze-wheeze* Minneapolis), you are actually buying a liability as you are legally bound to pay those taxes, no matter how much they increase. But the real risk is the unknown, i.e. – you never know how much property taxes are going to increase. Sadly, with city councils becoming progressively more and more leftist, it is likely property taxes for most homes in the country will go up in the foreseeable future.

This spells out the final and largest risk to home ownership – you might lose all of your investment.

Understand liabilities have no value. That's why you don't pay for somebody to punch you. It just doesn't make any sense. So why would anybody pay you for your house when your property taxes are $500 a month and increasing at five times the rate of inflation? Simple, they won't.

You may think this sounds incredibly cynical and pessimistic, but all one has to do is look at Detroit (or any inner-city). Crime and thuggery aside, Detroit has some of the highest property taxes in the country. Ergo, property in Detroit is not an asset, it is an legal commitment to keep paying the City of Detroit an unspecified and unlimited amount of property taxes into perpetuity. Consequently,

Detroit property prices reflect this as homes in Detroit sell for around the value of most liabilities...

$0.

This is the largest risk prospective homeowners must concern themselves with in modern day America. There is a chance you buy a house today for $250,000, spend (roughly) $450,000 on principal and interest over 30 years, only to have local politics drive its value down to $50,000. Not only did you lose $400,000, but the labor and money spent on maintaining your home. In short, local politics can easily wipe out the entire value of your largest investment, and given how politics has been trending left for the past 40 years this is an increasing probability. Therefore, you need to make damn sure you buy the right house, in the right neighborhood, and for the right reasons.

The Right Reasons

The truth is if you are single or young it is almost always cheaper to rent than own a home. The reason boils down to three expenses you don't have to pay while renting, but do have to pay if you own a home:

Maintenance
Property taxes
Insurance

These three expenses (again, depending on your local housing market and location) usually add up to more than what you'd spend on rent for a studio or one bedroom apartment. Therefore, unless you have expensive tastes in apartments, it almost always pays for the young and the single to rent.

Naturally, however, you won't remain single or young for the rest of your life. You'll start a family, you'll get a promotion, or some other significant life-change will occur, making homeownership a viable and beneficial option. And while there is no way to address everybody's personal situation, there are four general "reasons" or "cases" where home ownership makes sense.

#1 Family

While it is possible to raise a family in an apartment, it is not recommended. Kids need their own space, they need a yard, and even the husband and wife will need their respective places to get the hell away from each other. If you know you are going to start a family and have reasonably stable finances, then there really isn't a better reason to become a homeowner.

#2 You Absolutely Love Your Town

I live in a smallish community north of St. Paul.

I absolutely love it.

I am within walking distance to a lake, a handful of bars, a local city center, and am only 15 minutes from downtown St. Paul if I need to visit "the big city." And even though I may purchase a winter home in Florida, I will die in this town.

If you have such an affection and attachment for a particular town, that is another good and legitimate reason to consider becoming a homeowner.

#3 The Rare Job/Career

Most jobs are not reliable, long-lasting nor pleasant enough to suffer for more than three years. However, you may be one of those fortunate few who just absolutely loves their job and cannot ever see leaving it. Here it is your loyalty and love for the job that may rationalize purchasing a home. You may not love the town you're in, let alone the house, but if the job is that stable and that enjoyable (and the town is not on the precipice of becoming the next Detroit) it may be worth it financially to purchase a home, build up some equity during your tenure at the job, which you could (hopefully) sell at a profit should you retire or the company ceases operations.

#4 Retirement

Whereas the trend is to sell your house during retirement, this is primarily due to poor financial management where older people need to sell their home to put food on the table. Assuming you make wise financial decisions to avoid such a fate, having a condo or a small home in a town you love serves two purposes during retirement. One, to have an "HQ" where you base your operations out of and, two, you can store what worldly possessions you have. This allows you to go out, gallivant across the world, and enjoy your few remaining years on this planet, but still have a "home" to come home to.

Types of Housing

While the above paints a pretty black and white picture, the reality is of course a little more gray. Every person is different, every property is different, and every city is different. It is impossible to apply universal guidelines and rules to a topic as diverse as homeownership. Thankfully, the world of real estate is not so black and white and even though you may not be the nuclear couple with a reliable 30 year job in the same exact location, real estate is varied enough that it still might play an advantageous role in your financial life. Are you the entrepreneurial bachelor with a bit of carpentry skills? Perhaps rental property is an ideal situation for you. Do you have a keen eye for trends and know when to buy low and sell high? Then raw land might prove useful in your life. Not everybody needs the three bedroom, two bath, cookie cutter suburbanite home.

To that end, we will look at the five main types of property people buy and hopefully provide you some options when it comes to housing, as well as real estate investment options.

Single Family Homes

Single family homes are precisely that.

Homes for a single family.

This is your stereotypical view of a house in the suburbs. White picket fence, adequate yard for kids to frolic in, and an old beat up tire-swing, hanging from a tree.

Normally such houses are used to house and raise a family and unless you decide to have an inordinate amount of kids, most will suffice. The trick is finding one that will work for you, meet the demands of raising a family, maintain its value, and can then either serve as a retirement home or can be liquidated on the market as you downsize.

Condos/Townhomes

If you're not going to raise a family, but want to settle down, you may want to consider a townhome or condo. Essentially instead of renting an apartment you are going to buy one. Condos and townhomes make sense for younger people, childless families, or older people who wish to retire. In short, you don't want to waste money on rent, but you don't have the need for a five bedroom, four bathroom ranch with 50 sprawling acres.

The biggest drawback of living in a condo or townhome is that you have to answer to an "association" and pay monthly "association dues." The association is basically a committee of people who also live on the premises and are responsible for managing the communal property. Lawn care, maintenance, roofing, the parking lot, plowing, etc. For some this is a benefit (old people don't have to shovel, mow the yard, etc.), but you still have to pay and sometimes association dues can be more than $1,000 per month! Worse, if you have a poorly managed association, they may delay necessary repairs or undercharge people for their dues, resulting in random and large increases in association dues (one friend of mine had an association due of $4,000 in one month because the association failed to budget for roof repairs). These drawbacks aside, condos and townhomes do have their place in the real estate market, and if chosen wisely can help get you into the housing market.

Rental Property

Not everybody fits into the cookie cutter world. Chances are if you are reading this book you do not brook incompetent bosses, politics at the office, and thusly are not capable of affording the perfect house in the suburbs. However, with the help of renters you may be able to afford yourself a home, and rental property helps the independent minded individual achieve that American Dream.

The concept is very simple. Buy yourself a duplex, triplex, or a quadplex, and then live in one unit while renting out the others. Ideally, you would have other people pay for your mortgage, allowing you to live rent/mortgage free. After 30 years of reliable mortgage payments, you then have yourself a nice tidy asset that was bought and paid for by other people.

However, simple as the concept of rental property is, there are a bevy of problems. Most notably, other people. Realize that the single largest threat and risk in society is not tornadoes, hurricanes, earthquakes, or fire, but rather other human beings. And when you own rental property you get to deal with that single most volatile risk. This highlights the biggest drawback of rental property – other humans.

When you own rental property you get to deal with:

Late tenants.
Loud tenants.

Psycho tenants.
Abusive tenants.
Violent tenants.
Destructive tenants.
Tenants that like to sue.
And tenants who call at 4 AM because the light bulb burned out.

Making matters worse is that people are getting worse. People are not as reliable as they were 30 years ago. People are not as responsible as they were in 1947. And people are not as respectful as they were in 1962. The quality and caliber of the average American is decaying and that is the market you are committing yourself to when you purchase rental property.

Finally, realize that most local and state laws are against the property owner and for the renter. You are, of course, the "evil, rich, greedy" landlord, and your tenants (no matter how much meth they brew in their apartment) are the "poor, disadvantaged, abused" victim. If they decide to sue you, the legal system is heavily skewed against you and it will cost you money.

Because of all these rental property risks the **single most important thing** you **_have to do_** is thoroughly screen your tenants. I have an unlimited number of stories from landlords who failed to vet their tenants properly, turning their American Dream into an "American Nightmare."

Holes punched in the wall.
Cops called late at night.
Marijuana being grown in the basement.
Flooded basements.

Death threats.

Tenants can wreak more havoc on you and your property than an F5 tornado.

So be smart. Spend the money on a tenant screening agency, background checks, credit reports, and so forth. Also be willing (and able) to go a month or two without a renter, because losing out on four months' rent is still better than a destructive tenant who owes you six and threatens your dog.

The headaches of rental property do not end there as you have to deal with maintenance, additional tax work to account for rental income, not to mention tenants who ignore your rule about "no cats." But if done right rental property can bring a man from the poorest caste of society into solid "upper middle income" territory. The key is to purchase the right property and rent to the right tenants.

Investment Property

Should you have a particular penchant for property, you may want to make it your profession. This could mean a career as a realtor, a real estate developer, or, if you have the carpentry skills, a builder. In other words, you may not view property as a source of lodging, as much as you would a source of income. If this is the case then you may wish to look into investment property.

However, because of the cost of property (multiple hundreds of thousands of dollars) if you choose this route you will have to be committed to it, or at least until the point in time you can sell yourself out of the business. This is where many young men fall and fail as they may certainly be talented carpenters or tradesmen, but lack the financial and business skills to make a profit off of real estate. Thus, if you decide to go into investment property, it is not merely required that you can swing a hammer or lay some mean tile, but that you also are intricately aware of the financial aspects of real estate, real estate development, mortgages, and banking.

That being said, pursuing real estate in this capacity can certainly pay off. The plurality of rich people in America made their fortunes through real estate, and you don't have to make "$10 million dollars" to be considered successful. Simply building your own house or making enough money to buy a house with cash can be considered a great success. And though there is no guarantee you will be hob-knobbing with Bill Gates chatting about your multi-billion dollar real estate empire, if you pursue real estate as your profession and do it right, you can certainly work less and make more than the average cubicle slave.

Like any market, there is always a limitless number of ways to make a profit. But investment property falls into four general areas or subcategories.

One of these venues has already been addressed – rental property. However you will not be "super-rich" merely owning yourself a duplex, paying it off at an accelerated rate over 15 years. You need to get multiple multi-unit properties, committing yourself to be a full time landlord and property manager. The ideal goal of this approach would be to buy as many rental properties as possible, have them paid off through the rental income generated over the years, and when the mortgage/s comes due 30 years later, you have a real estate empire you own outright and can sell for millions of dollars.

Though not as grandiose, another approach is "flipping." This concept is familiar where you buy a "fixer upper" on the low, and post-renovation sell on the high. The benefit of this approach is that you are technically never unemployed. You are constantly working, only for yourself, to improve and build up a property, the payoff of which comes when you sell it for a significant amount more than what you bought it for. While this approach relies on a stable housing market and housing prices, it can pay huge dividends to those with good carpentry skills and a keen eye for property. It can also provide you the house of your dreams should you find a house you really like. The only drawback to flipping is that your paycheck is anything but regular as you only get paid when you sell a house.

Third, you could become a real estate developer. This is where the big bucks are. You're not building a paltry house or flipping a measly duplex. You're building entire suburbanite developments. You're building a $25 million condo project. You're building strip malls and luxury homes. And you're going to pocket a nice tidy 20% on each development as profit.

This requires not only skill, but experience in real estate to know when is a good time to build and when is a good time to hold off (nearly every real estate developer I knew, even the experienced ones, filed for bankruptcy because they lacked the economic skills to identify the housing bubble in 2008). Being a real estate developer also requires a lot of capital. Unless you have the money, you're going to need to borrow the money to finance your developments and projects. This may be hard to come by if you have no track record and cannot convince banks to lend you the money. But if you start off as a carpenter or general contractor, gain experience, build a good reputation, and then start with a small development (say two houses) you can expand from there until you get the larger projects.

None of this will be possible until you are at least 30 (assuming you started immediately at 16 working on homes, gaining 14 years experience). You need not only the skills, but familiarity with the real estate market to know what you're doing. But if you're serious about it and are willing to learn the financial/business side of it, you can have yourself a very promising and lucrative career.

Finally, if you have no interest in using the real estate market as a means of lodging, but still like the prospects of investing in real estate you may want to consider "non-human dependent" real estate. While the majority of real estate is based on housing, lodging, or accompanying humans, there are other forms of real estate that avoid humans altogether.

Parking lots.
Storage facilities.
Farm land.
Etc.

While these may require a certain set of entrepreneurial skills, they do avoid that one key and highly risky variable that sinks all real estate investments – humans.

A parking lot houses cars on a daily basis.

Storage facilities store all the "stuff" humans have accumulated over their lives.
And farmland is merely a place to plant crops or raise livestock.

But none of them store or house humans.

This is what makes "non-human dependent" real estate much less risky than rental property, condoplexes, or strip malls. Cattle is unlikely to sue. Stored couches do not punch holes in the wall. And cars cannot cause any real damage to a flat, concrete parking lot. Thus, if you aren't a people person, but still want to make some money on real estate, consider these alternative forms of real estate.

<u>"Live in a Van, Down By the River"</u>

A final, though minimalist, approach to real estate is to "live in a van down by the river." Not that you'd actually live in a van by a river, but you would live in a trailer, RV, or mobile home of some sort instead of a fixed, physical structure. Normally, when people hear "mobile home" they picture Cleetus the Slack Jawed Yokel, brewing moonshine in the trailer park, while determining if his daughter is his sister or both. However, stigmatism of mobile homes aside, they do provide a great housing option for some people.

First, they are much cheaper than nearly any other form of traditional housing, though you can easily spend over $100,000 on luxury RV's. Second, most state laws do not consider them "homes" which means you don't pay property taxes on them nor are they subject to building codes or ordinances. Third, they are mobile which means you can wake up to mountain vistas, sunrises over the ocean, or the silence of the rolling South Dakotan prairie. There's a reason so many old people have "tour around America in their RV" on their bucket list. Why wait till you're nearly dead to do the same? Finally, they offer the potential to go off-grid. Many trailers and RV's can be rigged with solar panels, deep cell batteries, and other MacGyver-like amenities for people who want to get by on the most minimal of incomes.

Naturally, there are also some drawbacks. Showering, sewage, and electricity becomes a logistical issue. You need to either own land, rent land, or find free land where you can park your RV. And your social status will take a hit as people will associate you with the citizens of the Trailer Park Capitol of the World – Evansville, Wyoming. These considerations aside, mobile housing provides the free-spirited individual with a cheap housing option that lets them pursue their dreams.

Finding a Home

The number one thing you must do when considering a home purchase is spend a lot of time researching and looking at homes. As it is the largest single asset you will ever purchase in your life, not to mention you will sign your life away for 30 years on a mortgage, you need to make sure it is a:

- house you want,
- a house you can afford,
- with no major maintenance or structural problems,
- in a town you like,
- that you will be in for a while.

Again, because this is the single largest purchase in your life, it is the most likely thing to destroy your finances and ruin your financial life if you make a bad decision.

It is here a little bit of arrogance and selfishness is called for. Not just to protect you from a huge financial mistake, but if you are being asked to drop $300,000 on an item, then that item better damn well be what you want. It's almost akin to picking a spouse. Therefore, you are well within your rights to spend years looking for a home, insisting on certain amenities, and investigating that house (and the neighborhood) as much as possible.

While there is no right or wrong way in going about choosing a house, if you take a methodological approach, you will certainly save yourself a lot of time and money. Also, in thinking things through first and knowing precisely what you want, you will endear yourself to the people needed to help you purchase a home (mortgage broker, banker, realtor, etc.) instead of wasting their time, and consequently, pissing them off.

<u>Location</u> – The first decision you need to make is where you want to live. This will depend on many factors, but you will want to consider the following variables:

- How close are you to work? Commuting sucks and is the single largest waste of people's lives as well as a contributing factor to divorce. Ideally, you would be able to walk to work.
- What are property taxes like? You can look up property taxes on any county's or city's website. You should also be

able to look at historical property taxes to see how much they've grown over time.
- Is the city council Republican or Democrat? Not to bring politics into this, but if you're being asked to spend $300,000 on a house, you must consider politics as it will inevitably affect your property's value. And to be blunt, you do not want a Democrat city council. They will vote to raise your taxes, putting you in a situation similar to Detroit.
- Is the house in a *county* that has a major metropolitan area in it? If it is, yes, the city council might be Republican, but the county commission is likely Democrat due to the fact large metro-areas can outvote the typically Republican suburbs. This means your local taxes (via the county) can still go up.
- What is crime like? Consult the local police department for reports on crime, as well as historical trends.
- What is the spending per pupil at the local school district? Typically, the single largest item on your property tax bill is the local school district. You want that to be as low as possible and a good way to determine that is how much the school district spends per pupil.
- What is the quality of the school district? Ironically, while schools increase property taxes, parents' number one concern when buying a home is the quality of the school district. This results in richer people willing to pay higher property prices (and taxes) to ensure their precious little children are in the "best" schools. This also results in a balancing act wherein you'd ideally find a cheap school district with a good reputation. Thankfully, spending per pupil does NOT correlate with performance so you should

be able to find a highly ranked school district that also has a low spending per pupil amount.

There certainly are other variables, most of which will center around your personal preferences (lake shore, parks, etc.), but following the above will at minimum put you in a safe neighborhood, put your kids in a good school, and protect the value of your home from politics.

Type of Home – Once you select a location (or several locations) you can now refine your search by determining what kind of home you'd like to have. Do you want a duplex? Do you want a single family home? Do you want a condo? You need to know this before you approach a realtor.

Budget/Pre-qualification – The single largest thing that pisses off realtors is when somebody expresses interest in a house, tells the realtor they want to buy it, only to find out they can't get qualified for a loan to afford it. If you are like the millions of naïve homebuyers that do this, you not only are the bane of realtors' existence, but you are wasting their time as they could be talking to people who could actually afford the home. Do your realtor the most simplest of favors and get pre-qualified.

What "pre-qualification" is, is when you go to a bank or a mortgage broker and find out what the absolute maximum loan amount you would qualify for. You simply go to your local bank, fill out some paperwork, and in about a day or two they will let you know that amount. This then gives you your maximum budget to purchase a home and allows you to further refine your search to homes under that amount.

<u>Auction/Foreclosures/Repossession</u> – Your fourth step will then be to see if you can find your dream home on the cheap. You can pay full "retail" price by buying a newly constructed home or a home from a reliable person who's made all of his mortgage payments regularly, or you can find "distressed properties" – i.e. – properties where the previous owner failed to make payments, and the bank (or county) repossessed it.

These "repossessed" or "distressed" properties are a good thing because they cause nothing but headache for the banks and counties that own them. Banks are in the business of lending money. Counties are in the business of managing the county. Neither of them are in the business of property management and real estate investment. They want to get rid of these properties.

It is here a little bit of research will be required on your part as each county and location is a little different. But in short, you should be able to find out when repossessed properties come up for auction, either at the county or your local bank. You may also want to walk into your local bank and see if they have any properties in "OREO" (other real estate owned) that they are looking to sell.

Ideally, you will find your "dream home" on the cheap, but keep in mind distressed properties are usually in a state of disrepair. The previous owners were not responsible enough to make their payments on time, and consequently were unlikely to do (or afford) basic maintenance and repair. Also, previous owners have a tendency to get angry when they find out they're being foreclosed on, and take that anger out by destroying their own home.

Assuming they didn't destroy the furnace or foundation, however, a skilled handyman can fix most foreclosure-related damage.

Realtor – After you've done all your homework, know what you want, and how much you can afford, it is now time to approach a realtor. However, contrary to conventional wisdom, you don't really need a realtor when you are the buyer. The reason why is that you can educate yourself about the paperwork necessary when purchasing a home rendering the realtor unnecessary. This can pay dividends as the commission on the sale of a home is 7%. All 7% technically goes to the seller's agent, but this is then split 50/50 with the buyer's agent. In other words, not using a realtor when buying a home saves you 3.5% of the purchase price.

However, if you are a complete novice when it comes to real estate or don't have the time to do it right, then it is definitely worth paying a realtor to represent you. Understand, a realtor doesn't just take 3.5% for some lousy paperwork. He or she is (or at least, should be) an expert in the local housing market and should be able to show you homes that best meet your tastes and desires. They should also be aware of market prices and know when selling realtors are asking for too much or when it might be a "steal." This alone could be worth more than their 3.5% commission.

Inspector – After consulting a realtor he or she will come up with a list of houses that may pique your interest. They will show them to you and sooner or later you are going to find a house you like. At this point, though optional, it is HIGHLY RECOMMENDED you have it inspected by a housing inspector. While it may cost you $300 or so, it is money well-spent as an inspector has a trained eye to look for problems, issues, damage or anything else that may be wrong with the house. This is a vital service as sellers are prone to hide repair issues, structural problems, etc., that can cost you much more than $300.

There is a problem with inspectors, however.

Most of them do a poor job.

I alone have had inspectors fail to identify cracked foundations, cut support beams, fire hazards, and a host of other problems. Large problems that even I (a housing construction novice) could identify with the naked eye.

Because the costs of buying a damaged home is so high, you may want to pay for TWO inspections, or spend the time to find the meanest, most curmudgeony old man housing inspector you can. These men don't care about people's feelings, are incredibly detailed, and will go over your house with a fine-tooth comb. It may take some digging to find an inspector like that, but that is the guy you want.

***

After all is said and done, hopefully you will have found a good house, in a good neighborhood, and in good repair. Once you decide it's the house for you, you (or your realtor) will make an offer to the selling agent. There may be some negotiations and counter-offering, but once accepted, you will go into the realtor's office, sign some paperwork and officially become a homeowner.

Applying for a Mortgage

A "mortgage" is nothing more than a loan you take out to finance your house. Chances are you don't have $300,000 in cash lying around, so you take out a mortgage instead. There are many types of mortgages – ARM's, 30 year, 7 year, interest only, etc. – but your two main types are the 30 year mortgage and the 15 year mortgage. Over the life of the mortgage you pay interest and principal, slowly paying down the loan balance. However, in addition to principal and interest, you will also pay insurance and property taxes as well. After 30 (or 15) years of reliable payments, the balance should be down to zero and you officially own your home free and clear.

On the face of it a mortgage should be a simple thing.

You want to buy a house. You need to borrow money to pay for it. So you go to your local bank and apply for a mortgage. The bank approves the mortgage and you buy your house.

Sadly, it is anything but that simple.

Today, the mortgage industry is much more complex, not to mention integrated with the federal government as well as the financial markets on Wall Street. This complicates matters and makes applying for a mortgage anything but straight forward. And though technically it isn't necessary to understand all these under-workings of the mortgage industry, it really helps so you know precisely what banks are looking for, how to increase your chances of approval, and to assuage the frustration when you might be declined for a loan.

The key thing to understand about the mortgage industry is to realize that it is very unlikely your mortgage is "held" at your local bank. It might have originated there. You may have signed your documents there. But rarely do banks "hold onto" the loan. They usually sell it to another bank or financial institution on the "secondary market."

You might ask,

"Well, if they weren't going to hold onto my mortgage, then why would they sell it? Heck, why did they lend me the money???"

The reason is diversification.

Imagine your small local bank only lent to homeowners in that town. By default that bank is then COMPLETELY dependent upon the health of the local economy. So if the local coal mine shuts down or the local car plant leaves, the townspeople get laid off, they can't afford their mortgages, and the bank consequently goes belly up. To avoid that, banks will take their loans, sell them on this "secondary market" and in turn buy mortgages from other areas in the country to lessen this risk.

This is completely normal, and actually quite smart, because if the coal mine or car plant does get shut down, the bank can keep operating. This does, however, fundamentally change how banks do business when it comes to mortgages. They are no longer really "banks" as much as they are now brokers. i.e. – they will make or "broker" the deal, but won't hold onto it.

To that end, in order to sell your loan on the secondary market banks must comply with the secondary market's standards and requirements. And these standards and requirements can be quite confusing as the secondary market is constituted of thousands of other banks, financial institutions, and the federal government. However, in general for a loan to qualify it must meet the guidelines set forth by "Fannie Mae" and "Freddie Mac," two federal government agencies. If your application meets these standards it is considered a "conforming loan" and can be sold on the secondary market, and therefore likely meet approval. If not, it is considered a "non-conforming loan" and is likely not to be approved.

To be a "conforming loan" you need:

1. A 20% down payment for the house
2. A decent credit score
3. Proof of income that you can afford the loan
4. Reliable income history
5. Conformance with the lending limits of Fannie Mae and Freddie Mac

There is certainly some leeway and interpretation based on each bank, but in general you must have the above, otherwise you will be considered a "non-conforming" loan. If this is the case, however, it doesn't mean you can't get a mortgage.

Enter the mortgage broker.

While a bank may not approve your loan based on whether it is conforming or not, that doesn't mean there aren't financial institutions that will. There are mortgage lenders, mortgage divisions within banks, hedge funds, you name it, hundreds of companies out there willing to make mortgage loans. The trick is to find them and mortgage brokers help you do exactly that.

It is here the world of mortgage lending gets a little shady.

If you are like millions of people, you pay your bills on time, are capable of affording a mortgage, but you have this one trait or variable that is preventing you from becoming a "conforming loan" applicant.

- You're self-employed.
- You don't have any credit cards or debt, and therefore (ironically) have a very low credit score.
- You don't have the nearly impossible 20% down payment banks typically require.
- Etc.

Whatever the case, you are still a good credit risk and there are companies (as well as a bevy of federal government programs) out there willing to work around your technicalities. And mortgage brokers will set you up with them.

However, realize mortgage brokers are **brokers, not investors.** They do not hold onto your loan. They only want to make the deal and collect their commission. This being the case, some really don't care if you can pay your mortgage or not. They will attempt to qualify you for as much as they can, some even suggesting you lie on your application, which can put you in a very bad financial situation (just look at the millions of naïve first time homebuyers that were sold on the idea of "ARM's" in the buildup to the 2008 housing bubble).

Because of this you want to make sure you understand the mortgage you're getting yourself into and ensure you can afford it. You also want to make sure they aren't charging or hiding excessive fees in the paperwork (I had one mortgage broker try to sneak a random $5,000 fee into my paperwork). To ensure this, there's nothing wrong with consulting your bank's mortgage lender, even though they're not the ones making the loan. If you're already a client, they will (likely) be happy to look over the terms of the mortgage for you and see if there is anything nefarious about it.

The final major hurdle you will face when it comes to qualifying for a mortgage will likely be your down payment. Traditionally banks have required a 20% down payment which is pretty much impossible for any first time homebuyer. Still, to meet this 20% requirement many people will borrow from family, take money out of their retirement accounts (IRA's, 401k's, etc.), or perhaps get a second mortgage. However, such measures may be unnecessary as many lenders today will accept a down payment as low as 5%. The only drawback is that they will then require you purchase something called "mortgage insurance."

"Mortgage insurance" is an extra payment you make that insures against you failing to make your mortgage payment. It is very expensive (easily $300 a month) and is an unfortunate consequence of being a younger, first time homebuyer who simply doesn't have the required $60,000 down payment needed for a $300,000 home purchase. Naturally your first goal should be to pay down the mortgage balance below 80% at which point in time you can cancel the mortgage insurance. However, thousands of people simply FAIL TO REMEMBER TO CANCEL THE INSURANCE. Make sure you are not one of these people and pay attention to your loan balance.

Refinancing a Mortgage

Over the course of a 30 year mortgage a lot can happen in the economy or your life that might make refinancing your mortgage a good idea. If the interest rate on your mortgage is 8% and interest rates drop down to 4%, you might want to refinance. If you have a 30 year mortgage, but got a huge promotion at work, you may want to consider refinancing with a 15 year mortgage. There are other reasons, but in short refinancing can lower your payment, lower your interest rate, get the house paid off sooner, or a combination of all three.

The process of refinancing your house is the exact same as when you applied for a mortgage the first time. You are simply paying off your current mortgage with a new one, so you will have to meet all the previous requirements discussed above. But keep in mind there are two drawbacks to refinancing. First, if you had a 30 year mortgage and refinance it with a new 30 year mortgage you simply reset the clock for "amortizing" (look it up) your loan. I almost laugh at times watching people in their 60's refinance their homes with 30 year mortgages because they are likely to die before paying off the mortgage. i.e. – they are forever going to be owned by the bank. Ergo, while most people are focusing on their payment, you should also be focusing on how quickly you can pay off the bank. Second, just like your first mortgage, you get to pay a bunch of fees. Normally, these are inconsequential if your payment is lowered enough, but if you're only going to shave ½% off of your mortgage, it isn't worth it. The general rule of thumb is if you can lower your interest rate by 2% then a refinance is worth it.

A Miscellany of Advice

Mortgage Interest Deduction – A benefit you will receive in owning a home is that you can write off the interest from your taxes. This can play a significant role in your personal financial planning, but it can also be used to subsidize the purchase of assets, namely through the use of a "HELOC" or "home equity line of credit." What a HELOC is, is essentially a credit card that uses your house as collateral. However, unlike a credit card, since the HELOC is technically a mortgage, you get to write the interest off on your taxes. So if you need to buy a car, pay your kid's way through college, or make some improvements to the home, you might want to consider a HELOC.

Most Realtors Are Salesmen, Not Economists – To be blunt, the majority of realtors are people who could not find jobs elsewhere. They are attracted to the position because it doesn't take much to become a realtor, but if you're good at it you can make millions. To work as a realtor you need to take some classes, get your license and you're off to the races. But the majority of this training is about ethics, code of conduct, law, regulations, and paperwork. They do not teach them economics, property valuation techniques, research, financial analysis, etc. In other words, unless they have extensive experience, they only know how to list, sell, and show properties. Because of this I recommend choosing a realtor who is older, has many years of experience, or has a financial background.

<u>One Story Home</u> – Unless you really need it, I strongly recommend sticking with only one-story homes. The reason is simple – safety. Over the course of owning a home you will inevitably have to paint the house, side the house, clean the gutters, all of which means you have to access the roof. But if you have a two story house, with a walk-out basement in the back, you need to be on a ladder that is three stories tall. One slip and you can die, or worse, be paralyzed from the neck down (which did happen to a person I know). Be safe, stick with one-story houses.

<u>No Trees</u> – Trees are pretty. Trees are nice. Trees add value to your property.

As long as they're **not on your property.**

Trees are, frankly, the largest pain in the ass I ever had to deal with in terms of property maintenance. There were ONLY TWO trees on my property, but they shed enough leaves that it would take two full days of raking to clean up what was a very small yard. But what was infinitely worse was the amount of leaves, brush, twigs and seeds the trees shat upon my roof which ended up clogging the gutters. This necessitated a twice-annual gutter cleaning that took an additional two full days out of my finite and dwindling life.

Ensure if there are any trees they are on your neighbor's property. Not yours.

<u>Live Someplace Warm</u> – Like raking, shoveling snow sucks. Also, as you get older, your fond childhood memories of having snow days will recede as you battle rush hour during snow storms, heating bills, frozen pipes and other blessings of winter. Life is too short to

suffer winter. Consider Arizona, Florida, Texas or any other state south of the Mason Dixon line.

Municipal Infrastructure – To be blunt, the previous generation has very poorly managed the finances of the country. They have spent money on all sorts of social programs while letting the infrastructure deteriorate. Therefore, your local town might have really nice "community center," but its sewer system is in a desperate state of disrepair.

To shore up their finances, however, many cities are now requiring home owners pay for public utilities that were normally paid for by taxes. This varies from city to city, but you will DEFINITELY want to know what public infrastructure you are responsible for in your home. Do you have to repair any sewage lines that run from the street to your house? Are you responsible for the sidewalks? Do you need to pay for the median? In general you can assume it is lefter-leaning towns that have these financial and infrastructure problems, but you will want to go to city hall and find out for sure.

You Need a Garage – As a younger person, especially if you live in the city, you will get accustomed to parking your car on the street. A garage will be a luxury, so much so you will likely completely forget about them. Thus, when you go looking for your first home, you won't even be thinking about garages. You'll just be "excited" if there's ample parking on the street simply because you don't have to search for a parking space late at night.

Demand more. Insist on a garage.

You will want to have a garage because as you age you will want to get things like a motorcycle, a spare car, and you will inevitably start to desire to work on them. You will also take on other projects that require tools and craftsmanship, needing a place to work on your hobbies and store your tools. But the main reason you need a garage is resale value. Most buyers insist on a garage, and if you don't have one, when it comes time to sell, you will have to significantly lower your price.

Homes are Like Motorcycles – The housing market is very seasonal with the majority of purchases occurring during spring and summer and a dearth of sales during the winter. Because of this homes are a lot like motorcycles in that you can pick them up on the cheap during winter. Consider contacting your realtor in January. Besides, chances are he'll appreciate a bit of business during slow season.

Section 8 – If you own rental property never, ever rent to section 8 tenants. Section 8 is a government program that guarantee's the rent of tenants. So if your tenant doesn't pay, the government will. Naturally, the quality and caliber of Section 8 tenants is what you'd imagine – scum. They will destroy your property, harass other tenants, threaten you, increase other people's taxes, and just make your life hell. They are parasites that deserve to be on the street, not in your house.

Roommates – If trustworthy, they can make affording a home, and thus your finances, a lot easier. Plus, unlike tenants you can kick them out at any time because they are sharing your living space, not a separate legal rental unit. But the best benefit of having roommates is comradery. Some of the happiest times I ever had was hanging out at a buddy's house who rented his spare rooms to all of his friends. He lived there for free, had a "surrogate" family of friends, and we all got hammered playing Halo every night. Matter of fact, I can't imagine a better living situation.

<u>Get Renter's Insurance</u> – If you are renting, ensure you have renter's insurance. Don't ask, just do.

<u>Get LA and NYC Out of Your System</u> – As a young person you will likely want to live in New York City, LA, or some other such media-glorified town because the media told you to. Don't even think about housing until you live there and get it out of your system. Truthfully, you will be let down when you realize such towns are not all they were cracked up to be. But at least you won't live the rest of your life wondering and regretting had you never followed your dreams and lived there in the first place.

<u>Get Denver, Montana, Europe, or Paraguay Out of Your System</u> – Unlike the stereotypical 22 year old, you may realize all the hype about living in LA or New York is precisely that – hype. But this doesn't mean you don't have personal dreams like I did about hiking in the mountains (Denver), fishing great rivers (Montana), backpacking in Alps (Europe), or fossil hunting in an exotic country (Paraguay). Not only should you do these things before you buy a home, but you should do these things before you even have a career. Remember, nobody is going to take you seriously until you're 35, so throw all your worldly belongings in a backpack, head out, and live your dreams.

<u>Only Finance in One Spouse's Name</u> – If you are married and you decide to purchase a home it is very wise to put the mortgage in

only one person's name. The reason for this is in case either you or your spouse run into financial problems and the house is repossessed, that foreclosure will only affect the credit of that spouse. This then allows the other spouse to purchase another home as their credit is not tarnished by the foreclosure.

<u>Do Not Over-Extend Yourself</u> – The biggest mistake novice rental property owners make is taking on more properties than they can effectively manage. While the appeal of having 10 rental properties to make 10 times the profit is appealing, realize a significant amount of time needs to go into managing, maintaining and financing that real estate empire. If you fall behind in managing just one of those properties, the financial consequences can easily wipe out your entire empire through foreclosure, repossession and bankruptcy. Organically and naturally grow your real estate empire. Do not rush it.

<u>Never Take on a Business Partner</u> – Because property is expensive many people come up with the idea of partnering up with other people to pool their resources and purchase properties. In nearly 100% of these cases one partner ends up doing all the work, while the other partner does nothing. Worse, in 99.9% of these cases, the "bad" partner embezzles money, steals from the partnership, and flees the state. If you are going to get into investment properties ensure you can do it by yourself or only with a person you have the utmost of faith in.

<u>No Longer Any Shame in Filing Bankruptcy</u> – There may come a point in time where you lose your job, you run into health issues, or some other major economic catastrophe occurs and you simply

can't pay your bills. You'll face losing your house, losing your car, and may have to consider...

bankruptcy.

Historically, there has been a tremendous amount of shame associated with filing for bankruptcy. Not anymore. With the real estate bubble, the corrupt banking system, and the general moral decay in society, bankruptcies have become so common it is perfectly acceptable to file for bankruptcy. Besides, after seven years bankruptcy is removed from your record and banks will gladly lend to you again. However, because of the legal complexities involved with filing for bankruptcy, you will want to consult a bankruptcy attorney about your particular situation before doing so.

<u>How I Would Have Done It</u> – Since the age of 24 I have owned two houses, both rental properties. I foolishly operated from the principle that if I worked hard and was a loyal employee I could work up the money to have them paid off by the time I was 30. My plan was then to retire and live off of the rental income, travelling around the world.

Theoretically it was a good plan and a feasible plan. Running various amortization calculations and detailed personal financial projections it was mathematically possible. But it had two major flaws. One, I lived in a liberal town where the property taxes increased so much I was no longer making money on my renters, but having to subsidize them. Two, I assumed because I graduated at the top of my class in a practical field that I would have a stable job and a successful career. These two flaws torpedoed my dream to escape poverty and enjoy my life.

Instead of retiring at 30 I scraped by, making my mortgage payments, but never paying down the principal due to a lack of any decent paying jobs. Worse, the ever-increasing property taxes made it so my house would never appreciate in value, and made it difficult to sell. In the end, all I managed to do was become a prisoner of my own home and effectively waste my 20's.

Do not make the same mistakes I did.

If I were to do it again I would operate from the premise that life is not "indoors" but "out there." I would treat housing as purely a place for me to sleep and store what meager possessions I had. I would have fit everything into a backpack, grabbed myself a laptop, and rented rooms for around $200/month. I would have travelled the world and done whatever I wanted to do on the cheap. And only after wandering the world for 20 years and finding out what my true calling/career was in life, as well as what part of the country I was absolutely in love with, would I consider purchasing a home. Even then, given the confiscatory risks our national debt and socialist political trends present us, I'd be somewhat loth to become a homeowner.

Ultimately, homeownership will be up to you. But in general I suggest you live as cheaply as possible until it becomes absolutely necessary for you to purchase a home.

CHAPTER 9
CARS AND TRANSPORTATION

Since the day you reached cognizance you have been bombarded with advertising, marketing and other social pressures to want one thing, and one thing only:

A super, powerful, fast, and awesome car.

Be it Hot Wheels cars when you're a toddler, TV shows like "Knight Rider" when you're an adolescent, or movies like "Fast and the Furious" when you're in your 20's, more money has been spent on convincing you to purchase a sports car than all of money spent on aid to Africa. Reinforcing this, however, is genetics. Men are genetically programmed to want things better, faster, and stronger. We aim to achieve excellence, and once we achieve that we aim to go even further. Always pushing boundaries. Always pushing limits. Always breaking records. It is in man's nature to improve, progress, and accelerate.

This is a good thing as it is this drive that has advanced society. Men's desire to go faster has resulted in inventions like the automobile, bullet-trains, motorcycles, speed boats, planes, and rockets. And without these inventions we consequently wouldn't have cell phones, nuclear power, satellite TV, video games, the internet, and so on. But while it is in our innate desire to be better, get stronger, and go faster, not all of us can actually experience and enjoy the cutting edge of speed. We all can't be Chuck Yeager piloting the X-1. We all can't afford our own personal XR-71 Blackbird. And we all can't be Felix Baumgartner.

Thank God for Henry Ford.

Henry Ford did all men a favor when he introduced the assembly line, making cars affordable to the masses, and consequently making it possible for every man to enjoy the pursuit of speed. Maybe not every man could break the sound barrier. Maybe not every man could orbit the planet at 7,000 MPH. But every man could stealthily speed on flat open stretches of Wild West highway and every man could go as fast as he and his machine possibly could on the Bonneville Salt Flats.

There is a problem with cars, however. The faster you want them to go the more expensive they get. This issue is further complicated as society places a huge demand on men to own cars as a sign of "social status," further increasing the price. And while your average compact will more than adequately suffice to provide reliable and safe transportation, a Chevy Cobalt will not satiate a man's desire for speed or unhinge a girl's bra like a Mustang GT500. This puts men in a quandary. Do they approach cars in terms of transportation, or as a toy to help satisfy their desire for speed...and a tool to unhinge bras?

The answer is "transportation."

The "Status Market" Trap

Understand when you decide to purchase a sports/luxury car you are unwittingly committing yourself to do battle in the "Status Market." For when you buy a sports car or a luxury vehicle you are not so much buying "transportation" as much as you are status. But there is a problem with "status" – it is incredibly elitist, snooty, and competitive. And unless you are absolutely in the top 1% of men you are going to lose this battle.

The reason why is the men you're going up against and the women you're trying to attract.

What kind of men buy Mercedes, BMW's, Lexuses and the like?

Very rich men.

What kind of girls chase after men based on the car they drive?

Very picky girls.

This presents the average young man an impossible situation. First you can't afford to go toe to toe against a 42 year old elite investment banker who actually has the money and can afford a luxury vehicle. The best you can hope for is to get a car loan, buy a used, five year old Lexus and hope women can't tell the difference. Second, women *can* tell the difference. They are ACCUTELY aware of what the latest models are as their entire existence and value is derived by dating the "richest" man with the "fanciest" car. They know the difference between a 2014 7-Series and a 2008 5-Series, just as they know the difference between a Rolex watch and an Omega. In other words, you aren't fooling anyone. Women in the "status market" will look at your used car (not to mention your clothes, your cologne, your hair style, your shoes, etc. etc.) and know you really don't have the money. Besides, you wouldn't be able to keep up the charade anyway as you take her to low-end restaurants, asking her to go Dutch, while your better-financed competitors fly her to Lake Havasu for the weekend.

The real question you need to ask yourself is what you are ultimately using the car for? If it's to impress girls (which 95% of the time it is) then that means you are ultimately using it to get sex. If that's the case then some simple math and logic is required. To lease an S-Class Mercedes costs around $1,400 a month. For that amount of money you could, bluntly, rent yourself three quality prostitutes a month. Over the course of a three year lease that's 108 different women you could sleep with, not to mention you don't have to waste your time and money on dates, insurance, gas, upkeep and listening to the ditzy, painful blather of "status market" women.

But there is a more important lesson here for you. Realize most guys who rely on their car and status have absolutely no game. If you are relying on your car you are a loser. You have no charm, you have no charisma, you can't get a girl to laugh. Your time would be better spent watching Cary Grant flicks, mimicking Walter Matthau, hitting the gym, and reading up on philosophy to become a more interesting and engaging person. In all honesty, I was most successful with women when I was my poorest. I lived in a basement, drove a 1985 Cutlass Supreme, but knew how to salsa dance and knew how to tickle a girl's fancy, getting her to constantly laugh, occasionally blush, and sometimes unhinge her own bra. Devastating wit and charm will always outdo the most luxurious and fastest of cars.

The Car You Need

This isn't to say, however, there's anything inherently wrong with wanting to own a luxury car. If you have the money and it doesn't impair your finances, then by all means, certainly buy yourself whatever car you want. But most men, especially young men, don't have the money. And in trying to purchase high end cars, even "nice" cars, you can easily torpedo your finances, wreaking as much damage had you gotten a Doctorate in Peruvian Lesbian Poetry. Therefore, it is a very good idea to be like Jason Statham in "The Transporter" and have some "rules" when it comes to buying cars.

Rule #1- NEVER Buy a New Car

The AVERAGE price of a new car in 2013 was $31,252. That not only is a tidy sum of money, it's INSANE. That is enough to pay for a four-year college degree, food for a decade, and rent for five years. What makes new cars worse is that they immediately lose 30% of their value after you drive it off the lot. It is the single largest purchasing mistake you can make for consumer items. **Never** buy new cars.

Rule #2 – Your Car is for Transportation Only

You need your car to reliably and safely transport you to where you need to go.

That's it.

It isn't to impress chicks. It isn't to race your buddies. It isn't so you can turn it into a hotrod.

It is there to transport you to where you need to go.

To that end it doesn't have to be fancy. Just a small, fuel efficient compact car that gets you from A to B. It can even be dinged up a bit in that dinged up cars are usually sold for a lower price, despite their engine and innards being pristine (for good dinged up cars, consider "salvaged" or "insurance" vehicles). Ensure when shopping for a car you do not let anything but "transportation" affect your judgment.

<u>Rule #3 – Ensure That if Your Car is Stolen, Damaged, or Destroyed, You Won't Care</u>

One of the largest advantages of owning my 1985 Cutlass Supreme, my 1990 Chevy Caprice Classic, and my 1988 Ford Escort EXP was when somebody dinged them, scratched them, slashed their tires or stole them, I didn't care. I paid $1,200 for the Cutlass, $500 for the Chevy, and $2,000 for the EXP. Those three cars lasted me 18 years and cumulatively 300,000 miles. So when my EXP was totaled, the Cutlass stolen, and the Chevy vandalized, I didn't care. I had spent so little on them it didn't matter to me. Matter of fact, it was more the annoyance of having to replace them than their loss that bothered me.

There is, however, another benefit of having a car you don't care whether it gets stolen or not – a lot less worry.

Have you ever seen one of those snobs who park their car in the back of the parking lot and across two spaces to make sure it doesn't get scratched? You ever see somebody melt down when their car gets keyed or dinged? The worry and fret is just not worth the price. You're going to park your jalopy, lock it up, and get on with your day without a worry in the world about your car.

Rule #4 – You Only Get Liability Insurance

By law you need to have auto-insurance. There are three types of auto insurance you can get on your car:

Liability
Collision
Comprehensive

"Liability insurance" only insures against damage you may cause in an accident or while driving your car, and is the minimal amount of insurance you are required to have by law. "Collision insurance" covers any damage caused to your car, either by yourself or somebody else. "Comprehensive insurance" insures your car against anything else that may cause it damage – vandalism, hail, tornadoes, etc.

Thankfully, since you don't care if your cars are destroyed, this affords you the luxury of getting by on liability insurance only. This can easily save you hundreds of dollars a month, all because you were smart enough to buy a car you really don't care about.

Rule #5 – Get the Club

Even though you don't care about the car, it is a pain in the ass to replace one. Spend the $50 on "The Club" or a club-like device and use it. Lots of thieves target colleges and neighborhoods where young people live. Young people who are likely poorer and can't afford to lose their car.

Rule #6 – Do All The Required Maintenance on Your Vehicle

The dumbest girl I ever dated drove a Chevy Cavalier. She had owned it for several years when she asked me,

"How often do you change oil?"

I said,

"Every 3,000-5,000 miles."

"Oh," she said.

"Why?" I asked.

"Well I haven't changed it in 50,000 miles."

Please do not be this incomprehensibly stupid. Not only should you do basic maintenance like oil changes and air filters, but consult the manufacturer's "scheduled maintenance" and religiously adhere to it. Auto technology is such today that if you do the proper and required maintenance on a vehicle it can easily last 200,000 miles.

Rule #7 – It is Worth Driving 2,000 Miles for a Good Car

It is worth your time and effort to go online and search for a car, even if it might be 2,000 miles away. The reason why is that, yes, it may cost some money to have a mechanic look at it, and, yes, you might have to fly or road trip out there to get it, but that time and cost is worth finding a car with 30,000 miles less on it than any comparable car near your area. The time savings alone will more than compensate you for your time and effort retrieving the car, not to mention, result in you having a more reliable car.

Rule #8 – Keep Your Car Clean

A truly good woman will not care what kind of car you drive. She will, however, care if you kept it clean or have a half-eaten, petrified BigMac from 2008 sitting in the back seat.

Clean your freaking car.

Rule #9 – Always Have Two Vehicles

Because you will likely be driving older cars it is wise to have two of them. This may at first seem odd as it would double your auto expense, but it is worth spending a paltry $1,000 to have a "back up beater" when your "primary beater" breaks down (which it will). This will save you when you have to be at work, have an interview, or need a car with a working heater because it's January. However, beyond purchasing the car, there are no additional expenses. Your insurance (assuming its liability only) will not go up because you "can't drive two cars at the same time." Plus, having a backup car allows you to try to fix your primary, instead of desperately paying a mechanic to fix it as it is your only means of transportation. I also strongly recommend one of these vehicles be a truck so you can easily move during your 20's as well as barter its use for favors from other people.

Rule #10 – You Are Not Going to Save the Environment

Let us be very clear about this. Hybrid and electronic cars are NOT cars that environmentally conscious people drive. They are luxury vehicles rich liberals buy so they can arrogantly lord their supposed "superiority" over non-hybrid drivers. Unless you are a rich liberal you will merely be paying an extra $10,000 for a car, not to mention a maintenance headache when the batteries need replacing. Do not succumb to the brainwashing you were fed during K-12. Think independently and buy a Rio or Yaris instead.

* * *

If you follow these ten simple rules you will at minimum avoid the fate millions of young men suffer every year – ruined financial lives because they bought a car they couldn't afford. At best, however, you will have solid transportation on the cheap, significant savings, as well as the serenity and peace of mind that comes with owning cars you can afford to lose.

Motorcycle Salvation

Assume you religiously follow all of the above 10 rules. You never buy new, you find a car that if it gets dinged or stolen you don't care, you only use it for transportation, and never as a means to score chicks or make a statement about yourself. Chances are you are going to end up with a small, fuel efficient compact, with a little body damage, and nothing that is going to turn heads, let alone be fun to drive.

How fun is that?

While you may be smart enough never to compete in the status market, that doesn't mean you don't want a nice car for yourself. Additionally, addressing the previously-discussed genetic desire men have for speed and performance, how is your Ford Fiesta going to put the fire in your soul as you bury the needle at 43 MPH?

Simple. It won't.

But a motorcycle will.

Motorcycles are the salvation of all young men. Like beer and video games, they are a gift from God and he wants you to ride them. Their importance to a man's life cannot be overstated. First, they are cheaper than cars in terms of cost, maintenance, and insurance. Second, they are much more fuel efficient (and manly) than hybrids. Third, they are easier to store and park making them ideal for city living. Fourth, they are easier to work on than cars. And, of course, fifth, they are *fast*. If there is a vehicle that is going to meet your need for speed, motorcycles are it. But their biggest advantage is one that most men are unaware of.

You can now go toe to toe with that 42 year old investment banker in the status market.

Understand that while you cannot *financially* compete against truly rich men who can afford a Mercedes S-Class, you can compete with them on a motorcycle. Matter of fact, you are in a league above them. You are the bad boy. The underdog. And if there's something women viscerally want more than a polished little Amber-Crombie and Fitch boy from the suburbs with his sales job and his Audi, it is the rough and tumble biker, with his scuffed-up leather jack, his "I don't give a fuck" attitude, and that fast and powerful two-wheeled machine beneath him.

Chicks dig motorcycles.

Because of these benefits, it is my humble opinion that the *single best bit of advice in this entire book* is to:

GET

A

MOTORCYCLE!

And not just get one, but learn to ride it as soon as possible.

Forget competing against the 42 year old investment banker. Knowing what I know now I would have deployed this tactic in high school and competed against the varsity football captain. I would have competed against the frat boys during college. The allure of a motorcycle is so strong for women, you can use it as a crutch when you are younger and have no game. Of course, your mother is going to complain loudly when she finds out her 16 year old son wants to get his motorcycle license, and perhaps you may have to wait until you're 18 and out of the house, but that doesn't change the fact a motorcycle makes pursuing the ladies an infinitely easier task, and consequently makes your life infinitely easier.

Don't Be a Dumbass

However, do you know why your mother is protesting so loudly against you getting a motorcycle?

It's because a bunch of young dumbasses, just like yourself, decided it would be really "cool" to go 100MPH in a 45MPH without a helmet and completely destroyed the lives of their mothers when they wrapped themselves around a tree and died. Your mother isn't protesting your ownership of a motorcycle because she doesn't want you to have fun. She is protesting because she loves you and the ABSOLUTE WORST THING to happen to her (and your father) would be to lose you. However, you can abate her fears by simply not being a dumbass.

"Not being a dumbass" meaning:

- Wear a helmet
- Wear other protective gear
- Take the motorcycle safety courses
- Pay attention/driving defensively (middle aged women in SUV's are the worst)
- Never speed (unless it's on the highway out in the middle of nowhere and nobody finds out)
- Do not take risks
- Drive only in acceptable weather

There is certainly *much more* to riding motorcycles, and I STRONGLY recommend taking at least two safety courses before riding. But if your goal is to impress women, merely owning one and safely driving on backstreets achieves the same thing as unnecessarily doing 120 MPH on the interstate. Ergo, there is no reason to hotfoot it or take the risks. Take your time, learn to ride, do it safely, and you'll still impress the chicks.

Besides, it will make your mother happy.

A Miscellany of Advice

Rent Sports Cars – Even if you own a motorcycle and do 150 MPH in the empty plains of Wyoming (which I highly recommend), you will still have the desire to drive a sports car. But why drive one sports car when you can drive many and at a fraction of the cost?

Here's the truth about sports cars.

They are a lot like women you can't afford. They may be hot, they may perform great in bed, but they're expensive, they're costly to maintain, and truthfully you don't want to own one. On top of it, even if you did own one, you'll find the novelty wears off, you get bored with it, and you'll soon yearn for another one (sports car that is, not a woman).

So why buy when you can rent?

I'm not talking about a three year lease or some kind of arrangement where you take long term possession of the car, but rather when you travel and rent a car for a couple of days or a week. You're already on vacation. You're going to die in a short 40 years. Why not live it up a bit and rent yourself a sports car?

This is my personal policy. Anytime I'm on vacation I try to rent a sports car I have not driven before. I have rented a Mustang, a

Mustang GT, a Dodge Challenger, Dodge Charger, and several convertibles, the total cost of which has been minimal. However, I have probably driven more sports cars than most sports car-owning men as they are relegated to the one car they own. Besides, if you play your cards right the day will likely come where you can pay cash for a sports car. Thankfully, you'll have rented enough sports cars during your vacations to know precisely which one you're going to buy.

CHAPTER 10
MAINTENANCE AND REPAIR

Divorce has many bad and horrible consequences. Wrecked marriages, ruined families, dysfunctional children, a larger state. You name it, "divorce" will be cited by historians as one of the primary reasons Western Civilization collapsed. However, it is also responsible for another (though, less serious) problem – the lost art of maintenance and repair.

With the custody of children being awarded in the majority of cases to women, you now have nearly three generations of men brought up under female-headed households, with only weekend visitation rights to their fathers. Making matters worse, with the outsourcing of manufacturing to countries like China, most fathers today work in white collar professions and therefore don't know the first thing about auto-repair or construction. Because of this millions of men, young to middle-aged, never had their dad show them how to change the oil on a car, how to roof a house, or how to replace a hard drive.

This is a tragic loss as learning the basics of maintenance and repair is more important and valuable than having an advanced liberal arts degree. And that's not hyperbole or rhetoric. It's true. Learning how to fix your own car, repair your own house, and trouble shoot your own computer will provide a far higher return on investment than a Master's in 17th Century French Architecture. You will easily spend thousands of dollars on the most basic of car repairs. You will spend a similar amount on geeks to fix your computers. And you will spend at minimum $50,000 on maintaining and repairing your home. Developing the skills to do these things yourself will likely save you $100,000 over the course of your life (which is certainly more than the $8/hour your Masters in French Architecture will pay working as a barista). But without fathers around, who will teach you these valuable skills?

Daddy YouTube

In the olden days, (and by "olden days," I mean pre-internet) if you wanted to learn how to repair or fix something you had to find somebody charitable enough to teach you or pay for some kind of training. If you were young or poor you couldn't likely afford the training, and so you were at the mercy of friends who were mechanics, carpenters, or tradesmen to show you. Unfortunately, these friends were hit up for free work, free advice, and free help all their lives, and, consequently, developed a revulsion and distaste for friends who kept asking them for help (no doubt you know a curmudgeonly computer geek or mechanic who gets impatient with your lack of computer or mechanical skills). However, with the advent of the internet you no longer have to sheepishly approach these people for help.

You have YouTube.

YouTube is a godsend for all men and boys today. It is full of instructional videos that hold your hand, carrying you step by step on how to do pretty much anything when it comes to home repair, auto-mechanics, computer repair, appliances, and everything else. I successfully removed, cleaned, and reinstalled my first carburetor following a YouTube video and could probably successfully complete open-heart surgery if there was a YouTube video on it. Regardless, because of YouTube the average man is now capable of mastering any kind of repair, construction, or maintenance and never has to pain somebody to personally instruct him ever again.

This is an invaluable advancement as the primary difficulty in repair was not so much its cost, but finding a person to do it on the cheap or be charitable enough to show you. But since finding that person and their know-how is now just a phrase search away, that time can be spent doing the repairs yourself.

There is just one minor problem.

Tools

In order to be able to do repairs you need to have a significant inventory of tools. And tools aren't cheap. You can easily spend over $50,000 on tools and still come nowhere close to what a specialist shop has (say, Danny from the show "Count's Kustoms"). Of course, you won't be rebuilding hotrods from the ground up, so all the "average man" needs is a basic set of tools falling into three categories:

Automotive
Computer
Carpentry

Since you won't own a house until you're older, the two most important tool sets you'll need as a young man are automotive and computer tools. Thankfully, computer tools are small and a complete set of them will fit into a pouch the size of a book. But automotive tools are heavy, varied, not to mention you'll need a ramp or a jack of some kind to get underneath a car. This is all fine and well if you have a garage to store them in, but if you're a college student or just a young bachelor living in a studio apartment, jacks and ramps can get in your way.

If this is the case, you have a couple options. Ideally, you will have followed my advice and bought a truck. This will allow you to install a truck bed toolbox which should provide more than enough room to store all your ramps/jacks (as well as tools). If you don't have a truck, hopefully you can find a co-op garage that lets you rent their work bays out for a cheap hourly rate. If you have neither, you'll either have to store them at home or find somebody kind enough to let you use theirs.

The issue of ramps, however, highlight another problem you are going to face – balancing the tools you need with the space you have. If you are a minimalist you will likely have a very small place to minimize rent. However, in being a minimalist, you will also want to do all your repairs and maintenance yourself. To this end you'll want to maximize the use of your space including your vehicles. There may be no room in your apartment for your toolbox, chainsaw, sander, and power drill, but there should be adequate room in the trunk of your car or the truck bed toolbox. Keep in mind, however, if you do decide to store all your tools in your car, you will want to ensure your car does not get stolen. Use a club or a sturdy lock to protect your investment in tools.

Finally, when it comes to the acquisition of tools it is best to buy a complete tool set, instead of buying tools as you need them. It may cost more up front, but the time and gas you'll save making a trip to the hardware store once as opposed to 30 times over the course of your life will alone pay for all your tools.

Ancillary Benefits of Self-Taught Repair

Beyond the obvious financial savings, there are other fringe benefits to becoming a skilled tradesman. Fringe benefits that will not only make your life easier, but significantly better. Remember, in learning a skill or a trade you now have a fungible skill that other people want, resulting in additional opportunities.

Disproportionately Higher Savings When Younger – When you are younger, especially during college, your wage will likely be very low. The problem this presents a young man is that he will have to work many hours at $8/hour to work up the $100/hour rate the mechanic is going to charge to fix his car. It won't be so bad when you're an older professional, making $40/hour, but while you're younger it REALLY pays to be able to do your own auto and computer repair.

Cash on the Side – In being the local handyman on campus or in your circle of friends, you will likely be able to pick up a little bit of extra cash on the side. You will also be able to charge more than the $8/hour your boss at Starbucks is paying you. Truth is, if particularly skilled, you won't need to work a part time job at all during college if rumor gets out you're the go-to-guy to fix things on the cheap.

Manpoints – To fix things is manly. And girls love manly men (just look at Mike Rowe). So if a girl sees you working on a car in the campus parking lot, you stand a better shot at getting her on a date than Mortimer Snerd who wrote her a poem during his 18th Century Gay Latina Poetry class. But if you're smart about it, you will combine this bit of advice with advice from the previous chapter:

What if instead of working on a car in the dorm parking lot, the girls saw you working on...

your motorcycle?

You wouldn't have to go to one party or one bar to buy one girl one drink. You would just be there, all greased up, working on your bike, and they will be drawn to you like moths to a flame. Heck, your motorcycle doesn't even have to be broken. Just act like you're making some much-needed repairs and see how many bras unhinge themselves.

Bartering for Romantic Favors – In the same vein of thought, you can leverage your skills to cajole romantic favors out of girls (if you fix her car, she needs to make you dinner). There will be plenty of opportunities to woo women with your mechanical abilities because, truthfully, girls can't repair stuff to save their lives.

Increasingly Proficient – Like anything else you practice, you will get better at it the more you do it. This not only cuts down on the time you'll need to complete repairs, but increases the quality of your workmanship. This will pay huge dividends, especially when you're a homeowner as you can increase the value of your home significantly with your higher quality craftsmanship.

Nearly Free Electronics – If particularly skilled in electronics and computer repair, a young man can pretty much get all of his electronics nearly for free. Realize most people are too lazy to learn how to replace a bulb in their big screen TV, put heat sinks in their Xbox 360, or install a new hard drive. Like most Americans they simply throw it out, assuming it's broken, when a cheap $10 fix would bring it back to life. Therefore, it may be in your best interests to do a little dumpster diving, visit Goodwill, or go on Craig's List to see if you can't score a "broken" 52 inch flat panel TV. You may not be able to repair everything, but if successful you would wipe out what is normally a young man's third largest expense behind tuition and vehicles – electronics.

Pride – There is no better feeling than fixing something and doing it right for the first time. It gives you pride in your work and confidence in your abilities.

The Tools Every Man Needs

After purchasing your motorcycle, the immediate next thing you will purchase are your tools.

Computers
- Standard computer repair kit
- A used "A+ Computer Repair" book (any version will do)

Automotive
- Socket wrench set, metric and standard, ¼, 3/8, and ½ drive
- Wrench set (including Tubing and Allen wrench sets)
- Adjustable wrench

- Jack or ramps
- Screw drivers (Phillips and Flathead)
- Torque wrench
- Pliers
- Compression tester

Carpentry
- Tape Measure
- Speed Square
- Chalk Line
- Utility Knife
- Hammer
- Saw (handsaw, hack and circular)
- Drill (cordless)
- Framing Square
- 2' Level
- 4' Level
- Socket Set
- Wrench Set
- Screwdriver Set
- Pliers
- Air compressor (with basic pneumatic tools)
- Table Saw

A Miscellany of Advice

Master These Skills Before Graduating From High School – Because you will likely be poorest when you first move out of the house, it's best to develop these skills before graduating from high school. Again, when you're a 53 year old lawyer, bringing in $300/hour, changing your own oil won't make sense. But in the meantime to derive the most benefit from these skills, it would be ideal if you mastered them before the age of 18.

However, people may question whether it's possible to learn all this stuff while in high school. If that's the case, you may want to consider whether your social activities at school (marching band, high school newspaper, etc.) are going to yield the same lifetime benefits had you spent that time teaching yourself about computer repair. The truth is most high school activities are a 100% waste of time. Do not waste such precious time learning how to twirl a baton when you could be learning how to frame and sheetrock instead.

Take a Class – The impersonal nature of YouTube (not to mention its lack of hands on experience) warrants the consideration of paying for a class. Not that you would get a degree or certification in the field, but your local community college or community education program should have an affordable class that teaches you the basics of computer repair, auto-mechanics, etc. It also helps to get out of the garage or basement and socialize with other people. You don't want to be the stereotypical computer geek residing in his mother's basement, never seeing the day of light, as he tinkers with his computers all day.

Don't Worry About Breaking It – The biggest hurdle to maintenance and repair is psychological. Namely, the fear of breaking it. Whether it's knocking out sheet rock or removing the gas tank, the rookie repairman is apprehensive, fearing they might cause further damage, making it irreparable.

Have no fear.

It's already broken.

Is this to say you can't make it worse? Of course not. You can totally make things worse. But being too timid to break something apart is only going to insure it will never work again and you'll never learn. So be bold and swing that sledge hammer and disassemble that wheel assembly. You can always call a professional for backup.

CHAPTER 11
INVESTING AND RETIREMENT PLANNING

The largest oppressor in your life will likely not be the government, but rather your employer. The government does not compel you to show up in person, every day at the same place for 40 years. The government does not compel you to stay at that place for eight hours a day, ensuring you spend more time there than with your family. And the government does not put one of its agents personally in charge of you, requiring you to take orders from that person. The only entity in your life that will do that is your employer. Naturally, your employment is voluntary and you are compensated for your time. But that doesn't change the fact that in terms of both time and control over your personal life, your employer is by far the largest and most invasive oppressor.

Of course, employers are a necessary evil as without them you wouldn't be able to survive. You do need a job to put a roof over your head. And you do need income to put food on the table. But because employers are by nature "oppressive," they still run contrary to human nature which is to be free. This is why most people don't like work. This is why most people would rather be at home than the office. And this is why most people's goal in life is to retire as early as possible. For when you retire you are technically and truly free. There is no boss. There is no authority. There is no one or no thing you have to answer to. And assuming you live in a reasonably free country, your retirement years are likely to be the most enjoyable.

But retirement, especially early retirement, doesn't "just happen." It's something that needs to be planned. Something that needs to be worked at. And as you'll read later, something that is fraught with risk and is no longer the guarantee it used to be. Therefore, to ensure this very important part of your life is enjoyable you need to understand how to plan for retirement, how retirement works, and what pitfalls await.

The History of Retirement

In the olden days retirement was very simple – it didn't exist. It wasn't an option. The vast majority of people throughout human history have worked until they were either dead or physically incapable of working anymore. If you were lucky, some of your children survived to become productive adults and respected you enough to take care of you in your old age. But the vast majority of humans on this planet never retired. They simply worked until they were dead. It wasn't until the industrial and agricultural revolutions was society capable of producing the economic surplus necessary to afford people the luxury of retirement. But once retirement became an economic possibility, it became the goal of most workers.

At this point in history (early 1900's) retirement was pretty straight forward – save up enough money to support you until you died. But thanks in part to the labor movement, employers also started to contribute to the retirement of employees, namely through pensions. You would loyally work 35 years at the same company, put in your dues, and upon a certain age you could retire and collect a small monthly stipend, aka "a pension." Government also got involved in 1935 by offering every citizen in the United States a pension called "Social Security." Between savings, the company's pension, and Social Security it was now possible for nearly everybody to retire and avoid the horrible fate of working until death.

But two trends in the economy resulted in further changes to the retirement system in the US. The first was a fundamental change in how businesses operated. Between outsourcing, internationalization, product development and a whole host of things, the idea of working for the same employer for 35 years became obsolete. People were laid off. Companies were bought out. It was impossible to "have the same employer" for such a long time and therefore impossible to qualify for a pension. The second thing was that the pensions were horribly managed. Statisticians called "actuaries" who were responsible for calculating how much pensions would cost the company (and thus how much the company should put away for paying future pensioners) failed to account for increased life expectancies of the pensioners. Underestimating how long they would have to pay out a pension, companies' pension funds ran dry, sometimes bankrupting the company (just look at General Motors).

To account for both of these trends, the federal government came up with two general retirement plans – the 401k and IRA. Like a bank account, these retirement programs were specific to the individual, not the company. This allowed a worker to work for as many employers as he wanted and still keep his retirement plan. The 401k and IRA also solved the under-funded pension problem by switching the primary retirement program from a "***defined benefit***" plan (a pension) to a "***defined contribution***" plan (401k's and IRA's). What this meant was unlike a pension, where the company was legally responsible to pay a potentially unlimited amount of money until you died, it would instead make fixed, defined contributions to your 401k while you were still working and be done with it. This eliminated the risk of not having enough money in the pension fund to pay pensioners as there was no fund. The company made its contribution up front, and it was now up to the individual to manage it effectively. To sweeten the pot, the federal government granted employees various tax breaks for investing in these retirement programs, providing additional incentive for people to save adequately for retirement.

This is the state of retirement planning today. While some employers do offer pensions, the majority of retirement plans being offered are 401k's. You are expected to sock away a certain amount per paycheck into this retirement account and (hopefully) your employer makes a matching contribution as well. For people who are self-employed or whose employers do not offer a 401k plan, they are allowed to set up their own "Individual Retirement Accounts," aka, "IRA's." Like the 401k you are expected to make contributions to this account over the course of your life. Hopefully, by the time you retire, you will have enough saved up in these accounts to support you until your death.

The Basics of Investing and Retirement Planning

While the above provides a very general and top-down explanation of retirement planning, it does not explain the specific steps, tools, and details needed to start preparing for retirement. It also does not explain all the people, players, and processes you will be interacting with to help you invest and save. And although such topics are ***incredibly*** dry and boring, they are an unfortunate and vital requirement for successful retirement planning. If you do not take the time to understand these things you run the risk of becoming an ignorant investor. This makes you more susceptible to scams, thieves, con artists, or just outright lousy investments. This can easily torpedo your retirement and make your golden years a nightmare. It, therefore, behooves you to take the time to understand and comprehend everything below.

Securities

When most people think "investing" they think "stocks and bonds." But stocks and bonds are just two out of a nearly limitless number of different investments. There are hedge funds, there are futures contracts, there are commodities, there are REIT's. There are scores of different classes of investments you can invest in. However, whether they are "pork bellies futures" or "IBM stock" they all fall under the same category – "securities."

"Securities" has nothing to do with being safe or "secure." It is a catch all term that describes any kind of investment or "financial instrument" sold on the financial markets. So a "bond" is a "security" just as a "mutual fund" is a security. But to understand these securities and precisely what you are investing in, you need only to know about three basic securities:

Stocks
Bonds
Commodities

These three securities are the basic "building blocks" or "key ingredients" of the securities world. Every other form or variant of a security out there is either composed of, or based off of, these three securities. And if you can understand these three securities you can intuitively understand the rest.

Stocks – Stocks (or a share of stock) is merely a fractional ownership in a company or a corporation. While most business ventures can be started with money the owner has on hand, some business ideas require millions, sometimes billions in capital. Since most entrepreneurs don't have a cool billion laying around, they have to go to the "stock market" to raise the money. However, investors do not simply hand over money without something in return. If they are going to give the entrepreneur money they are going to require ownership in the company and a percentage of the profits proportional to their investment. They receive "shares" which entitles them to voting rights and their share of profits. It is these profits that then drive the price or value of the stock.

(I strongly recommend at this point watching the YouTube video "How the Stock Market Works" which can be found here: http://www.youtube.com/watch?v=GnJCOof2HJk)

Bonds – Bonds are nothing more than a loan. Instead of investing in a company (like you do with stock), you decide instead to loan the company money. But because you are loaning and not investing, you are not entitled to a share of the profits. Instead, you are promised to be paid a fixed amount of "interest" on the loan. The benefit, however, in being a "bondholder" (as opposed to a "shareholder") is interest has to be paid to you first, before any profits are paid out to the shareholders. Additionally, bonds are less risky because in the case the company goes bankrupt, you and other bondholders have first rights to any assets the company may have.

There are many types of bonds. There are corporate bonds (say you loan IBM some money), government bonds (do you have any "savings bonds" from when you were a child?) municipal bonds (your school district is likely financed by them), even celebrities like David Bowie have issued personal bonds. But ultimately their value is determined by the rate of interest they pay and the ability of the borrower to pay you back. Thus, when researching bonds you not only look at the interest rate being offered, but the quality of the borrower. This is where "bond ratings" come in where companies like Moody's or Standard and Poor's have the "AAA+" or "CC-" ratings you have likely seen. There is certainly more to investing in bonds, but the key thing is to realize you are lending money, not buying a piece of ownership in the firm.

Commodities – Commodities are raw materials that do not pay dividends or interest, but have value unto themselves. This "intrinsic value" is derived from some kind of practical use the commodity has. For example, timber is considered a commodity because it can be used to construct houses. Gold and silver are considered commodities because they can be used in jewelry and electronics. Cattle are considered a commodity as they have use as food. And copper is a commodity because of its use in plumbing. The prices of commodities are determined simply by the supply and demand for them. If there is a housing boom going on, timber is likely trading at a higher price as builders demand more wood. If a huge new supply of oil is discovered, oil prices go down as there is now an increased supply of the stuff. Understand, when you buy commodities you are not "investing" in them as much as you are "speculating." They pay no dividend, they pay no interest. You are merely hoping the price of commodities goes up so that you may sell it later for a profit.

***

In understanding these three basic building blocks of securities, you can now understand most other securities as they are nothing more than a combination or a derivation of the three. However, the average investor is unlikely to use elaborate or exotic securities such as "hedge funds," "futures contracts," and "options." Instead, most people will very likely use the following five securities:

Mutual Funds
Indexed Funds
Exchange Traded Funds
Real Estate Investment Trusts
Annuities

Mutual Funds – Mutual funds are nothing more than a combination of two or more securities. Technically the mutual fund could be composed of just one stock and one bond, but usually they are composed of at least 20 or more different underlying securities. The purpose of mutual funds is to provide something that individual securities can't – diversification.

Say you had $10,000 to invest. It would be foolish to invest it all in one individual stock or one individual bond. What if the stock did poorly? What if the company went bankrupt? If that happened you could very easily lose all of your investment. But if you spread that $10,000 across a score or more of securities, you diversify your investment. Some securities will do well. Some will do bad. But overall the average return on your investment should be positive.

The problem, however, in individually investing in 20 or more stocks is that it's cumbersome. You would have to spend the time researching 20 different securities, not to mention spend the time making 20 separate trades. Worse still, you have to pay a "commission" on each trade which can easily run $20 a trade. $20 times 20 trades is $400, a full 4% of your original investment already eaten up in trading costs. A mutual fund bypasses these problems by allowing you to make one trade and immediately be invested in all those different securities.

Of course, mutual funds don't do this for free. They charge various fees (12b-1 fees, administration fees, "loads," etc.), but because they are doing it for the entire fund, it is a fraction of the cost had you tried to replicate this on your own. Regardless, because of their relatively low costs and diversification benefits, mutual funds comprise the majority of investments for pension funds and other retirement programs.

Indexed Mutual Funds – In addition to diversification, mutual funds, in theory, offer another benefit – superior returns. When you pay those fees you aren't just paying to keep up the operations of the mutual fund, but you are also paying the *mutual fund manager* to manage the fund – i.e. – to research and choose the underlying investments of the fund in the hopes of providing the highest possible rate of return.

Some of these managers become famous as they pick great underlying securities and provide excellent rates of return. Peter Lynch's Magellan Fund rose to prominence in the 1980's earning him financial fame and Warren Buffett's "Berkshire Hathaway" company has earned him the reputation of the world's greatest investor. However, the truth is the majority of mutual fund managers do not provide superior rates of return. Depending on which study you cite, around 80% of mutual fund managers are no better at picking stocks and bonds than drunk monkeys throwing darts at the Wall Street Journal.

The question then becomes,

"If these professionals can't provide a superior rate of return, then why should I pay them?"

The answer is,

"You shouldn't."

Enter the "Indexed Mutual Fund."

"The Index" is a phrase you will commonly hear in financial circles and refers (typically) to the S&P 500 Index. This index is the top 500 publicly traded companies in the United States and is used as a benchmark to compare the performance of mutual funds against. The idea being,

"If you can't beat the S&P 500 Index, then why should I pay you, when I could go and invest in the S&P 500 myself?"

But can you?

The answer is "Yes, through 'Indexed Mutual Funds'."

Indexed Mutual Funds aim to do precisely that – invest in the index and nothing more and nothing less. The goal is to merely provide the same exact rate of return the index does and in doing so beat out the vast majority of mutual fund managers. However, because you are merely mimicking the S&P 500 Index, it requires no research, no analysis and no stock picking. You just invest in the 500 stocks that compose the S&P 500 Index. This not only makes the mutual fund manager's job a lot easier, but lowers the managerial fees you have to pay to invest in indexed funds.

But it gets better.

The S&P 500 Index is only one index of hundreds. There are indexes for every imaginable group or amalgamation of securities. There is the "Barclay Bond Index" which is the benchmark index for bonds. There is the "Golden Dragon Index" which is benchmark index for Chinese stocks. There's even the "HUI Index" which is the index for gold mining companies. In other words, you are not relegated to only investing in US stocks when it comes to indexed funds. There are indexed funds for pretty much every security, country, and industry out there.

When you combine these benefits (lower costs, superior returns, and wide selection) it is really hard to beat indexed mutual funds as your default go-to investment for your 401k or IRA. They're cheap, they don't cause any headaches, and they really simplify investing. However, there is nothing wrong with wanting more. If you can find a mutual fund that is part of that 20% that beats the index, then you can get rates of return superior to the index. But how do you analyze a mutual fund composed of 200 different securities or more?

Simple, you don't. You use "Morningstar" instead.

Since it is impossible to individually analyze and stay on top of 200 or more securities, you compare mutual funds based on two simple measures:

1. Historical performance relative to its respective index
2. Fees

Morningstar does both (and much more).

If you go to their website you can look up any mutual fund you want. Morningstar will then provide a report that, among other things, will show you an "expense ratio" and a chart showing the mutual fund's performance against its corresponding index. The expense ratio is the amount of your investment you can expect to spend each year on fees. It can range from as low as .8% to 5%. Naturally you want the lowest expense ratio as possible. The chart Morningstar displays merely shows whether the fund is beating the index or not. These two variables are the only ones you need in order to determine whether it is worth investing in a mutual fund or not.

Exchange Traded Funds (ETF's) — Without going into mind-numbing detail there is an even cheaper way to invest in the index — "Exchange Traded Funds" or "ETF's." ETF's are just like indexed mutual funds but are managed slightly differently. Because of this they have much lower operational expenses than mutual funds, but still provide the same rate of return as the index. The only catch is that unlike a mutual fund, you have to pay a commission when trading ETF's much like you do when you trade stocks. This means if you are only going to buy $200 of ETF's here and $200 of ETF's there and are paying $20 in commission for each trade, you are losing 10% of your investment right off the bat. Therefore, if you do decide you're interested in investing in ETF's it is best to make sure you buy at least $1,000 worth of ETF's at a time.

Real Estate Investment Trusts (REIT's) – When you mention investing in real estate, most people think of their home or perhaps rental property. However, you can still invest in property without having to shell out $40,000 for a down payment and committing yourself to a 30 year mortgage. You can invest in a "Real Estate Investment Trust" (REIT).

A REIT is simply nothing more than a mutual fund, but instead of being composed of securities, the REIT is made up of a portfolio of properties. This is great for anybody who would like to invest in real estate, but doesn't have the money to buy a whole piece of property outright. Additionally, just like a mutual fund, a REIT is diversified across multiple properties so if one goes belly up or doesn't perform as well, the rest of the properties compensate. So if you are a 25 year old, just starting in his career, would like to get some investment exposure in real estate, but can't afford a house, no worries. Just invest a couple thousand dollars in a REIT instead.

Annuities – Annuities are nothing more than "income insurance." Just as you pay an auto insurance company money every month to insure against a car crash, you pay an annuity firm a certain amount of money today to guarantee you a certain amount of income in the future.

So for example, you agree at the age of 20 to make monthly payments of $200 for the next 20 years into an annuity. In return for those payments, the annuity company GUARANTEES that starting at the age of 60 you will receive monthly payments of $400 until your death.

Usually what you pay into the annuity seems less than what the annuity pays. However, there are two reasons for that. One, inflation. $200 at the age of twenty could actually be worth more than $400 at the age of 60 when you've had 40 years of inflation to whittle away at it. Two, the annuity company doesn't just take your money and throw it in a vault. They invest it, hoping to make more than what they promised to pay out to you. This way they can honor their guarantee to pay you and make some profit for their shareholders.

But perhaps the most confusing thing about annuities is just how varied they can be. Traditionally, annuities paid out until you died. Now you can specify they only pay for 10, 20, or 30 years. Sometimes after you die, the annuity can be passed onto your spouse, sometimes it can't. Maybe you pay in $300 for 15 years, other times you pay in only $200 for 25 years. But regardless of what terms the annuity is offering you can be guaranteed of one thing:

They are making money off of you.

Understand that if annuity companies WEREN'T going to make money on offering annuities, they wouldn't do it. If it isn't profitable, then the company wouldn't be around. So whatever the terms are, chances are had you invested that money yourself, you would statistically be likely to come out ahead. But understand this important point about annuities:

They are not investments. They are *insurance.*

When you buy an annuity you are paying to ensure you have a basic level of income in the future. That's it. Any surplus that may be left over gets to be kept by the annuity company. Many people find this disagreeable, thinking it is "your money," but that was not the purpose of the annuity. As long as the company honors its guarantee and pays you what was agreed upon, it has done its job and delivered the service you were promised. Ensure you understand this before purchasing an annuity.

Purchasing Securities

There are two general ways the average person invests in securities – either through their retirement plan or through a brokerage. If you have a retirement plan the investing is automated. A fixed amount of each paycheck is withheld and invested in whichever mutual funds you designated when signing up for your company's retirement plan. However, if your company doesn't offer a retirement program or you would just like to invest on your own you then need to go through a brokerage.

A brokerage is very much like a bank, but instead of holding onto your money, it holds onto stocks, bonds, mutual funds and any other securities you might invest in. It will also place and execute trades for you allowing you to buy and sell securities. But unlike banks they have advisors who will consult you and recommend different investments. These individuals are called "brokers" and are the people you deal with when you want to invest in the financial markets.

There are varying levels of brokerages in terms of service and quality. At the top end are your elite firms such as Goldman Sachs, Merrill Lynch, JP Morgan, etc. These companies are considered "full service" brokerages and will consult you, advise you, trade for you, even manage your family's estate. They will also let you trade in anything you want – options, currencies, pork bellies, Guatemalan timber, you name it, they'll trade it. However, since they are a full service brokerage they are also the most expensive. Depending on the trade, commission can easily run $200 a pop.

Beneath the full service brokerages are "discount brokerages." These firms charge significantly less (around $30 a trade), but do not provide investment advice. They only offer trading services, allowing you to invest in securities and nothing more. They also are unlikely to trade in some of the more exotic securities such as options and commodities (though some do specialize in such securities). Because of this they suit the "average man" more than the elite brokerages. Most people can afford the commission and really only need to buy either stocks, bonds, or mutual funds. Examples of such brokerages are Charles Schwab, Fidelity, and Vanguard.

Even more stripped-down than discount brokerages are your "online brokerages." Not that discount brokerages or the full service brokerages don't offer their clients the ability to trade online, but "pure" online brokerages *require* you place your own orders online. There is no broker you can call to place your trade, and there certainly isn't a broker who is going to provide you investment advice. They may have a support hotline to help you with technical issues while trading, but you are the one doing all the work, research and trading. Because of this, however, trading costs are minimal with commissions averaging around $7. Scottrade, TD Ameritrade, and ShareBuilder are examples of such brokerages.

As for which one is the best, it really depends on the person. You may enjoy doing your own research, don't need the advice of a broker, and you absolutely hate going to the bank in person. If that's the case, online brokerages are for you. Or you may be really busy working as a doctor, don't have time to manage your money, and are happy to pay a premium to outsource your investing to a professional. If this is the case, a full service brokerage is for you. However, before you commit to one type of brokerage or another, remember one very important thing:

The majority of investment professionals fail to beat the index.

This is one of the most important bits of information in this book because it makes investing incredibly simple and incredibly cheap. If the majority of brokers can't beat the index, then why would you pay for a broker when you yourself can invest in an indexed mutual fund or an ETF? Technically, there shouldn't even be brokers anymore because their entire profession has been rendered obsolete by index investing. Therefore, unless you really need to have your hand held or you think your broker can actually beat the index, there is no reason to pay $200 a trade for a full service brokerage. Most people just need a platform to trade with and online discount brokerages provide exactly that.

Regardless of which type of brokerage you go with, once you choose one it's only a matter of a few simple steps to start trading. First, you need to apply for an account. This requires filing out some paperwork, signing some documents, and mailing them into the brokerages. Once approved for an account you need to fund it. You can't trade without money so you have to either mail in a check, cashier's check, electronic funds transfer, or fund your account with a credit card payment. Upon confirming your check cleared and the brokerage has your money, they will authorize your account and "POOF!" – you are ready to trade.

Retirement Plans

While you may be tempted to set up a brokerage account right away, you should first ensure to take full advantage of any retirement programs offered to you at work. They offer tax benefits that a regular normal brokerage account doesn't and therefore should be your first foray into investing. However, while we've already mentioned "IRA's" and "401k's" there are actually nearly a score of different retirement programs out there.

401k's, IRA's, Thrift Savings Plans, 403b's, 457's, Roth IRA's, Traditional IRA's, 529 Plans, Keogh Plans, SIMPLE IRA's, the list goes on.

It can be very confusing which plan is best for you, but regardless of the plan, all of them have some key things in common. These traits vary depending on the plan, but will ultimately help you decide:

Tax Benefits – All retirement plans have some kind of tax benefit. You can either write your contributions off from your taxes or not pay "capital gains" taxes when you cash them in. These tax benefits can be significant and should be considered when choosing a retirement plan.

Contribution Limits – Because you can write off your contributions, you could in theory contribute all your income and pay a 0% tax rate. The government knows this and so they limit the amount you can contribute each year (though they do adjust it to account for inflation). Different retirement programs have different contributions limits, and sometimes your contribution limits will be dependent on how much you make. However, this doesn't mean you can't invest beyond your contribution limit. It just means you won't get the tax benefit for contributions beyond that limit.

Withdrawal Penalties and Requirements – All retirement programs require you keep the money in them until a certain age. If you withdraw money from your accounts before that age you will have to pay a (typically) 10% penalty (though sometimes this fee is waived if you qualify under certain "hardship" requirements). You will also be penalized if you wait too long to withdraw money from your accounts (typically you are mandated to withdraw at 70 ½ years of age). In short, the government wants to ensure your investments go to pay for your retirement.

"Matching" – "Matching" is where your employer "matches" your contributions by investing an equivalent amount in your retirement program. Usually they will limit their total contributions to a few percentage points of your gross salary, but it still can prove a tremendous help to your retirement planning. Note, however, not all retirement programs have this option and not all employers match.

"Vesting" – If your employer does match your contributions, however, realize you aren't immediately entitled to that portion of your retirement fund. You usually need to work for them for a certain number of years to prove your loyalty and that you are "vested" in them. Some employers don't bother with vesting, where you are immediately 100% vested and therefore entitled to all the money in your account. Other's scale it by 20% over five years, allowing you to incrementally become vested overtime. I personally insist on being 100% vested immediately with any prospective employer.

These traits vary with, and thusly define, all the different types of retirement programs. However, with nearly 20 different retirement programs it is beyond the scope of this book to address each and every one of them. To that end, we will only discuss the four most common retirement programs you are likely to run into:

The "Traditional" 401k
The "Roth" 401k
The "Traditional" IRA and,
The "Roth" IRA

and leave it to you to research the other more obscure ones.

The "Traditional" 401k – The first thing to note about the 401k is that there are other "401k variants" out there, namely the 403b and the 457. All three of them operate pretty much identically, with the only major difference being that the 401k is for private employers and the 403b and 457 are for public sector or non-profit employers. Regardless, their basic operations are the same.

You are allowed to contribute up to $17,500 (in 2013) to your 401k (or 403/457). This retirement program being a "traditional" retirement program, that contribution is tax deductible. This will lower your taxable income by $17,500 which will in turn significantly lower your tax bill. Upon turning 59 ½ you can start to withdraw money from your account, but because it's a traditional retirement program you will have to pay income taxes on those withdrawals. Any withdrawals before you turn 59 ½ are taxed at an additional 10% as a penalty.

The "Roth" 401k – Everything about the "Traditional 401k" applies to the "Roth 401k" except for the tax benefit. The contribution limits are the same, the penalties are the same, and the required age of distribution is the same. However, instead of getting to write off your contribution from your taxes, you do not have to pay income taxes when you retire and start withdrawing. This makes the Roth version of the 401k (and any other Roth retirement programs) preferable to younger investors as their investments have more time to grow, and thusly save more in taxes should they not have to pay taxes on their withdrawals.

The "Traditional" IRA – Not every employer is going to offer a retirement plan. And if you're self-employed you can't set up your own 401k plan. To remedy this the government established the "Individual Retirement Account" or "IRA."

Like the "Traditional 401k" you get to write off your contributions from your taxes. And like the 401k you have to wait until you're 59 ½ to retire or face the 10% penalty. However, the only real difference between the 401k and IRA is the contribution limits. In

2013 you can only contribute $5,500 to your IRA account. Additionally, since the IRA is independent of an employer you need to contact either a bank or a brokerage and set up an IRA account through them. It will act exactly like a brokerage account, except it is designated as an "IRA."

The "Roth" IRA – Logically, you can likely deduce what the Roth IRA is. It has all the same contribution limits and traits of the Traditional IRA, but instead of being able to write off your contribution from your taxes, you don't have to pay income taxes on your withdrawals when you retire.

***

Again, there are certainly more retirement plans out there, but it is nearly guaranteed you will use one of these four. But regardless of which retirement plan (or plans) you choose, you have one final responsibility – choosing what to invest in.

Understand for the most part you can't just "invest in whatever you want." When you have a 401k or an IRA it is usually "hosted" or "managed" by another financial firm and that financial firm usually limits your investment options. This is not for nefarious or evil reasons, but economic. Unless they are a full service brokerage (which sometimes they are), they don't have the capacity or staff to allow every single participant to invest in whatever they want. To that end they usually have a list of pre-approved mutual funds you can invest in.

This list will be presented to you by your HR rep when you sign up for your 401k plan or by a financial representative from the brokerage hosting your IRA plan. It will include mutual funds that fit into different types of investment categories – growth, value, fixed income, bonds, international Asian, European, commodities, etc. You will then determine what funds you want to invest in and what percentage of your contribution should be invested into each. Usually the people managing the plan do their best to pick the best funds with the highest performance, but they also usually include indexed funds for people who want the ease of index investing. However, if you are really lucky, they will also offer you a "self-managed account" option.

A "self-managed account" (SMA) is where you can invest outside the "approved list" of mutual funds. Usually SMA's are offered with IRA's in that IRA's are typically hosted by brokerages. These brokerages have the capacity to invest in stocks, bonds, mutual funds, ETF's and more, and consequently so does your IRA account. SMA's, however, are not as common with 401k plans in that they are not typically managed by a broker. But if your employer does offer an SMA option with your 401k, you should not only avail yourself of it, but be incredibly thankful.

As for what to specifically invest in (what percent bonds, what percent stocks, what percent international, etc.) that again depends on you, your age, and how much risk you like to take. But a good starting point is to consult the investment allocations recommend by Fidelity's "Freedom Funds." These mutual funds are considered "target date" mutual funds and have the recommended allocation for people retiring in different years. So if you plan on retiring in the year 2030, you would look up the allocations for Fidelity's 2030 Freedom Fund. If you plan to retire in 2043, you would look up the allocation for Fidelity's 2045 Freedom Fund (as they round to the nearest five year increment). Of course, not everybody is the same and the allocations for your particular retirement date may differ from somebody the same age, but it is a good proxy to start with.

Insurance

The final, and often forgotten component to investing and retirement planning, is insurance. Not necessarily car or renter's insurance, but rather insurance to protect against the risk you become disabled or are no longer able to work. This not only compensates you in case you become disabled, but also any children or other dependents you may have. It also protects your family from the financial burden of supporting you should you become disabled.

There are three general types of insurance you should consider as part of your retirement planning:

Disability
Nursing Home (aka "Long Term Care")
Life

And though they may seem the same, there are some differences.

Disability Insurance – Disability insurance covers you when you become disabled and are no longer able to work. Upon becoming disabled the insurance company will pay the monthly benefit until the point in time you can return to work or the benefits run out. Since you can get injured at any point in time, it doesn't matter if you're 18 or 81 – if you are working and need your monthly income to survive (especially if a family is dependent upon you) disability insurance is a wise investment, certainly wiser than that brand new SUV the wife demands.

Nursing Home Insurance – Nursing home insurance covers you when you need to go into a nursing home or some other kind of long term care facility. Like disability insurance it pays the pre-determined monthly benefit and lasts either until death or when the benefits run out. Unlike disability insurance, chances are you will not need this coverage during your youth. However, even during middle age you may wish to consider buying a policy as cancer, Alzheimer's, and other ailments can strike as early as 40. Besides, it is still a better investment than that brand new SUV wifey demands.

Life Insurance – Life insurance covers you in case you die. At first this may not make sense because if you're dead, then what use would that money be to you? However, it isn't for you. It's for your children or any dependents you might have left behind. Therefore, if you are a childless bachelor, life insurance makes absolutely no sense. But if you are married or have children that rely on you, it is certainly something to consider. Fortunately (bar some pre-existing condition) life insurance is very cheap and certainly more affordable than that brand new SUV wifey demands.

Beyond these three "late life" types of insurance there really isn't much else that would be part of your retirement planning. If you were to purchase all three you would be well-ahead of most of your financial planning peers. But before you start buying policies there are three things you'll want to consider.

First, there is a fourth and much better type of insurance than all three – healthy living. Realize that 70% of sicknesses are caused by life-style choices. Smoking, drinking, sedentariness, bad diet, etc. If you can commit yourself to eating healthy, avoiding vice (within reason), and exercising regularly you will not only save a lot on insurance, but you will live a better life.

Second, it isn't a matter of just choosing a policy. You need to choose the right insurance company. Like banks or any other business, they can go bankrupt and fail to deliver on your policy. Thankfully, companies like Standard and Poor's and A.M. Best rate insurance companies based on their financial strength and ability to honor their policies. Unfortunately, they usually charge for these ratings, but the site below allows you to look up Standard and Poor's ratings for most insurance companies for free:

http://www.insure.com/articles/interactivetools/sandp/newtool1.jsp

Finally, deep down inside you know you are spending money on something that is absolutely frivolous compared to these useful types of insurance. And while statistics may be in your favor, all it takes is a slip from a ladder or a bad gene that results in a crippling disease to send you and your loved ones into the poor house. Therefore, before you buy the latest video game console or your wife buys that brand new SUV, ensure you have the necessary insurance to protect your life and your family.

Retirement Planning in the "Perfect World"

With all of the above in mind, you can now put together a comprehensive retirement program. The first step of which is to estimate the amount of money you are going to need to retire. The truth is, however, this number cannot be known. The reason why is that your retirement funds need to last you until you die, and you simply don't know when that's going to be.

At first you might think, *"Well, I'll just assume I'll die at 78 which is the average life expectancy of a man,"* but there is a problem with that:

What if you live beyond 78?

This highlights the most common mistake people make when assessing their retirement needs. They never account for the chance they may live a longer-than-average life. And while living longer than average is great, running out of money when you're old and decrepit is a nightmare. To prevent this you need to do a little research into your family's health history, your own personal health habits, and then err on the side of caution to ensure your retirement funds last you till death.

For example, if your mom lived till 90 and your dad lived till 85, longevity runs in your family. You can expect to die around the same age as well. But what if you eat healthier than your mother? What if you exercise more than your father? Chances are, especially with technology, you could live to 100. If you were planning on retiring at the standard age of 65, that means you need enough money to last you 35 years. Had you foolishly assumed, however, you would live the average life expectancy, you would have ran out of money by 78 and had to work the next 22 years as an old decrepit man. Therefore, a rule of thumb I recommend is taking the average time your parents were alive and adding 10 years to that. If your parents are still alive, look to your grandparents and add 15. This should give you an age you are very unlikely to live past and if you budget for that age, you will likely not outlast your retirement funds.

The next thing you need to figure out is when you want to retire. While certainly easier to calculate than when you're going to die, it's not as easy as you think. Most people just assume 65, but what if you like working? What if your parents both lived to 100? In either case, it would be foolish to retire at 65. Conversely, you may have very low life expectancy. Your mom died at 49, you're dad at 60, and you like smoking and drinking. You won't make it to 65, so why bother saving at all?

But the real reason it's difficult to predict when you will retire is because life is constantly changing. Many people can't wait to retire, only to find out when they do they're so bored it's worse than working. They soon return to the labor force out of sheer boredom. Some people unexpectedly come into an inheritance or a lottery, allowing them to retire much sooner than planned. An oopsie baby can make a happy late 40's couple have to delay retirement, and a problem child you desperately feared for, makes it rich and retires his beloved Ma and Pa. But to make retirement planning work you do need to come up with at least some kind of estimated retirement age. It can always change, but then your financial planning must change correspondingly. And unless you know for a fact it should be something different (say you plan on living till 100), 65 is as safe a starting point as any.

With these two numbers (life expectancy and retirement age) you now know how many years you roughly have to save up for. The next step is to calculate how much money is needed to support you during that time. You can do this by sitting down for about four hours, listing all of your potential expenses, and programming complex Excel spreadsheets

or

you can use one of the many retirement calculators available for free on the internet.

A simple Google search will pull up scores of different calculators, all varying in detail and complexity, but for the beginner I recommend Bankrate's retirement calculator:

http://www.bankrate.com/calculators/retirement/retirement-calculator.aspx

Retirement Calculator — How much to retire.

30000	Annual Income Required (today's dollars)
15	Number of years until retirement
25	Number of years required after retirement
0.0	Annual Inflation (%)
7.5	Annual Yield on Balance (%) (average)

Calculate

You simply fill in five variables, hit the "calculate" button, and "POOF!" You have a reasonably good estimate of the amount of money you need to save up before you retire:

Required Income (Current Dollars)	$20000.00
Required Income (Future Dollars)	$0.00
Number of Years Until Retiring	32.00
Number of Years After Retiring	20.00
Annual Inflation (on Required Income)	3.00%
Annual Yield on Balance	7.50%

You will need $707208.13 ($69899.87 invested today)

There is, however, some confusion about the different variables you plug into this (and any other) calculator, and thus a review of each variable is called for.

"Required Income (Current Dollars)" – This is the amount of money you estimate you'll need to live off of each year *during retirement*. It is NOT the amount of money you need to live off *today* as you will likely not have a mortgage, children, and other expenses when you're retired. Additionally, you'll need to account for the fact you may be collecting a pension, Social Security, or an annuity at the time. This extra income needs to be SUBTRACTED from this amount to provide you the "net" figure your retirement funds must provide for. Notice it is also in "current dollars," which means you do not adjust for inflation. Merely enter the amount of money you think you would need to live off of annually when you retire in today's dollars.

"Number of Years Till Retirement" – Simply take your estimated retirement age and subtract your current age. You may want to vary this number to run different scenarios for different retirement ages to see how it affects the total amount of money you need saved up.

"Number of Years After Retirement" – Here you merely estimate the number of years you'll live from retirement to death. Like the "number of years till retirement" you'll also want to vary this number to account for different scenarios.

"Annual Inflation" – Inflation can cause a lot of confusion because a seemingly low inflation rate (say, 7%) can greatly distort your final retirement dollar figure. Because of this I recommend running three different scenarios. The first one set the inflation rate to 0%. This will result in a number in "today's dollars" and will give you the most accurate idea of how much money you'll have to save up had you retired "today." The second scenario set the inflation rate to 3%. This is likely the inflation rate you'll experience between now and retirement, and will yield a dollar amount closest to reality. The final scenario set the inflation rate to 7%. This will assume a "high inflation economy" and can show you the effects of inflation.

"Annual Yield on Balance" – This is a poorly termed phrase, but it means *"what kind of annual rate of return do you expect to get on your investments."* Again, like the other variables, you will want to run "pessimistic, normal, and optimistic" scenarios. Historically, investments average around 7.5%, but there have been bouts where the markets have provided negative rates of return, and bouts where they have provided 25% rates of return. I recommend plugging in 3% for pessimistic, 7.5% for normal, and 11% for optimistic.

Naturally, if you plug in multiple variables for multiple scenarios you will have multiple amounts you need for retirement. As for which one to choose, and therefore plan on, it is really up to the individual. I personally take the average between my "normal" and "pessimistic" scenarios, but this is primarily because I want to make doubly sure I do not run out of money when I retire. The key thing is to make sure you're comfortable with whatever scenario and final dollar figure you choose. If you still have some nagging doubt or a "twinge" in your stomach, that is your intellectual honesty telling you, you are being too optimistic. Remember, there is no worse outcome than running out of money when you are old and cannot work. Ensure it doesn't happen.

With a final number, you can now start to figure out how much you need to sock away each year for retirement. To do this you can use "future value of an annuity" and reverse engineer the formula to solve for price:

$$FV = \left[\frac{(1+r)^n - 1}{r} \right] P$$

or

you can use Bloomberg's online calculator that does this for you:

http://www.bloomberg.com/personal-finance/calculators/retirement/

Retirement Plan

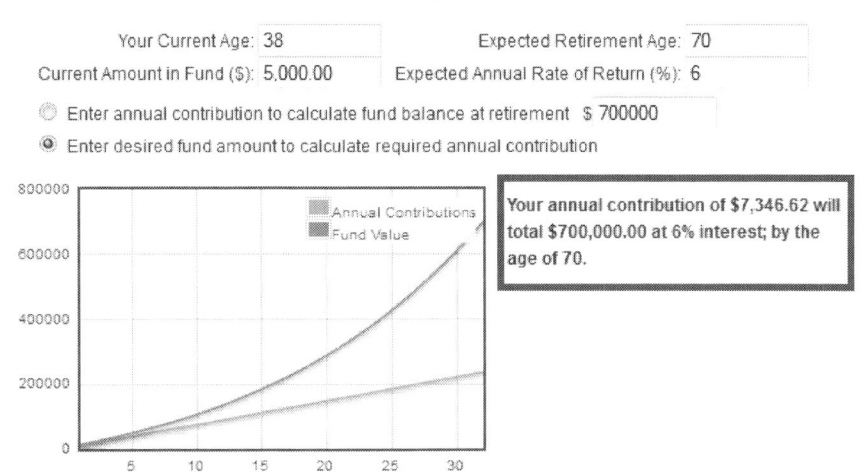

Your Current Age: 38   Expected Retirement Age: 70
Current Amount in Fund ($): 5,000.00   Expected Annual Rate of Return (%): 6

○ Enter annual contribution to calculate fund balance at retirement $ 700000
◉ Enter desired fund amount to calculate required annual contribution

Your annual contribution of $7,346.62 will total $700,000.00 at 6% interest; by the age of 70.

Like the Bankrate calculator, you simply enter a couple numbers and the Bloomberg calculator will provide you with the amount you need to save each year. Once you have this number it is merely a matter of incorporating it into your personal budget and ensuring you invest the required amount in your retirement account each and every year.

Beyond that, there is nothing more to retirement planning. However, what is important to understand is that despite all the numbers, despite all the formulas, retirement planning is not an exact science. You could do everything by the book, run every calculation, and religiously invest the required amount each year, and still end up running out of money when you're 82.
The reason for this is because while we use math as the tool to estimate and calculate our retirements, the real world is not so precise or mathematical. It is dynamic, chaotic, and constantly changing. But because of the mathematical nature of retirement planning, people are misled to believe retirement is a precise science. However, once people realize that their retirement isn't

100% completely under their control and there is a large element of chance, they fret, they worry, and they start to lose sleep. But realize to do so is pointless. As long as you did what you're supposed to, as long as you did your best to position yourself financially, then you have done all you can do. It is up to the fates what will happen next, and since that is not under your control, you should never worry and never lose sleep over your investments.

Retirement Planning in the "Real World"

Take everything you just read in the previous section about retiring in the "perfect world" and throw it out the window. The reason why is you can read all the financial planning textbooks you want, fill out a thousand online retirement calculators, and follow the advice of finance professionals to the letter, it won't change the fact that the country's retirement system, and the economy in general, is horribly flawed, which renders traditional retirement planning obsolete.

Most people find this a hard pill to swallow, especially those who are already heavily invested into the current system. And investment professionals will scoff at this, claiming its sensationalism, gonzo journalism, and hyperbole designed to drum up sales. But just like the housing bubble, the Dotcom bubble, and the education bubble, there is a retirement bubble. And most people have neither the foresight, nor courage to see it, let alone act on it. Fortunately, you will. This isn't to say that you should not be investing in 401k's or that you shouldn't be planning for retirement at all. But it is to say you need to be aware of the problems and risks that threaten the current retirement system so that you have an effective "Plan B" in place should it collapse.

Problem #1 – Underfunded Pensions

Most people today are thankful to have a pension. Because of their costs (or rather, the difficulty in estimating their costs), most companies have shifted away from pensions and replaced them with defined contribution plans (like the 401k) instead. Still, millions of people have pensions and a handful of employers still offer them. But just because you may be one of the lucky few to have a pension does not mean you can depend on it when it comes time to retire. The reason is simple – employers have failed to sock away enough money to pay for them.

Be it poor actuarial work (where, once again, actuaries fail to account for life expectancy, etc.) or poor stock market performance (where the underlying investments of the pension do not perform as expected) pensions in the United States do not have enough money in them to make good on all the payments they promised. Estimates vary, but companies in the S&P 500 alone have a cumulative shortfall of $500 billion. However, the private sector is the least of the pension industry's worries as municipal and state pensions are estimated to be underfunded by $5 trillion.

What this means for you is that you cannot rely on the payments (especially if you are a government worker) promised to you by your pension. To this end, your financial planning should assume you will receive only a fraction of your pension benefits and if ever given a buyout option for your pension to take it (assuming the offer is acceptable).

Problem #2 – Social Security and Medicare

Social Security (and to a lesser extent, Medicare) are nothing more than the world's largest pensions. And just like most other pensions they too are underfunded. But by how much depends on who you ask.

Some say neither are underfunded. Others claim they could be underfunded by as much as $220 TRILLION dollars. But saner actuarial figures post Social Security at a $20 trillion deficit and Medicare at a $100 trillion deficit (and even those figures will be hotly contested). Regardless of the veracity of the figures, Social Security and Medicare are indeed underfunded by at least 10's of trillions of dollars and therefore pose the same problem regular pensions do – they are unlikely to deliver on their promises.

To that end you should plan accordingly. Assume you are only going to receive a fraction of what politicians promise you, and truthfully, if you are under 45 you might as well plan on receiving absolutely jack from either of these programs.

Problem #3 – The Retirement Bubble

An important question to ask about the retirement system in the United States is:

"Why Securities?"

Why are stocks, bonds, mutual funds and their derivations considered the official, default investment for everybody's retirement? In the olden days if you wanted to retire you did so either with cash you saved up, selling the farm, or handing your business off to your children for a compensatory cut of the profits. But today everybody is expected to just blindly invest in "stocks and bonds" without considering the side-effects of making them the one and only vehicle for retirement.

Unfortunately, there are side effects, namely a retirement bubble.

Without going into a long and lengthy discussion about finance and economics, a bubble is quite easy to identify because you can always compare three things to determine if there is one:

1. The price of something
2. What you get in return for owning that something
3. What has the ratio between the two historically traded at

For example, consider rental property. Say you bought a duplex for $200,000 and that duplex would rent out for $20,000 a year. By comparing what you paid ($200,000) to what you get ($20,000) you get a ratio:

$200,000/$20,000 = 10

This ratio simply means you paid 10 times the amount of rent that the duplex generates.

However, this concept can be applied to any asset or investment and is officially called the "Price to Earnings Ratio" or "PE" for short. You take the price of an asset, divided it by the earnings that asset generates, and you get a PE ratio. But while you can certainly use it on property, it is more commonly applied to stocks. Stocks are an asset. They generate profits. So to see how "expensive" or "cheap" a stock is you can look at its PE ratio.

Historically, the average US stock (as measured by the S&P 500) has traded at a PE ratio of around 15. Literally translated this means you would pay $15 in stock price to be entitled to $1 in earnings. However, since the advent of 401k style retirement plans (1978), the S&P 500 has traded above its 15 PE average despite (severe) stock market crashes in 1999 and 2007-2009.

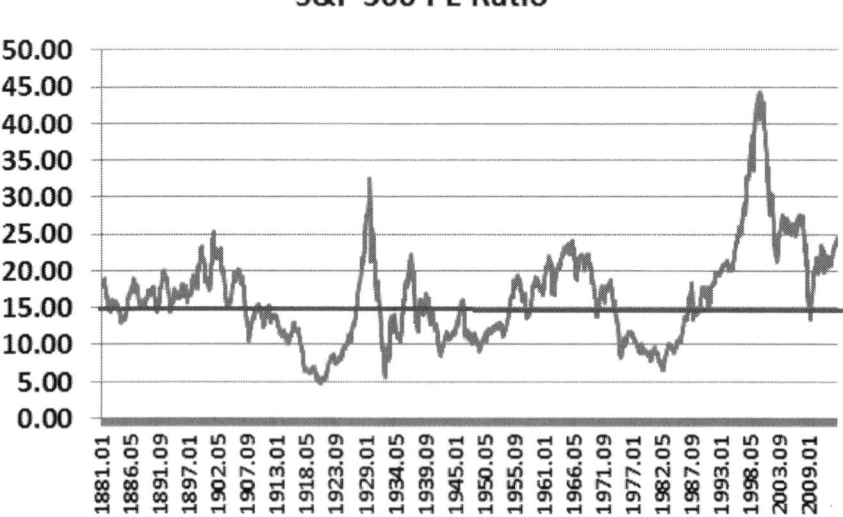

S&P 500 PE Ratio

Only during a brief three month period in the depths of the 2007-2009 crash was the US stock market "fairly" valued. Since then stocks have risen faster than earnings to the point people are paying 62% more for stocks than they historically have. This would be no different than if you were to pay $5 a gallon for gas, $6.84 for a Big Mac, or $651 for the brand new PS4.

However, it gets worse.

Technically, shareholders don't get paid all of the earnings a stock generates as most corporations reinvest some of those profits back into the firm. Whatever profits remain after *that* is paid out to shareholders in the form of a dividend. Since the dividend is technically the only profit a shareholder sees, a more appropriate PE ratio would be the "dividend yield."

The "dividend yield" merely shows what percent rate of return a shareholder receives in the form of dividends. Mathematically, it is the dividend a company pays divided by its current stock price (making it the inverse of a PE ratio, technically an "EP" ratio). Historically, an investor could expect to receive a 5% rate of return on average in the form of dividends. But, once again, since 401k style retirement plans were introduced in 1978, the S&P 500 has traded well below that average, currently only paying a paltry 2.03% dividend yield. Compared to the historical 5% rate of return, this implies stocks are more likely 246% overvalued (just imagine paying $10.33 for a Big Mac).

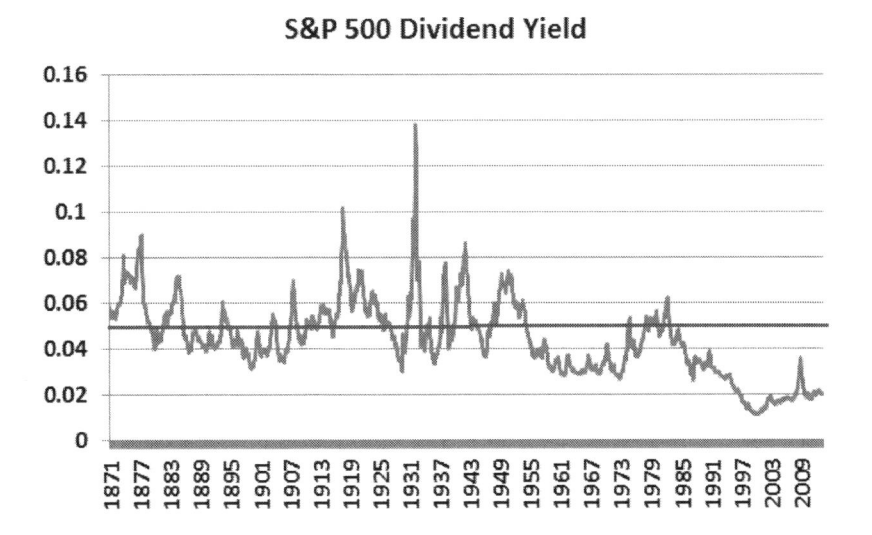

S&P 500 Dividend Yield

The question is what is making the stock market so overvalued? And the answer is retirement programs. Since the advent of 401k's, 403b's, IRA's, etc., TRILLIONS of dollars have flooded the markets that normally would have not otherwise. This has driven the price of stocks up while earnings (and dividends) have remained relatively stagnant.

The problem this poses to you or anybody else wishing to plan for retirement is that you are effectively buying into a bubble. Between the PE ratio and dividend yield, stocks are roughly trading at twice the price they should be. Making matters worse, most of the money that inflated the bubble came from the Baby Boomer generation over the past 20 years – Baby Boomers who are on the verge of retiring. Once they start retiring (or switching from stocks to bonds as they age), they will sell their stocks putting downward pressure on prices, lowering the value of your investments. This isn't to say there aren't good investments out there, or that there aren't reasonably priced stocks, but you will certainly face an uphill battle to find them.

(For additional research into the effects retirement plans have had on stock market valuations, please read the article "When You Abandon Fundamental Value" on Captain Capitalism.)

<u>Problem #4 – Time is Not On Your Side</u>

But before you worry too much about buying into bubbles, you have more pressing matters. Namely, you need money to invest in the market in the first place. And most of the younger generations don't. The reason is in part due to the poor economy, poor labor market, and an aging managerial class that just refuses to retire and free up some jobs. But there is a much larger hurdle preventing younger generations from participating in the retirement system – progressive credentialism.

In the olden days your "timeline" for retirement looked something like this:

```
0      18                              65      78
[------|==============================|########]
Born   Work                           Retire  Death
```

You would go to school until you were 18. Most jobs only required a high school diploma, so you were qualified to immediately go to work. Thankfully, the economy was growing at twice the rate it is now, so your job would pay enough to afford a house and a family on ONE income. Over the next 47 years you would work up enough money to pay for your expenses, plus enough to pay for your retirement. You'd retire at 65 and live the remaining 13 years until your likely death.

Today the time line is completely different.

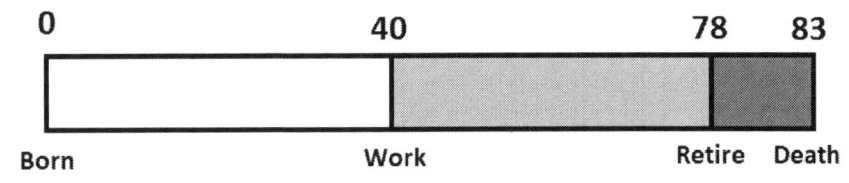

```
0                    40                78     83
[--------------------|==================|######]
Born                 Work              Retire Death
```

Today you have to go to school until you are 25. Not because you weren't qualified to work at the age of 18, but because employers now all demand college degrees. The problem, however, is that everybody has a college degree. So, in addition to your bachelor's degree, you need either a master's degree or two years of additional training and apprenticeship. But, even if you do get a job, you really can't start saving for retirement because you have all those student loans to pay off. Further complicating matters is the economy is now growing at half the pace it was 50 years ago, taxes are twice what they were 50 years ago, and housing costs effectively twice as much as well. And did I forget to mention you can't rely on pensions, Social Security, or Medicare if you're under 45? All these factors, combined with a hefty student debt load, will ensure you can't effectively start saving for retirement until you're 40. This gives you 25 short years to save up for a retirement that (if you live to the improved life-expectancy of 83) is going to last 18 years, which would require a salary of around $100,000 a year. Since this is unlikely, you will unfortunately have to postpone your retirement to about 75 when you might have enough money saved up to enjoy your last five years of life.

In short, because we constantly require more and more education before giving somebody the simplest of jobs, we increase the incubation time of labor to nearly a quarter century. This shrinks the amount of time people have to work and save for retirement from 47 years to just 25. However, further albatrossing our younger generations, we saddle them with crippling levels of student debt, which when combined with a poor economy and poor job prospects, means men today cannot really save for retirement until they're already half dead. The only solution is one where people are forced to work well past the traditional age of 65, and suffer a much shorter retirement as a consequence.

Problem #5 – Confiscation

The US national debt currently stands at $17 trillion (and is certainly higher as you are reading this now). It is so large that it is a guarantee we will suffer economic consequences sometime in the future. Maybe not today. Maybe not tomorrow. But one day, the country will suffer the costs of this debt.

In the meantime, politicians will do whatever they can to postpone this inevitable suffering in a bid to stay in power. They will borrow money from the Chinese. They will inflate the currency by having the Federal Reserve buy US bonds. They'll do anything to avoid forcing the American public to pay the full price of what we've promised ourselves. The problem they face, however, is they are running out of money, and are therefore becoming more desperate to find new sources of revenue.

So desperate they are starting to eye your nice little 401k over there.

Estimates vary but Americans have roughly $8 trillion sitting in their IRA's, 401k's, 403b's and private pensions. That $8 trillion is too tempting for your typical amoral, corrupt politician to care if it's yours or how hard you worked for it. He needs to bribe his constituency with Obama phones, free day care, WIC, and EBT so they will vote for him. And it's more important he or she stay in power than you have enough money to retire.

Naturally, this seems incredibly cynical, even conspiratorial. What country would raid the retirement accounts of their citizens?

For starters try:

Argentina
Poland
Hungary
Greece

And if you want to see a really audacious move, look at Cyprus where the government just decided to steal 45% of all bank deposits. It's happened before, it's currently happening in Europe, and it can certainly happen here.

Of course, the modern day psychologies of most Americans are,

"Well this is America! We're Americans! It can't happen here!"

Oh really?

http://online.wsj.com/news/articles/SB122662401729126813
http://www.wnd.com/2012/11/now-obama-wants-your-401k/

While nothing overt has been stated, there is enough political chatter to know that confiscating the retirement plans of Americans is definitely on the minds of our politicians. Combine this with the sheer mathematical reality of our debt, and the "nationalization" of your retirement plan is a very real and serious threat. A threat you should take seriously and make contingency plans for.

"Plan B"

Considering the problems plaguing the current retirement system, you need to come up with a "Plan B." And while I'd like to say the alternatives are just as good as your options under the traditional system, they aren't. However, these alternatives do have one key advantage over the currently broken retirement system – they're based in reality and will work. Ideal as it would be to retire early at 55 on a government pension, with full benefits of Medicare and Social Security, it just isn't mathematically feasible. It's a day dream. It actuarially impossible. Thus, it is better to have a plan that doesn't sound as good, but is realistic, than a plan that sounds great, but will never work.

Work Till You're Dead – While work for the most part sucks, what a lot of people find out upon retiring is that "not working" sucks even more. This is why you have a lot of retirees return to the labor market. Not for money, but for engagement, intellectual stimulation, and the sense of having purpose or agency.

This is actually a win-win for most people in that, even if it's a part-time job, the extra money goes a long way in bolstering your retirement finances. It also pays great dividends in terms of psychological and social benefits. Yes, many people genuinely loathe working and are perfectly happy staying at home, never to work again. But the majority of people, especially after being psychologically conditioned for 70 years to engage others, will need to participate in some kind of productive activity. A part-time job fits the bill perfectly and serves as a steroid to your retirement finances.

Spending Control is the New Investing – While the focus of retirement planning has been to "save" or "invest" enough, very little attention is paid to spending. And while both have equal importance in retirement planning, spending has one HUGE advantage over investing:

Your spending is 100% under your control.

If I invest in a stock, bond, or mutual fund I am rolling the dice and throwing my investment to fate. It could quadruple in value, or I could lose it all, but that is entirely up to factors outside my control. However, I do control, with 100% certainty, whether I buy that car, purchase that new video game, or take that flight to Phoenix.

This is important because with the stock market being inflated with previous generations' retirement dollars, you are unlikely to realize the required rate of return needed to make traditional retirement programs work. Combine this overvaluation with slowing economic growth and a stock market that has yet to recoup from its 2007 high (adjusting for inflation), the potential for an adequate rate of return just isn't there to make 401k's and IRA's viable. Therefore, since the potential for investment returns is limited, it puts the onus of retirement planning on spending.

Thankfully, this is where a minimalist lifestyle comes in handy. Not that you would be living in a van down by the river, but you would refuse to purchase luxury items, rent or buy more housing than you need, splurge on a worthless degree, or any one of the many mistakes that can impair your finances. At first it may seem such cheap living is a "lower" standard of living. But remember that the only thing that matters in life is other humans. Not material wealth.

Keep Your Retirement Amounts Low – While at this point in time it is speculation your retirement plans would be confiscated, because of the leftist nature of American politics, it is likely if they do decide to nationalize people's retirement plans they will (like Cyprus did) spare poorer people and target richer people. Therefore, if you keep the balances in your retirement accounts relatively low, you will likely avoid having the majority of your funds stolen. Of course, the government could just nationalize all the retirement plans outright (like Argentina), but if the partial nationalizations of Europe are any indication, it is unlikely the US would do something so extreme.

Fully Avail Yourself of Matching – About the only glimmering hope in the entire retirement system is when a company decides to match your contributions to a 401k, 403b, or 457 plan. This is essentially free money that immediately doubles your investment. Even with the risk of confiscation or the 10% early withdrawal penalty, it pays to make the full contribution to the limit that your employer will match.

Overseas – If you have considerable assets, it may pay to look into diversifying outside of the US. Not in terms of investing in foreign stocks, but setting up foreign bank and brokerage accounts. If the US government gets into the confiscatory mood, your entire life's work and life's savings could be stolen. Additionally, it is always good to have multiple accounts in multiple countries in case things become so politically hostile here you need to move for your safety. Understand, however, you would not be using overseas accounts to avoid taxation. You will still be responsible to pay for any taxes on income or interest from these accounts while in the US. This is merely a move to protect your assets from being stolen.

Silver/Gold/Booze/Guns/Bullets – Regardless of whether your 401k is confiscated or not, EVERYBODY should have a certain amount of gold, silver, or other precious metals on hand. This is just a simple insurance move in case the economy collapses, as well as a good hedge against an inflating currency. However, the key is to ensure you physically hold these investments. If the economy does collapse or the currency does hyper-inflate, it won't do you any good having gold ETF's or silver mutual funds in your brokerage account. The government can merely confiscate your investments from the brokerage as they are merely electronic records. Additionally, if the economy REALLY collapses, good luck redeeming your paper ETF for the gold it entitles you to in a mine over in China. As the saying goes,

"If don't hold it, you don't own it."

I also strongly recommend having a small gun collection consisting of a pistol, shotgun, hunting rifle, and semi-auto rifle with a commensurate amount of bullets. Guns and bullets not only maintain their value much like gold or silver, but they can also serve to protect your family and your home in case of emergency.

The Smith and Wesson Retirement Plan – Depending on which source you cite, roughly 80% of your health expenses are consumed in the last six months of your life. Additionally, while in your terminally ill days, you will consume a plurality of your retirement savings, not to mention a plurality of taxpayer's money through various government programs. These expenses are, bluntly, the primary reason for all western nations' financial problems as the majority of people consume way more in end-of-life expenses than what they paid into the system.

But imagine if you didn't have these expenses.

Not only would it make planning for retirement infinitely easier, but it would save the taxpayer and future generations trillions of dollars. It would even make the US economy viable again. All it takes is 35 cents.

How does 35 cents save millions of dollars?

Simple. It buys a .45 caliber bullet that you can permanently retire yourself with.

At first, people are abhorred I would dare suggest such a thing. But you need to take emotion out of it and replace it with logical and mathematical thought.

What is life about? Slaving away when you're young for decades to build up enough money that will hopefully pay for six painful, lousy, drugged up months? Or is it meant to be lived to its limits, enjoyed while it can be, and then when your time comes, you don't fight it, but go peacefully and with dignity?

What many people fail to realize is just how much of their enjoyable youth they sacrifice to pay for lousy and pain-filled old age. When you're young your wage is likely very low. But when you're old an hour of hospice care or nursing home care can easily run into the hundreds of dollars. You are merely exchanging hundreds of hours of enjoyable youth for 30 minutes of miserable old age. This exchange is, frankly, stupid.

This doesn't mean you buy a gun and off yourself at the first sign of cancer, but that you do consider euthanasia as a legitimate means to severely lessen the amount you need for retirement. Not only will it free up a considerable amount of your youth, as well as lessen the pain you'll endure in old age, but it will also lessen the financial burden you place on the taxpayer and future generations.

A Miscellany of Advice

No Children Make Retirement Easier – Children cost around $250,000 each. That's enough dough that your life and retirement planning is a lot easier without them.

Government Work & Early Retirement – Though public sector pensions are most at threat for being cut, consider working for the government anyway. The benefits are much better than the private sector, plus you can (usually) retire at 55 instead of most normal, productive adults who have to work till they're 65.

Can I Have Both an IRA and 401k? – Yes

Currency/Options/Day Trading – There is a lot of press about "day traders" or "options trading" which is a natural follow up to stocks and bonds. However, for the most part, options trading or day trading is not for the average person. This isn't to say you can't do it, or that it doesn't make for a fun hobby. But if you do decide to do it, ensure you take several classes before you do.

Investopedia – Investopedia is a great web site that not only serves as the best encyclopedia for every type of finance or investing term out there, but also offers people a free online trading simulator. I strongly recommend using their simulator to get an idea what it's like to trade stocks before putting actual money down on a real brokerage account.

"Stocks, Bonds, Investing: Oh My!" – It is impossible to address every aspect of financial planning and the investing world in one chapter. And while this chapter does a decent job in addressing the basics, it does not delve into the necessary detail to get you to the point you can start taking action. If you are that interested in investing, however, I strongly recommend taking my online class "Stocks, Bonds, Investing: Oh My!" It is an introductory investing class offered through many different community colleges and community education programs online. Go to www.ed2go.com and search for the title to find a class near you.

"The Analysis and Valuation of Stocks" – If you are interested in investing in stocks, I strongly recommend my other class, "The Analysis and Valuation of Stocks." This will not only teach you how to research and invest in stocks, but give you a great lesson in basic accounting and financial statement analysis. I would almost argue that skill is more valuable than knowing how to invest in stocks itself. You can also find it by searching for it at www.ed2go.com.

"Enjoy the Decline" – While briefly addressed in this chapter, there is much more to the underlying fundamentals of the US economy that will affect your retirement planning and investing. And though not necessary to start planning for retirement, it is good to have a more in-depth understanding of these fundamentals in that it will provide you additional vision and perspective. To that end I recommend reading "Enjoy the Decline," specifically chapter two which goes into great detail about the current economy and how it affects society today. You can find it on Amazon.com.

CHAPTER 12
WIFE AND KIDS

Notice this chapter, "Wife and Kids," comes after:

Philosophy
The Basics
Education
Career
Girls
Entrepreneurship
Housing and Lodging
Maintenance and Repair, and
Investing and Retirement Planning

That wasn't done by accident or happenstance. It was done on purpose and it should be the same way in your life.

Not until you have gone to school, dated a ton of girls, found gainful employment, established yourself a career, and started saving for retirement, should you even consider starting a family. The reason is that until you achieve these things in life you are not capable, nor prepared, to get married and raise children. You will either yearn to date other women, never have the money to adequately provide for your family, or you just plain won't have enough time to spend with your wife and kids. Raising a family is going to be the single largest responsibility in your life and you need to make damn sure you can do it effectively and do it right.

However, there are three much more important reasons why you need to have your shit together before starting a family. First, you have an obligation to society. Realize and understand that the vast majority of problems plaguing society today are due to failed families. Single parent homes, divorced parents, absentee parents, or just plain dysfunctional (i.e.-abusive) families breed children who are prone to crime, drugs, poverty, dependency, welfare, depression, suicide and a whole host of other social ills. If you fail to raise good children, you are sending damaging and dysfunctional people into society.

Second, if you have children, you have now brought an innocent human being into this world. This human, though separate from you, has the exact same capacity for emotions, feelings, dreams, and sentience that you do. However, just like you, he or she didn't have a say as to whether they were brought into this world. You brought them into this world. That makes you 100%, completely responsible for their upbringing. Sadly, however, all too often children are viewed as a physical purchase, like a nice armoire. They are dumped in daycare, treated as a disposable pet instead of a human, and forced to suffer an insufferable childhood. To prevent this you need not only the time and money to raise your children, but the altruism and selflessness to put them ahead of your own life. Otherwise you will be responsible for the ruination of an innocent human life. This will haunt you for the rest of your days, and you will never be able to forgive yourself for it.

Finally, since humans are the most important thing in the world, and your wife and kids the most important humans in your life, that makes them the single greatest potential source for happiness...

as well as the single greatest potential source for misery and pain.

I have seen men with a permanent glowing smile on their face, knowing that behind that smile is a hot wife with interesting, intriguing, and curious children. I have seen men walk through life like a zombie – lifeless, indifferent, and depressed – knowing behind their lethargy there's an overweight wife at home who nags him, berates him, and does not obey. And then I've seen men completely incapacitated. These men lost their wives, lost their children, and suffer a constant and unending emotional pain akin to being burned alive, but without the merciful benefit of death. Some end their misery through suicide, others limp through life impaired, crippled, and dysfunctional, all because they failed to raise a good family. In short, there is just too damn much riding on a family for you to botch it up, because if you do, it is a guarantee it will destroy you.

Ergo, take this chapter very seriously and do not fuck it up.

Before You Commit

A simple solution to the risks and threats failed marriages and failed families present is simply to avoid them altogether. Remain a perpetual bachelor or "MGTOW" (Men Going Their Own Way). There's nothing wrong with this lifestyle and, frankly, it's quite enjoyable. You have no financial obligations to raise children, you have no wife nagging you when you get home, all of your money is yours, and 100% of your free time can be spent however you'd like. In short, the childless bachelor (or bachelorette) lifestyle is the freest life there is.

However, while most people view such freedom from the perspective of a beleaguered, hen-picked husband a la

"Wow, it must be great being able to go play poker and get drunk whenever you want!"

there are significant and very unappreciated benefits of this maximum level of freedom.

First, there is no cheaper unit to field in the world of humans than a bachelor. Whereas most bachelorettes require a:

- Fully furnished luxury apartment,
- High end VW,
- "Flirtini's" and sushi every night,
- Prada hand bags,
- Premium cable subscription to the Hallmark Channel,
- Jimmy Choo shoes,
- King sized bed,
- Thrice weekly therapy sessions,
- Monthly spa treatments,
- Pedicures,
- Manicures,
- 900 cubic feet of clothing,
- A tea cup dog, and
- 40 gallons of creams and lotions,

a bachelor needs:
- A place to sleep and shit
- A car for transportation

This not only makes for cheap living, but puts the average bachelor in the enviable position of "not needing the money." He can bluff for higher pay, and if he doesn't get it, he walks. He doesn't have to tolerate an abusive boss because he has no mortgage, wife, or children to behold him to the job. And while his married counterpart is knocking out 60 hours a week, he knocks out 20 at his part-time job, while spending another 20 working on his book, business idea, or pilot's license. The bachelor is his own man and like Steve McQueen he answers to no one.

This leads to the second, often under-appreciated, benefit of bachelorhood – the freedom to pursue your own interests. A bachelor not only enjoys a stress-free career and stress-free finances, but has the free time to start a business, travel, and explore the world. He has the money to live life and take risks. Thus, while his married-man counterpart is slaving away as an accountant to pay for wifey's SUV, the mortgage, and diapers, all while subserviently taking abuse from his boss, the bachelor is biking across Europe, motorcycling out to Alaska, tangoing in Argentina, hiking the Grand Canyon, composing a new jazz piece, and writing a best-selling book about it all.

In short, being a bachelor allows you to avail yourself of your one and only life. In choosing not to follow the crowd and saddle yourself with a wife and kids, you are allowed to treat the planet as your own personal playground, full of limitless adventure and potential. This not only guarantees your life will be infinitely more enjoyable and interesting than the conformists, but it is the conduit to the third, and largest, benefit of bachelorhood – greatness.

If you look at "The World's Most Interesting Man" he did not achieve his greatness by doing what he was told or following the crowd. He set off on his own and did his own thing. In doing so he not only led a much more interesting life (because he is, after all, The World's *Most Interesting* Man), but exceled and achieved greatness in several fields. Some of these achievements were physical feats (climbing mountains, swimming across oceans), others were financial (though it is a secret as to how he affords his lifestyle). But what is really interesting about greatness is how accidental it is. If you look at most "successful" people it was largely by accident they came across their fortunes and success. Edison was not as much a money-hungry capitalist as he was a tinkerer. Steve Jobs was not a multi-billion dollar CEO as much as he was an IT geek eccentric. And Richard Branson is first and foremost an adventurer whose interests just so happened to make him billions of dollars on the side. The larger point is you will never achieve greatness in any field if you are just like everybody else – anchored to a job, a mortgage, a spend-happy wife, and money-burning children. You need to set off on your own unique path and achieve greatness in your own right. This doesn't mean you can't at some point in your life have a wife and children, but once you do, realize any potential to achieve your individualist dreams are severely impaired.

Finally, there is one final reason you may want to consider committing to the bachelor lifestyle: the quality and caliber of today's modern women is, to be blunt, atrociously poor. Corrupted by societal viruses like feminism, socialism, and a whore-worshiping media, women have become overweight, unattractive, narcissistic, unfeminine wrecks that no self-respecting man would ever commit to. Even if they do manage to maintain their physique, they are usually so mentally damaged it renders commitment impossible (and currently 25% of American women are on some kind of mood-altering drug). Combine this spoiled crop of women with their propensity to divorce, unfavorable divorce laws towards men, not to mention the damage you would be causing any would-be children brought into this world, marriage in most instances is simply not worth the risk.

Drawbacks of Bachelorhood

There is, however, a problem.

While the bachelor lifestyle may seem like a slam dunk decision, unfortunately society does not operate that way. And while living your dreams, gallivanting across the world, and going on worldwide adventures in your 20's seems great, there are four major factors outside of your control that can make married life preferable to swinging bachelorhood:

Attrition
Peerlessness
Reject Society and
Nature

Attrition

When you're a bachelor, friends are your family. It's just you and the guys kicking ass, taking names, living a life of drinking, playing video games, and chasing skirts. You'll go through thick, you'll go through thin, you'll enjoy highs, and you'll suffer lows, and though girls will come and go, your friends will always be there for you. Because of this, you will develop a fierce loyalty to them and think that they will be around forever. You'll view them as your surrogate family, and because of all you've endured together you'll be supremely confident nothing will break up the ole gang. You'll start to like the idea of working hard during the day, and knocking about with the guys at night, and you'll see yourself doing this till the day you die.

Then "she" walks in.

Your best friend who was your best drinking buddy, mentions a girl he just met. All of a sudden he starts talking dopey, frilly, girly shit. Crap about "love" and "feelings" and "family." You try beating it out of him with a full fifth of Jack Daniels. Then you try to talk some sense into the guy by going nightclubbing, hitting the strip clubs, and ending it with an all-night campaign session of MW3. Still, nothing gets through to him. He's in love and before you know it he's spending more time with "her" than he is with the guys.

You lean over to your other buddy to talk about the condition of your traitorous friend, only to find out he's making eyes with some drink of water he brought to the poker party. Wait a minute! What's this broad doing at the poker party?! You stand up to protest!

"HEY! What's a girl doing here at the poker party!!!! There ain't supposed to be no dames here! It's guy's night!!!"

But he explains in a wimpish tone, *"Come on guys, she's alriiiiiiight. Just this onnnnnnce. Let her stay, pleeeeease???"*

Then you realize it isn't just a coincidence. All the guys are getting googly eyes for some girl or another. Before you know it you're in the Battle of Britain and all of your buddies are getting picked off like German Messerschmitts. You dive, you roll, you provide cover, but it's no use. The squadron is breaking up due to the ill-fates of marriage.

The larger point is simply this – as fun as the swinging bachelor life is, it is heavily dependent on a critical mass of other bachelors being present. This (for better or worse) is a temporary situation as most men are programmed to want to get married and have kids and will soon leave "the squadron." This puts a true "life-long bachelor" in a situation where his social network is constantly suffering from attrition, requiring he continually replenish his social circles. But it doesn't get any easier as you age. Because most bachelors are in their 20's, the longer you remain unmarried, the less you'll have in common with the likely incoming replacements. Soon you're not 23 years old anymore, doing shots, staying out till 3AM with a score of guys, but a 43 year old trying to pry your friend from the clutches of his wife so you two can simply get "a" beer on Tuesday.

In other words, your surrogate family is a fleeting condition that will not last much past the age of 30. After that, having the social network of equally free and unattached bachelors (and bachelorettes) becomes increasingly difficult and most of your "free nights" are spent alone. It is the price you pay for being unique and may drive you to consider marriage yourself.

Peerlessness

Along the same lines is peerlessness.

Let's say you buck the marriage trend either out of choice or necessity. You don't have the money to get married. You can't hold down a job. Or you just plain aren't done playing anymore. You like being single, you enjoy having your free time to yourself, and you are not done exploring this planet yet.

So off you go on your adventures. You climb many mountains, you visit many countries, you sleep with many women, you start several companies, and you master a lot of hobbies. In doing so (intentionally or not), you surpass your contemporaries in interestingness and skills. Soon, your life is envied by all, and when you go to a party you are the center of attention as the words and stories coming out of your mouth are more engaging and intriguing than anyone else's. You grab the hottest girl in the club and salsa dance, returning to the table that is now flabbergasted as you failed to mention you were a competition ballroom dancer. More questions are asked, the entirety of focus is on you, and you soon realize with girls leaning into you, hanging on every word coming out of your mouth, you are the real world incarnation of "The World's Most Interesting Man."

So what do you do the next day?

Nothing. You sit and do nothing.

The reason why is that while 12 hours ago you were the life of the party and you genuinely were the most interesting person there, 99.9% of the people in attendance were normal people with normal lives. They had to go home and relieve the baby sitter. They had to wake up the next day to go to work. They couldn't afford the next drink because they have kids they can barely afford. And so while it was nice to sleep in till 10AM, log into your online accounts to see how much money you made, in the end you are alone. Who do you talk to? Who do you discuss your adventures with? No one, because there is nobody that can compare to you let alone relate to you.

This then sets off a wicked spiral for the adventuresome bachelor. Since there is no human you can relate to or talk to, you decide to pick up another hobby or go on another adventure to keep your mind engaged. You climbed that 13,000 foot peak, why not a 15,000 foot peak? You bought yourself a motorcycle, why not build a chopper from scratch? You're OK at playing tenor sax, but you dedicate yourself for three hours a day to improve to the point you can join the open jam session at the local jazz club. You get a fix, or least a reprieve from having your mind sit and atrophy, and in doing so become an even *more* "Most Interesting Man in the World." But what you don't realize is in becoming "more interesting" you are now even further removed from the average person. You have less in common with them, have less patience for them, and you find their observations elementary and boring. This drives you to find new intellectual and physical adventures – auto racing, UFC fighting, getting a doctorate, something to give you that mental fix you need...which only perpetuates the cycle and removes you from humanity even further.

In the end, yes, you are an incredibly interesting person. And yes, you are the epitome of peerless. But you are so unique, such a statistical anomaly, you are also...

a freak.

Albeit a very accomplished and interesting freak, but a freak nonetheless.

What you'll soon discover is that, yes, while your life was much more interesting than most, it is so extreme, there is nobody who can keep up with you. You can't find anybody to go mountain climbing with because they are not in as good of shape as you. You can't find anybody to take a motorcycle ride to Alaska with you, because they have not the time, nor the money. And you can't find anybody to lift weights with because they're already too exhausted from work. You have unintentionally alienated yourself from society through excellence and in doing so are lonely.

Like any other drug-addict, it isn't until you hit bottom will you realize what is truly important in life. But when you do, either placing first in an autocross, making your "next $10 million," or renovating your fourth hotrod, and that fix doesn't do it anymore, you'll realize it is other humans that are the most important thing in life. And at that point you may entertain marriage as a viable option.

Reject Society

If the loneliness that comes from attrition or peerlessness doesn't convince you, a quick peek at the singles scene for 40-60 year olds will send you SCREAMING into the arms of marriage. Because despite all the media touting "cougars" and "50 being the new 30," the truth is most 40+ single people are the rejects of society. And you only have to attend two different types of events to see proof of this – single "Meetup" groups and ballroom dance clubs.

Understand marriage really is a market. A game of "musical chairs" if you will. And the people left "unpurchased" or "left standing" are at the bottom of the barrel. Desperate single 50 year old men, who live in their mother's basement, using ballroom dancing to compensate for their utter lack of charm or ability to speak to women. Christian singles groups, full of 47 year old librarian women who are "saving themselves for Jesus," but never thought to hit the treadmill, shave down below, or learn to fellate. Both groups sport their best clothes from the 80's in a vain hope to recapture their youth, and if they were to breed you wonder if the result wouldn't be *devolution*.

This isn't to say there aren't cool or attractive 45 year olds. This isn't to say you can't find a normal 50 year old woman that would make for a good wife. But it is to say good, quality marriage candidates not only get picked off early, but stay married never to return to the dating market again. i.e. – most single women 35 or older are rejects in one way or another and have some kind of deal-breaking damage. Ergo, if you want to score a keeper you can't wait until you're 47, looking to land a virginesque 26 year old computer programmer. Your options are going to be more along the lines of a 37 year old single mom with two divorces and a stripping career under her belt.

Nature

Arguably, the single most damaging thing feminism and feminists have done to women is lie to them about their nature and their biology. In short, feminism tells women they do not need men. And not only do they not need men, but they are weak and not true women if they dare to desire a husband or be a stay-at-home mom.

The consequences have been horrible.

The lives of nearly two generations of women have been ruined as they abandoned their genetic programming and instead pursued what they were told by a political movement. They dumped their children at day care centers while they pursued careers they were none-to-good at. They subordinated their husbands to those same careers, not to mention the state and government checks. And in failing to put their families first, they have caused an epidemic of divorce that has spanned and damaged three generations of child-victims.

Do not make the same mistake. Do not deny your nature.

Just like women, *most* men also have a natural desire to get married and have children. And though men receive nowhere near the propaganda women do to avoid marriage, there still is a fair amount of media that portrays the bachelor lifestyle as preferable. Patrick Harris in "How I Met Your Mother," Charlie Sheen in "Two and a Half Men," or George Clooney in...well...just being George Clooney, it is always the cool swinging bachelor that seems to have all the fun and get all the girls, while the reliable, nerdy married square gets shafted, begging his battle-ax for permission to have a night out with the guys. However, this is not the real world, this is Hollywood. This isn't to say being a bachelor can't be fun (George Clooney will testify to this) or that being married can't be hell (just ask my dad), but it is to say not to let a Hollywood-made parody override your genetic desire to get married and have children. If you do, you will deprive yourself of one of (if not "the") greatest joy in life and suffer just like women who swallowed feminism whole.

(For a perfect example of believing a sitcom is the real world and then making a real-life decision on it, research all the women who moved to New York because of the show "Sex in the City.")

Wife

Fun as it is to date and nail a lot of chicks, even the best players will suffer from "player burnout." The reason is simple – dating sucks. While at first it's great, going out, flirting with girls, getting them drunk, and cajoling them to go back home with you, the novelty wears off after a couple decades because most women are a royal pain in the ass. The drama, the mind games, the crying, the lying, the scheming, the painfully idiotic conversations, and all the other bullshit, not to mention the time and monetary expense it takes to pursue them, will wear down the lothariest of Lotharios. Soon you'll be 32, sitting there on a Friday night with the option to go out to yet another night club, and will instead choose to watch Fire Fly or go grab a beer with a buddy. If that's the case, it's about time to start thinking about potentially contemplating looking into the possibility of studying the feasibility of theoretically getting a wife.

Of course, some men will be fortunate enough to have met a girl during their dating days that just compels them to propose. But unless you are one of those lucky few, you will have to start screening for wife material and not another piece of meat to take home for the night. And if you thought getting a girl to sleep with you was difficult, just wait till you try to find a girl that's tolerable enough to spend the rest of your life with.

Wife Selection

There are no universal rules or laws on how to go about choosing a wife. You'll wake up one day and "you'll know." However, even with this industry-standard advice, 50% of marriages still end in divorce. Therefore, it behooves the prospective husband to be very discerning when selecting a wife to make sure he does it right the first time, ensuring there isn't a second, third, or fourth time.

The first step is to make sure you choose your wife and that she does not choose you. Specifically, you want to avoid women who trick men into marriage. Though incredulous, there are MILLIONS of women out there who have no problem tricking men into marrying them. They do this usually by getting a man to impregnate them and then force him to "do the right thing" by marrying them. This means anything from poking holes in condoms, lying about being on the pill, or even getting impregnated by somebody else (or in vitro fertilization) and then claiming the child is his. Obviously such deceitful women make poor wives, so you'll want to avoid a life of misery with them by guarding your sperm like Fort Knox. Use your own condoms, flush the used condoms down the toilet (women have fished used condoms out of the trash to then inseminate themselves), or consider getting a vasectomy.

Once you avoid that veritable marriage-trap, you can further refine your search, but understand the impossible task you're about to take on. The vast majority of American women are absolutely abysmal when it comes to marriage material. I've dated well over 300 girls in my life and no more than THREE, 1 in 100, could have been considered "wife material." The reason I point this out is because it is a guarantee as you date scores of women you will start to think you're having incredibly bad luck. You'll constantly self-analyze yourself, trying to find out what you're doing wrong and why you're attracting such batshit insane women. You'll get so desperate you'll even consult your mother and without fail she will say,

"Well, maybe **you** just attract the wrong type of women."

Or

"Well, **you** must be looking in the wrong places."

But the reality is you're doing it absolutely right. It's just that nearly all women (especially in their teens and 20's) are worth nothing more than a sexual fling, if that even.

This is not to slam on women or be misogynistic, but to candidly warn men about the statistical REALITY they are going to face. It is also to protect your sanity and psychological health as millions of men have spent billions of hours worrying there was something wrong with them, and worse, tried changing themselves when they weren't the problem. You aren't the problem – the women are. However, realize because nearly 99% of women are not qualified to be wives, that makes the 1% of women who are all that more precious and why you should genuinely appreciate your wife when you are fortunate enough to discover her.

The final thing you have to do is prepare and commit yourself to the search. You are going to have to kiss a lot of frogs before finding your wife. This not only means having to go out or pick up a social skill like ballroom dancing, but spending a significant amount of time on dating sites, approaching women in public, and statistically increasing your chances of finding that 1 in 100. It will almost feel like a part-time job, and the 99 out of 100 women will make sure it does, but it will be worth it if you're lucky enough to score that 1%.

Beyond the psychological fortitude and commitment you're going to need to find a wife, there is no general strategy or approach to take. It will depend on you, your preferences, your guile, your environment, and luck. But there are some key red flags or "do's and don'ts" that will help expedite your search, not to mention help screen out all the unqualified candidates.

Divorced/Single Mom – If the girl has been married before or already has another man's kid, it's a good bet she is not "the one." She's already been somebody else's "the one" and if she has a kid you are, once again, default-ranked 2nd in her life. Remember, this is your one life. You deserve your very own wife, not a time share. The only instance you should consider a woman with kids is if she is a widow. The hierarchy is:

Never married, no kids
Widow, no kids
Widow, kids
Divorced, no kids
Divorced, kids
Divorced, multiple kids
Divorced, multiple kids from multiple fathers
Never married, multiple kids, multiple fathers

Insist on never married with no kids, with the widow clause as an exception.

Tattoos/Piercings – While I have had many fun times with tatted and pierced up women, none of them were marriage material. This doesn't mean you can't find a girl with a discrete tattoo, hidden away somewhere that wouldn't make a good wife. But if she looks like she's on a roller-derby team you should pass. Usually when women have an excessive number of tattoos, piercings or other forms of body mutilation they have underlying psychological problems. Psychological problems that aren't yours.

Born Again/Newly Religious Women – There is absolutely nothing wrong with marrying a religious girl. Truth be told, they probably make better wives. But you do want to avoid, with all your might, the "born again Christian" or a newly religious woman.

Like felons, most women who all of the sudden "find Jesus," do so because there was a crisis or problem in their lives that was 100% their own fault. An illegitimate child, bankruptcy due to spending, injuring somebody while drunk driving, etc. However, they are such intellectual weaklings and their egos so fragile, they cannot accept responsibility for their failures. This is where religion makes the perfect scapegoat.

No matter how atrocious their actions, some guy in a cloud "forgives them of all their sins." No matter how evil they were, "Jesus loves her no matter what." And the most disgusting and dishonest aspect of religion they cling onto is fate, abdicating them of any responsibility of their horrific mistakes because, "the lord has a plan." But what makes born again women particularly vile is they have no problem sanctimoniously "lording" their religion over you in an effort to seem more righteous or moral, when deep down inside they are merely abusing the religion to manipulate and control you.

Do not have anything to do with born-again girls. They are the textbook definition of psychotic.

Worthless Degrees – Most girls major in stupid shit. This would be fine if college didn't cost anything, but it does. This more often than not means ~~some sucker~~ the engineering-majoring husband gets to bail his wife out of her Master's in Chicano Studies. But worse, even though the degree was complete fluff, complete bunk, and could be completed by a 3rd grader, the degree gives the girl an underserved superiority complex. They will view themselves as intelligent, perhaps even superior, when they are anything but. You don't need twice the student debt, and certainly not any of the attitude. Find a nice IT girl, an accountant, or a mechanic.

Incapable of Orgasm – A blaring red light is a woman that cannot achieve orgasm. The reason could be any one of a million underlying psychological issues, but it basically boils down to one thing – she is incapable of enjoying sex. This not only is going to make your sex life less than what it should be, it is a guarantee you'll be dealing with psychological issues that aren't yours.

Views Lingerie as "Degrading" – The most psychologically healthy and enjoyable women I've dated LOVED being women and consequently LOVED lingerie. Some of them just wore it because they liked being feminine and wanted to lounge around in it. Others, however, found it degrading and insulting if I dared suggest they doll themselves up in it. Invariably, I would receive some lecture about feminism, and how she wasn't an object, blah, blah, blah. And invariably I would never call them back. Regardless, women who don't like lingerie don't like being women. And since it is a woman you want to marry, lingerie is a great test to see if that is the case.

No Blow Jobs – 95% of the fun of sex is variety and doing wild ass crazy shit. But you cannot get to the "wild ass crazy shit" stage if your wife refuses to give you a blow job, or uses it as a rare currency to extract favors from you. If this is the case, not only is your sex life going to suck (or not suck, actually), she usually has some underlying issues with intimacy and control that will plague your marriage. Before you get on your knee, she better get on hers.

Weddings/Rings – You will want to attend at least one extravagant wedding with a potential wife-candidate to see her reaction to the blatant and egregious waste of money. Ideally, without prompting, she'll point out just what a waste of money it is and then say something about a "small wedding" or "eloping." Bonus points if she talks about how stupid diamond rings are. This means she is not only financially astute, but knows what's important in life – other people (namely her theoretical husband). If your wife-candidate pines wistfully about "her day" or "destination weddings" and obsesses over the party favors, she is no longer a candidate.

Liberal, Leftist, or Feminist Women – Nearly all young girls upon graduating from high school, will swallow the brainwashing they received and claim to be "feminists, "leftists," or "liberals." The truth is they are too ignorant to know what they truly are, and it only takes a few dates to find out they're really conservatives or libertarians underneath. So just because they "say" they're a "feminist" or a "liberal," chances are they're anything but. It's up to you to convince them of their true convictions.

However, if they are a genuine liberal, leftist, or feminist, they are antithetical to being wives because, consciously or not, they vote to replace men with the state. Like nuns to the church, they are first and foremost wedded to the state and not you. Therefore, any self-respecting man will simply refuse to marry, let alone, support somebody who actively votes against him, his success, and his liberty.

Hyphenated Names – Along the same lines, if a woman insists on hyphenating her name, you run the other direction. Do not stop at "Go." Do not collect rent. Matter of fact, one of the first questions you should ask when courting a girl is what she thinks about hyphenated names. It will save you a lot of time and money.

Where's the Father? – I was about 25 at the time and things had gotten so bad I was about to insist on meeting a girl's father before taking her out on a date. The reason was simple – the girls that had the most problems either hated their dad or he wasn't involved in their lives. You want to find a girl whose dad is around and she is on good terms with. The best women I've dated were those with reliable and loving fathers in their lives.

Good Front Game – Women have an AMAZING ability to act like somebody they're not for long periods of time. This is called "front game" and women will run this game to either hide major flaws or their true personality in order to lull the guy into proposing. Because of this you will want to court for a LOOOOOONG time, and not just a long time, but cohabitate as well. Inevitably she will break and her true demeanor will shine through. *That* is the true woman you will be marrying, not the Oscar winning performance she put on for the five years previous.

Cats – Red flag. Don't care how much she claims "he's just like a dog." Red flag.

Support or Nag – All women nag. It is a darwinistic skill they've developed over the years to cope with men who are stronger and faster. They are not aware of it, they are completely unconscious when they do it, and they will do it until the sun supernovas and consumes the Earth. However, some women nag so much, it borders a psychological problem because it's a control issue.

If this is the case, you drop her like a hotcake. Women, especially your wife, should support you. Without question, without interrogation, and without audit. You don't have the time, money, patience, or life expectancy to tolerate a woman who constantly hounds you, questions you, gets in your way, and challenges your authority. I know several men only half-jokingly contemplating suicide because their wives do not support them, but nag them. It makes for a miserable home life and a great case to file for divorce.

***

We could certainly go on, but the number of "red flags" and founts of wisdom are literally endless. It will be up to you, your skills of perception, as well as experience that will help you make the right choice. However, I strongly recommend consulting men who have been married a long time. Be they family, friends, or even complete strangers, ask for their advice and if necessary buy them a beer for it. Besides, 16 oz. of prevention is worth $125,000 in a divorce settlement.

Wife Training

After a long and hard search, you will finally settle on a wife. And unless you are incredibly lucky to find a girl that really understands marriage, is capable of selflessness, and has her shit together, your job is not done by a long shot. The reason has nothing so much to do with "women" as much as it is combining two separate people with two separate personalities. Just like you may have had disagreements with roommates in the past, it is a guarantee you will have issues with your spouse. This isn't "bad" or a "deal breaker," it's just the natural consequences of having two people merging their lives together.

To navigate and manage this effectively, however, you need to do a fair amount of "wife training." Not in the condescending sense of "dog and master," but holding her to and insisting on various standards that will only serve to improve the marriage and ensure it is a successful in the long run. This is where most sensitive 90's men fail as they try to approach everything in terms of "compromise" or "co-leading. Instead of insisting on absolute standards, they give in here, give in there, and soon you have an amorphous and intangible set of rules that results in a dysfunctional marriage, a dysfunctional family, and a divorce suit eight years down the road. To avoid this it is vital you understand the biggest lie told about male and female dynamics:

No matter what they say.
No matter what Oprah tells you.

No matter what legions of single moms and psychologists tell you,

women don't want to lead or be leaders,

women want, nay, *crave* to be led.

Yes, they will put up a big kerfuffle contesting otherwise. Yes, they will scream, shout, and insist otherwise. But in the end, historically and empirically, women want men to lead. All the protesting is merely a big massive "shit test" to see if you have the confidence, spine, and temerity to be a real man and stand up to them.

To this end, you simply need to develop the spine and commit yourself to declaring and insisting on these standards when married. If not, your wife WILL run over you, commandeer the family from you, and ironically get angry at you and start to detest you, because you aren't being a real man. She will then find another man who does stand up to her, and likely leave you for him. Ergo, for every prospective husband it is not an option to be "the man in the family." You *must be* the man in the family, because if you aren't, who will be? Thus, the importance of training your wives.

There Can Only Be One Leader – Leadership, by its nature and definition implies one person. You need one goal, one mission, one objective. To achieve that goal or objective you need ONE PLAN and to interpret and execute that one plan, you can ONLY HAVE ONE LEADER.

Once you have more than one leader, you now have multiple interpretations of that goal, not to mention multiple opinions on how to go about achieving that goal. This, with a 100% guarantee, results in conflict between the various leaders, and renders them ineffective as they spend more time arguing amongst themselves, rather than marshalling and deploying their resources to achieve that goal.

The same thing applies to the family.

There can only be one leader. This doesn't mean other members of the family are denied input, but in the end, if a final decision has to be made, there must be an ultimate authority. Historically, this has been the husband. The man was the final arbiter of all decisions. However, sometimes it is the wife who makes a better leader. There is nothing wrong with that as you've certainly known the couple where the wife wears the pants and it works out great. But whether it is the husband or the wife, there MUST BE ONLY ONE LEADER.

To this end (and assuming it is the man who is the leader), you must ensure your wife understands this. That you are the head of the household, you will make the final decisions if necessary, and after a thorough and honest discussion of issues, you will have the final say in complex matters. However, this does not mean you're a tyrant, telling her it's your way or the highway (though it may come to that). You also consider her input and her desires. Because of this, the best model for leadership in marriage is Star Trek's "Captain and First Officer."

If you look at Star Trek (either the original or next generation) there was Captain Kirk and First Officer Spock.

Did Kirk ignore Spock, telling him to shut up and make him a sandwich?

No, of course not. Kirk consulted with Spock, respected Spock, and nearly always weighed Spock's advice heavily. But if there was an emergency, or the Klingons were attacking, Kirk was without a doubt the supreme and absolute leader. Such an arrangement is key to a happy marriage, so ensure there is only one Spock and one Kirk in the family.

Need to Be an Honorable Gentleman – If in the position of power, you cannot abuse it. You must think of her needs just as much as yours, perhaps even more. This is where the test of a true gentleman is. Are you capable of altruism? Are you capable of selflessness? Are you capable of being fair and just? Sadly, many men aren't and end up abusing their power to unfairly benefit from their (presumed) beloved wife. If this is the case you are not mature enough to be married and will only (though slowly) send her into the arms of another man, not to mention, ruin the lives of any children unfortunate enough to have you as a father.

The Division of Labor – The division of labor is actually unnecessary until you have kids. If you have no kids, nobody has to stay at home to take care of them. Both the husband and wife can work, have lots of money, have sex in any room in the house, and live a rather pleasant and enjoyable life. But once kids come into the equation, both you and the wife now must subordinate yourselves to your children's lives. Namely, somebody needs to stay home and raise them.

Again, I don't care what the "experts" say, children need their parents to raise them.

Not day care.
Not government preschool.
Not a nanny.

Their PARENTS.

To this end, ONE PARENT MUST STAY AT HOME TO RAISE THE CHILDREN. This will become a point of contention if you have not discussed this with your wife previous to proposing. However, if you have properly trained your wife, she will understand that either you or her are staying home, and the family will live within the confines of a single-income budget.

Finances – Women are absolutely horrible at managing their personal finances. They are most prone to blow $100,000 on a worthless master's degree, they will spend more on clothes than they will rent, and they are the only sex that will go without health insurance so they can own a horse (true story). In short, one of the largest risks women pose to prospective husbands is their poor finances can easily torpedo the man's otherwise healthy finances.

Because of this you need to insist she is debt free before marrying, and that the finances are under your command. Unless she has proven particularly frugal, the wife should never be in charge of the purse strings. This, again, will cause great contention, but considering tight finances is the primary cause of divorce you need to lay down the law on this one.

Get Rid of Her Shit – Because women spend money at a rate of five times that of men, she is likely to have five times the amount of shit. And since it is men who are likely to own a home while women rent luxury condos, when you decide to combine your assets, she will be tempted to view your home as a storage facility for all of her worthless trinkets, keepsakes, and matching furniture set.

This will turn your house into a cramped storage facility that will drive you insane or necessitate you buy a larger, more expensive house that you frankly can't afford and don't need. To that end you need to train your wife to get rid of her shit.

This will prove harder than you think as women have a psychological, even emotional attachment to material items. Theories are abound, but it is likely the fact that having "lots of things" meant their husband was a great provider and it makes them feel more secure. Studies have also shown that women use frivolous material items to display and attain status among other women. Whatever the underlying psychological reason, and no matter how psychologically valid it is, it's completely 100% unacceptable bullshit in the real adult world.

You need to deliver that dose of reality to her.

The reason why is not so much to save money on rent or mortgage (though those are reasons enough), but because if she insists on holding onto all of her worthless shit, then she loves her material items more than you. And just like a feminist is wedded to the state first and foremost, a woman who is married to her physical possessions first and foremost is antithetical to being a wife.

Get the Fuck Out of the House – Your wife could be the perfect genetic combination of Sophia Loren, Jennifer Aniston, with a dash of naughty Jenna Jameson. And you could be the perfect combination of Hugh Jackman, Sean Connery, with a bit of real guy Mike Rowe.

You're both going to get on each other's case and drive each other nuts.

Because of this, you both need to get away from each other, but the wife will typically assume the worst and think you don't like her or are losing attraction. You need to train her to understand that not only is it good for you to get away and have a weekend with the guys, but that it's good for her to get away from you and have a "girl's night out."

But there is a more important reason to escape from the Mrs. – you both need to maintain your individuality.

While the pastor or the priest will say, "you are now one" at your wedding, that doesn't erase the past three decades of life you both spent becoming individuals. You have your own friends, you have your own tastes, and you have your own lives. To abandon them is not only disrespecting yourselves, but is the quickest way to psychological problems. To that end, I not only recommend the occasional "guys night of poker" or the occasional "flirtini night" for girls, but a full month, even two away from each other. Not only will this reinforce your individuality and remind you of who you are, their absence will also make you appreciate your significant other all that much more.

Expectations Management – Between Oprah, the Hallmark Channel, Hollywood, women's magazines, women's studies departments, and the public education industry, women are brought up to have completely unrealistic expectations of a husband. You're supposed to be rich, but not commanding. You're supposed to be strong and confident, but sensitive and caring. You're supposed to ride a Harley and bench press 220, but not want sex, unless she wants it, but you'd better be gentle, unless she wants it rough, in which case you should "just know" without her saying anything. The fact "Fifty Shades of Grey" will forever be a more popular book than this one is proof positive modern day women are completely delusional about men. Once again, you need to train them in.

How you deprogram them and install more realistic expectations of men and husbands, I frankly do not know. Taking them to the beach to show them what the "average guy" looks like is one way. Pointing out Bureau of Economic Analysis data on income distribution to mathematically prove to them billionaires account for less than 1% of the male population is another. Whether any of this sticks, is anybody's guess. But I do know being confident and doing your own thing will solve most of these problems.

Understand while women may *think* they want "Christian Grey," if a confident man comes along, doing his own thing, completely indifferent about what the woman thinks, her impossible-check list will be thrown out the window and simply be replaced with:

"That guy who is ignoring me and doing his own thing."

Yes, you may not be a billionaire. And yes, you may not be a pilot. But your confidence, agency, and aloofness will make her quickly forget her unrealistic expectations of a man, as you become her real world "Christian Grey" that (unlike the fictional character) is attainable.

Physical Fitness – Sex is the most important thing to men on a darwinistic level. Denying this will only result in a lesser (and most likely) absolutely miserable life. Therefore, it is an absolute requirement you not only be physically attracted to your wife, but that she MAINTAINS HER PHYSICAL BEAUTY OVER TIME. If she doesn't it is a 100% guarantee one of two things will happen:

1. You will cheat and put your marriage at risk
2. You won't cheat, but will be miserable with a wife you no longer find physically attractive

Unfortunately, most women do not place as much value on sex as men do, and thusly let themselves go after marriage. Furthermore, with all the female-centric brainwashing they've received over the decades, they actually believe you should only like them for their personality and "inner beauty." Matter of fact, they're so brainwashed you'll be accused of being "shallow" for daring to suggest a physical requirement to love and sex. Therefore, you need to convey to them just how important it is to you that they stay in physical shape.

This is often a very sensitive topic to broach with women, as they are very self-conscious about their weight and looks. But while convention says you should approach the topic gingerly, adroitly, and as kind as possible, that never works. You need to be blunt and direct.

"Dear, sex is very important to me and I need you to maintain your physical beauty. It is a REQUIREMENT for me to be in a committed relationship."

"Dear, if you don't lose weight I will leave you."

"Dear, if you don't lose weight, I will be tempted to find a younger, thinner girl."

"Dear, if you get fat, I will view it as grounds for divorce."

It may not be pretty, and I guarantee you tears will fall, but there will be a lot less tears, strife, suffering, and depression doing it this way than if you were to get divorced or busted cheating.

<u>Your Own Damn Training</u>

While "wife training," as well as the overall tone of this book would suggest it is the women who need the most amount of work, that is not the case. Since you are ½ of the equation in marriage, by default you have the same amount of responsibility to your wife. This means abiding by the exact same standards you apply to her. You need to let her live her own life. You need to let her do her own thing. You need to provide for the family. You need to stay in physical shape and you need to rock her world in bed. The key thing, though, is to simply ask her what she wants. Every woman is going to be different and therefore have different demands, but the simplest and least of things you can do for the woman of your life is make an attempt to make her happy. This may mean flowers, this may mean nice dinners, this may mean suffering going to some stupid play that you absolutely LOATHE and do not want to go to. But if it makes her happy, you can afford to be selfless and do it anyway.

There is certainly more to being a good husband, and myself not being married I can only largely speculate or go based off of my experience courting girls. But for more direct advice on what it takes to be a good husband I highly recommend reading the blog "Married Man Sex Life" by Athol Kay. The blog specializes in husbandry and comes from a man with 16 years' experience in a successful marriage.

Kids

The first thing that needs to be stated about children is that they are unnecessary. No matter what tradition, society, or your family tells you, you do not need to have kids. They may be nice to have, and you certainly may have a genetic desire to have them, but today's economy and technology allows for people to live successful, happy lives without them.

This is an important financial point to make because (unless you buy a really expensive house) children are the single largest expense you will ever have in your life. Each one runs around $250,000 and that does NOT include paying for college, rent, insurance, or any other form of aid you may give them after 18. Pro-rate this amount by the average 1.9 children each woman has today and this is easily a cool $500,000 in savings. That money, especially if used wisely early in life, can solve practically all your personal financial planning problems forever.

Because of this every man should seriously consider the childless life. You have extra money and time for travel, food, and other luxuries in life. You don't have to work as hard or be as loyal to your employer. Retirement planning is a breeze. And your health will improve being able to sleep more (not to mention never having your kid come back from the petri dish – aka "daycare"- passing on communicable diseases). Still, kids can be the most rewarding experience in your life. You are certainly programmed to want to have them, and no matter how much they poop, fart, belch, cry, and vomit, they can be the single largest source of happiness and meaning in your life. Because of this, children can absolutely play a role in your life and should if you genuinely want them.

Severity of the Decision to Have Kids

However, the decision to have kids is not one to be taken lightly. Matter of fact, it is the most important and serious decision you will ever make because you are now creating human lives. Lives that didn't exist before, lives that had no say as to whether they were born into existence, which makes you completely responsible for them.

It is here most modern day parents fail. As alluded to before, most people today have children not because they want to have another human being experience a wonderful and rewarding life, but simply because "*they* want them." Most parents give little, if any consideration as to whether or not they are capable of being truly good parents. They never consider what kind of environment they are bringing their children into. They don't spend a second of thought contemplating whether they can provide for their children. And few, if any ask themselves if they are prepared or capable of raising children to become functioning, mentally healthy adults, who can then go on to live enjoyable lives themselves. It is a sad fact that most parents today view "children" merely as physical items to have, no different than an SUV or a highly functional dog. In short, the emphasis is on how can children bring joy to the parents, and not the other way around.

This is the question you, and every other potential father, must look deep into your heart, and answer before having children. Do you and your wife merely "want" children or do you want to "raise children?" If your familial plans include dropping your kids off at daycare or paying a nanny to raise your children while you both work, then frankly, fuck you. You're scum. Why did you have children in the first place, if you had no intention of raising them? You don't care what emotional or psychological experience that child is having because you love yourself and your career more than your child. That child is nothing but a "thing" to you. Ergo, you're nothing as noble and righteous as a "parent," as much as you are just a selfish breeder. Your child/ren will remember your poor upbringing, they will remember you dropping them off in daycare, and they will drop you off at a lonely, never-to-be-visited nursing home. But if you do want to *raise* children, if you really want to put the effort into being a good father and are willing to commit to it, then there is just one thing you have to do – put your child ahead of yourself.

This means ensuring there is one parent who stays home to raise the child. This means being able to work to support your family, no matter how much you hate your job. This means dispensing tough fatherly love instead of merely BFF-ing your children. It even means sticking it out in a marriage you hate, with a wife your loathe, "faking it" until your youngest turns 18, before you divorce. In short, you must realize and accept that upon bringing a child into this world your life is officially over, and it now must be dedicated raising that child. That is the price of having kids and if you're willing to pay it, then, and only then, can you have them.

Being a Good Father

Not to be crass, but men have penises and women have vaginas. Men cannot lactate, but women can. And men are physically strong, whereas women are physically weak. In short, men and women ARE different no matter what feminists, leftists, liberals, politicians, teachers, and media types tell you. But while these various groups view these differences as a "bad thing," the truth is the differences between men and women is the greatest thing about life. Where women are weak, men are strong. Where men suck at doing things, women excel. And where men like to play with boobies, women like having their boobies played with. It is this complementary nature men and women have that make relationships mutually beneficial and has made humans the dominant species on the planet.

Child rearing is no different.

Children need BOTH a father and a mother. They are going to run into both males and females in life when they grow up, and therefore having a role model for both sexes will prove vital for their success. Unfortunately, various political forces want to eliminate the difference between fathers and mothers. They want to destroy the nuclear family, replacing it with single-parent homes, and some want to go so far as to replace parents altogether with the state (and this is not a scare tactic, just read Karl Marx's view on the family, or, more bluntly and tragically, look at the black community). However, political agendas and ideology will never replace nature. Therefore, it is vital that if you have children you be a FATHER, not some castrated co-parenting, asexual, wimp.

There are certainly some obvious basics to being a good dad. Spending time with your kids, being part of their lives, financially providing for the family, etc. But the true art of fatherhood has been lost over the past 50 years of anti-male, anti-masculine, new-age type tripe. This has skewed child-rearing to have a heavy "motherly" bias. You never discipline, you never yell, you only have "time outs,' you even resort to bribery to cajole good behavior out of them. It's only positive reinforcement and never negative reinforcement. Naturally, the consequences of "mother-only" rearing has been nearly three generations of soft, weak, adults who can't find a job, suffer mental problems because they can't handle the real world, end up living at home, and likely collect a government check. In order for your children to avoid this fate you need to reintroduce "tough fatherly love," being the one who says "no," metes out punishment, and ultimately holds the children to standards.

However, being a father goes beyond just "play bad cop," spanking your kids, and saying "no."
You have an even larger obligation – you need to guide and lead them. You need to prepare them for the real world.

Unfortunately, I don't know one father that does this. Most dads think once they bring the bacon home, discipline their children, and toss the ball a couple times their job is done. But this does nothing to prepare your kids for the future. You need to sit down with your children, regularly and at different stages in their lives, and pass on the wisdom and knowledge you've gained over the years to ensure they make wiser decisions that you did. This may not seem like much, but it is invaluable. Imagine if you could relive your life, avoiding the mistakes you made. How much better off would you be? You would have avoided that divorce and the $500,000 settlement. You would have avoided that worthless degree in communications, and instead become an accountant, with $200,000 in a 401k instead of $50,000 in unpaid student debts. And when you were 21 you would have purchased rental property instead of that Corvette you couldn't afford and would be looking at early retirement instead of having to work past your 70's.

This is the true benefit of taking the time to impart your fatherly wisdom and advice upon your children. You ensure your child has a better life than you did. It takes time, it takes selflessness, and they certainly won't appreciate you trying to teach them the benefits of auto-maintenance when they're 14, but the payoff is worth it. Your child will grow up to love and respect you when they're 30 because they'll realize and appreciate all you and your wisdom did for them. Meanwhile, the parents who aimed to be their children's BFF in the "tween" years and were too lazy to be real parents, are guaranteed to have spoiled, entitled adult-children, who all have mental problems, constantly ask for money, and ultimately hate their parents.

Divorce

Divorce is the absolute worst thing that can happen to a family. It emotionally destroys both spouses, typically financially cripples the man, and absolutely devastates the children. The risk of divorce can be abated by selecting the right woman, ensuring both yours and her finances are secure, and postponing children until you are absolutely ready and prepared to have them. But even if you take all the precautionary and preventative measures, divorce can still become an unfortunate reality.

To prepare for this contingency there are various actions you can take both before and during marriage that will help lessen the emotional, financial, and psychological damage a divorce is guaranteed to wreak. It won't solve all of your problems, and any divorce will still certainly ruin your life, but it will lessen the pain most divorces cause.

<u>Prenups</u> – A prenuptial agreement is a good idea for anybody considering getting married. Not so much because you do not trust your partner (although that is a good enough reason), but because in having a prenup you are guaranteed to make divorce less messy. The reason why is that prenups provide sort of a pre-determined "ground rules" for divorce. Therefore, when you get divorced there is little to argue over as the terms of divorce have already been established.

There is, however, another compelling reason for all men to consider getting a prenuptial agreement:

Again, women are absolutely HORRIBLE with money.

Usually it is the man who brings a real career and real tangible financial assets to the matrimonial table, while it is women who bring spending problems, student loans, credit card debt, and immaterial earnings potential from some kind of faux, non-profit "career." It is also the man who usually thinks about things like 401k's or retirement planning, while it is women who buy the dumbest, most worthless shit to clutter a house with. Because of this, in a very general sense, most men are a financial asset, while most women are financial liabilities.

You need to protect yourself from those financial liabilities.

Not because you may have to bail her out of her Master's in Literature or support her horse farm addiction, but because of something much more simple – self-respect. You sacrificed a significant percentage of your life to get where you are financially and she likely relied on others. You majored in engineering while she majored in education. You spent money on a seminar about retirement planning, while she went and bought shoes. And you spent time repairing the house, while she had flirtini's at ladies night. Of course, there are women who are the fiscally responsible one in the relationship, but for the majority of cases it is men who make the majority of sacrifices in life and earn the majority of money. Ergo, a prenup does not so much protect the fruits of a man's labor, as much as it ensures he did not work in vain because a divorce rendered him nothing more than a slave to his ex-wife.

(Note – In order for a prenuptial agreement to be effective it is ABSOLUTELY NECESSARY for both you and your to-be-wife to have your own lawyers before drafting and signing one. Also, you do not

have to be getting married to have a prenuptial agreement. Anytime two people intend to own asset communally, a prenuptial agreement can be used).

<u>Stay Married Until the Kids Are Out of the House</u> – If you have children and you desperately want to get a divorce, do your kids the least of dignities and stay married until they move out of the house. Just because you ruined your lives, try your best not to ruin the lives of any innocent children unfortunate enough to have you and your wife as parents. Suck it up, stay married, put on the show, and stick it out. It's the least you can do for the children you should have never had.

Of course, this does not sound like "taking the sting out of divorce" (matter of fact, it sounds like making life even more insufferable), but there is a very compelling reason to do this:

Your children will actually remain in your lives.

Yes, your wife may be an insufferable bitch. Yes, you may have to go outside of the house and live a separate sex life with your girlfriend. But if you get divorced while your children are young, they will never forgive you and they will simply never return once they leave the house. They may call, they may show up for Christmas, but they will have no loyalty to you or your wife which means no support in your old age, and no visits in the nursing home. And it is that horrible fate, one where your children want nothing to do with you, that makes faking a marriage until they're out of the house worth every ounce of pain and suffering you'll endure doing so.

Choose Your State (and County) Wisely – In general there are FOUR MAIN THINGS you are going to be concerned about when getting divorced:

Assets, debts, children, and alimony.

Namely, who gets them or gets to pay for them.

The problem, however, is that there are no "universal, federal laws" governing divorce. Divorced is governed at the state and county levels. Therefore, you can be in one state and forced to pay your wife lifelong alimony (i.e.-income to provide her the lifestyle she was accustomed to while married to you), while another state may deny your ex-wife alimony altogether. You could be in a county where debts accrued by your wife are still hers, while another county would demand you pay half. The larger point is that it is vital you consult an attorney about the local laws in your state AND county to see if it isn't worth moving, changing residences, or getting married in a particular state instead of the one you're currently in now. It may seem inconsequential now, but it can literally mean the difference between paying your ex alimony for a year versus alimony for the rest of her life. It can also be the difference between being a free man or being thrown in jail.

Plan Your Escape – While it may sound cynical and overly cautious, the day you get married, start preparing for divorce. Specifically, stash away cash. Many men (and women) who are facing divorce will hurriedly and hastily start trying to hide assets, realizing their soon-to-be-ex will get half. Unfortunately, by this time it is too late. Courts, through accountants and auditors, will be able to tell you've been hiding assets and will still force you to give your wife half despite your claim "you don't have any assets." To avoid this you need to stockpile inconsequential amounts of money starting day one. Take out inconspicuous and varying amounts of cash that you would likely spend at a bar. Purchase gold, silver, or some other kind of physical investment that holds its value. And if you're really tricky, find a friend or family member you implicitly trust, start a business with them, but have the business in their name. There are other tactics you can use, but the key thing is to start immediately and not wait for divorce to be over the horizon. Besides, if your wife proves to be your "one true love," then you can surprise her with all that money you were "secretly" saving up for that "special European vacation."

<u>In Charge of Finances</u> – You need to be in charge of the finances. Not only because women are horrible with money, but because women have been known to rack up TONS of credit card debt before divorcing as a form of spite. They do this knowing the court will likely force the husband to pay for half of the debts because debts are consider "marital property." This effectively forces you to pay for half of her things.

<u>Consult an Attorney</u> – Before marrying, even if you love your fiancée, you need to consult an attorney. Not only will they advise you on the pros and cons of state and county divorce law, but they will be able to help you in terms of protecting your finances and investments, as well as put you in a better position for a custody battle. It isn't romantic, and it isn't something you want to think about, but with 1 in 2 marriages ending in divorce you need to consult an attorney. Do not let love blind you to the risks of marriage, and do not be so cheap as to let a $500 price tag deter

you from getting some preventative legal advice that could easily save you $500,000 in the future.

A Miscellany of Advice

<u>Vasectomy</u> – Your sperm is the riskiest thing you carry. If any of it comes in contact with an egg you are (in the words of Tom Leykis)

SKA-ROOD!

Thus, the nanosecond you know you don't want kids or you've had all the kids you're going to have, get a vasectomy.

A vasectomy is a surgical procedure that cuts the tube (the "vas deferens") from your testicles to your shaft. It is NOT the removal of your balls. It merely makes it impossible for sperm to travel beyond your testes.

You can still get erections.
You can still have orgasm.
You can still lovingly give your wife or girlfriend a facial.

You just can't get her pregnant.

However, 1 in 100 vasectomies FAIL. Your tubes can repair themselves, growing back and once again allowing sperm to flow out of the testes. Because of this you want to regularly test your virility. This can be done with over-the-counter test kits you can order online, or if you want to make doubly sure, a test at your local clinic (though it costs more).

Finally, be warned there is a huge anti-vasectomy mentality among society and the medical community. Understand on a darwinistic level, society wants men to breed. It not only provides for more children in the future, but forces men to work hard and be productive. This may sound far-fetched, but you would be amazed at how many people get viscerally angry at men who have vasectomies. They are called "selfish" and "greedy," and I personally have been lectured multiple times about my "duty to society" and how dare I enjoy the childless bachelor life. Because of this, expect a backlash from family, friends and strangers when you decide you want a vasectomy. Also expect resistance from your doctor. Some doctors will question whether you are making the right decision, some will try to persuade you not to do it, and some will just outright refuse.

But the one thing you need to know is this. Despite all the scare tactics they'll throw at you about the "serious and PERMANENT decision" you're about to make, and that you'll never be able to have children, and your family line will die into obscurity...

you can still have children.

Just because you had a vasectomy doesn't mean there isn't any sperm in there. There are surgical procedures that can extract sperm from your testes and then via in-vitro-fertilization impregnate your wife. Yes, it may be painful, but it's certainly less painful than the 18 years of poverty an ill-timed child will wreak on you. To that end, it may be the best thing for all men to get vasectomies, ensuring they will only have kids when they want to (though you will still want to consult a doctor).

People Do Regret Having Children – No parent in the history of parents publicly confessed to regretting having their children. They have always said,

"They're the best thing that happened to my life."

But while that may be true for the majority of parents, there are still some who do indeed regret it. Whether it is bad parenting, a psychologically damaged child, or just plain bad kids, some children can, and do, cause more pain and suffering to their parents than joy and happiness.

Because of this, you will want to ensure you are indeed a good parent. You will also want to ensure you do what you can to minimize the risk of down syndrome or other birth defects by having children before the woman is 40. But even with these precautions taken, realize there is no guarantee your child will be a good child. Children, just like you, are independent, sentient beings with their own minds. Some of them, regardless of the best parenting in the world, will still choose to be evil.

Wife Loves the Kids More – A sad fact is that once kids are born many women will love their children more than their husbands. This relegates you to merely a sperm donor, is an unacceptable insult, and puts you in the impossible situation of competing against your kids for attention. Unfortunately, there really isn't anything you can do about it as there is no way to force somebody to like you. But you can screen out women who are prone to love the children more than you. Do they have a ton of pets? Do they prefer their cats over other people? Does she obsess over wanting children, to the point she ignores real world factors like affordability or preparedness? If that is the case, she is likely viewing you merely as a sperm donor and perhaps a meal ticket to pay for her "mommy-fantasy."

Forcing Religion Down Your Kid's Throats – Do you want your kid to go to church when he's a kid, but never as an adult? Then shove religion down his throat. It's a great way to make sure your child leaves the church the day he leaves home.

Deteriorating Environment – Though it will be addressed in more detail in a later chapter, realize what kind of social and economic environment you are bringing children into today. Economic growth is half of what it was 50 years ago, the national debt is at an all-time peace-time high, the labor market offers nothing to youth, and when considering things like "unfunded liabilities" any child being born today is immediately saddled with $300,000 in debt. Also realize the people themselves are deteriorating as well. Dependency ratios are up, illegitimate birth rates are up, divorce is up, Miley Ray Cyrus is a household name, and if you look around you can empirically see people getting dumber every day.

Is this the environment you want to bring your child into?

Understand the United States (and western civilization) is in decline. It is no different than the Roman Empire, and like all empires, it will collapse. The question is whether now is the time to bring new and innocent children into this world, right before a new "dark age." Realize your children, and their children, are VERY unlikely to enjoy the economic environment you were brought up in. Also realize they are not going to be surrounded by as mature and moral people as you were (have you seen other parents' kids???). And while it's absolutely possible the economy and society may not outright collapse, the numbers (as will be displayed later) indisputably prove we are in decline. Therefore, you need to ask yourself if you can still raise a child to have an enjoyable life in this increasingly hostile environment, or if you would merely be bringing in another innocent soul to suffer a declining society.

Cohabitate/No Legal Marriage – Unless you are going to have kids there is no real good reason to get married. Aside from merely making a commitment to each other, marriage does nothing more than add an additional and unnecessary layer of bureaucracy (be it the church or the state) on a relationship that is a private matter. Because of this you may want to consider merely cohabitating or getting married by the church, but not making it legal. Your relationship with your loved one is none of the state's business, and attaching legal strings to it provides no advantage (besides, it's fun to "live in sin" – irks all the right people).

Foreign Brides – With the quality of American (and western women in general) so poor, a logical conclusion would be to find yourself a bride overseas. These "mail order brides" are viewed with much derision by American women, not so much because men who get them are "lame" or "can't get any," but because foreign women are competition. But while a mail order bride may make logical sense, nearly every foreign bride I've seen is indeed a scam. They do not care to marry a "nice sensitive American man," as much as they want to escape their shithole country and get a green card. I've seen mail order brides divorce their American husbands the day they attained citizenship, and one even brought over a child she forgot to mention she had. Furthermore, you have to worry about them becoming "Americanized." Once introduced to the culture, foreign women invariably start to exhibit the behaviors and traits of their American sisters, rendering them unmarriageable.

If you really want a foreign bride, your best bet is to live overseas for a long period of time and find a woman in her native country. However, with that amount of effort and expense, you should in theory be able to find a quality wife here.

<u>Betting Liberal Chicks</u> – A common problem in wife selection all young men will face is that nearly all young women are liberals or leftists. Again, deep down inside they probably aren't, but you will have to contend with the fact they believe they are. To deal with this an INCREDIBLY effective tactic I used during my 20's was betting.

Understand most young women think just because they went to college they are "smart," but most are woefully ignorant about basic economics, government finances, etc. Predictably, they will disagree or argue with you about something political or economic. But to prove them wrong, and at the same time deliver a **devastating** blow of charm, bet them something sexual.

One of my favorites was to bet a liberal girl a night where she'd come over to my house and clean in lingerie if she was proven wrong. Even if they don't take the bet (most won't), they are charmed (and a bit impressed with your bravado) to the point they'll blush and usually end up going out with you anyway.

<u>You Will Never Rid Yourself of the Desire to Nail Other Chicks</u> – Boys, you are not only programmed to want to have sex, but to have sex with as many hot chicks as possible. This is how it works,

there's no denying it. It will be that way until you're dead. Unfortunately, this is antithetical to marriage (or any exclusive relationship) and will cause at least some frustration. Historically, men have had mistresses, prostitution is of course the oldest profession, and affairs are abound. But unless you have an explicitly open relationship (kudos if you can get it!), you must realize the immense pain and suffering you will cause your wife if you do cheat on her and she finds out. This is where you must once again, be a gentleman, be selfless, and train yourself to be a good husband, realizing the love for your wife is stronger than your urge to nail other chicks.

<u>If You Cannot Take Care of a Dog, Don't Have Kids</u> – Dogs are like kids, except better. They are loyal, they don't give you guff, they don't carry communicable disease for humans, and you can sell them if you don't like them. However, they also serve as a great proxy to see whether or not you have the capacity, patience, and ability to raise kids. If you can't take care of a dog, then you can't take care of a kid. Nearly everybody should get a dog first as a trial run before having kids.

CHAPTER 13
LEGAL

In addition to divorce the average man is likely to need the services of a lawyer in other capacities in life. Sometimes it will be for a good reason (starting a business) sometimes it will be for a bad reason (getting arrested), and sometimes it's merely boring and procedural (drafting a will). Whatever the reason, it is good to have a basic knowledge about the legal system, the different type of lawyers you're likely to need, and what kind of services they offer.

Avoid the Legal System

But before we begin, there is a cardinal rule you need to know about the legal system:

Avoid it if you can.

Understand the difference between what a legal system is supposed to do and what it actually has become. A legal system is to mete out justice. It is to make things fair. It is a system that is used to resolve differences between people. Without it a society cannot progress. Contracts would not be honored, crime would go unpunished, employers could abuse employees, and employees could steal from employers. Frankly, without a legal system you wouldn't even have an economy, let alone society. You'd have complete anarchy and chaos. But with a legal system you have order. You have rules society operates by. If Bill signs a contract with me, but fails to hold up his end of the bargain, I can sue him in court. If Kristy punches me in the face and then comes at me with a knife, I can call the cops and she will be thrown in jail and tried for her crimes. That is how it's supposed to work, and it does to an extent, but not really.

In the real world the judicial system is prone to corruption just like any other industry or institution; banking, congress, academia, corporate America, etc. And because of its increasing corruption, it's increasingly failing to serve the people it was intended to. For example, unless you are assigned a public attorney, the legal system is prohibitively expensive to the average person. Lawyers can easily bill out at $400/hour and have no problem stretching out the amount of time they need to work on your case. Also, the sheer number of procedural actions that can be taken in a court case multiply the length of time (and billable hours) it can take to resolve a case. In short, you can have the strongest of personal finances, but all it takes is one lawsuit and you are in the poorhouse forever.

Second, it is not fair or impartial. Judges are humans too, and even though they're "supposed" to interpret the law unbiasedly, more and more of them are merely using their position to advance a political agenda. This can be seen, even in our highest court, The Supreme Court, where "democrat" and "republican" justices vote along ideological lines. The fact there is even such a thing as "democrat" or "republican" Supreme Court justice shows you how unconsciously politics have corrupted our judicial system. And if the land's highest court is so politicized you can expect such bias to be rife all the way down.

Third, the legal system is becoming a racket. Its participants (lawyers, judges, politicians, etc.) view it more as a means to advance their careers than find innocence, guilt, or justice. For example, there's more than one aggressive prosecuting attorney who doesn't care if he or she sends an innocent man to jail as long as it's a win for their resume. There's no end to ambulance chasers who will sue just to make a buck. And there are political crusaderists who instead of using the taxpayers' money to fight real crime, will use the justice system to advance their own pet cause.

In the end, the judicial system is slowly turning into a self-serving entity much like education. It is not there for the people, it is not there to help its clientele, it is there first and foremost for itself, and the price you will have to pay to access it is not worth any kind of benefit you might receive in return. Ergo, it should be your LAST RESORT when trying to solve your legal problems.

Still, you will likely have brushes with the law, and for some aspects of your life you WILL need a lawyer. Because of this it is important to know the basics, what you're getting yourself into, and what legal services you will likely need in your life.

Bankruptcy

Be it bad luck, health issues, or the sudden loss of a job, there is a chance you may have to file for "bankruptcy" in your life. Bankruptcy is simply a declaration on your part to your creditors that you cannot pay them back or are at least having troubles paying them back. In "declaring" bankruptcy you are then given a reprieve from your creditors and allowed to reorganize your finances to the point you can either pay your creditors back, pay them back partially, or have your debts forgiven altogether.

There are two primary types of bankruptcy an individual can file – Chapter 7 and Chapter 13 – both of which have some pro's and con's depending on your individual situation.

Chapter 7 – Chapter 7 is considered the most "severe" of bankruptcies in that you simply cannot afford to pay back your debts. This being the case, what assets you do have are sold off, and the proceeds are then used to pay down your debts as much as possible. While you may lose all your assets, the good news is that all your debts (bar child support, alimony, student loans, and other "unforgivable debts") are forgiven. Additionally, most state laws protect what are considered "vital" assets like your house or your vehicle. This allows you to have shelter and transportation for employment. You can then "start your life anew" without the burden of debt you had previously.

Chapter 13 – Chapter 13 is a "less severe" form of bankruptcy in that your financial situation is not so dire that you need to have your debts completely forgiven. You still have some ability to pay them, but you either need more time or need to find some other source of income to do so. In this case your bankruptcy is not so much a "bankruptcy" as much as it is a restructuring of your debts. Usually this "restructuring" results in a 3-5 year payback plan with your creditors where you either pay back all or most of your debts. Additionally, since you are paying back your debts, creditors cannot confiscate your assets, and therefore a Chapter 7 style liquidation does not occur.

Regardless of which chapter you decide to file under, understand there is one major drawback to filing for bankruptcy – ruined credit. You will not qualify for any kind of loan (at least not one with a reasonable interest rate) until at least three years pass. Also, understand filing for bankruptcy can have a negative effect on your career. With more and more employers demanding they pull your credit report as a contingency to employment, a black mark like bankruptcy can cost you a job.

However, realize these costs are actually becoming progressively inconsequential in today's society. With "The Great Recession" of 2007-2009 practically an entire generation filed for bankruptcy. And so, whereas in the past, there was great shame and ridicule attached to filing for bankruptcy, today it's like "who hasn't?" It is so common it no longer raises a brow. So common in fact credit card companies will still extend you credit just a year after filing for bankruptcy, and banks will approve you for a mortgage in seven. The truth is the biggest cost to bankruptcy is not a lowering of your credit score or lesser chances of finding a job, it's the shame and mental strife you put yourself through contemplating filing it. I've seen people go through incredible depressions, losing sleep and health, some people even driven to suicide by their finances. However, this shame and strife is completely unnecessary. Given the decay in the quality of people in society, not to mention skyrocketing tuition costs and abysmal employment opportunities, there no longer is any shame in having financial problems (let alone anything). So do yourself a favor and avoid that undue strife. Contact a bankruptcy attorney and get on with your life.

Landlord Tenant Law

Whether you're a tenant or a landlord, it is helpful to know a little bit of landlord-tenant law, even have access to a lawyer that specializes in the field if you own rental property. Like divorce, landlord-tenant laws vary by state, county, even city and it is something you definitely want to investigate before purchasing any kind of rental property. However, especially when you're younger, it is wise to consult the basic laws governing leases and tenantship as renting will be your most likely form of lodging. This doesn't require you consult a lawyer, but it does mean you should research the basics of tenant law on the internet, or consult any one of the numerous "tenant's rights groups" that exist in nearly every major city. It could mean the difference between having shelter or being thrown out to live on the streets in the middle of January.

Employment Law

As you spend nearly a third of your waking life at work, there is a good chance you will have a legal problem over the course of your career. However, it will not be so much between you and your employer as much as it will be you and another employee. Understand most companies are smart enough to obey employment law to the letter. It's why they dedicate entire legal and HR departments to the cause, ensuring they do not discriminate, have air-tight contracts, and in general avoid nearly all legal problems. But the same cannot be said of employees.

Be aware that because of the general decay of society it is almost a guarantee over the course of your career you will offend some soft-skinned, professional-victim who will purposely take something out of context, file a complaint against you, and demand either you be fired or there be some kind of reprimand. Also be aware that even if the complaint is completely bogus or the epitome of petty, employers are so sensitive to (and afraid of) lawsuits they will heed it and investigate it. It may not be fair. It may not be right, but that is the world we live in today. However, while there are many types of complaints or legal problems you can potentially run into, the most common one a man will face is sexual harassment.

Understand through constant media, government propaganda, and 20 years of schooling, women are brainwashed to believe they are oppressed and discriminated against. They are also so pampered via these institutions many of them have attitude problems to the point they are full-blown narcissists looking to take umbrage. This makes women in the work place (especially younger ones) ticking time-bombs ready to go off at the slightest, misperceived sleight. But understand this isn't hyperbole or rhetoric. This is a real and genuine threat. All one has to do is look up "Dongle-Gate" where a girl, who wasn't even employed at the same company, got two men fired for cutting "Dongle and Forking" jokes at a convention. There was another instance where a girl was "offended" by an off-colored joke at a bar, complained, and got the bartender who cut the joke fired. The reason I highlight these two instances is to show you the mentality that has infected young women today – they're not only preprogrammed to think of everything in terms of harassment, they're not only actively looking to be offended, they are so far gone they think it's their place and right to get people fired from companies *they're not even working at*.

Because of this veritable mental disease, it is vital you follow the aforementioned advice in this chapter – avoid the legal system at all costs. When you go to work, you shut up and you work. When you interact with women, you say nothing that could even be construed as harassment. You don't even participate in after-work social events or company Christmas parties. And for god's sake, NEVER DATE A CO-WORKER. Because if you get a complaint filed against you, bogus or not, it can cost you your job. And if you want to get your job back, that means you have to go to the legal system…where you likely fail because you are, of course, an "evil, sexist man who harassed a poor girl."

Finally, in addition to the legal threats sexual harassment poses during employment, there is always the chance (albeit it unlikely) your employer screws up. They let it slip you were passed over for promotion because you were young. They ask you how old you are during an interview. Your boss actually says something off-color or offensive. If this is the case, you sue the living hell out of them. Remember that companies and employers have absolutely NO loyalty to employees today. They have no problem firing people by the thousands, not to mention forcing the scourge of progressive credentialism down your throat, and lying to your face about the job description and duties. They should not be viewed as a place to "hang your hat" or start a career, but instead should be viewed purely as a Machiavellian tool to advance you personally. Therefore, if they screw up and give you the opportunity, you pull a Lester Burnham and sue.

Do, however, consult a lawyer before you do.

Criminal

Men commit crimes at roughly nine times the rate of women. We have testosterone, we have a sense of pride, and we drink more alcohol. This combination does not bode well for us and the result is us making stupid decisions, some of which land us in jail. If that is the case, you need a "criminal attorney," but again, following the aforementioned advice at the beginning of the chapter, avoid the legal system at all costs.

We addressed this in the subsection "Don't Do Stupid Shit" in chapter three. Namely, control your environment, don't hang out with bad people, and make wise choices so you don't accidentally fall into crime. Still, either through bad luck or stupid decisions you might find yourself in the back of a squad car and facing jail time. If this is the case you are already screwed, but because of how the legal system works, you can actually make yourself even more screwed. Mouthing off to cops. Talking too much. There are many mistakes you can make when getting arrested.

To that end, there are two things you can do to prevent a bad situation from getting worse. One, take a class or read up on how to interact with police or how to behave when you're getting arrested. There are many articles, tutorials and YouTube videos about the topic so you will want to consult those. Two, download or get yourself a copy of the ACLU's "Busted Card." It goes over what rights you have, do's and don't's when being arrested, and many other important legal facts that can save you a world of hurt down the road.

Beyond avoiding the law and knowing how to act while interacting with the fuzz, it doesn't hurt to know a criminal lawyer personally. Most men don't go out "planning on getting arrested" that evening and so the demand for a criminal lawyer is very much an abrupt and unexpected event. Having one pre-programmed into your cell phone will prove very useful should you ever get arrested.

Firearms/Carry Conceal Specialist

Along the same lines of having access to a criminal lawyer, many men carry guns and therefore need a lawyer who specializes in gun possession/carry conceal law. Realize owning and carrying a gun adds considerably additional legal risk, and should you ever be confronted with the situation of having to shoot somebody, you will **emphatically** need somebody to legally defend you. Doesn't matter how right you were. Doesn't matter how evil your assailant was. You WILL be going to jail that night and the local DA (especially if a liberal) will do their best to put you behind bars for good. Therefore, if you're going to carry a gun (and dare to have the audacity to protect yourself) it is equally vital you know a lawyer who specializes in defending people who have killed in self-defense.

Business Law

Should you have an entrepreneurial streak in you, it's a pretty good bet you will start a business. And just as it is good to have a thorough and complete business plan, it is also good to have a business attorney. A business attorney can provide a lot of benefits that will more than compensate you for the couple hundred dollars you'll pay him for some basic services.

First, they usually have the business acumen to determine whether you have a good business idea or a bad one. They may not be accountants, but they have seen enough good and bad businesses either succeed or go belly up and can usually stop you in your tracks if you're on track to start a failing business. Second, they're versed in contract law. Should you have to hire somebody, contract a consultant, get a vendor, purchase some property, or anything else that involves signing or drafting a contract, a business attorney can not only draft those documents but audit and edit them in your favor. Third, they also know the tax benefits and consequences of forming different types of business. Your business attorney will know, considering your personal finances, whether it's best to form an LLC, a holding company, an S-corp, or a C-corp. And if they're particularly good they will be able to explain to you in everyday language why. Finally, a business attorney will be able to prevent you from making a suable mistake. You may have a great idea. You may have a creative thought. And you may have absolutely no intention of doing something illegal. But even the slightest of mistakes can result in somebody or some company suing you. Play it safe and spend the money on a good business attorney.

Intellectual Property Law

Depending on the type of business you're planning on starting, you may need to hire an attorney that specializes in intellectual property law. The reason is that not all businesses are simply redoing what has been done a million times before:

Sports bar
Nail salon
Trinket boutique

You may have a completely new and revolutionary idea.

A vaccine that cures warts
The next "Angry Birds"
The cure for cancer

The problem is that once you come up with an idea, anybody can replicate it and therefore effectively steal it. Therefore, you need to protect it by either copyrighting it, trademarking it, or patenting it.

Copyrighting is used to protect any kind of media works. Literature, music, film, software, etc. A trademark is used to protect any kind of brand name, art, or logo. And a patent is used to protect an invention or procedure. But regardless of what your idea is and what specific legal measures you need to take to protect it, it's a good idea to have an attorney help you in that process. While you can do it yourself, it may be worth the extra couple hundred of dollars to have a lawyer do it professionally, making sure you did it right. They will be able to ensure you filed your patent (or copyright or trademark) correctly, ensuring your intellectual works are thoroughly protected. And if done correctly, they will prevent any future lawsuits or attempts to steal your intellectual property in the future. Again, it may seem like an insignificant, almost unnecessary procedure, but imagine if Bill Gates had not copyrighted Windows. Spend the time and the money making sure your creations and ideas (and the ensuing profits) are yours and yours alone.

Estate Planning

You are going to die. No two ways about it. You, like the previous 50 billion humans that have lived on the planet, will die. The problem is that while most people prepare for their retirement, they do nothing to prepare for their death. Specifically, they don't consider what happens to all their stuff once they die. This is important as it is likely you will leave behind a significant "estate." And one of the best things you can do in your life is allocate your wealth to help improve the lives of others after you have long passed.

To help you in this endeavor it would be wise to consult an estate planning attorney. Estate planning attorneys are lawyers that help you legally pass on all the wealth you've accumulated over your life to family, friends, and loved ones. They will not only help you draft up a will, but will consult you about what you can do while you're still alive to pass on your estate to your benefactors with the minimal amount of taxes and complications.

But there is a more important reason you may want to consider buying the time of an estate planning attorney – incapacitation.

Understand not everybody dies quickly, suddenly, and painlessly. Many people die slowly and over long periods of time. Worse, many people lose their mentality and their ability to think clearly long before their death. The problem is this puts the law in an odd situation. You are still alive, but you are incapacitated. You have Alzheimer's, you have dementia, or you have just plain lost it. You cannot make wise decisions about your estate, but because you are still alive, who has legal or moral authority to determine what happens to your estate and (more importantly) what happens to you?

This is the true benefit of consulting an estate planning attorney. Not so much to help you bequeath your material possessions, but to manage your own self should you have the unfortunate fate of becoming a vegetable. You need to have an attorney draft a "living will" that expressly states your desire, that in the case of incapacitation, you are allowed to die. You also need to designate somebody with the "power of attorney" who can make both health and financial decisions for you (because, once again, you are incapacitated). These things are vastly more important than "who gets your car" in that being alive, but paralyzed from the neck down, or being in a conscious comma, is an infinitely worse condition than having your hated sister get your comic book collection.

Fortunately, this is an issue you can address right now. You don't need to accrue an estate to get a living will as it isn't your estate you're protecting, it's yourself. So consider contacting an estate planning attorney to draft a living will, as well as who to designate the "power of attorney" to.

Choosing a Lawyer

Most lawyers are scum. And the reason why is because the caliber and quality of the average person who becomes a lawyer is also scum. Understand most people who set out to become a lawyer actually didn't intend to as a child. They weren't idealistic children who had a passion for law, justice, and fairness, desiring to make the country a better place. Instead, they usually started out as a lazy senior in high school who absolutely wanted nothing to do with rigor, challenge, discipline, self-supportation, math, and real work. Because of this they chose an easy major, typically a liberal arts degree. But upon finding out that degree would not get them a job any better than flipping burgers, they then turned to graduate school. Some chose simply to double down and get an advanced degree in that same worthless field. The rest went to law school. Not because of any particular passion for law, but because it "just seemed the thing to do."

This is an important point to make as it shows the majority of law schools are not there churning out the latest generation of Perry Masons, but are first and foremost nothing more than overpriced degree mills. They're extracting insane amounts of money out of worthless, talentless, lazy adult-children in exchange to feed their egos by awarding them "advanced degrees." However, while giving these adult-children a piece of paper that says, "you're really smart" does indeed feed the ego, it does not change the economic fact that the market is over-flooded with lawyers and they're only making $30,000.

This cannot stand.

Because of all the effort they put into getting an advanced degree, not to mention all the youth they wasted on it, their egos simply cannot abide the fact they've got "a law degree," but still only make $30,000 a year. And so to rationalize this, most lawyers invariably abandon ethics and do anything they can to make money, achieve status, and therefore validate their investment. Some, with adequate parental resources become politicians and run for public office, not because they altruistically care about society, but because they want an easy job. Others, who are not so lucky, turn to more desperate and amoral means to validate their career choice. Some become ambulance chasers, others join non-profits that never solve any problems, and some join political crusades, but regardless of what route they choose, realize the one trait they all have in common – they don't do so because they care about their clientele, the "people," the "environment," or the "poor starving children." They are doing it 100% and solely for themselves. They are the textbook definition of sociopaths and they will stop at nothing, even if it destroys lives, to validate their ego.

Realize when you go into the world of lawyers this is the lion's den you're entering. They are a sad, pathetic, depraved, and desperate group of losers. They are not only talentless, but they are also egotistical, making most of them full-blown narcissists who will put themselves ahead of everybody else, including you. Because of this you need to choose a lawyer wisely, and it is a process that can take years. Therefore, it is very wise to search for a lawyer NOW instead of waiting for a legal emergency to force you to choose one in haste which may be the greatest mistake you make.

You have several options when it comes to finding a lawyer, but the best way to do it is find a "general practitioner" or "family lawyer" that you trust. Not because you need a family lawyer, but because they know other lawyers that they trust and can refer you to. Understand, family lawyers are just like family doctors. They are general practitioners, they know a little bit of everything, and are also familiar with your personal situation. However, your demand for legal services, just like health services, will probably require a specialist at some point (estate planning, patent law, criminal law, etc.). If this is the case, your family lawyer can recommend a specialist in that field.

The key to doing this, however, is to find a family lawyer YOU TRUST. You do not want some ambulance chaser that merely refers you to other incompetent cronyistic reprobates. You need to research them on the internet, find out if they are indeed successful lawyers, see what political organizations they belong to, fake-facebook friend them to see what they're saying behind "presumed" closed doors, and whatever else you can to determine their mettle, honesty, and morality. It may take some doing, but just like drafting a living will, it is something you can (and should) start doing now.

Being a Good Client

Lawyers (at least the good ones) are busy people. And just like you, they can't afford to work for free. They also need to put food on the table, pay for rent, and clothe themselves and, therefore, you are going to have to compensate them. However, there are various ways you can pay for a lawyer.

Ideally, they will do your work "pro-bono" – i.e. "free." Usually, a lawyer will only do this if there's some kind of prestige or non-monetary reward for taking on your case. Your case is in new, uncharted law which would give him experience in this embryonic field. Your case is particularly "charitable" and if he takes it his reputation will improve. Or your case has some kind of personal meaning to the lawyer and he, in a genuine act of charity, takes it on. However, most lawyers cannot afford to work pro-bono all the time, and thusly will require some form of compensation.

"Contingency" is the "next best" form of compensation. It's very simple – if your lawyer wins, you pay him. If he loses, you owe him nothing. I prefer this form of compensation because it ensures your lawyer does his or her job right. It also prevents you from wasting a lot of money. However, many good lawyers will refuse to work on a contingency basis because there is no guarantee they'll get paid and they can, frankly, find a paying client elsewhere. Therefore, you want to make sure your lawyer is competent, not desperate, if they're offering to work on a contingency basis.

Finally, you can just pay as you go. This is the most common form of paying a lawyer. You usually are asked to put down some money in the form of a "retainer" to ensure you have some skin in the game and that your lawyer is also compensated. You are then billed at regular increments for any additional work your lawyer does beyond what the retainer afforded. If you refuse to pay, your lawyer simply stops working.

Regardless of the pay arrangement you and your lawyer agree to, and beyond simply having the decency to pay your bills on time, there are other things you can do to be a "good client" and make your relationship with your lawyer a better one. Most of these things are the same things you'd want to do with your accountant or realtor:

Be on time
Pay your bills on time
Have your shit together
Promptly provide paperwork
Clearly think through the question you want to ask so he or she can answer it quickly and succinctly

These basic courtesies not only make their jobs easier, but it can also save you a lot of money as they don't have to spend an extra five hours either hunting you down for an answer, paperwork, or trying to interpret what you want. Be as professional with your lawyer as you would want him to be to you.

A Miscellany of Advice

<u>"White Shoe" Law Firms</u> – If you failed to find yourself a good family lawyer you trust, but suddenly need legal services, it may be worth paying the extra money for a "White Shoe" lawyer. "White Shoe" is a reference to the top lawyers and law firms in the country. They are very expensive, easily charging $500 per hour. However, they may be worth consulting first because of one simple thing:

They don't need your money.

Understand these lawyers and law firms are dealing with multi-billion dollar companies. Senior lawyers bill out at $800 per hour. Partners in $1,000+ range. They are in demand and have no problem finding work. This is a good thing because if they don't think your case stands a shot, they'll tell you because they don't want to waste their time. Contrast that with a desperate, incompetent lawyer, who will lie to your face, even if your case doesn't have a prayer, because he desperately needs the money. Ergo, the $500/hour you may drop on **ONE hour** of consultation with a white shoe will be cheaper than the $200/hour you drop on **50 hours** on a shyster.

<u>"Tier One" Law Schools</u> – Like "White Shoe" law firms, you may want to consider only hiring lawyers who graduated from a "Tier One" law school. "Tier One" refers to the top 14 law schools in the US and unlike most other law schools, are definitely not degree mills. They are serious law programs, fully intent on producing high-quality lawyers. This doesn't mean there aren't any good lawyers that come from "Tier Two" or even "Tier Three" law schools, or that it's a guarantee your "Tier One" lawyer is good, but

it is another way to statistically improve your chances of finding a good lawyer.

Accountant – Just as it is important to know a good general practitioner lawyer, it is equally important to have a good accountant. Unless your taxes are very simple, having an accountant that is familiar with your personal tax and financial situation is worth the money you pay them. However, just like a lawyer, you will do yourself a great service in being a good client. Do not file extensions, be on time, provide your accountant all the financial information they need ASAP. I have worked with accountants and they WILL charge you less if you are less of a headache for them, and WILL charge you more if you are an irresponsible pain in the ass.

What's My Legal Budget? – My lawyer said something very profound to me and will answer most of your legal questions. Simply ask one question:

"What's my legal budget to solve this problem?"

If it's $0, then don't do it.

David and Goliath – If your lawyer ever utters "David and Goliath" referencing him (or her) against a large legal firm, get rid of your lawyer and find a new one.

You Can Fire Your Attorney – Attorneys, especially bad ones, will be very friendly and charming as they use their personality to compensate for their lack of skill. You will feel bad about getting rid of them, but don't. They are not your friend. They are your lawyer.

If they are not winning cases or you get the feeling they're costing too much, fire them. Realize the pool of sociopathic, narcissistic scum you are dealing with and make sure you are not taken advantage of.

CHAPTER 14
ECONOMICS

Study all the annual reports you want, master the art of minimalism, become a certified public accountant with a Doctorate in Accounting, you will still be missing a very important and vital piece to managing your financial life – economics. Realize that your personal financial life exists within an economic environment. And while you can directly affect and control your personal finances through wise decision making and thoughtful planning, the economy can also affect your personal finances. There's just one problem – you don't control the economy.

You can make all the right decisions, follow the advice of experts, and be in great financial shape, but all it takes is a crushing recession, a drop in the stock market, or a government defaulting on its debts and you can lose everything. But while you can't control what the economy does, you can study it in an attempt to predict what it is likely to do and, therefore, respond to or hedge against it. Thus, it is vital every man study, research, read, and stay on top of the economy and economics.

However, understanding economics goes well beyond merely bolstering your strategic financial planning. It serves a much more noble and important purpose. Specifically, stewardship to your country, your future, and your children.

Realize that since you live in a democracy it is you, the individual, who is ultimately responsible for the governance and leadership of the nation. You are responsible for picking the people in society to lead us and therefore it behooves you to inform and educate yourself about which people and which governmental policies are best for the country and the best for our future. Unfortunately, this decision is ALWAYS obscured, confounded, and blurred by politics, corruption, and just plain evil. People who couldn't care less about the future of the country look to politics for an easy and lifelong career. People who are immoral look to government as a means to enrich themselves. People who are just plain power hungry egomaniacs become politicians instead of selfless, altruistic statesmen. And the way these amoral scum get into office is very simple – they lie.

They lie about reality. They lie about the economy. They lie about their intentions. They lie about lying. It is nearly impossible to tell who is telling the truth, let alone what precisely is the truth. But there is a way to cut through all the propaganda, deceit, and falsehoods – economics.

Economics is the MANDATORY tool for any responsible citizen who cares about his country and the future. Economics is apolitical. It is unbiased. It is impassionate. It is math, and it is emotionless. It does not ask:

"What would be nice?" or *"How can I unfairly benefit from this situation?"*

It merely asks,

"What is reality?"

Because of this, economics is very much like "the red pill" from the movie "The Matrix." It will allow you to see the government and political world for what it truly is. The question is whether you are capable of taking the red pill. Can you get rid of any political biases, desires, or preferences, and accept the empirical data, statistics, mathematics, and facts economics produces? Can you admit that despite you claiming to be a "Republican" or "Democrat," you never studied economics, you never truly knew what you were doing, and thus you were a hypocrite when you voted? It is not until you commit yourself to KNOWING (not merely "thinking" or "feeling") what the economic reality is will you be able to make an informed decision while voting and, therefore, be a capable and worthy steward of the country and our future.

To achieve this "epiphany" is very simple. You need to be intellectually honest with yourself. You need to commit yourself to finding out the truth. And you have no excuse not to because the internet makes finding the truth incredibly easy. But the real reason you should commit yourself to finding the truth and studying economics is not out of shame or guilt for being an ignorant or hypocritical voter. It's the simple fact you have something vastly more important at stake:

Your future, and (if you have any)
Your children's futures

If your voting and stewardship is based in lies, misinformation, and propaganda from politicians, media, unions, and lobbyists, and not the truth, then you will ruin, or at least lessen, your and your children's futures. There will be lower economic growth, lower employment, less income, and less freedom. Not to mention all the unfathomable psychological, emotional, and financial pain that comes from recessions, debt crises, unemployment, bankruptcies, and foreclosures. Because of this you need to study economics. Not just for your own personal finances, but out of duty to your fellow countrymen and your children.

Basic Economics

Before we delve into boring statistics, charts, and vocabulary, it is important to know precisely what economics is and what it's all about.

Thankfully, it's very simple. Economics is all about "stuff."

Professors might make it more complicated. The news and media might make it so much more complex. And politicians will insist only they are smart enough to understand it. But all of the books, all of the formulas, all of the statistics, and all of the research that economics entails is simply about one thing, and one thing only.

Stuff.

This might be a bit confusing at first, as most people think "money" or "riches" is what economics is all about. But participate in a simple mental exercise and imagine:

a world with no stuff, but...

tons of money.

Precisely what would you do with the money? Nothing, because there's no stuff to buy with it. You could be sitting on top of a billion dollars and two billion in gold, but without anything to buy or services to purchase, the gold and the money are completely worthless. Ergo, economics is not about "money." It is **100%, COMPLETELY ALL** about the stuff it can buy. Money simply serves as a tool of exchange.

Therefore, the true measure of how "wealthy" or "rich" an economy is, is not the amount of money it has. It is the ability of that country to produce stuff or what economists call "wealth." This is why Adam Smith wrote "The *Wealth* of Nations," not "The *Money* of Nations" (though I would have preferred "The *Stuff* of Nations"). He was not speaking to a country's ability to mint gold or print currency. He was talking about the country's ability to produce things that would support and improve the lives of its people. If you can understand this, then you already are light-years ahead of most people when it comes to understanding economics.

The next step is how do we produce the stuff? What is the optimal economic system that produces the most amount of stuff and therefore enriches the most amount of people?

And it is here there is a bit of debate.

In the olden days, understand, there was no debate. Wealth was gained either through theft or slavery. You would be working in your village one day and the Vikings or the local warring tribe would come in and take your goats, bread, and a lot of times, your women. Or, you would be in your village, and soon a raiding party would grab you, drag you off to some faraway land and force you to build their stuff for them for free. But after the Enlightenment, the American Revolution, the Civil War, two world wars, and other significant historical events, society has evolved to the point the debate about producing stuff falls into two general camps today – capitalism and socialism.

Capitalism is the idea that the individual produces the stuff and gets to keep the vast majority of the stuff he produced.

Socialism is the idea that everybody should produce as much stuff as they want, but then all the stuff is redistributed equally or at least "more fairly."

And to be blunt, one is based in mature-adult reality and the other in child-like idealism.

The reason for such a confident and patently biased statement is because capitalism stands up to logic, history, empirical data, and evidence, whereas socialism does not. And if you try to understand economics through socialism, you will simply fail. Economics and the road to a rich and prosperous society will forever elude you. This is not to brainwash you one way or another. Nor is it to advance a political agenda. But it is to have the decency and respect to treat you like a full grown man, not waste your time, and tell you how the real world works. You should, by all means, confirm and verify everything I state here (even try to prove me wrong) for your own convincing, but in the meantime, for the sake of expediency, we cannot treat socialism with the same level of impartiality and dignity as capitalism. It just doesn't hold muster.

First, the most obvious failing of socialism is logic. You don't need to be getting your Master's in Logic (real degree, not kidding) to quickly realize that if all the income is spread around to the point everybody makes the same, then why would anybody work? You'd make just as much money as a janitor as you would a surgeon, so why try? The natural consequence of these perverse work incentives is people pursuing easier professions or just refusing to work at all, which further translates into little-to-no stuff being made. This is why there were always shortages of bread, cars, toothpaste and everything else in the Soviet Union, while American grocery stores were filled to the brim. Since it didn't matter how much or how little you worked, most Soviets logically chose to work less which lowered the overall economic production of their economy and gave them standards of living a mere third of Americans.

Second, you just have to look at history. Bar some Scandinavian countries, socialism has a horrible track record. It has killed more people during peacetime than the Nazi's purposely did during war. And for those people it didn't kill it severely lessened their standards of living compared to their capitalist counterparts. East Germany suffered standards of living 2/3rd's *less* than their Western German counterparts. China experienced economic growth of only 3.65% per year under communism vs. 8.24% post Deng Xiaoping's capitalist reforms. Cuba only enjoys a GDP per capita of $9,500 vs. another Caribbean island, Bermuda, which has $69,000 in GDP per capita. And perhaps the "purest" comparison we have in the field of economics is the Koreas. North Korea has an abysmally low GDP per capita of $1,800, while the South enjoys a standard of living 18 times that - $32,800.

Third, statistical evidence. While the above figures are indeed statistical evidence, they are anecdotal (though compelling unto themselves). When you look at all the countries with enough historical economic data and compare the size of their governments (as measured by spending as a % of GDP) to their long term economic growth there is a negative relationship.

15 Yr GDP Growth Rates vs. Gov't Spending % GDP for OECD Countries
(Source: OECD)

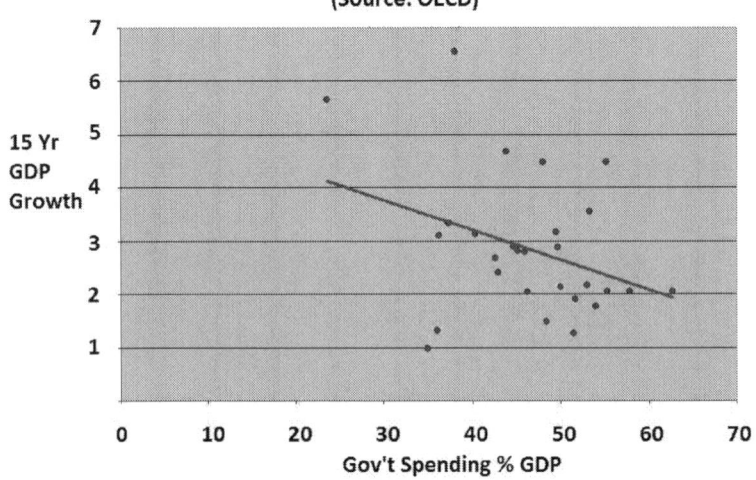

Additionally, within the United States, as the government has grown larger (again, as measured by spending as a % of GDP) our long term economic growth rate has slowed.

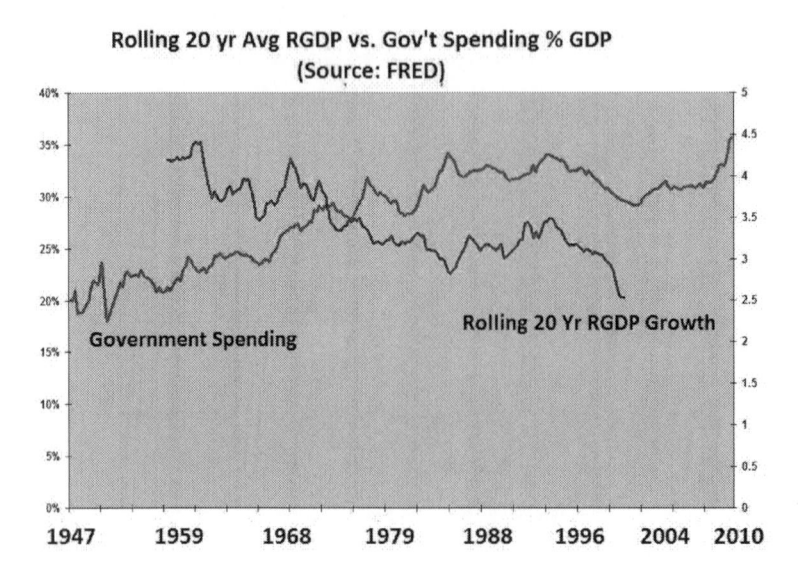

Rolling 20 yr Avg RGDP vs. Gov't Spending % GDP
(Source: FRED)

Both data sets only make sense because as the government consumes a larger and larger share of the economy, it **by default must** crowd out the private economy and thus slow economic growth.

Fourth, morality. Realize the only way genuine, tyrannical oppression of people can occur is through the "state" or the "government." Yes, one person can individually oppress another (say a possessive husband, or an overbearing wife), but the only entity capable of oppressing an *entire nation of people* is the government because it is the ultimate monopoly of society and (more importantly) controls the military. Our American forefathers knew this and is why they wrote so many rules into the Constitution and Bill of Rights, limiting the power of government. But when people vote for socialism, regardless of what the constitution might say, they consciously or not give the government more money and more power. Sometimes (though rarely) this power isn't abused (e.g. – the Scandinavian countries), but more often than not it is. The Soviet Union's KGB was no different than the Nazi's Gestapo, arresting and killing people for merely disagreeing with socialism. The East German "Stasi" would regularly spy on its citizens, murder dissenters, and even have children spy on their parents. North Korea flagrantly oppresses its people when it's not too busy killing them in concentration camps. And Cuba celebrates a mass murderer like Che Guevara. This isn't to say voting for socialism guarantees a country will immediately devolve into a totalitarian dictatorship, but that historically governments have been so predisposed to become tyrannical, that in voting for socialism you do at least enable them to do so.

Finally, there is a gapping flaw in socialism. It simply puts the cart before the horse. Ask yourself the question – what came first? The government or the people? You'll logically conclude that people came first and not government, because without people, why would you have a government? What would it govern? Where would it get its taxes? Therefore, it is the government that relies on the people, and not the other way around.

This is an important point to make because it shows that people are the ultimate source of production, economic growth, and success. Therefore, if you are going to have an economic system it needs to focus on the people, not the state. Socialism simply fails to do this. Socialism believes the state is not just the source of economic growth, but the solution to all of society's problems.

Economic growth is slowing?
"The government must do something!"

Poverty is increasing?
"The government needs to give more money to the poor!"

Oil prices are too high?
"The government needs to stick it to Big Oil!"

It is never the *people* that must do something.

Capitalism, however, does the opposite. It realizes the government is merely a tool of the people. That the only role government should serve in society is that of "governance" and not "engine for economic growth," simply because it can't. Capitalism, therefore, focuses its efforts on incenting the people to produce with things like low taxes, economic freedom, property rights, and other things enumerated in our founding documents. It is, therefore, no surprise that capitalist economies, which are based in reality, always manage to produce more wealth than socialist ones, which erroneously put their faith in the state.

***

If you take what I've said at face value, you may ask why is there even a debate? If capitalism is so patently, empirically, and obviously superior to socialism, then why are most western nations drifting towards socialism? Why is there so much passion, argument, debate, even violence on the news and in society when it comes to the debate as to "how to produce stuff?"

And it is here psychology enters the equation.

Realize while you may have the intellectual honesty and temerity to study economics, conduct your own research, and unbiasedly discover the truth for yourself, most people don't. Most people are too lazy to study economics or put forth the effort required to thoroughly and fully think through their ideology. Worse, some of these people start to take on an emotional attachment to their political beliefs. These people usually live inadequate lives, have nothing else to offer society, and find a mental solace, even purpose or meaning in political ideologies much like zealots do in religion (for example, environmentalism, feminism, veganism, organic, etc.). Thus, when you encounter them, be it in person or watching the news, it is a guarantee they are going to disagree with you, often violently.

But understand why there is disagreement.

It's not because you're right and they're wrong. Or that they have the right data and you don't. It's because you are arguing from empiricism, logic, fact, and math, while they are arguing from feelings, emotions, simpleton logic, even a zealous faith. In other words, it's like mixing oil and water. You're not even on the same page and therefore will never be able convince them, just as they will never be able to convince you.

The reason I bring up this impasse between capitalists and socialists is because if you don't realize this it can be maddening to try to understand economics and politics. You will have all the data, you will have all the research, you will have thoroughly thought through your economic philosophy to the point it's airtight. But you will still get vehement resistance from your socialist counterparts. This will make you think they're either insane or you completely missed something in your economic analysis, when in reality, the entire debate about economics is couched not in empiricism and research, but emotion and psychology. The truth is economics is quite easy to understand. Just takes a little research, a decent understanding of the basic principles of "stuff" and "wealth," and an intellectually honest mind. The hard part, and where the forefront of economics and politics is being played out, is in understanding the emotions and psychology of socialists, leftists, and people in general. That is where you will cut your teeth as an economist.

Key Economic Statistics

From here on out mastering the study of economics is pretty straight forward. You already have the intellectual honesty and commitment to discover reality. You have a functional and theoretical understanding of what economics and economies are all about. All that's left is to pull data and statistics to actually see what is happening in the economy.

There is a problem, however.

There are practically a limitless number of economic statistics and variables you can use to analyze the economy. Labor statistics, production statistics, price statistics, value statistics, growth statistics. There are as many statistics as there are people studying economics. However, the profession has largely settled on some "key" ones that can give you a very comprehensive idea of how the economy is performing. They certainly are not the end-all-be-all list of statistics, but in familiarizing yourself with these basic statistics you will not only be infinitely more informed than the average American, but able to further expand your studies into more interesting and intriguing areas of economics.

Gross Domestic Product

You already know what "Gross Domestic Product" (aka "GDP") is.

It's stuff!

Specifically, all the stuff a nation produces within its borders within one year, or more generally referred to, "the economy."

This is arguably the single most important variable in all of economics because it is the best measure we have of wealth and an economy's production. As GDP goes up, then so does the standards of living of the people.

Currently the US produces about $17 trillion worth of stuff each year. However, this number can be misleading due to inflation. GDP does not automatically account for price increases and so the real number we are interested in is "REAL Gross Domestic Product" or "RGDP" (GDP is the solid line while RGDP is the dotted line).

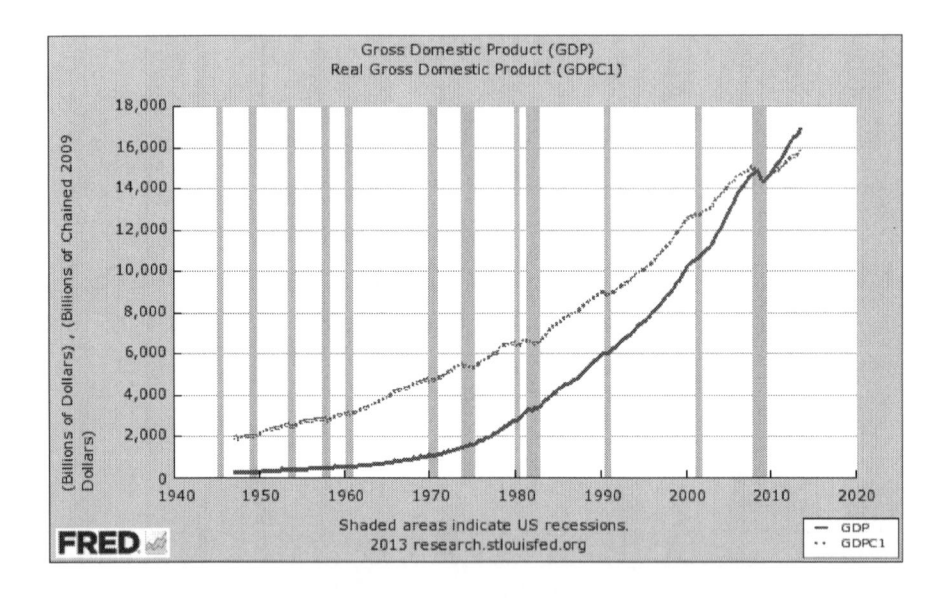

Ideally, you would want GDP growing as much as possible. The more stuff we make, the better. However, the economy does not always grow. Sometimes companies make bad investments (Dotcom Mania), sometimes people make stupid mistakes (the housing bubble), and sometimes the government tries to help, but just makes things worse (The Great Depression). These investments do not pay off and, thusly, the economy shrinks or "contracts." When RGDP decreases for two or more quarters in a row you officially have a "recession."

If you look at the chart above you can see some gray vertical lines. Those lines indicate when the economy was in recession. However, because of inflation and the length of time the chart covers, you really can't visually discern when RGDP was decreasing. To see this more clearly economists focus on the *percent change* in RGDP rather than just looking at it nominally:

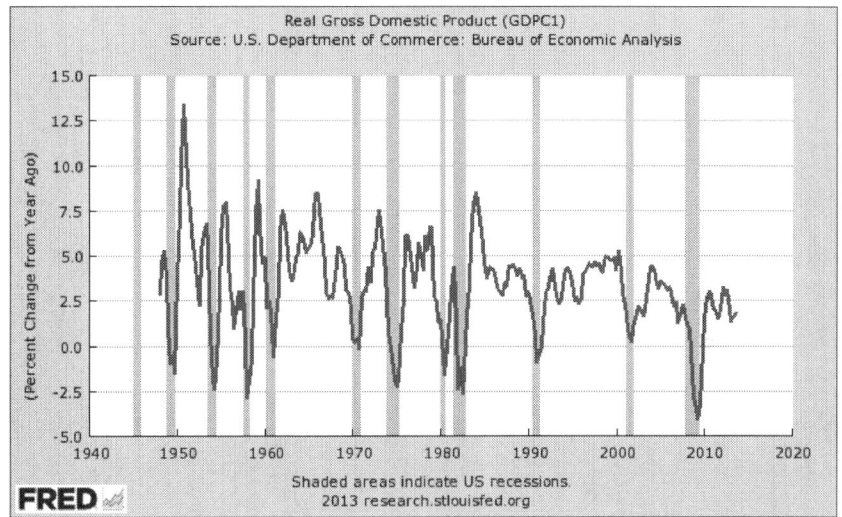

Like the charts above, recessions are denoted in the gray shaded areas, however, you can now more clearly see recessions when RGDP is converted into percent growth rates.

The variant measures of GDP do not stop there, because technically, we aren't even interested in RGDP as much as we are RGDP *per person* or *"per capita."* This is an important distinction to make because you can have an economy grow by 5%, but if its population grew by 10% then standards of living are actually decreasing. Thus, we divide RGDP by the population of the country to get "RGDP per capita."

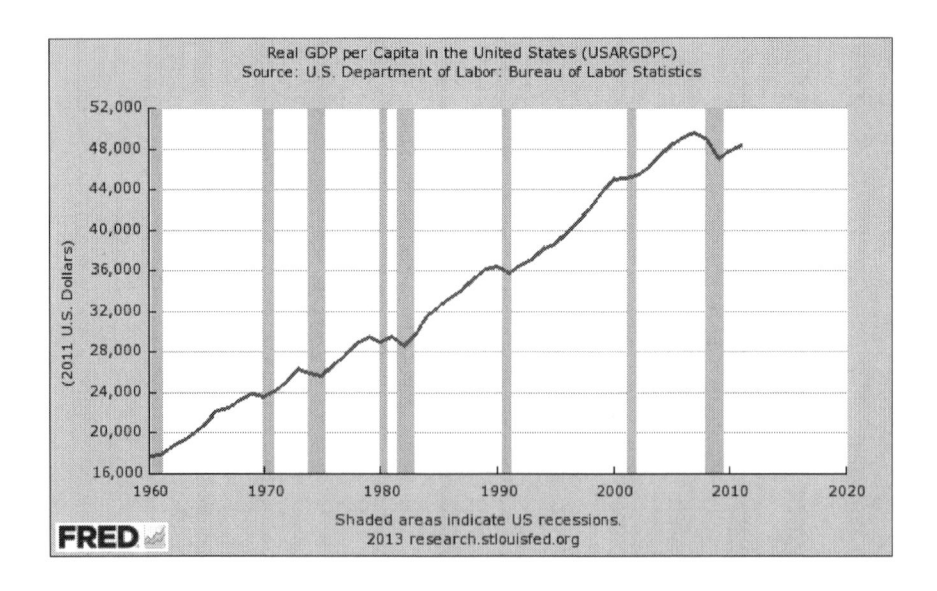

Real GDP per Capita in the United States (USARGDPC)
Source: U.S. Department of Labor: Bureau of Labor Statistics

Shaded areas indicate US recessions.
2013 research.stlouisfed.org

FRED

This measure is more or less the universal economic statistic to gauge standards of living. While it does not directly translate into "income per capita," for most analytical purposes it does. Additionally, not everybody makes $48,000 per year. Retirees make considerably less and children make nothing, some people make $12,000 a year, others make $120,000, but overall the country does produce roughly $48,000 of stuff each year per person.

Finally, though not studied or followed by most economists, a very important statistic is the long term average economic growth rate. Ideally, a country would be growing faster, thereby improving people's lives faster. Of course, this is ideal and not many countries are so lucky, so most people would be OK if the economy just maintained its historical average economic growth rate. What we DON'T want to see, however, is a *decline* in the country's long term economic growth rate. This means there's something chronically or fundamentally wrong with the economy akin to having cancer, and if not reversed the decline and inevitable collapse of the country is guaranteed.

However, as seen before economic growth is very volatile, so there is no discernable trend as to whether it's increasing or decreasing to the naked eye. But you can adjust for this volatility to get a long term economic trend by averaging economic growth over a significant number of years. When we do this for the United States over a 20 year period, the picture is not pretty:

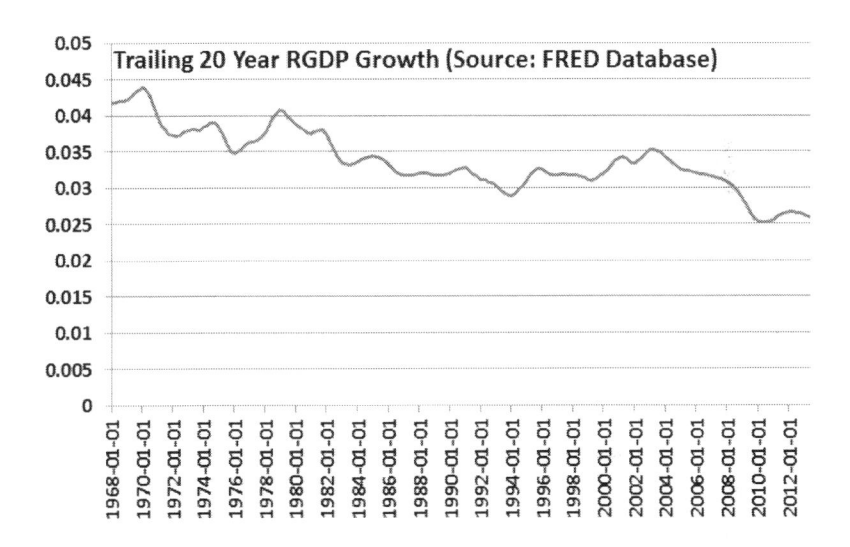

Trailing 20 Year RGDP Growth (Source: FRED Database)

Economic growth in the country has been declining since the 1940's-1960's era. Back then the US economy grew at a rate averaging 4.4%. Today we have shaved nearly 2% from that rate and currently only enjoy a 2.6% growth rate. This may not seem like much, but when considering the power of compound mathematics, it is. Had the US continued to grow at its 1940's-1960's average our GDP today would have been closer to $26 trillion, resulting in a RGDP per capita of *$99,832 per person*.

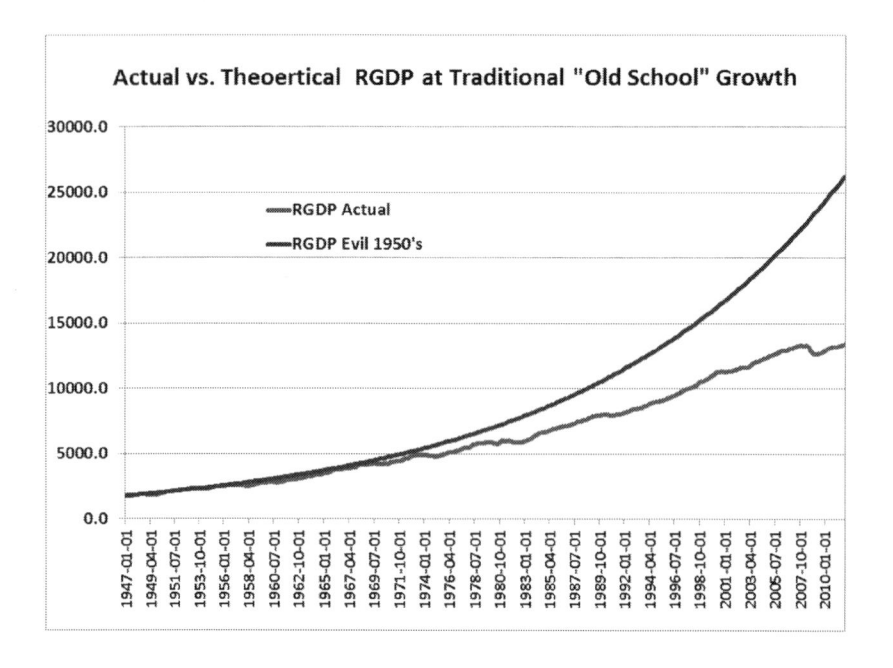

[Chart: Actual vs. Theoertical RGDP at Traditional "Old School" Growth, showing RGDP Actual and RGDP Evil 1950's from 1947 to 2010]

Labor/Employment Statistics

The most commonly cited labor statistic is the "unemployment rate." This obviously ebbs and flows with the economy, increasing when economic times are bad and decreasing when economic times are good (note the shaded recession areas).

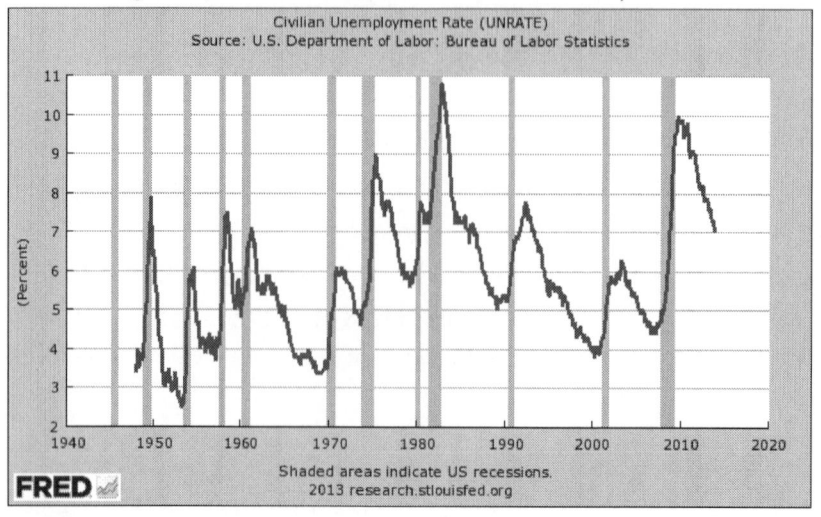

[Chart: Civilian Unemployment Rate (UNRATE), Source: U.S. Department of Labor: Bureau of Labor Statistics, 1940–2020. Shaded areas indicate US recessions. 2013 research.stlouisfed.org]

However, the unemployment rate is arguably the MOST misunderstood economic statistic there is. Most people erroneously assume it's the percent of the population that is unemployed. But what about children that make up $1/3^{rd}$ the population? Or what about retirees who make up $1/5^{th}$ of the population? That would result in an unemployment rate of over 50%, not the 7% it currently is today. Thus, the unemployment rate doesn't measure the percent of the population that is unemployed, it measures *the percent of people who want to work that can't find jobs*.

This is confusing at first, but important to understand as that description describes what is called the "labor force." The labor force is quite simply people who want to work. Maybe not everybody has a job, but as long as they want to work they are considered part of the labor force. The *percent of the labor force that cannot find jobs* is what the unemployment rate really is. So today, 7% of the people who want to work cannot find jobs or are currently without one.

The question then becomes if the labor force only consists of people who want to work, then what percent of the population wants to work? This is called the "labor force participation rate" and is actually more important than the unemployment rate. The reason why is that it shows what kind of a work ethic a country has. The higher the percent of people who want to work, the better. However, there are three main categories of people taken out of the equation when calculating the labor force participation rate:

Children (because they're too young to work)

Retirees (because they're retired and by definition don't work) and Disabled people (people who physically can't work even if they wanted to)

Thus, a more refined definition of the labor force participation rate is the *percent of able-bodied people who **can work** and **actually want to work***.

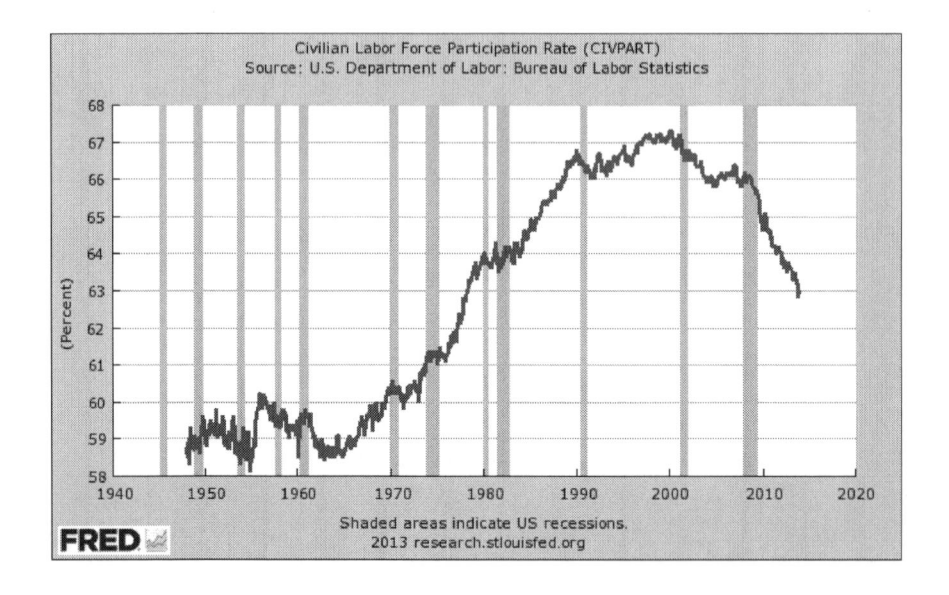

Civilian Labor Force Participation Rate (CIVPART)
Source: U.S. Department of Labor: Bureau of Labor Statistics

Shaded areas indicate US recessions.
2013 research.stlouisfed.org

The most notable thing about the labor force participation rate is that it increased dramatically from the late 60's to the early 00's. This was primarily due to women entering the work force. Unfortunately, the trend reversed staring in the early 00's and accelerated during "The Great Recession." This was due to more women choosing a family life over a career and men just getting completely decimated by "The Great Recession." Since the start of "The Great Recession" we have lost a full 3% of our labor force, 5% if you go back to the Dotcom Recession of 1999-2000. This is an important trend to pay attention to because it directly addresses the declining economic growth. With fewer people willing to work it is unlikely the US can continue to increase its standards of living, let alone pay its debts and future obligations.

Finally, just because somebody is employed does not mean they are working at their full potential. This is a common problem for younger people especially as previous generations have forced "progressive credentialism" on them, requiring they get degrees, training, and educations they will never use on the job. Ergo, you have the person with a master's degree working at the local fast food joint. To measure this economists have come up with "U6," often called the "*under*employment rate."

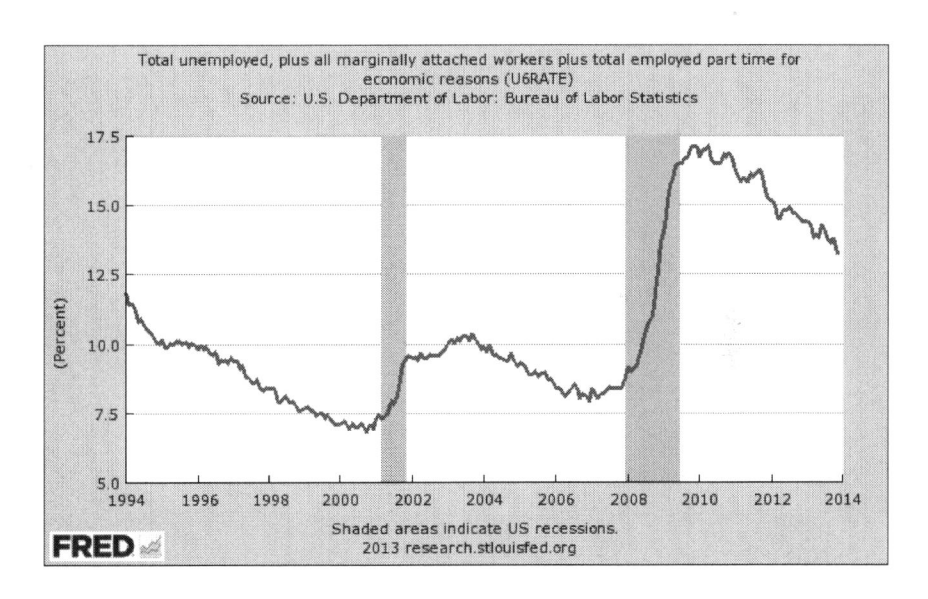

Total unemployed, plus all marginally attached workers plus total employed part time for economic reasons (U6RATE)
Source: U.S. Department of Labor: Bureau of Labor Statistics
Shaded areas indicate US recessions.
FRED — 2013 research.stlouisfed.org

Unfortunately, when considering underemployment, the real rate of unemployment is closer to 13% than its current 7%. However, this includes people of all ages. The underemployment rate for youth is significantly worse. There are no official U6 statistics for youth, but various estimates put the underemployment rate for people 25 and under anywhere from 25% to as high as 50%.

Finally, the duration of unemployment. Looking at the unemployment rate or the underemployment rate only tells you one side of the story – how many people at that point in time are out of work or not working at their full potential. It doesn't tell you how long people have been out of work. This is an important statistic, because it shows how long potential labor has been sitting idle, not producing stuff. It also testifies to the severity or mildness of a recession:

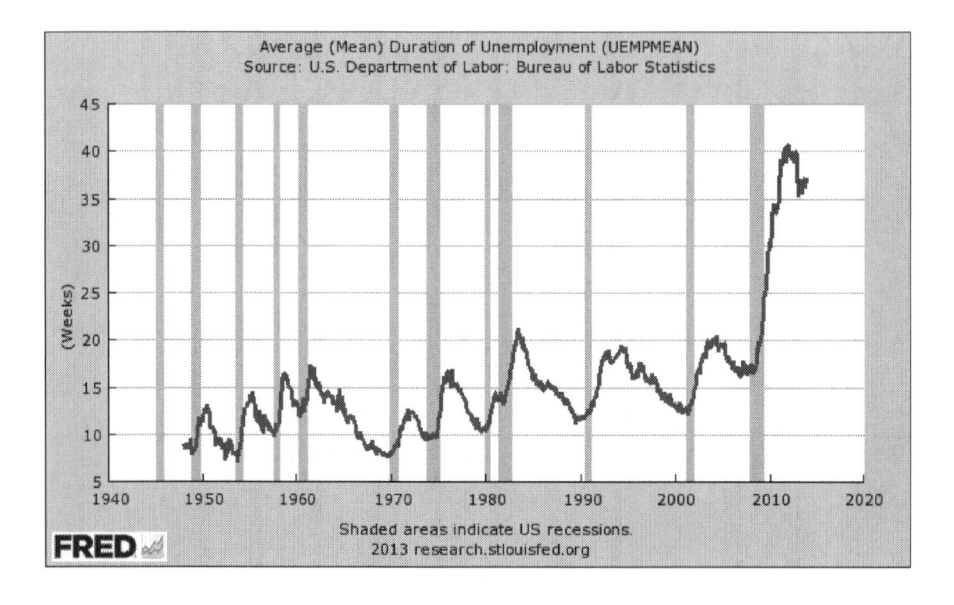

Obviously, "The Great Recession" is much more severe than what politicians and media would indicate, but this particular data set shows you an important overall lesson about economics – why you need to look at multiple statistics. Had we just looked at unemployment and RGDP growth, we would have concluded while "The Great Recession" was severe, it wasn't that bad. But in looking at the duration of unemployment (not to mention the labor force participation rate), we realize this recession is actually quite severe, very likely the worst since the Great Depression.

Inflation

Inflation is a simple concept – how much did prices increase (or decrease) by? Ideally you would like prices to be stable, or even decreasing as dropping prices would increase your purchasing power. However, the Federal Reserve likes to set a target inflation rate of around 2%. This keeps prices relatively stable, but is enough that it does two things:

1. Forces people to invest so "inflation doesn't eat away at their savings." This increases the amount of money available to entrepreneurs and businesses to invest and expand
2. Erodes the real value of the national debt

Inflation is measured by the "Consumer Price Index" or CPI. The CPI is calculated by taking the prices of thousands of goods and services and then calculating their percent change in price. These numbers are then indexed to one number giving you the "overall" price level for goods and services in the economy. There are about 40 different variant CPI measures focusing on anything from agriculture to electronics, but the two key CPI's we're interested in are the "Nominal" CPI and "Core" CPI.

The Nominal CPI includes items that have volatile prices (food and energy). The Core CPI excludes those volatile items to get a more "real" rate of inflation. Though the Nominal CPI is more volatile than the Core CPI the two do parallel each other quite closely:

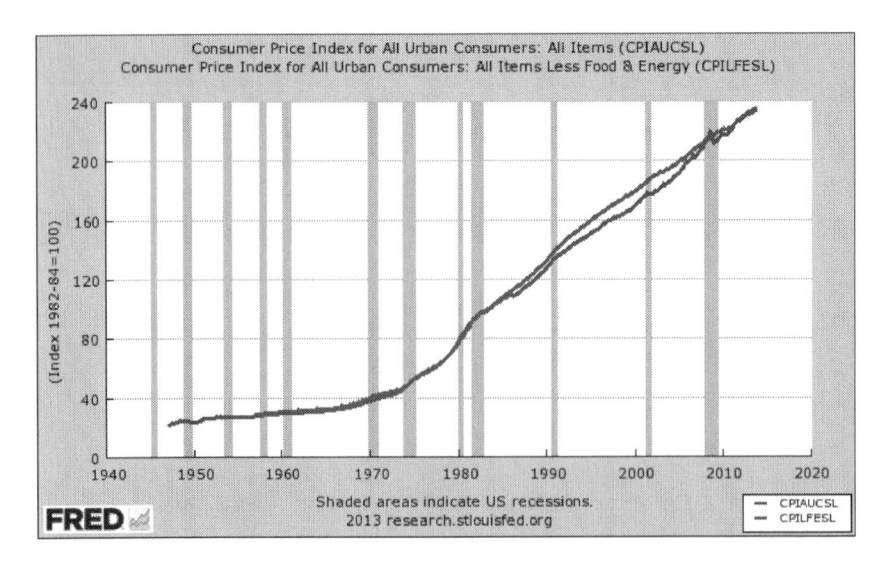

[FRED chart: Consumer Price Index for All Urban Consumers: All Items (CPIAUCSL) and Consumer Price Index for All Urban Consumers: All Items Less Food & Energy (CPILFESL), 1940–2020, Index 1982-84=100. Shaded areas indicate US recessions. 2013 research.stlouisfed.org]

In general, inflation is a bad thing. Constantly increasing prices lowers your purchasing power, not to mention makes it difficult for companies to plan for investing. If a company doesn't know what prices are going to be two years from now, then it is reluctant to invest. However, as long as inflation remains relatively low and stable it will not impede economic growth.

New Housing Starts

Though obscure, housing starts are actually a reliable indicator of the future of the economy and labor force. The reason is two-fold. One, in housing starts being "housing **STARTS**" that indicates at least three months of future construction spending as it usually takes anywhere from 3-6 months to build a house. Two, new houses don't sit empty. They usually need to be furnished. So not only is a housing start an indicator of 3-6 months future construction spending, but 1-2 years of additional consumer spending as wifey picks out new drapes, new furniture, new appliances, new chairs, new dogs, new cats, a new husband, and new everything.

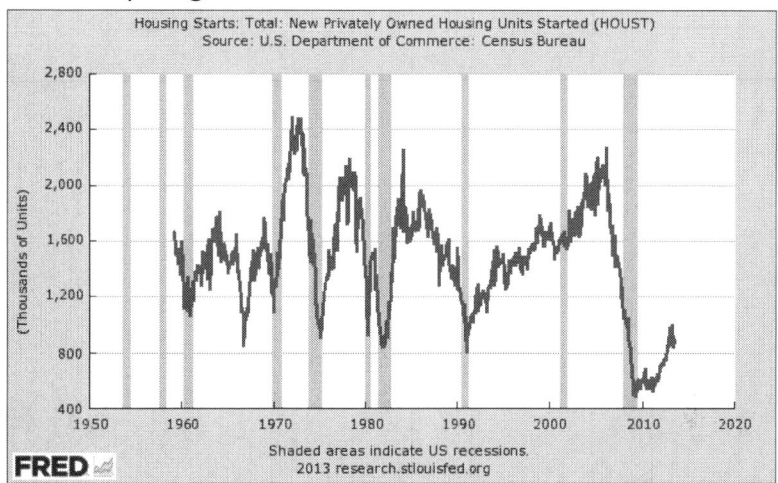

Though the chart below looks a little busy, you can actually see the predictive value of housing starts. Housing will usually lead unemployment by 6-12 months. Thus, when housing starts tank, you can see unemployment spike a year or so later.

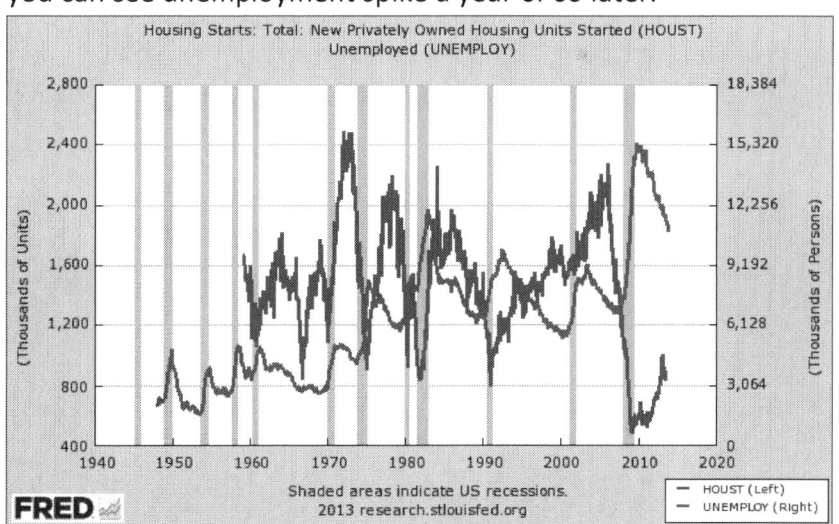

There are certainly other "leading economic indicators" that foretell either a recession or a recovery, but housing starts is arguably the best one. It is definitely a statistic you will want to pay attention to.

The National Debt and Deficit

Though often confused, there is a difference between the deficit and debt.

The *deficit* is the ANNUAL amount the federal government (or any government) spends in excess of what it took in. On the rare occasion it takes in more than it spends it is called a "surplus" (but the last time that occurred was under President Clinton, and before that, Nixon).

The *debt* is just the culmination of all deficits. So if the government runs a deficit of $10 each year, after 10 years it would have a $100 debt.

Unfortunately, the federal government has been running deficits a wee little bit more than $10 per year. It's closer to around $1 trillion per year (though recently was "only" $680 billion).

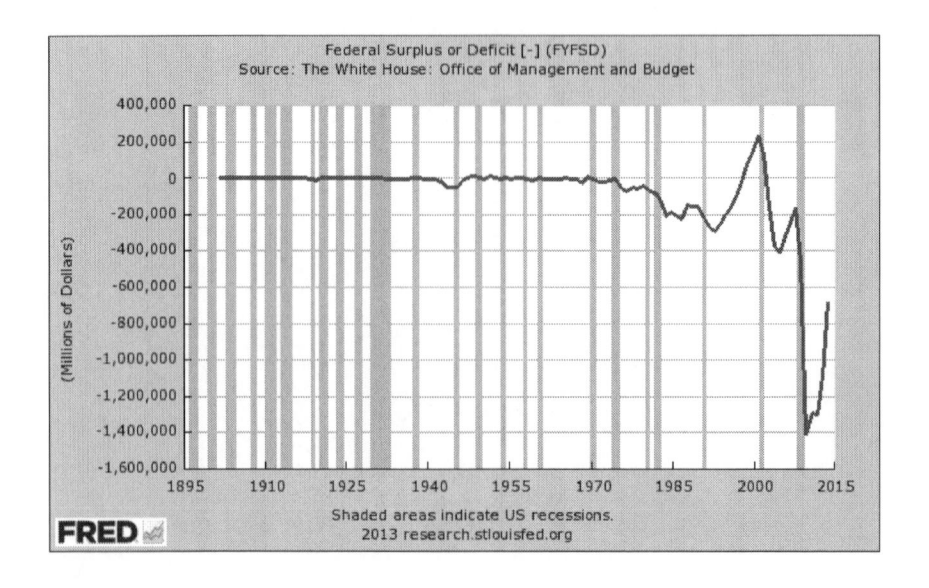

Like GDP, you will notice an exponential like increase in the size of the deficit. This isn't because everything was great and then all of a sudden, BAAM! Things got really bad in the past several years. Instead this is due to inflation. All one has to do to get a perspective on this is note the two little "blips" during 1914-1918 and 1941-1945. Those barely-observable blips are WWI and WWII, respectively. Obviously, both wars were much more severe than the relative peace time we have today, but because there's been so much inflation since then the "nominal" deficits we ran back then seem inconsequential.

The national debt is the same thing:

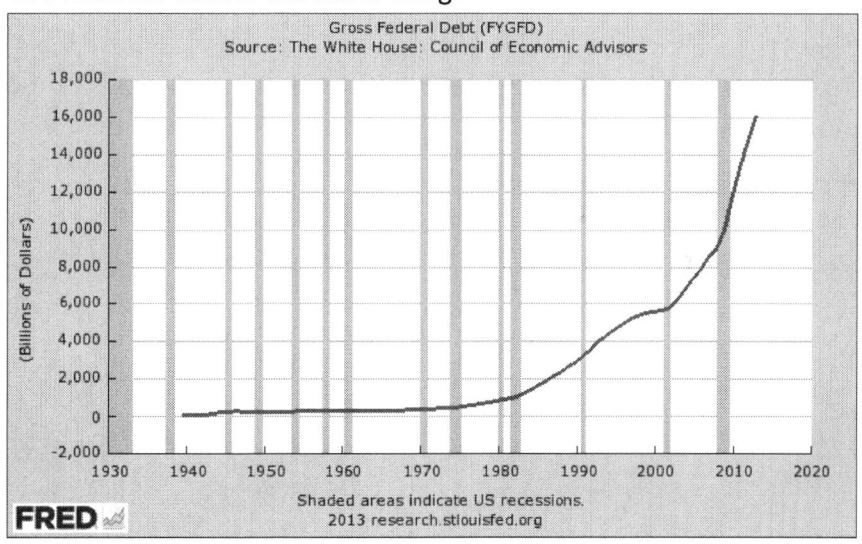

Again, it wasn't like everything was hunky dory up until 1980 and then, BAAM! The debt skyrocketed. The US government has always had a sizeable debt, it's just that it hasn't been adjusted for inflation.

However, there is a problem in merely adjusting the US deficit and debt for inflation. It doesn't account for two other major factors that distort them. One, the population has increased significantly over time. And, two, the economy has also grown significantly during that time. This often causes much confusion because precisely how then do you adjust the deficit and debt to account for

inflation,
population growth, and
economic growth,

turning it into an understandable and digestible number?

Enter in "% of GDP."

Since GDP is basically the income of the entire nation, a lot of economists will use it as a base to compare other numbers to in order to see how severe or inconsequential different aspects of the economy are. And truth be told, these comparisons are nearly identical to simple, basic personal financial calculations you might do for your own finances.

For example, the "national deficit." Currently, it is $680 billion and our GDP is $17 trillion. These numbers may seem large (and they are), but if you were to put it into "human terms" it would be like you making $17,000 per year, but borrowing an extra $680 that year. In other words, your deficit was equal to 4% of your income.

The national debt you can do the same thing. Currently, the national debt is $17 trillion, the same amount as our GDP. This would be like you making $17,000 per year, but having all our loans add up to $17,000. In other words, a 100% debt to income ratio.

But how do you know if these figures are "good" or "bad?" How do you know if they're too big or too small? To do that we look at both of these figures historically.

With the national deficit as a percent of GDP you see that while we are running the largest deficits during peacetime, we ran much higher deficits during WWII. This only makes sense because when your nation is threatened by war, you will spend whatever is necessary to defend it. Ergo, while the 10% deficit to GDP we run today is absolutely abysmal (especially for peacetime), it doesn't compare to the 30% deficit to GDP we ran during the depths of WWII.

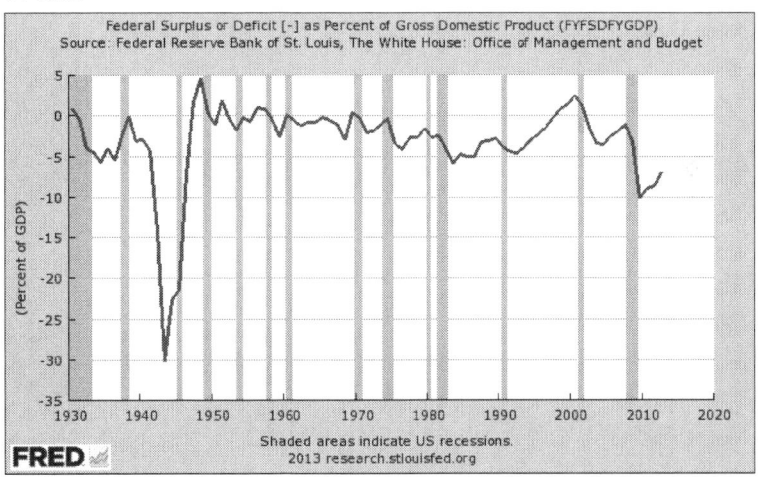

However, while deficits equal to 10% GDP may not spell the end of the world, consistently running such deficits overtime do. And thus, when we look at the national debt to GDP we can see just what kind of havoc chronic and consistent deficits can wreak:

Debt to GDP (Source: FRED)

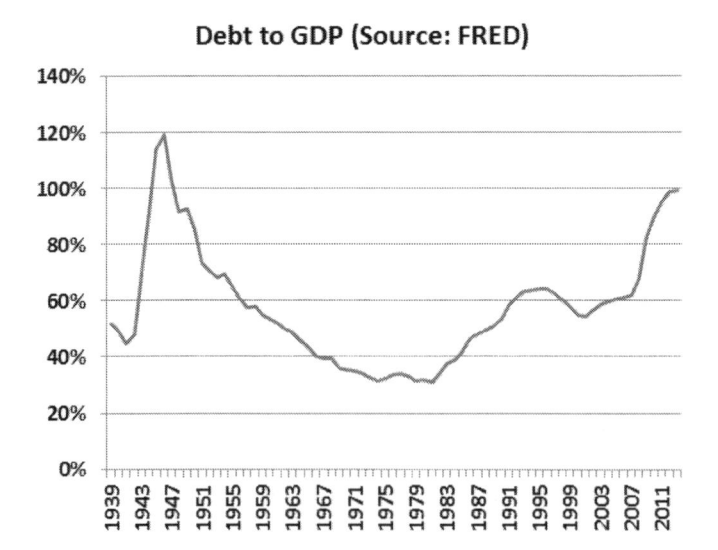

While our deficits roughly average only 4% per year, those deficits have been adding up over the course of three decades, driving our national debt to an unacceptable 100% GDP. What's worse is the recent acceleration when the US went from a relatively low debt level to one that now threatens the economy. George Bush Jr. and Barack Obama alone took on more debt as a percent of GDP than the 10 presidents who preceded them combined! Add to that the fact we are engaged in nothing approaching the severity of a world war, it is a despicable testament to our politicians' mismanagement of the government treasury.

More on a % of GDP

Commoner people will immediately jump to accuse military spending as the primary reason we have burgeoning deficits and debts. But this is a good opportunity to exercise our newly-found desire to be intellectually honest and research what is fact. Not to mention, use our new trick of converting things into a percentage of GDP.

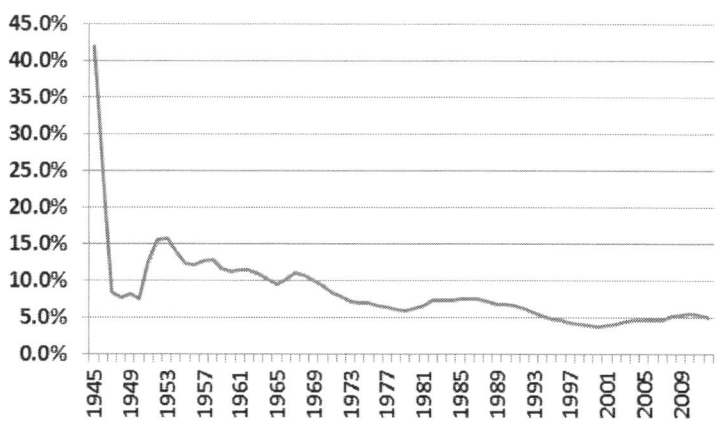

Military Spending % GDP (Source: FRED/US Govt Spending.com)

As you can see, military spending, despite the war on terror, is a meager 5% of GDP. This is nothing compared to the 42% we spent at the peak of WWII and is only half of what we spend on the much-larger Vietnam War. Matter of fact, the trend in military spending has been a downward one (though in intellectual honesty the above figures do not include money spent on Homeland Security). But with the presumed culprit of our exploding national debt not being the droid we're looking for, what is to blame for this inexcusably high level of debt?

% of US Budget that Goes to Wealth Redistribution (Source: Federal Budget)

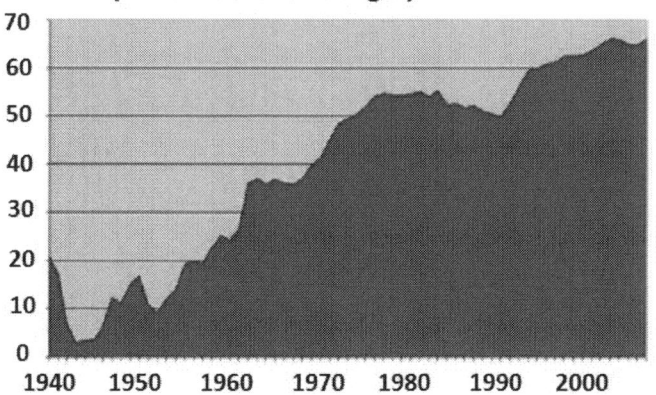

We can go on, but notice what we did with only two charts, a bit of honesty, and the ability to convert various economic statistics into a percent of GDP. We were able to explain, with numerical clarity, just how much military spending truly is. We were able to find out, indisputably, what the primary cause of our nation's debt problem is. We were able to debunk, empirically, what passes for "common knowledge" amongst most people. And most importantly, should we find ourselves in a disagreement with a cute liberal girl we'd like to sleep with, we have armed and informed ourselves to the point we can now use the betting technique discussed in Chapter 12.

Humor aside, realize the power and insight converting various statistics into a percent of GDP. You can figure out just how important, irrelevant, large, small, increasing, decreasing, etc., an aspect or variable of the economy is. You can use it to calculate what percent of our nation's income is spent on health care, just as you could calculate what percent of GDP is spend on video games (if you really wanted to get into the NIPA accounts). Regardless of what you'd use it for, the ability to calculate things as a percentage of GDP provides infinitely more insight and clairvoyance into economics than any college class ever will.

Consumer Confidence

A huge component of economics is faith. Faith, specifically, in that there is a future. If you do not believe there is a future or that dire economic times are ahead, there is a plethora of economic behaviors that will ensue that do not bode well for the economy. For example, children. If you think the economic future bodes ill, you will not breed, resulting in less future economic production. If you have no faith in Wall Street, you will be less likely to invest, depriving companies of capital they need to expand and advance. And if you think you're only a day or two away from losing your job, you will cut back on spending, depriving businesses of future revenue. In short, a lack of faith can result in a viscous downward spiral that can shut down an economy and send it into a crushing recession, becoming a self-fulfilling prophecy.

Because of this the government, corporations, Wall Street, and pretty much anybody with the slightest interest in economics pay attention to "consumer confidence." Consumer confidence, or the "Consumer Confidence Index," measures the optimism people have in the US economy and their financial futures. Though it doesn't directly translate into "faith in the economy," for most practical purposes it does. It is a good predictor of future spending and investment, just as it is a predictor of tightening of belts and recession.

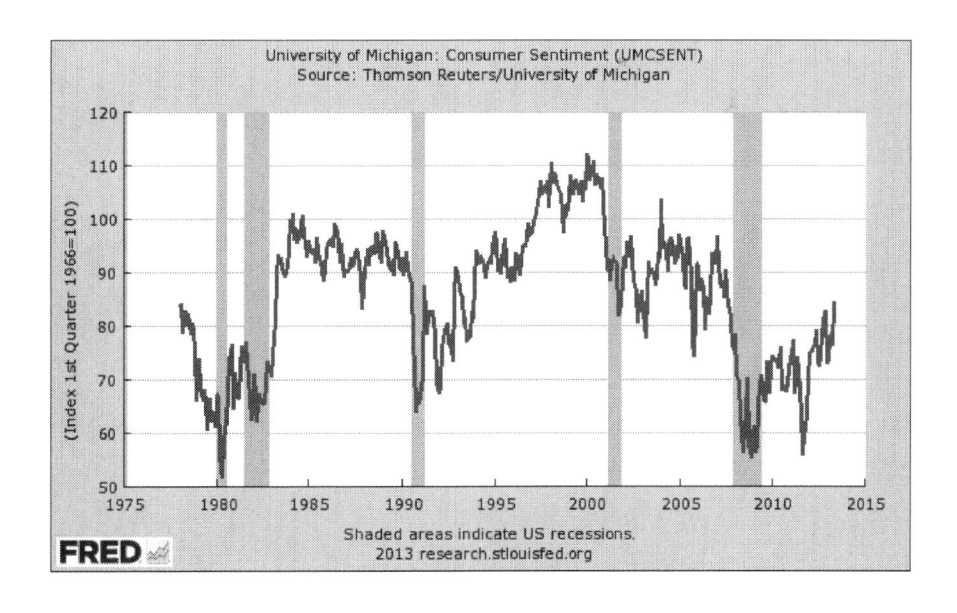

Social Security/Medicare

Though not necessarily an economic statistic, two major and related economic issues will play an increasingly dominant role over US economics and politics – Social Security and Medicare. These two items are so huge, so large, that no other economic debate matters. If they are not resolved all other economic issues will be rendered moot as the US economy will collapse.

Realize previous generations have made promises to themselves. Promises they cannot afford. They have promised themselves a "guaranteed" level of income through Social Security and promised themselves free healthcare in the form of Medicare. Unfortunately, they did not adequately save to pay for these things. Matter of fact, they've frivolously spent so much money on other (veritable) crap we now have a national debt equal to 100% GDP *and most of them haven't even retired yet*. Therefore, the only way these two items are going to be paid for is on the backs of younger and future generations. It isn't fair. It isn't right. But it "is."

Unfortunately, Social Security and Medicare aren't cheap. They account for 22% and 23% of the federal budget, respectively, each more than what we spend on the military. However, the real issue isn't what it costs now, but what it's projected to cost in the future. As a percent of GDP Social Security and Medicare combined today cost just under 8%. But as the baby boomer generation retires costs are expected to increase to 12% GDP in 2030 and 14% GDP 2040.

Social Security and Medicare % GDP
Source: SSA

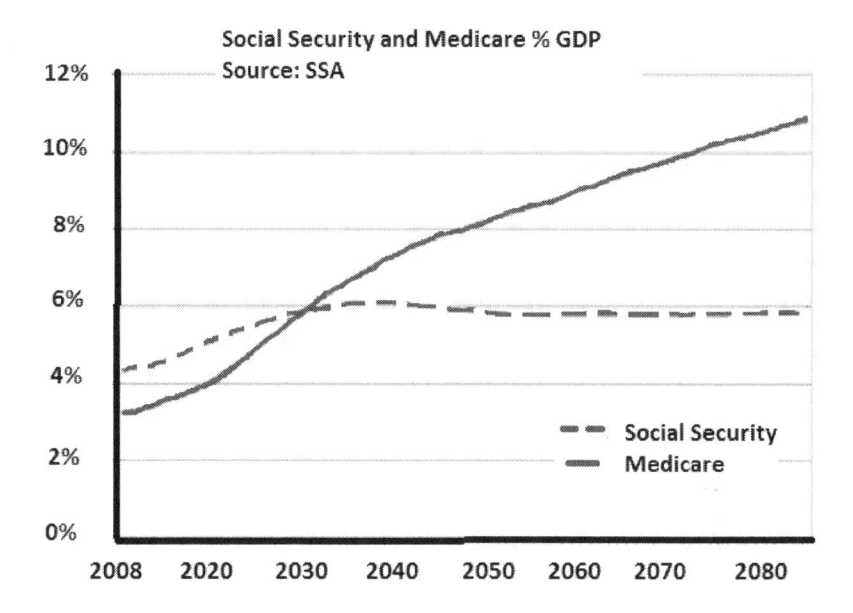

This ever so roughly translates into an additional 10% tax rate on what is already about 40% for the average American. It only gets worse as there are NO economic projections that show Medicare ever decreasing which means future generations will not only have to pay for the livelihood and healthcare of the dying, but will (in theory) essentially become full-time slaves by about 2200.

Of course, this points out the absurdity and impossibility of our current retirement system. It simply is not mathematically feasible. It will, at some point in time, collapse. However, older people are hands down the most powerful (and greedy) political group in the country and will easily vote out any statesman who dares to have the courage and honesty to suggest reorganizing the retirement system into one that is sustainable. Unfortunately, this means most older people would rather destroy the country, destroy the futures of younger generations, so that they can collect their government check. And with amoral politicians beholden to them for their careers, neither group is going to give up their goods so that the country might actually have a future.

This essentially (and unfortunately) relegates you to a role of observer. Between the political cache senior groups like AARP have, the lack of genuine statesmen who have the spine to stand up to them, and the desire of neither to consider people other than themselves, it is pretty much a guarantee Social Security, Medicare, and other forms of "unfunded liabilities" will destroy the US, as well as all other western economies. Not to deter you from pursuing your newfound interest in economics, but that is the 800 pound gorilla of economic reality Social Security and Medicare are.

***

As mentioned before there are hundreds of different economic statistics. You can literally spend weeks studying them all and learning about them, only to find out there's a couple score more you missed. However, for the average man who wishes to merely become "adequately savvy" about economics, the above statistics will suffice. You will be able to interpret the news, more effectively plan your personal finances, as well as become an informed voter and good steward of the country.

Resources

With the advent of the internet, the amount of economic data and information out there is infinite. Matter of fact, I would contend the entire economics profession is more or less obsolete because anybody can through self-study become just as good, if not, a better economist than those who were brainwashed at school.

However, the key is to maintain, above all else, intellectual honesty. Therefore, you must focus on data, and not opinion. Evidence, and not editorial. Because of this, true economists do not watch the news (or at least base their theories and opinions on the news). Be it right-leaning Foxnews or the veritable communist mouthpiece of the government, NPR, both are biased and cannot be trusted. To this end economists rely on data and databases. It's not as enjoyable, and certainly not as fun as looking at the hot news-babes of Foxnews, but it does screen out bias and allows you to more quickly get to the truth.

Databases

The FRED Database – The FRED database is arguably one of the most comprehensive and user friendly databases out there. It has practically ALL of the major and minor economic statistics of the United States in one convenient and chartable location. I strongly recommend making the FRED database our first stop. www.stlouisfed.org.

BLS (Bureau of Labor Statistics) – The BLS is the authoritative source of labor related data. Unemployment, labor productivity, etc. It is a bit cumbersome to navigate and its data is somewhat poorly organized, but with determination you can find the data you're looking for about the US labor market. www.bls.gov.

BEA (Bureau of Economic Analysis) – The BEA is more or less the exact same thing as the BLS, but for a larger, more general set of economic data. Equally cumbersome, equally disorganized, but with determination you should be able to find what you're looking for. www.bea.gov.

The Census Bureau – The Census Bureau is a GOLDMINE of various economic, population, and sociological data. It does start to wander from the world of economics into sociology, but if you ever have a question about various groups within the US (women, men, minorities, children, immigrants, etc.) it is indispensable. Unfortunately, the Census Bureau suffers from information overload and is one of the most complicated databases to navigate. However, if you're willing to put the time into it you can become reasonably proficient at finding the data you need. www.census.gov.

The Organization for Economic Cooperation and Development (OECD) – If you are looking for international data or data on other countries, there is no better database than the OECD. It is horrendously complex, but the amount of data they have is amazing. It allows for international comparisons, longitudinal studies, and anything else you can imagine. www.oecd.org.

The International Labor Organization (ILO) – the ILO is a combination of the OECD and the BLS. It has a plethora of labor data, but it's all international. Therefore, if you're interested in studying the labor market across different countries, the ILO will be your first stop. www.ilo.org.

Nation Master – Though not an official government or internationally recognized site, Nation Master is a VERY EFFICIENT and quick way to do quick comparisons and studies against different countries. It has an impressive menu of not just economic statistics, but sociological statistics, ranging from GDP per capita to water filtration quality. Because of its ease of use I recommend starting at Nation Master if you're doing any kind of international research. www.nationmaster.com.

Blogs/Publications

Though they are guaranteed to have a bias because they are human, not data, I still recommend reading blogs and publications about economics. Not so much to drum up economic data for analytical purposes, but because it is only humans and their opinions that can provide the theoretics and philosophy that would result in working models that fully explain economics. In other words, data tells you whether or not you're right. Humans and their philosophies give you something to be right or wrong about.

Zero Hedge
Mish's Economic Global Analysis
Captain Capitalism
The Economist
Vox Day
Free Domain Radio

Economists

Along the same lines, it is good to read the philosophies and ponderings of others. No human just sets out on his own and independently drafts and develops their own economic theories out of whole cloth. It helps immensely to read the works of others who have done the footwork for you, which not only accelerates your understanding of economics, but also allows you to further advance the field if you so desire.

Peter Schiff
Robert Schiller
Thomas Sowell
Dr. Walter E. Williams
Stephen Molyneux

A Miscellany of Advice

Million, Billion, Trillion – For the love of the Patron Saint's name of Frick, know the difference between a million, a billion, and a trillion. It is appalling how many people don't know this basic math, but still insist on spouting off opinions about government spending and economics. If you don't know the difference, then you won't be able to understand even the simplest aspects of government finances and you certainly shouldn't be voting.

Bogus Statistics – Obviously there is a huge political incentive for politicians to manipulate and just outright lie about different economic statistics. Argentina is notorious for lying about their GDP figures, Venezuela laughably lies about their inflation, and China is always treated with a bit of circumspect when they release their economic growth figures. To circumvent this some very crafty economists look to alternative measures that more directly measure a country's economic growth and production.

For example, many economists prefer to look at electrical consumption instead of China's "official" GDP figures. Many economists prefer to call in to friends they have in Venezuela to ask about prices for a handful of goods to calculate their own CPI for Venezuela rather than believe the government. And Alan Greenspan even distrusted his own government (to an extent) that he preferred railroad tie replacement to actual GDP growth figures. Whatever the case, realize there is a huge political incentive to lie about economic growth figures and so all of those stats you see at the BLS, the BEA, and the FRED database could very well be tainted.

To this end you may want to consider Shadowstats.com, a website that does its own independent economic calculations. This isn't to say it's right or that the official statistics released by the US government are wrong, but it is to say that you need to realize there is HUGE political incentive to distort economic figures and, therefore, you need to rely on our own intelligence, observations, and honesty to figure out what is the best approximation to the truth.

Overall Tax Rates – Revisiting the lesson about converting things into a percentage of GDP, one of the best uses of this technique is that it clearly and plainly explains what the true tax rate people in any one country pay. Between income taxes, social security taxes, property taxes, and sales taxes, it's nearly impossible to add up, individually, all the taxes you pay to see what precisely is the price you're paying for government. However, while such a bottom-up approach is nearly impossible, a top-down approach is actually quite simple.

If you think about it, any money transferred from the people to the government is a tax. Doesn't matter if it's officially called an "income tax" or if it's a fee you pay for a fishing license, any money that transfers from private hands to the government is a tax. So all one has to do is take the total amount of revenue a government receives, divide it by GDP and you have your "overall effective tax rate."

Federal Revenue as % GDP (Source:FRED)

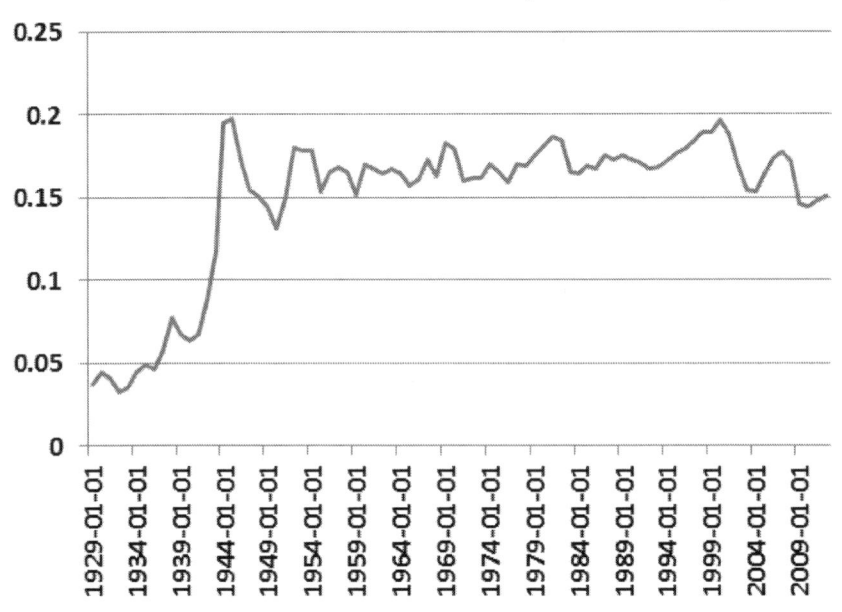

On the onset, our tax rate seems pretty reasonable. 15% isn't the "worst" thing to pay for roads, infrastructure and defense. However, realize there is a major problem with looking at just "REVENUE." It says nothing about spending. While we may only be taxing our citizens at a 15% tax rate, the government is spending a lot more than that. The way it makes up for this deficit is through borrowing. But just because we borrow money, doesn't mean those debts go away. It merely defers those taxes into the future for future generations to pay for. This means the TRUE tax rate is not REVENUE as a percent of GDP, but SPENDING as a percent of GDP.

Federal Spending % GDP (Source: FRED)

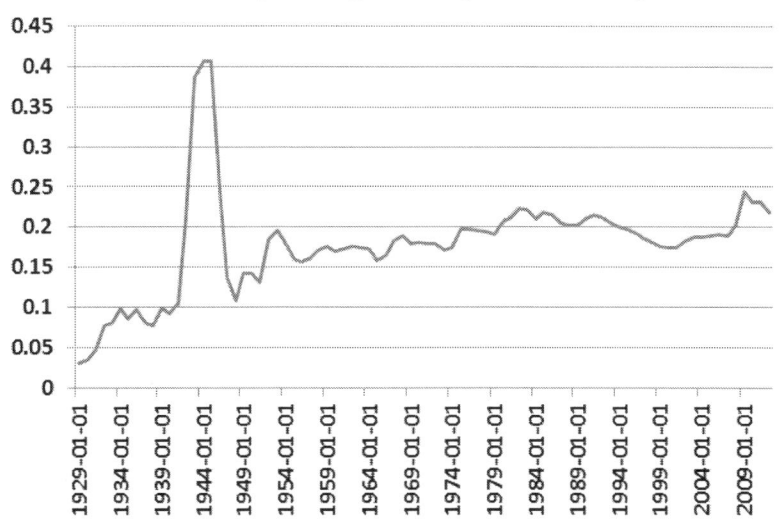

This is a more accurate reflection of your overall tax rate. Nearly 1 in 4 of your dollars go to support the federal government today. Unfortunately, that's just the FEDERAL government. This doesn't even address the real tax rate people face as they also have to pay local and state taxes. When you include these, it gets a little more drastic:

Total Gov't Spending % GDP (Source: OECD)

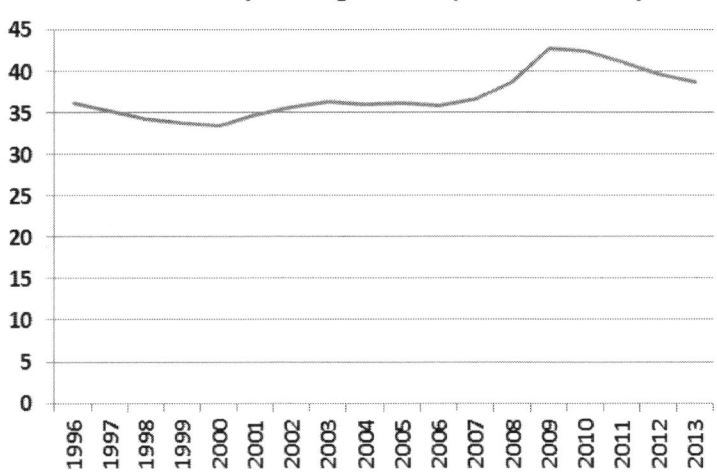

You can expect between income taxes, social security taxes, property taxes, fishing licenses, deer hunting fees, and all the other payments you make to the state, federal, and local forms of government to pay an effective tax rate of about 40% over the course of your life. You can also competently argue against somebody who says the US is a capitalist country the next time you have a debate.

Additional Resources and Books

There is a limitless number of books, articles, and resources you can read and research to advance your understanding of economics. And while I am of the philosophy one should just go to Wikipedia and explore where their heart takes them, it doesn't hurt to read a couple books or articles that would help structure your learning. To that end I recommend the following:

The GLEOC Model – By Captain Capitalism
Economics in One Lesson – By Henry Hazlitt
Freakonomics – Steven Levitt
Wealth and Poverty – George Gilder
Capitalism and Freedom – Milton Friedman

CHAPTER 15
END OF LIFE PLANNING

The irony about retirement planning is that the entire focus is on preparing for retirement, but not enjoying retirement. Everybody is so obsessed with saving up the money necessary to retire they lose the forest from the trees and then literally do not know what to do with themselves once they stop working. Additionally, just as people inadequately prepare themselves to enjoy retirement, they equally fail to prepare for the final stage in life – death. Not so much in terms of "preparing your soul" or "setting things right with the world," but doing what they can while they're alive to make it easier for those they'll leave behind when they pass on. Therefore, just because you cross the magic finish line of "retirement age" doesn't mean your life is over, nor that it still doesn't need to be managed.

This "end of life planning" stage usually consists of four things:
1. Downsizing
2. Having fun during retirement
3. Estate planning
4. Not letting death ruin our life

And while there may be some other aspects you may wish to address in your own personal life, if you dedicate the time and effort to address these four things you will not only have a more enjoyable retirement, but make the financial and managerial aspects of your death easier on your family.

Downsizing

When people mention "downsizing" in the context of retirement they are usually referring to their home. The kids are out of the house. Everyone has moved away. And you've gotten rid of most of your stuff (though maybe you vainly keep one of your children's rooms "just the way it was" in the hopes they come back to live with you at the age of 43). But nostalgia aside, you inevitably realize you and the wifey are officially "empty nesters," and logically conclude you no longer need a five bedroom, three bathroom home. You sell the house, taking only a fraction of the proceeds to purchase a smallish, two-bedroom condo and put the rest of the proceeds into your IRA.

However, while the house is typically the focus of most people's downsizing, in actuality it is your entire life that needs downsizing. Without a family, without a mortgage, and without a career, your life dramatically changes once you retire and switches from one where you were slaving away to pay for all the expenses and infrastructure to support a family, to one where you no longer have to work and just need to support you and Ma Kettle. This not only requires you liquidate most of your physical assets, but it also requires a mental adjustment. You are no longer required to stay at and maintain that home. Matter of fact, you are quite free to do what you want. And in a very minimalism sort of way, the more stuff you can get rid of then the less money you'll need, the cheaper your housing expenses will be, and the more freedom you will have during retirement.

Of course, over the years many people will have grown attached to their homes and all the keepsakes they've adorned them with. And some people just simply cannot leave the home that their entire family was raised in. It means too much to them. And if this is the case there is certainly nothing wrong with that. But while sentimentality may weigh heavily in your mind, you must also consider the counter-argument. Namely, one of mortality and your own enjoyment in life.

You've spent all that time selflessly raising your family, rearing your children, and supporting a household. With the kids gone and you officially retired, your life's focus, by default, reverts back to you. Ergo, you need to let yourself have some fun and enjoy life before you pass on. But if you are obsessed with physical items like your home, your trinkets, or pictures of your children, you are forever beholden to those **things** and therefore deny yourself the ability to enjoy this final stage in your life. You won't permit yourself to move to warmer climes. You won't permit yourself to take those trips you wanted. Besides, unless your kids live nearby, you will merely be enjoying *memories* of them in the old house, looking at their pictures, instead of enjoying their *actual presence and company*. Because of this, you must seriously consider eliminating as much stuff as possible from your life. This will not only allow you to go and enjoy your last days on this planet as you see fit, but grant you the mobility to visit and spend more time with the only thing that truly matters – your children (and grandchildren if you have any).

But there is another, very important reason to consider liquidating as much stuff as possible and pursuing retirement in a minimalist fashion. If you don't get rid of your shit, then your kids will have to when you die. And it is a BITCH of a job to do.

I was in Phoenix, Arizona visiting a buddy of mine. He was working for the local "old man" who collected and repaired classic cars. I got to his property and was quite impressed with what I saw – five acres of rusty old cars, semi-trailers full of car parts, transmissions laying in the sun, and several warehouses full of tools, lifts, and everything automotive. The "old man" was kind enough to show me around and explain how he made his fortune. He was incredibly interesting and very successful, but there was just one problem.

The man was 85 years old.

And despite his amazing mechanical ability, there was no way he was ever going to use even $1/10^{th}$ of the junk laying around his property before he died. It was a guarantee that his children would be burdened with getting rid of all of his stuff which was about the worst "going away gift" you can leave somebody.

Not that you have five acres of scrap and junk laying around, but you will do your children a great service to clean up your estate as much as possible making it easier for them to clean up after you when you pass on. Additionally, you will do your children a great service having some key legal and financial files organized and easily accessible. In other words, prepare your home and estate as if you were going to go away on a permanent vacation, because...well...you are.

Having Fun During Retirement

The irony about retirement is that it takes work. You slaved away all those years to finally retire, only to find out the act of retiring requires work unto itself. Not so much in terms of physical labor or commuting to an office, but deprogramming yourself from 50 years of structure, organization and routine. This should not be taken lightly because after 50 years of anything, your brain will not only "adapt" to it, but be programmed to become ADDICTED to it. So much so many men go through a severe depression after retiring. This only makes sense, as their entire life purpose, their entire agency, their entire meaning was defined by and vested in their career or what they did for a living. And to naively think a man can just simply "flick a switch" and turn from

"full time provider of the family, head of the household, and supreme strategic planner"

to

"old man in Florida wearing Bermuda shorts drinking pina coladas"

is not only laughable, but outright impossible.

Because of this you need to make some mental, physical, and philosophical adjustments in order to transition into and enjoy retirement. For some people it's easy, for some it's incredibly difficult (if not, impossible), but for most it will take a little bit of doing.

<u>Mental Retooling</u>

The biggest hurdle to enjoying retirement is the mental retooling you'll need to do. After 40 years of commuting, working, buying groceries, fixing the home, etc., your brain has been so thoroughly conditioned to work that if you drop it into a new environment of leisure it won't know what to do with itself. Worse, because work was the way you directly attained security and survived, your hindbrain will unconsciously think because you're not working starvation and strife are just around the corner, even if you have $50 million socked away for retirement. To this end, you need to deprogram your brain from one of work and reprogram it into one of leisure.

How to do that is anybody's guess. Sitting down, thinking things through, talking with your wife, even meditating or consulting a therapist, if necessary. But what helps in general is to realize what your larger goal is – to be able to enjoy life like you did as a child. After 13 years of school and 40 years of work, most people lose the ability to have fun like they did when they were children. And if you think back to what you wanted to do as a kid and how your lived your life, it at least gives you a goal or an ideal to aim for.

Prioritizing

Having priorities in life is no different than having agency. However, whereas your first priority was likely your career (out of a larger priority to your family), with that gone you now have to reprioritize your life. Naturally, your wife (if you have one) will be your number one priority. She will be your companion, and if you're lucky, she'll outlive you, providing you companionship until your death (or in other cases, driving you to your death). Your second priority will be your children and grandchildren. You'll want to spend time visiting them, enjoying holidays together. The real challenge, however, will be what do you prioritize after that?

Understand without a job you will have a lot more time than you do priorities. And with your wife also in the same retirement boat as you, not to mention you would drive your children nuts if you spend too much time with them, you'll still need to fill about 10 hours a day with activities. What those activities are depends on what's most important to you after your wife and children.

It is here you need to know what your dreams are. You need to compile your bucket list. And not just compile it, but actively pursue it. How anybody can sit in a retirement community, wasting away, doing nothing but the local senior's pilates class and Tuesday night bingo is beyond me. Would "The World's Most Interesting Man" live his last days on this planet just sitting there at cribbage night, drinking milk? You need to get out and do things, whatever those things are. And if you don't know what those things are it is vital you sit down and figure them out. If you don't, you will stagnate and mentally rot away during retirement.

Regimen and Structure

Unless you're incredibly wealthy and in incredible shape, you will not be able to ride your motorcycle to Sturgis, race boats on Lake Havasu, bike across Europe, and salsa dance in Madrid 24/7 during retirement. Your budget, let alone your physique, just won't allow for it. Because of this you will have a lot of downtime and free time. Free time that if left unoccupied, will spell mental death for you.

While you can reprogram your brain to go from a labor mode to a leisure mode, it is pretty much impossible to undo what 50 years of school and work has done to get your brain addicted to regimen and schedule. This isn't necessarily a bad thing because people need structure, they need organization, and they need regimen in their lives. If they didn't have it, nothing would get done and nothing would be achieved. But while work and school were the sole providers of this structure, without them it is up to you to force-place structure and regimen on your own life.

This can mean anything like having a regular sleep schedule, your morning cup of coffee, or your daily walk. And it can be something as minor as drafting up a "daily to do list" with three small items on it, or a detailed "militant to do list," outlining your schedule to the minute. But without SOME self-structure it is nearly a guarantee you will slip into an inactive, sedentary lifestyle, and worse, mental depression.

Regardless of how you invariably structure your day, there are some key things that you need to make part of your daily regimen.

Exercise – It is vital not only for your body, but your mind, that you keep physically active. Sloshing around in the pool to Richard Simmons or going for a quarter-mile "power walk" will not cut it. You need to be able to run three miles, cycle 20, or if your joints are bad, swim two. You need to lift weights not just to remain attractive to your wife, but to ensure if you take a fall you have enough structural integrity you won't crack a hip. And you need to work out everyday. Not that you'd run four miles, lift weights and play tennis every day, but you need to get the blood flowing daily via exercise and have the brain dump those work-out endorphins into your system. Not only will you look better, you'll feel better.

Healthy Diet – You're old. Pay attention to your diet. It can be the difference between a long and enjoyable retirement, a very short-lived retirement, or worse, a long, but stroked-out paraplegic one.

Hobbies – Men cannot play all day. It just isn't in our psychologies. You will need to produce something of value, even though you're retired. However, instead of slaving away at a job you hate for a boss you loathe, you get to choose what work you'll do. These are called hobbies. Wood whittling, computer repair, trading stocks, saxophone, some kind of craftsmanship or skill that stimulates the brain and challenges it. It doesn't have to make money, but don't be surprised if it does.

Conversation – No matter how many hobbies you have or how much you work out, you will still need intellectual stimulation. And the only way you can get this is through conversation. Thus, you need a social network and a group of friends you can talk to regularly, go have coffee with, and spar with intellectually. However, this has to be in addition to your wife. While she certainly will be your primary converser, like all other marriages, she will drive you nuts. You need to get out, join the local poker game with the guys, hide out at the local cigar lounge, or just get out and golf with the gang. Besides, you're likely driving her nuts too, so get out of the house.

<u>Go Back to Work</u>

Finally, some men are just incapable of retiring. You take them out of their work environment and they just cannot cope. Either they are unable to sustain the loss of agency or their career was really that enjoyable, perhaps even providing him with a second family very near and dear to his heart.

There is absolutely nothing wrong with going back to work and never retiring. The truth is if you enjoy work that much, you are one of the luckiest people in the world as you got to spend 40 years doing what you love. The key is to realize that you might be one of these people and not to force retirement on yourself. The risk of depression and, sadly, suicide just isn't worth it. If you're not happy being retired, go back to whatever it was that made you happy.

Estate Planning

While we have already discussed the importance of having a will, a living will, and designating a loved one with the "power of attorney," there are some other aspects of passing on your estate to your loved ones. This is important because taking the time to understand some basics about estate planning, as well as consulting an estate planning attorney can mean the difference between millions of your dollars going to the people you love or the government.

Asset Protection

As it stands right now, unless your estate is worth more than $5.25 million, or you plan on your estate being worth more than $5.25 million by the time you die, you don't have to worry about the government getting your money instead of your children. The reason is that there is currently a $5.25 million exemption on estates. Only if you pass on more than that do your inheritors pay the 40% tax rate on the difference. However, that does not mean if you have less than $5.25 million you are in the clear. The reason why isn't because of tax law today, but what it's likely going to be in the future.

Revisiting Chapters 11 and 14, remember that the government has HUGE and unfunded liabilities in the form of Social Security and Medicare. Also remember that the US government is running enormous deficits to finance its spending today. But the point in time will come that people will stop lending the government money, and like highlighted in Chapter 11, the government will be tempted to start taxing, aka, "confiscating" assets like Cyprus, Greece, Bulgaria, and Argentina. This means there is huge pressure to lower the exemption which means you may not have to worry about the estate tax today, but will likely have to worry about it in the future.

Because of this, especially if you are younger, you are going to want to consider what LEGAL moves you can take today to help lower your liability in the future. Some of these are simple moves like hoarding precious metals, others are very complex like setting up off-shore asset protection trusts. But regardless of your personal financial situation and what would work best for you, the key is to start now so that you can pass on the maximum amount of your wealth to your family and not the government.

Stockpiling Precious Metals – Whether you're rich or poor, something everybody can do is stockpile precious metals. Not only do they have the benefit of not being electronic or "paper" investments (and therefore not confiscatable), you can easily pass them onto your children or any intended beneficiary. Also, coin collecting is a great hobby for any child and is a great way for you to bond with your children or grandchildren.

Gifting – The IRS allows you to give people "gifts," tax free, of up to $14,000 each year. This amount is adjusted for inflation and will likely increase in the future. There is no limit on the number of people you can gift, so in theory you could deprive the government of any tax revenue by gifting away your estate by making thousands of $14,000 individual gifts to random people. However, the real reason you would use gifting is as a long term way to slowly mete out your estate while you're still alive. $14,000 for each person, every year, over the course of 20 years can add up to a significant sum.

Overseas Accounts – If you are particularly worried that the government may pull a "Cyprus" you may want to consider having an account overseas. However, realize once you get into "international banking" a whole host of issues arise. First, you need to make sure that bank does NOT have any kind of investment or physical presence in the US. The reason why is if an overseas bank does have a presence in the US, the federal government can simply hold those assets hostage and demand the bank does what it tells them, even if it isn't headquartered in the US (this is what happened to UBS, a Swiss bank). Second, you need to know what the laws are in that country as it pertains to inheritance and ownership of the account after you die. Because of these complexities, an overseas account may serve as a good hedge to protect your assets from a Cyrpus-like confiscation, but doesn't really make sense for the average man in terms of passing on his estate.

Expatriation – While the idea of expatriating and renouncing your US citizenship for greener economic pastures sounds nice, realize it isn't as feasible an option as you think. Not because you can't or that the IRS would stop you, but because for most people money isn't the most important thing in life. It's other people. Even if you are the most pro-capitalist, ardent anarcho-libertarian, the fact is that your personal relationships with your friends, family, and loved ones will inevitably overrule the taxes you loathe paying. The only real or feasible way to expat is to do it while you're young, don't have roots, don't have a family, or somehow are able to afford to move your entire family overseas (though you risk having a "Mosquito Coast" like lifestyle).

Regardless, expatriating may still be a viable option for you. And if you can find a tax-haven that doesn't have an estate tax, it may be a great place to raise a family. The key thing is to take the time to ensure the country you are taking up residency in is the one you want to live in. Unfortunately, this means you will have to spend an inordinate amount of resources researching, studying, even living in different countries. However, if you do all your homework and are absolutely sure you've found your new home, by all means, expatriate.

Asset Protection Trusts – "Asset Protection Trusts" or just "trusts" are legal entities that allow you to transfer your assets to a "trust," but designate somebody else as the beneficiary. Because the trust is a separate legal entity, the assets you place in it are protected from any lawsuits or confiscators that may be coming after you personally. This is a handy tool to have in estate planning as it gives you the ideal situation of "controlling everything, but owning nothing."

However, trusts can be INCREDIBLY complicated. You can have an LLC set up within the trust to manage it. You can have yourself be the beneficiary. You can have your son be the "trustee" of the trust. And you can have the LLC established in one country, while the trust is established in the other. In short, before you consider setting up a trust you will want to have a long and serious chat with your accountant and an attorney who specializes in trusts. It's a great tool to incorporate into your estate planning, but it is beyond the abilities of the average person to implement.

Attorney – Estate planning is horrendously complex. Do not try to do it on your own. You absolutely need to consult an estate planning attorney, even if you aren't rich. They know the law and the handful of money you spend on them can save your children and your bequeathed piles of money later.

Not Letting Death Ruin Your Life

One of the best bits of advice I've ever received in my life was from William Shatner. Not personally, but from his (surprisingly good) musical career. Specifically, the song, "You're Gonna Die." And it is the first lyric that is all anybody ever needs:

"Live life like you're gonna die, because you're going to."

Death presents a problem for most people in that they fear it. And during retirement it is probably a daily and increasingly worrying concern. The problem with death though is that it is not under your control. You can certainly postpone it with healthy living. You can certainly defer it with diet and exercise. But in the end everybody dies. The key is to not let this fact lessen or ruin your life.

However, that is easier said than done. How do you let your ceasing of existence, the ending of your consciousness, and your fear of the unknown NOT affect you while you're alive today? How do you just "accept" death without a bit of remorse, fear, concern, or sadness?

The answer lies in understanding the Serenity Prayer:

God, grant me the serenity to accept the things I cannot change,
The courage to change the things I can,
And the wisdom to know the difference.

The Serenity Prayer is a great prayer to know whether you're religious or not because once you understand it, it makes things a lot easier in life. You only control what is under your control. Therefore, as long as you did your best, there is nothing more for you to do. You need not worry. You need not fret. You need not try anymore, because it's out of your hands. Therefore, relax. Have peace. Have serenity.

Death is the same thing.

The only thing you do in worrying about death is lessen the quality of your life today. It's going to happen, it's already fated to happen, so you shouldn't waste even a second of your life over it. Besides, you have more important things to do with your life.

A Miscellany of Advice

<u>Reverse Mortgages</u> – There is a huge push for retirees to use the equity in their homes to subsidize their lives. These "reverse mortgages" allow you to make monthly withdrawals from your house, helping you make ends meet. When you die, the house is sold and the residual balance on the mortgage is then paid off. At first it may seem like a great idea because it's a convenient way to use the equity you built up in your house over the years, and it is. But realize what you are telling the world when you get a reverse mortgage:

"I'm a moron who couldn't do basic math, was irresponsible and didn't adequately prepare for retirement, and I'm not going to leave my children anything, by the way, where's my Social Security check?"

You should have great shame if you so poorly managed your finances you are now so desperate you need something as Jerry-Springer-esque as a reverse mortgage. Additionally, if you need to rely on a reverse mortgage to make ends meet, that means your finances are critically inadequate. Worse, they're inadequate during a point in time that you are progressively likely to be unable to work. Therefore, if you ever find yourself contemplating a reverse mortgage, you should instead get your ass back to the labor force and shore up your finances if you can. Otherwise prepare for a miserable retirement as you outlive your savings.

<u>Preplanning Your Funeral</u> – In addition to cleaning up your house and having your legalities in order, an additional kindness you can do for your family while you're still alive is pre-plan your own

funeral. Realize when you die your family will be in mourning. Unfortunately, however, your biological remains need to be buried reasonably soon which forces an unneeded and untimely chore on your bereaving family. If you can alleviate them of this chore you only make your death easier on them.

To pre-plan your funeral you can consult your local mortician. They have many options like pre-paying for a casket, selecting flowers and arrangements, they even have "funeral insurance." How "elaborate" or "cheap" you want your funeral to be is up to you, but on average you can expect to spend around $6,000.

Pay Your Fucking Taxes – Though addressed before, it is worth re-emphasizing the importance of paying your taxes. While the idea of overseas bank accounts, expatriation, and offshore asset protection trusts seems exotic and exciting, keep in mind none of that will matter if you already have troubles with the IRS. Your goal should be to ensure you have no tax problems with ANY taxing authority, and then, should you come into a lot of money or make it rich, LEGALLY use said tools of asset protection to lower your taxes. You will spend more money and time fighting the tax authorities than you would save if you cheat on your taxes. It just isn't worth the risk, and certainly not the headache.

Get a Second Passport – It is wise counsel to obtain yourself a second passport. The reasons are numerous. Your US passport is actually trackable allowing the government to essentially follow your every move. It will allow you to visit and reside in additional countries. And it will also be a requirement if you plan on expatriating. Overall, however, you will want to consider a second passport as an insurance policy against a collapsing or increasingly tyrannical state that you may have to escape at some point in time.

(I recommend contacting Jeff Berwick of Dollar Vigilante to assist in obtaining secondary passports).

Please Consider the Smith and Wesson Retirement Plan – Albeit the most dramatic bit of advice in this entire book, for the love of god don't destroy your kids' inheritance, let alone their sanity watching you painfully waste away in a nursing home. Have the decency and self-respect to euthanize yourself. There is no worse fate than being bed-ridden, incontinent, and demented. And it is painful for others to see somebody they love who was a great man, decay into a fraction of his former self. It is humiliating, disgraceful, undignified, and no way for a real man to die. Additionally, that $800 spent keeping you alive on the ventilator for **one hour** can pay a month's rent for your kid or grandkid, granting them **weeks** of time. You need to accept that your life is OVER. Do not unconsciously parasite and syphon off of, and therefore, deny your progeny their own lives so you can stay alive for another miserable month or two. It is the most honorable and final act you can do in your life.

Resources

Nomad Capitalist
Escape Artist
Fred on Everything
CIA World Factbook
Dollar Vigilante

THE END

RESOURCES

This resource list assumes you're a man and you are capable of "googling" these items instead of asking "how do I find these items?"

Educational
College Insurrection
The College Fix
Khan's Academy
Joanne Jacobs

Career
"An Army of Davids" – Dr. Glenn Reynolds
Progressive Credentialism

Health
Bold and Determined
Hawaiian Libertarian

Girls/Wife/Dating
Rollo Tomassi – The Rationale Male
The Art of Manliness
Return of Kings
Rooshv
Dalrock
Grerp
Haley's Halo
Tom Leykis

Housing
Mortgage calculators (bankrate recommended)
"Behind the Housing Crash" – by Aaron Clarey
Craig Kamman
The Thinking Housewife

Investing and Retiring
"Stocks, Bonds, and Investing: Oh My!"
"The Analysis and Valuation of Stocks"
Retirement calculators (there are many)
Andrew Henderson – Nomad Capitalist
Dollar Vigilante

Divorce
Divorce calculators
Spearhead
AVFM

Economics and Economists
Captain Capitalism
Vox Day
Robert Shiller
Peter Schiff
Kerry Lutz
Walter E. Williams
Thomas Sowell
Murray Rothbard
Ludwig Von Mises
Milton Friedman
Jerry Robinson

Books
"Worthless" by Aaron Clarey
"Enjoy the Decline" by Aaron Clarey
"The Way of Men" by Jack Donovan
The Bang Series – By Roosh V
"Economics in One Lesson" – Henry Hazlitt
"Capitalism and Freedom" – Milton Friedman
"The Road to Serfdom" – F.A. Hayek
"Bankruptcy of Our Nation" – Jerry Robinson

Radio/Podcasts
Davis Aurini
Dennis Prager
Garage Logic
Stephan Molyneux
FTM Daily Radio
The Clarey Podcast
Matt Forney's Podcast Extravaganza

SPECIAL THANKS TO

LESLIE EASTMAN OF "THE TEMPLE OF MUT"
Suzanne McCarley at A Voice for Men
Mrs. B at "The Lonely Conservative"
Marty Andrade at MartyAndrade.wordpress.com

SILVIO CANTO

DAVIS AURINI

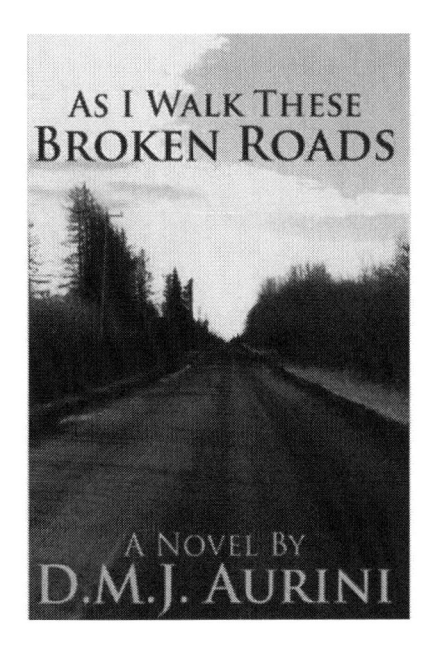

ROOSH V
(www.rooshv.com)

BANG

Roosh V

Worthless

Worthless

Copyright 2011

The Young Person's Indispensable Guide to Choosing the Right Major

By
Aaron Clarey

ENJOY THE DECLINE

ENJOY THE DECLINE
Accepting and Living with the Death of the United States
By Aaron Clarey

Marty Andrade
Martyandrade.wordpress.com

Richard Nixon's Guide to the Multiverse
Martin Andrade

Chris Pohl

www.commieobama.com

A BIG THANKS TO JORGE GONZALES FOR ALL THE ART WORK!

http://jegonzalezart.blogspot.com/

Printed in Great Britain
by Amazon